W9-BKG-826

Media Ethics:

ISSUES & CASES

SIXTH EDITION

Philip Patterson
Oklahoma Christian University

Lee Wilkins
University of Missouri–Columbia

Higher Education

Boston   Burr Ridge, IL   Dubuque, IA   Madison, WI   New York
San Francisco   St. Louis   Bangkok   Bogotá   Caracas   Kuala Lumpur
Lisbon   London   Madrid   Mexico City   Milan   Montreal   New Delhi
Santiago   Seoul   Singapore   Sydney   Taipei   Toronto

Higher Education

Published by McGraw-Hill, an imprint of The McGraw-Hill Companies, Inc. 1221 Avenue of the Americas, New York, NY, 10020. Copyright © 2008. All rights reserved. No part of this publication may be reproduced or distributed in any form or by any means, or stored in a database or retrieval system, without the prior written consent of The McGraw-Hill Companies, Inc., including, but not limited to, in any network or other electronic storage or transmission, or broadcast for distance learning.

This book is printed on acid-free paper.

1 2 3 4 5 6 7 8 9 0 DOC/DOC 0 9 8 7

ISBN: 978-0-07-351189-4
MHID: 0-07-351189-7

Editor in Chief: *Emily Barrosse*
Publisher: *Frank Mortimer*
Sponsoring Editor: *Suzanne Earth*
Marketing Manager: *Leslie Oberhuber*
Developmental Editor: *Craig Leonard*
Production Editor: *Karol Jurado*
Production Service: *Jean Dal Porto*
Manuscript Editor: *Jan Nickels*
Designer: *Andrei Pasternak*
Media Project Manager: *Ron Nelms, Jr.*
Production Supervisor: *Dennis Fitzgerald*
Composition: *10.5/12 Times New Roman by International Typesetting and Composition*
Printing: *45# New Era Matte, R. R. Donnelley & Sons*
Cover image: *Wetzel and Company*

Library of Congress Cataloging-in-Publication Data
Media ethics: issues and cases/[edited by] Philip Patterson, Lee Wilkins.—6th ed.
    p. cm.
Includes bibliographical references and index.
ISBN-13: 978-0-07-351189-4
ISBN-10: 0-07-351189-7
1. Mass media—Moral and ethical aspects. I. Patterson, Philip. II. Wilkins, Lee.
P94.M36 2007
175—dc22   2007010797

The Internet addresses listed in the text were accurate at the time of publication. The inclusion of a Web site does not indicate an endorsement by the authors or McGraw-Hill, and McGraw-Hill does not guarantee the accuracy of the information presented at these sites.

www.mhhe.com

To Amy, Andrew, Miranda and Joshua
Our equally bright and now-grown children,
unequally distributed between us

CONTENTS

5 *Public Relations: Standards of Advocacy*   123

6 *Privacy: Looking for Solitude in the Global Village*   147

FOREWORD

CLIFFORD G. CHRISTIANS
Research Professor of Communication
University of Illinois–Urbana

The playful wit and sharp mind of Socrates attracted disciples from all across ancient Greece. They came to learn and debate in what could be translated "his thinkery." By shifting the disputes among Athenians over earth, air, fire and water to human virtue, Socrates gave Western philosophy and ethics a new intellectual center (Cassier 1944).

But sometimes his relentless arguments would go nowhere. On one occasion, he sparred with the philosopher Hippias about the difference between truth and falsehood. Hippias was worn into submission, but retorted at the end, "I cannot agree with you, Socrates." And then the master concluded: "Nor I with myself, Hippias. . . . I go astray, up and down, and never hold the same opinion." Socrates admitted to being so clever that he had befuddled himself. No wonder he was a favorite target of the comic poets. I. F. Stone likens this wizardry to "whales of the intellect flailing about in deep seas" (Stone 1988).

With his young friend Meno, Socrates argued whether virtue is teachable. Meno was eager to learn more, after "holding forth often on the subject in front of large audiences." But he complained, "You are exercising magic and witchcraft upon me and positively laying me under your spell until I am just a mass of helplessness. . . . You are exactly like the flat stingray that one meets in the sea. Whenever anyone comes into contact with it, it numbs him, and that is the sort of thing you seem to be doing to me now. My mind and my lips are literally numb."

Philosophy is not a semantic game, though sometimes its idiosyncrasies feed that response into the popular mind. *Media Ethics: Issues and Cases* does not debunk philosophy as the excess of sovereign reason. The authors of this book will not encourage those who ridicule philosophy as cunning rhetoric. The issue at stake here is actually a somewhat different problem—the Cartesian model of philosophizing.

The founder of modern philosophy, René Descartes, preferred to work in solitude. Paris was whirling in the early 17th century, but for two years even Descartes' friends could not find him as he squirreled himself away studying mathematics. One can even guess the motto above his desk: "Happy is he who lives in seclusion." Imagine the conditions under which he wrote "Meditations II." The Thirty Years' War in Europe brought social chaos everywhere. The Spanish were ravaging the French provinces and even threatening Paris, but Descartes was shut away in an apartment in Holland. Tranquility for philosophical speculation mattered so much to him that upon hearing Galileo had been condemned by the Church, he retracted parallel arguments of his own on natural science. Pure philosophy as an abstract enterprise needed a cool atmosphere isolated from everyday events.

Descartes' magnificent formulations have always had their detractors, of course. David Hume did not think of philosophy in those terms, believing as he did that sentiment is the foundation of morality. For Søren Kierkegaard, an abstract system of ethics is only paper currency with nothing to back it up. Karl Marx insisted that we change the world and not merely explain it. But no one drew the modern philosophical map more decisively than Descartes, and his mode of rigid inquiry has generally defined the field's parameters.

This book adopts the historical perspective suggested by Stephen Toulmin:

> The philosophy whose legitimacy the critics challenge is always the seventeenth century tradition founded primarily upon René Descartes. . . . [The] arguments are directed to one particular style of philosophizing—a theory-centered style which poses philosophical problems, and frames solutions to them, in timeless and universal terms. From 1650, this particular style was taken as defining the very agenda of philosophy (1988, 338).

The 17-century philosophers set aside the particular, the timely, the local and the oral. And that development left untouched nearly half of the philosophical agenda. Indeed, it is those neglected topics—what I here call "practical philosophy"—that are showing fresh signs of life today, at the very time when the more familiar "theory-centered" half of the subject is languishing (Toulmin 1988, 338).

This book collaborates in demolishing the barrier of three centuries between pure and applied philosophy; it joins in reentering practical concerns as the legitimate domain of philosophy itself. For Toulmin, the primary focus of ethics has moved from the study to the bedside, to criminal courts, engineering labs, the newsroom, factories and ethnic street corners. Moral philosophers are not being asked to hand over their duties to technical experts in today's institutions, but rather to fashion their agendas within the conditions of contemporary struggle.

All humans have a theoretical capacity. Critical thinking, the reflective dimension, is our common property. And this book nurtures that reflection in communication classrooms and by extension into centers of media practice. If the mind is like a muscle, this volume provides a regimen of exercises for strengthening its powers of systematic reflection and moral discernment. It does not permit those aimless arguments that result in quandary ethics. Instead it operates in the finest traditions of practical philosophy, anchoring the debates in real-life conundrums but pushing the discussion toward substantive issues and integrating appropriate theory into the decision-making process. It seeks to empower students to do ethics themselves, under the old adage that teaching someone to fish lasts a lifetime, and providing fish only saves the day.

"Media Ethics: Issues and Cases" arrives on the scene at a strategic time in higher education. Since the late 19th century, ethical questions have been taken from the curriculum as a whole and from the philosophy department. Recovering practical philosophy has involved a revolution during the last decade in which courses in professional ethics have reappeared throughout the curriculum. This book advocates the pervasive method and carries the discussions even further, beyond freestanding courses into communication classrooms across the board.

In this sense, the book represents a constructive response to the current debates over the mission of higher education. Professional ethics has long been saddled with the dilemma that the university was given responsibility for professional training precisely at the point in its history that it turned away from values to scientific naturalism. Today one sees it as a vast horizontal plain given to technical excellence but barren in enabling students to articulate a philosophy of life. As the late James Carey concluded,

> Higher education has not been performing well of late and, like most American institutions, is suffering from a confusion of purpose, an excess of ambition that borders on hubris, and an appetite for money that is truly alarming (1989, 48).

The broadside critiques leveled in Thorstein Veblen's "The Higher Learning in America" (1918) and Upton Sinclair's "The Goose Step" (1922) are now too blatantly obvious to ignore. But "Media Ethics: Issues and Cases" does not merely demand a better general education or a recommitment to values; it strengthens the communications curriculum by equipping thoughtful students with a more enlightened moral awareness. Since Confucius we have understood that lighting a candle is better than cursing the darkness, or, in Mother Teresa's version, we feed the world one mouth at a time.

PREFACE

As you glance through this book, you will notice its features—text, illustrations, cases, photos—represent choices the authors have made. I think it's as important to point out what's missing as what's there, and why. I'll begin with what's been left out and conclude with what you'll find in the text.

First, you'll find no media bashing in this book. There's enough of that already, and besides, it's too easy to do. This book is not designed to indict the media; it's designed to train its future employees. If we dwell on ethical lapses from the past, it is only to learn from them what we can do to prevent similar occurrences in the future.

Second, you'll find no conclusions in this book—neither at the end of the book nor after each case. No one has yet written the conclusive chapter to the ethical dilemmas of the media, and I don't suspect that we will be the first.

What, then, is in the book?

First, you'll find a diverse, up-to-date, and classroom-tested compilation of cases in media ethics. Authors from more than 30 institutions and media outlets contributed real-life and hypothetical cases to this text to help students prepare for the ethical situations they will confront in whatever areas of the media they enter. We believe case studies are the premiere teaching vehicle for the study of ethics, and this book reflects what we think are the best available.

Second, the text binds these cases together and provides a philosophical basis from which to approach them. While it intentionally has been kept succinct, the text introduces students to the relevant ethical theory that will help eliminate "quandary ethics," which often results when cases are used as a teaching strategy.

Third, you'll find built-in discussion starters in the questions that follow each case. The questions at the end of the cases were written by the authors of each case, with the instructions that they were to be like concentric circles. The tightest circle—the micro issues—focuses only on the case at hand and the dilemmas it presents. The next circle—midrange issues—focuses on the problem in its context and sometimes manipulates the facts slightly to see if the decisions remain the same. The most abstract level—the macro issues—focuses on issues such as truth, equity, responsibility and loyalty. Properly used, the questions can guide discussion from the particular to the universal in any case in a single class period.

The book may be used either as the main text for a media ethics course or as a supplementary text for ethics modules in courses on newswriting, media and society, advertising and public relations and photojournalism. The book works well for teachers who like to use the Socratic method in their classes or as resource material for lecture classes.

Our approach in this text is best illustrated by an anecdote from a class. One student had the last hand up after a particularly heated case study. When I called on her, she asked, "Well, what's the answer?" I was surprised that she asked the question, and I was surprised that I didn't have a ready answer. I joked my way out of the question by asking if she wanted "The Answer" with a capital "a" or a lowercase one. If she asked today, I'd respond differently. I'd tell her that the answer exists within her, but that it won't emerge in any justifiable form without systematic study and frequent wrestling with the issues.

That's what this book is about. The chapters direct you in some systematic way through the philosophy that has explored these questions for centuries. The cases will make you wrestle with that knowledge in scenarios not unlike ones you might encounter while working. Together, they might not enable you to find "The Answer," but they might help you find *your* answer.

For the authors and contributors,

Philip Patterson

ACKNOWLEDGMENTS

The ethical dilemmas that challenge us require a "moral compass" to help us find our way down the winding paths of life. My compass was given to me by my parents at an early age, and it has worked for more than four decades. No one can ask for a better gift than that, and I thank them for their part in placing me where I am today.

No book of this type is a solo effort, and this book is certainly the result of hard work and encouragement by many people. To begin, each of the authors in the text has been a pleasure to work with. Lou Hodges, Cliff Christians, Ralph Barney, Jay Black, Deni Elliott, and others listened patiently to the idea in its many stages and offered advice along the way. Over the years I have been privileged to attend workshops on ethics sponsored by the Poynter Institute, the Freedom Forum and the University of Nebraska. To Bob Steele, Ed Lambeth, Steve Kalish and Robert Audi I owe a debt of gratitude for helping me continue to learn about ethics as I seek to teach my students.

A special thanks goes to the Ethics and Excellence in Journalism Foundation and to McGraw-Hill Higher Education for grants to cover costs incurred in this edition of the text. Finally, I thank my wife, Linda, and my children, Amy, Andrew and Joshua: I love you all.

p.d.p.

When ethics entrepreneur Michael Josephson opens his public speeches, he asks audience members to think of the most ethical people they know. Those people set ethical standards for others, by who they are and by what they inspire. It's fair for readers of this book to know who's on my list.

First, my mother, whose sense of human connection and compassion has been only incompletely copied by her daughter. Second, my father, who is the most principled human being I have ever met. Third, my stepmother, Carrie, who's managed to love the family she's married into—a feat worthy of far more than a Kantian sense of duty. My dissertation advisor and friend, Jim Davies, affirmed for me the ethical connection between people and politics. My former colleagues at the University of Colorado, Russ Shain, Steve Jones, Sue O'Brien and Risa Palm, have proved that connection to be a very human one, as have my colleagues at the University of Missouri. They have also been willing to listen—*another ethical activity that too often goes unmentioned.* Barrie Hartman and the staff of the *Boulder Daily Camera* were wonderful reality checks.

I've received intellectual help as well. I've attended a number of conferences designed to teach me about ethics. The Hastings House, Gannett, the Poynter Institute and the University of Nebraska have done their best to educate me in this field. The people connected with those efforts deserve special mention. Among them, Ed Lambeth, Ted Glasser, Deni Elliott, Cliff Christians, Lou Hodges, Martin Linsky, Roy Peter Clark, Don Fry, Sharon Murphy, Jay Black, Ralph Barney, Steve Kalish and Robert Audi have helped most profoundly. Many of them you will find mentioned in various contexts on the pages that follow. All of them have a special place in my intellectual psyche.

Two sets of acknowledgments remain.

For the past 25 years, my students at the state universities of Missouri and Colorado have taught me much more about ethics than I have taught them. They have suffered through portions of this manuscript with me. Their questions and their insights are evident on every page of this book.

Then there are Miranda and David—my daughter and my spouse. For the smiles, the hugs, the reading of first drafts, the talking, the listening, the suggestions, the lecture about using "skin" names, the films and all of the rest that being a family means. Love and thanks. I could not have done this without you.

l.c.w.

1

An Introduction to Ethical Decision Making

By the end of this chapter, you should be able to:

- **recognize the need for professional ethics in journalism.**
- **work through a model of ethical decision making.**
- **identify and use the five philosophical principles applicable to mass communication situations.**

MAKING ETHICAL DECISIONS

Scenario #1: You work for a PR firm that represents pharmaceutical giant PharMedCo. The drug company has recently come across an herbal medicine that is being used successfully in Europe to lower blood pressure naturally. PharMedCo wants to package and sell it in the United States. They are planning a major national promotion that will cost hundreds of thousands of dollars, generating large fees for your firm. As part of the promotion, they want to use the "third-party strategy," hiring key opinion leaders in the medical world to help get the word out and create a buzz by talking up the advantages of herbal products in general. These third parties would not push PharMedCo's new herbal medicine directly. In doing some research on the herb, you discover a little-known piece of information: if used in combination with another readily available over-the-counter drug, the herb can be abused to get high. You tell PharMedCo about your findings but they want you to go ahead with the strategy without informing the third-party experts, who would probably have a duty to warn the public. What should you do?

    Scenario #2: You are the chief information officer for a large metropolitan police force, trained in media and public relations. Your job ordinarily consists of acting as spokesperson for the department and also representing the department at a variety of community events. Your city is three weeks into a sniper spree that has left 10 innocent people dead. Now comes a break. Police have determined that the suspects are driving a blue Chevy Caprice with New Jersey plates. If this information is released to the public, citizens could potentially spot the car and assist police in the capture of the suspects. However, releasing the information might also enable the suspects to dump the car for another and continue their spree. How would you advise the chief? If the local media somehow obtain the information before a decision is made to release it, do you verify it or deny it?

Scenario #3: You are the producer for the nightly newscasts of the third-rated station in a Top-30 market. Poor ratings have caused the station to pay the lowest salaries in the market, meaning that most of the staff, like you, are relatively fresh out of college. Hoping to gain more market share, your station has formed an investigative team, and "I-Team" ads are airing throughout the day. Within weeks, they capture their first exclusive story. The I-Team has staked out the local airport—a medium-size facility with many domestic routes and four international flights daily. They have found several glaring security breaches, which could allow terrorists to gain access to passenger planes, and they describe these breaches in detail. Running the story will expose the loopholes and possibly cause responsible parties to close them. However, in the short term, the story could give important information to potential terrorists who might try to exploit other airports with your information. It is obvious that such a story would give a big boost to your new investigative thrust. What do you do?

Scenario #4: You are the promotions director for a local television station that sponsors a large Christmas drive for all the charities that help the needy in your community. The station not only provides a large advance gift to start the campaign, but it also airs a feature story each night after Thanksgiving on a different charity receiving money from the drive. To avoid tying up staff resources, the station outsources the stories to a local public relations firm specializing in video news releases. About a week into this year's campaign you get a call from a woman who says that yesterday's video for the charity where she works (a food bank) was staged. In addition, the caller tells you off the record that the story stretches the truth of the amount of good the food bank does as well. You call a few of the other charities already profiled by the PR agency and detect a similar pattern: posed photos often using employees as "clients" and exaggerated stories. No one, however, wants to go on the record for fear they will be dropped from the list of charities receiving the funds. What do you do next?

The Dilemma of Dilemmas

The scenarios above are dilemmas—they present an ethical problem with no single "right" answer, even though the final decision is full of ethical ramifications. Resolving dilemmas is the business of ethics. It's not an easy process, but it is a process that can be anticipated and prepared for, and it is a process that has a wealth of theory to back up your final decision. In this chapter and throughout this book, you will be equipped with the tools to help solve dilemmas that arise in working for the mass media.

In the end, you will have tools, not answers. Answers must come from within you, but your answers should be informed by what others have written and experienced. Otherwise, you will always be forced to solve each ethical problem anew without the benefit of anyone else's insight. Gaining these tools also will help you to prevent each dilemma from spiraling into "quandary ethics"—the feeling that no best choice is available and that everyone's choice is equally valid (see Deni Elliott's essay following this chapter).

Will codes of ethics help? Virtually all the media associations have one, but they have their limitations. For instance, the ethics code for the Society of Professional Journalists could be read to allow for revealing or withholding the information in the airport scenario above, two actions that are polar opposites. That doesn't make the code useless; it simply points out a shortfall in depending on codes.

While we don't dismiss codes—and all branches of mass media, public relations, and advertising and their trade associations have them and post them on their Web sites—we believe you will find more help in the writings of philosophers, ancient and modern. We will turn to several of those writers in this chapter.

The goal of this book is to teach more than a set of rules. The goal is to give you the skills, analytical models, vocabulary and insights of others who have faced these choices, to make and justify ethical decisions.

Too many books insist that ethics can't be taught. It's situational, some claim. Since every message is unique, there is no real way to learn ethics other than by daily life. This analysis is partially correct. Most of us, outside of church or parental teachings, have learned ethics by the choices we've made or seen others make. Ethics, it is argued, is something you have, not something you do. But while it's true that reading about ethics is no guarantee you will perform your job ethically, thinking about ethics is a skill anyone can acquire.

While each facet of mass communication has its unique ethical issues, thinking about ethics is the same, whether you make your living writing advertising copy or obituaries. Each day at work, journalists make ethical choices, and some days those choices will have an influence far beyond a single broadcast or one newspaper's circulation area. Thinking about ethics won't make many of those choices easier, but, with practice, your ethical decision making can become more consistent. Ethics then will become not something you have, but something you do. A consistently ethical approach to your work as a reporter, photographer or copywriter in whatever field of mass communication you enter can improve that work as well.

Contemporary professional ethics revolves around these questions:

- What duties do I have, and to whom do I owe them?
- What values are reflected by the duties I've assumed?

Ethics takes us out of the world of "This is the way I do it" or "This is the way it's always been done" into the realm of "This is what I should do" or "This is the action that can be rationally justified." Ethics in this sense is "ought talk." The dual questions of duty and values can be answered a number of ways as long as they are consistent with each other. For example, if a journalist sees her primary duty as that of informing the public, she will place a high value on truth telling, tenacity in the pursuit of a story, etc. If a public relations practitioner sees his duty as promoting a cause, his choices would change accordingly.

It is important here to distinguish between *ethics,* which is a rational process founded on certain agreed-on principles, and *morals,* which are in the realm of religion. For example, the Ten Commandments are a moral system in the Judeo-Christian tradition, and Jewish scholars have expanded this study of the laws throughout the Bible's

A Word About Ethics

The concept of ethics comes from the Greeks, who divided the philosophical world into three parts. *Aesthetics* was the study of the beautiful and how a person could analyze beauty without relying only on subjective evaluations. *Epistemology* was the study of knowing, debates about what constitutes learning and what is knowable to the human mind. *Ethics* was the study of what is good, both for the individual and for society. Interestingly, the root of the word means "custom" or "habit," giving ethics an underlying root of behavior that is beneficial to the ongoing of society. The Greeks were concerned with the individual virtues of fortitude, justice, temperance and wisdom, as well as with societal virtues, such as freedom.

Two thousand years later, ethics has come to mean learning to make rational choices between what is good and bad, between what is morally justifiable action and what is not. Ethics also means distinguishing among choices, all of which may be morally justifiable, but some more so than others. Rationality is the key word here, for the Greeks believed, and modern philosophers affirm, that people should be able to explain their ethical decisions to others. That ability to explain ethical choices is an important one for journalists, who, in the course of reporting a single story, may have to make separate ethical decisions when dealing with sources, colleagues and, ultimately, the public. When an angry viewer telephones to ask why you broadcast the name of a rape victim, "It seemed like the right thing to do at the time" becomes a personally embarrassing and professionally unsatisfactory explanation.

Old Testament into the Talmud, a 1,400-page religious volume. The Buddhist Eightfold Path provides a similar moral framework.

But moral systems are not synonymous with ethics. *Ethics begins when elements within a moral system conflict.* Ethics is less about the conflict between right and wrong than it is about the conflict between equally compelling (or equally unattractive) values and the choices that must be made between them.

Immanuel Kant, the most influential philosopher of the 18th century, described this famous ethical dilemma: What should you do when a man carrying a gun arrives at your front door, asking the whereabouts of a second man (who is hiding in your closet) because he wants to kill him? Do you lie, or do you tell the truth? The Judeo-Christian moral system says that both killing and lying are wrong. Yet you are being asked to make a choice between the two, and Kant's solution is a surprising and perplexing one.

When elements within a moral system conflict, ethical principles can help you make tough choices. We'll review several ethical principles briefly after describing how one philosopher, Sissela Bok, says working professionals can learn to make good ethical decisions.

BOK'S MODEL

Bok's ethical decision-making framework was introduced in her book, *Lying: Moral Choice in Public and Private Life.* Bok's model is based on two premises: that we must have empathy for the people involved in ethical decisions and that maintaining social trust is a fundamental goal. With this in mind, Bok says any ethical question should be analyzed in three steps.

First, consult your own conscience about the "rightness" of an action. *How do you feel about the action?*

Second, seek expert advice for alternatives to the act creating the ethical problem. Experts, by the way, can be those either living or dead—a producer or copywriter you trust or a philosopher you admire. *Is there another way to achieve the same goal that will not raise ethical issues?*

Third, if possible, conduct a public discussion with the parties involved in the dispute. These include those who are directly involved, that is, the reporter or the source, and those indirectly involved, that is, a reader or a source. If they cannot be gathered, conduct the conversation hypothetically. The goal of this conversation is to discover *How will others respond to the proposed act?*

Let's see how Bok's model works in the following scenario. In the section after the case, follow the three steps Bok recommends and decide if you would run the story.

How Much News Is Fit to Print?

In your community, one of the major charities is the United Way. The annual fund-raising drive will begin in less than two weeks. However, at a late-night meeting of the board of directors at which no reporter is present, the executive director resigns. Though the agency is not covered by the Open Meetings Act, you are able to learn most of what went on from a source on the board.

According to her, the executive director had taken pay from the agency by submitting a falsified time sheet while he was actually away at the funeral of a college roommate. The United Way board investigated the absence and asked for his resignation, citing the lying about the absence as the reason, though most agreed that they would have given him paid leave had he asked.

The United Way wants to issue a short statement, praising the work of the executive director while regretfully accepting his resignation. The executive director also will issue a short statement citing other opportunities as his reason for leaving. You are assigned the story by an editor who does not know about the additional information you have obtained but tells you to "see if there's any more to it [the resignation] than they're telling."

You call your source on the board and she asks you, as a friend, to withhold the damaging information because it will hinder the United Way's annual fund-raising effort that is just under way and jeopardize services to needy people in the community for years to come because faith in the United Way will be destroyed. You confront the executive director. He says, if you run the story you will ruin his chances of a future career.

What do you do?

THE ANALYSIS

Bok's first step requires you to *consult your conscience.* When you do, you realize you have a problem. Your journalistic responsibility is to tell the truth, and that means providing readers with all the facts you discover. You also have a larger responsibility not to harm your community, and printing the complete story about the United Way director's actions might well cause at least some short-term harm. Clearly, your conscience is of two minds about the issue.

You move to the second step: *alternatives.* Do you simply run the resignation release, figuring that the person can do no further harm to the community and therefore should be left alone? Do you run the whole story but buttress it with board members' quotes that such an action couldn't happen again, figuring that you have restored public trust in the agency? Do you sit on the story until after the fund-raising drive and risk the loss of trust from readers if the story circulates around town as a rumor? Again, there are alternatives, but each has some cost.

In the third step of Bok's model, you will attempt to *hold a public ethical dialogue* with all of the parties involved. Most likely you won't ask the executive director, the story's source, average readers of the newspaper, a United Way donor, and your editor into the newsroom for a lengthy chat about the issues involved when you are on deadline. Instead you can conduct an imaginary discussion among the parties involved. Such a discussion might go like this:

EXECUTIVE DIRECTOR: "I think my resignation is sufficient penalty for any mistake I might have made, and your article will jeopardize my ability to find another job. It's really hurting my wife and kids, and they've done nothing wrong."

REPORTER: "But shouldn't you have thought about that *before* you decided to falsify the time sheet? This is a good story, and I think the public should know what the people who are handling their donations are like."

READER 1: "Wait a minute. I am the public, and I'm tired of all of this bad news your paper focuses on. This man has done nothing but good in the community, and I can't see where any money that belonged to the poor went into his pocket. Why can't we see some good news for a change?"

READER 2: "I disagree. I buy the paper precisely because it does this kind of reporting. It's stories like this that keep the government, the charities, and everyone else on their toes."

PUBLISHER: "You mean like a watchdog function."

READER 2: "Exactly. And if it bothers you, don't read it."

PUBLISHER: "I don't really like to hurt people with the power that we have, but if we don't print stories like this, and the community later finds out that we withheld the news, our credibility is ruined, and we're out of business." [To source] "Did you request that the information be off the record?"

SOURCE: "No. But I never thought you'd use it in your story."

REPORTER: "I'm a reporter. I report what I hear for a living. What did you think I would do with it? To use the same argument he used a minute ago, it's stories like these that allow me to support my family."

EXECUTIVE DIRECTOR: "So it's your career or mine, is that what you're saying? Look, no charges have been filed here, but if your story runs, I look like a criminal. Is that fair?"

PUBLISHER: "And if it doesn't run, we don't keep our promise to the community. Is that fair?"

NEEDY MOTHER: "Fair? You want to talk fair? Do you suffer if the donations go down? No, I do. This is just another story to you. It's the difference in me and my family getting by."

The conversation could continue, and other points of view could be voiced. Your imaginary conversations could be more or less elaborate than the one above, but out of this discussion it should be possible to rationally support an ethical choice.

There are two cautions in using Bok's model for ethical decision making. First, it is important to go through all three steps before making a final choice. Most of us make ethical choices prematurely, after we've consulted only our consciences, an error Bok says results in a lot of flabby moral thinking. Second, while you will not be endowed with any clairvoyant powers to anticipate your ethical problems, the ethical dialogue outlined in the third step is best when conducted in advance of the event, not in the heat of writing a story.

For instance, an advertising copywriter might conduct such a discussion about whether advertising copy can ethically withhold disclaimers about potential harm from a product. A reporter might conduct such a discussion well in advance of the time he is actually asked to withhold an embarrassing name or fact from a story. Since it is likely that such dilemmas will arise in your chosen profession (the illustration above is based on what happened to one of the authors the first day on the job), your answer will be more readily available and more logical if you hold such discussions either with trusted colleagues in a casual atmosphere or by yourself, well in advance of the problem.

Bok's model forces you to consider alternatives. It's in the pursuit of these alternatives that journalistic technique improves.

GUIDELINES FOR MAKING ETHICAL DECISIONS

Since the days of ancient Greece, philosophers have tried to draft a series of rules or guidelines governing how to make ethical choices. Obviously, in most ethical dilemmas such as the one above, you will need principles to help you determine what to do amid conflicting voices. While a number of principles work well, we will review five.

Aristotle's Golden Mean

Aristotle, teaching in the fourth century B.C., believed that happiness—which some scholars translate as "flourishing"—was the ultimate human good. By flourishing, Aristotle meant to exercise "practical reason" in the conduct of any particular activity through the setting of high standards.

Aristotle believed that practical reason was exercised by individuals. The *phrenemos,* or person of practical wisdom, was that human being who demonstrated ethical excellence through daily activity. For Aristotle, the highest virtue was citizenship, and the highest form of citizenship was exemplified by the statesman, a politician who exercised so much practical wisdom in his daily activity that he elevated craft to art. In contemporary terms, we might think of a *phrenemos* as a person who excels at one of a variety of activities—cellist Yo-Yo Ma, poet Maya Angelou, filmmakers George Lucas and Steven Spielberg. They are people who flourish in their professional performance, extending our own vision of what is possible.

*This notion of flourishing led Aristotle to assert that people and their acts, not
particular sets of rules, are the moral basis of activity.* His ethical system resulted in
the creation of what is now called *virtue ethics.* Virtue ethics flows from both the
nature of the act itself and the moral character of the person who acts. In the Aristotelian sense, the way to behave ethically is that (1) you must know (through the
exercise of practical reasoning) what you are doing; (2) you must select the act for its
own sake—in order to flourish; and (3) the act itself must spring from a firm and
unchanging character.

It is not stretching Aristotle's framework to assert that one way to learn ethics
is to select heroes and to try to model your individual acts and ultimately your professional character on what you believe they would do. An Aristotelian might well
consult this hero as an expert when making an ethical choice. Asking what my hero
would do in a particular situation is not necessarily a poor form of ethical analysis.
The trick, however, is to select your heroes carefully and still think for yourself
rather than merely copy behavior you have seen previously.

Aristotle's philosophy is often reduced to the somewhat simplistic *"golden
mean"* which is often phased like this: *Virtue lies at the mean between two extremes
of excess and deficiency.* Courage, for example, is a mean between foolhardiness
on one hand and cowardice on the other. But to determine that mean for yourself,
you have to exercise practical wisdom, act according to high standards, and act in
accordance with firm and continuing character traits. *In reality, therefore, the middle ground of a virtue is not a single point on a line that is the same for every individual.* It is instead a range of behaviors that varies individually, while avoiding the

Unacceptable behaviors (deficiency)	Acceptable behaviors	Unacceptable behaviors (excess)
Cowardice	Courage	Foolhardiness
Shamelessness	Modesty	Bashfulness
Stinginess	Generosity	Wastefulness

FIGURE 1.1. Aristotle's golden mean.

undesirable extremes, as shown in Figure 1.1., in examples from Aristotle's *Nichomachean Ethics.*

Continuing with the example of courage, this principle can be illustrated by considering two witnesses to a potential drowning. If one onlooker is a poor swimmer yet a fast runner, then it would be foolhardy for him to jump into the water and attempt a rescue, just as it would be cowardly for him to do nothing. For him, the courageous thing might be to run for help. If, on the other hand, the second onlooker is a good swimmer, it would not be foolhardy for her to attempt a rescue; in fact, it would be cowardly for her not to jump into the water. In each instance, both onlookers have done the courageous act, yet in radically different ways.

Seeking the golden mean implies that individual acts are not disconnected from one another, but rather that they form a whole that a person of good character should aspire to. A virtue theory of ethics is not outcome-oriented. Instead, it is agent-oriented, and right actions in a virtue theory of ethics are a result of an agent seeking virtue and accomplishing it. As Aristotle wrote in *Nicomachean Ethics:* "We learn an art or craft by doing the things that we shall have to do when we have learnt it: for instance, men become builders by building houses, harpers by playing on the harp. Similarly we become just by doing just acts, temperate by doing temperate acts, brave by doing brave acts."

Far from being old-fashioned, in this age of questions about character, Aristotle's concept of virtue ethics has been rediscovered by a variety of professions. As Kenneth Woodward (1994) states in a *Newsweek* essay entitled "What is Virtue?" a call for virtue is still relevant today:

> But before politicians embrace virtue as their latest election-year slogan, they would do well to tune into contemporary philosophy. Despite the call for virtue, we live in an age of moral relativism. According to the dominant school of moral philosophy, the skepticism engendered by the Enlightenment has reduced all ideas of right and wrong to matters of personal taste, emotional preference or cultural choice. . . . Against this moral relativism, advocates of the "ethics of virtue" argue that some personal choices are morally superior to others.

Kant's Categorical Imperative

Immanuel Kant's *categorical imperative* asserts that an individual should act on the premise that the choices one makes for oneself could become universal law. Furthermore, he states that you should act so that you treat humanity always as an end and never as a means only. Kant called these two maxims "categorical" imperatives, meaning that their demands were not subject to situational factors. Many readers will recognize the similarity between Kant's categorical imperative and the Bible's golden rule: Do unto others as you would have others do unto you. The two are quite similar in their focus on duty.

Kant's ethical theory is based on the notion that it is the act itself, rather than the person who acts, in which moral force resides. This theory of ethics is unlike Aristotle's in that it moves the notion of what is ethical from the actor to the act itself. This does not mean that Kant did not believe in moral character, but rather that people could act morally from a sense of duty even though their character might incline them to act otherwise.

For Kant, an action was morally justified only if it was performed from duty, and in Kant's moral universe there were two sorts of duties. The strict duties were generally negative: not to murder, not to break promises, not to lie. The meritorious duties were more positive: to aid others, to develop one's talents, to show gratitude. Kant spent very little time defining these notions, but philosophers have generally asserted that the strict duties (i.e., not to harm) are somewhat more morally mandatory than the meritorious duties (e.g., to render aid).

To some, Kant's ethical reasoning indicates that as long as you perform the right act based on what the categorical imperative and duty demand, the consequences of that act are not important. We prefer a somewhat less austere reading of Kant. While Kant's view is that the moral worth of an action does not depend on its consequences, those consequences are not irrelevant. For example, a surgeon may show moral virtue in attempting to save a patient through an experimental procedure, but the decision about whether to undertake that procedure requires taking into account the probability of a cure. This framing of Kantian principles allows us to learn from our mistakes.

The test of a moral act, according to Kant, is its universality—whether it can be applied to everyone. For instance, Kant would insist that the ethical person drive at a speed and in a manner that would be appropriate for everyone else on the same highway. Under Kant's categorical imperative, journalists can claim few special privileges, such as the right to lie or the right to invade privacy in order to get a story. Kant's view, if taken seriously, reminds you of what you give up—truth, privacy and the like—when you make certain ethical decisions.

Utilitarianism

The original articulation of *utilitarianism* by Englishmen Jeremy Bentham and later John Stuart Mill in the nineteenth century introduced what was then a novel notion into ethics discussions: *The consequences of actions are important in deciding whether they are ethical.* In the utilitarian view, it may be considered ethical to harm one person for the benefit of the larger group. This approach, for example, is the ethical justification for investigative reporting, the results of which may harm individuals even as they are printed or broadcast in the hope of providing a greater societal good.

In his 1977 work, *On Human Care,* Harvard ethicist Arthur Dyck claims that the appeal of utilitarianism is the "apparent advantages that accrue from identifying and specifying a single moral principle . . . that can be stated in an exceptionless form." In writing about Mill, Dyck (p. 55) claims:

TABLE 1.1. The Shifting Focus of Ethics From Aristotle to Mill

Philosopher	Known for	Popularly Known as	Emphasized
Aristotle	Golden mean	Virtue lies between extremes.	The actor
Kant	Categorical imperative	Act so your choices could be universal law; treat humanity as an end, never as a means only.	The action
Mill	Utility principle	An act's rightness is determined by its contribution to a desirable end.	The outcome

He took the view that the rightness or wrongness of any action is decided by its consequences. . . . His particular understanding of what is best on the whole was that which brings about the most happiness or the least suffering, i.e., the best balance of pleasure over pain for the greatest number.

The benefit of the "formula" as Dyck calls it, is that it provides a principle by which rightness and wrongness can be identified and judged, conflicts can be adjudicated and exceptions can be decided. The utilitarian calculus also has made possible the "quantification of welfare" Dyck says, allowing governments to make decisions that create the most favorable balance of benefits over harms.

With its focus on the consequences of an action, utilitarianism completes a cycle begun with Aristotle (see Table 1.1). Aristotle, in developing the golden mean, focused on the *actor.* Kant, in his categorical imperative, focused on the *action,* while Mill, in his utilitarian philosophy, focused on the *outcome.*

Utilitarianism has been condensed to the ethical philosophy of the greatest good for the greatest number. While this pithy phrase is a very rough and ready characterization of utilitarian theory, it also has led to an overly mechanistic application of the principle: Just tally up the amount of good and subtract the amount of harm. If the remaining number is positive, the act is ethical. However, when properly applied, utilitarianism is not mechanical.

To do justice to utilitarian theory, it must be understood within an historical context. Mill wrote following the changes of the Enlightenment. The principle of democracy was fresh and untried, and the thought that the average person should be able to speak his mind to those in power was novel. Utilitarianism as Mill conceived of it was a profoundly social ethic; Mill was among the first to acknowledge that the good of an entire society had a place in ethical reasoning.

Mill was what philosophers call a *valuational hedonist.* He argued that pleasure— and the absence of pain—was the only intrinsic moral end. Mill further asserted that an act was right in the proportion in which it contributed to the general happiness, wrong in the proportion in which it contributed to general unhappiness or pain. Utilitarianism can be subtle and complex. Mill acknowledged that the same act can make some happy but cause others pain. Mill insisted that both sets of consequences be valued simultaneously, a precarious activity but one that forces discussion of competing stakeholder claims.

Utilitarianism can be applied in both the specific and the general, what some philosophers have referred to as "act utilitarianism" as opposed to "rule utilitarianism."

For instance, one way of evaluating the ethical impact of investigative reporting is through the application of *act utilitarianism*. A producer might reason that an investigative report, while it would hurt the subject of the investigation, might further the general welfare. Crooks and cheats could be exposed, general societal problems aired. When the methods of obtaining information are ethical, investigative journalism can be justified because it contributes more to human happiness than it extracts in the pain it causes some individuals.

Rule utilitarianism, on the other hand, might be applied as follows. Take the assertion sometimes made that advertising itself is unethical. The rule utilitarian would note that in contemporary American culture advertising provides needed information about a variety of products and services. It is often entertaining, and it supports the media we enjoy. Of course, advertising sometimes can be in poor taste, it can be intrusive, and it can sometimes provide false or misleading information. When balancing the societal good against the societal harm, the rule utilitarian might well conclude that while the practice of advertising is ethical, certain forms of the activity—advertising products to children or advertising certain substances such as alcohol—should be regulated. Utilitarian theory does allow the sort of ethical reasoning that approves of particular activities while rejecting specific acts.

In utilitarian theory, no one's happiness is any more valuable than anyone else's, and definitely not more valuable than everyone's—quantity and quality being equal. In democratic societies, this is a particularly important concept because it meshes well with certain social and political goals. In actual application, utilitarianism uniformly applied has a way of puncturing self-interest, although critics have argued that, when badly applied, it can actually promote selfishness.

Utilitarianism also suggests that moral questions are objective, empirical and even in some sense scientific. Utilitarianism promotes a universal ethical standard that each rational person can determine. However, utilitarianism is among the most criticized of philosophical principles because it is so difficult to accurately anticipate all the ramifications of a particular act. Different philosophers also have disputed how one calculates the good, rendering any utilitarian calculus fundamentally error prone.

While we recommend utilitarianism as a theory, we do caution you against exclusive reliance on it. Taken to extremes, the act of calculating the good can lead to ethical gridlock, with each group of stakeholders having seemingly equally strong claims with little way to choose among them. Sloppily done, utilitarianism may bias you toward short-term benefit. And a view to the short term, in an ethical sense, can often be shortsighted.

Pluralistic Theory of Value

Philosopher William David Ross (1930) based his ethical theory on the belief that there is often more than one ethical value simultaneously "competing" for preeminence in our ethical decision making. Ross sets up this tension in the title of his 1930 book: *The Right and the Good.* In an essay entitled "Appreciating W.D. Ross," ethicist Christopher Meyers (2003, 84) says:

> As the book title suggests, Ross distinguished between the *right* and the *good.* The latter term refers to an objective, if indefinable, quality present in all acts. It is something seen, not done. Right, on the other hand, refers to actions. A right action is something undertaken by persons motivated by correct reasons and on careful reflection. Not all right actions, however, will be productive of the good.

In acknowledging the tension between the good and the right, Ross differs from Kant or Mill, who proposed only one ultimate value. To Ross these competing ethical claims, which he calls duties, are equal, providing the circumstances of the particular moral choice are equal. Further, these duties gain their moral weight not from their consequences but from the highly personal nature of duty.

Ross proposed these types of duties:

1. Those duties of *fidelity,* based on my implicit or explicit promise;
2. Those duties of *reparation,* arising from a previous wrongful act;
3. Those duties of *gratitude* that rest on previous acts of others;
4. Those duties of *justice* that arise from the necessity to ensure the equitable and meritorious distribution of pleasure or happiness;
5. Those duties of *beneficence* that rest on the fact that there are others in the world whose lot we can better;
6. Those duties of *self-improvement* that rest on the fact that we can improve our own condition; and
7. One negative duty: the duty of *not injuring others.*

We would recommend two additional duties that may be implied by Ross's list but are not specifically stated:

1. The duty to tell the truth, *veracity* (which may be implied by fidelity); and
2. The duty to *nurture,* to help others achieve some measure of self-worth and achievement.

Ross's typology of duties works well for professionals who often must balance competing roles. It also brings to ethical reasoning some affirmative notions of the primacy of community and relationships as a way to balance the largely rights-based traditions of much Western philosophical theory.

Ross's concept of multiple duties allows the ethical decision maker to appreciate and consider important aspects of a situation without losing the value of following some rules. Like Kant, Ross divided his duties into two kinds. *Prima facie* duties are those duties that seem to be right because of the nature of the act itself. *Duty proper,* sometimes called "actual duties," are those duties, that are paramount given specific circumstances.

Arriving at your duty proper from among the prima facie duties requires that you consider what ethicists call the *morally relevant differences.* But Ross (1988, 24) warns that it won't always be easy:

> I would contend that in principle there is no reason to anticipate that every act that is our duty is so for one and the same reason. Why should two sets or circumstances, or one set of circumstances *not* possess different characteristics, any one of which makes a certain act our *prima facie* duty?

Let's take an example using one of Ross's prima facie duties: keeping promises. In your job as a reporter, you have made an appointment with the mayor to discuss a year-end feature on your community. On your way to City Hall, you drive by a serious auto accident and see a young child wandering, dazed, along the road. If you stop to help you will certainly be late for your appointment and may have to cancel altogether. You have broken a promise.

But is that act ethical?

Ross would probably say yes because the specific aspects of the situation had a bearing on the fulfillment of a *prima facie* duty. You exercised discernment. You knew that your commitment to the mayor was a relatively minor sort of promise. Your news organization will not be hurt by postponing the interview, and your act allowed you to fulfill the prima facie duties of beneficence, avoiding harm, and nurturing. Had the interview been more important, or the wreck less severe, the morally relevant factors would have been different. Ross's pluralistic theory of values may be more difficult to apply than a system of absolute rules, but it reflects the way we make ethical choices.

Ross's concept of multiple duties "helps to explain why we feel uneasy about breaking a promise even when we are justified in doing so. Our uneasiness comes from the fact that we have broken a *prima facie* duty even as we fulfilled another. It helps explain why even the good consequences that might come from a failure to tell the truth or keep a promise do not always seem to us to justify the lie or breach of confidence" (Lebacqz 1985, 27).

Communitarianism

Classical ethical theory places its dominant intellectual emphasis on the individual and individual acts by emphasizing concepts such as character, choice, liberty and duty.

But contemporary politics points out the intellectual weakness in this approach. Consider the environment. On many environmental questions, it is possible for people to make appropriate individual decisions—today I drive my car—which taken together promote environmental degradation. My individual decision to drive my car doesn't matter very much; but when individual decisions are aggregated, the impact is profound. Furthermore, this environmental impact has consequences not for a single generation but for geologic time. Individual human beings cannot opt out of participating in daily living in the physical environment—unless they decide to live on the moon. While classical ethical theory acknowledges such problems, it provides little guidance for determining individual action or in understanding how individual actions fit within a larger whole.

Communitarianism, which has its roots in political theory, seeks to provide ethical guidance when confronting the sort of societywide issues that mark current political and business activity.

Communitarianism spotlights society understood holistically and dynamically. Communitarianism returns to Aristotle's concept of the "polis"—or community—and invests it with moral weight. People begin their lives, at least in a biological sense, as members of a two-person community. Communitarian philosophy extends this biological beginning to a philosophical worldview. "In communitarianism, persons have certain inescapable claims on one another that cannot be renounced except at the cost of their humanity" (Christians et al. 1995, 14). In modern parlance, communitarians assert that when issues are political and social, community trumps individuals but does not trample them.

Communitarianism focuses on the outcome of individual ethical decisions, understood not as disconnected choices but analyzed as the impact of the sum of the choices on society. "Nurturing communitarian citizenship entails, at a minimum, a journalism committed to justice, covenant and empowerment. Authentic communities are marked by justice; in strong democracies, courageous talk is mobilized into action. . . . In normative communities, citizens are empowered for social transformation, not merely freed from external constraints" (Christians et al. 1995, 14).

Communitarianism asserts that social justice is the predominant moral value. While communitarians recognize the value of process, they are just as concerned with outcomes. They formally acknowledge one of history's more difficult lessons, that "good" process—for example, democratic elections or the writing of constitutions—can produce "bad" outcomes—for example, the 1933 takeover of Germany by a minority party headed by Hitler or the inclusion in the original U.S. Constitution of the three-fifths clause (African-Americans were equal to three-fifths of a single European Caucasian colonist for purposes of population count to determine the number of representatives each state would have in the U.S. Congress). Communitarians measure individual acts against the normative standard of their impact in creating a more just society.

Communitarian thinking allows ethical discussion to include values such as altruism and benevolence on an equal footing with more traditional questions such as truth telling and loyalty. Indeed, game theory (refined by John Nash and discussed in Case 9-A) has demonstrated that cooperation, one of the foundation stones of community, provides desirable results once thought to be possible only through competition (Axelrod 1984). Cooperation is particularly powerful when something called the "shadow of the future" looms sufficiently large. The "shadow of the future" means that people understand they will encounter the outcome of their decisions, in the form of their impact on others, in readily foreseeable time.

Communitarian philosophy suffers from a lack of a succinct summation of its general propositions. Amitai Etzioni, one of the movement's leaders, suggests that communitarianism emphasizes responsibilities "to the conditions and elements we all share, to the community." Political theorist Michael Sandel arranges communitarianism as both an extension of and a counterpoint to traditional political liberalism. Like traditional political liberalism—as expressed in this book by the philosophy of John Rawls and, to a lesser extent, the utilitarians—a communitarian community would be manifest in the aims and values of its individual participants.

But it would differ from a traditional community in the sense that community members would include, as part of their understanding of self, their membership in the community. "For them, community describes not just what they have as fellow citizens but also what they are, not as a relationship they choose (as in a voluntary association) but an attachment they discover, not merely an attribute but as a constituent of their identity" (Sandel 1982, 150). Communitarian community resembles family more than it resembles town.

We believe that communitarianism is most helpful in discussing ethical issues that revolve around the journalistic role. Viewed this way, journalism cannot separate itself from the political and economic system of which it is a part.

Communitarian thinking makes it possible to ask whether current practice (for example, a traditional definition of news) provides a good mechanism for a community to discover itself, learn about itself, and ultimately transform itself into a more just and cohesive entity. Communitarian reasoning allows journalists to understand their institutional role and to evaluate their performance against shared societal values.

For instance, the newsroom adage "if it bleeds it leads" might sell newspapers or attract viewers, but it also might give a false impression of community and its perils to the most vulnerable members. Communitarianism would not disallow the coverage of crime but would demand context that would help viewers or readers decide if they need to take action.

Thinking as a communitarian mutes the competition among journalistic organizations while amplifying the collective effect that journalists and their organizations have on society and culture. Communitarian thinking can provide journalists with an effective justification for sometimes placing family before work, for including mobilizing information in a story about the local rape crisis center, or for inviting viewers and readers to help determine the sort of political stories in which they are most interested and then providing ample coverage of them.

Because communitarianism is a philosophy of ideals, it is difficult to find concrete journalistic examples of the theory in action. Many writers have linked communitarian philosophy with the civic journalism movement. But like the philosophy of communitarianism, the practice of civic journalism has not yet been embraced by the mainstream of society.

THE "SCIENCE" OF ETHICS

Life in the 21st century has changed how most people think about issues, such as what constitutes a fact and what does or does not influence moral certainty. We will explore those changes, and the changes they have led to in the lives of mass-communication professionals, in more detail in the next chapter. But for now, it suffices to say that ethical theory, with its apparent uncertainties and contradictions, appears to have taken a backseat to science in much of modern life. Part of the reason people have become so concerned with ethics is that they seek "the answer" to ethical dilemmas in the same way they seek "the answer" in science. In such an endeavor, the vagaries of ethical choice as contrasted with scientific knowledge seem unsatisfactory.

We'd like to offer you a different conceptualization of "the facts" of both science and ethics. Science, and the seeming certainty of scientific knowledge, have undergone vast changes in the past 100 years. After all, before Einstein, most educated people believed that Sir Francis Bacon had accurately and eternally described the basic actions and laws of the physical universe. But Bacon was wrong. Scientific inquiry in the 20th century searchingly explored a variety of physical phenomena, almost always uncovering new relationships, new areas of knowledge, and most importantly, new and expanding areas of ignorance. What modern humanity regarded as the certainty of scientific truth has changed fundamentally in the last 100 years, and humanity has every reason to expect similar changes in this century. Science and certainty are not synonymous, despite our tendency to blur the two.

Contrast these fundamental changes in the scientific worldview with the developments of moral theory. Aristotle's writing, more than 2,000 years old and with no fundamental changes, still has much to recommend it to the modern era, although, of course, there will continue to be new interpretations. The same can be said of utilitarianism and of the Kantian approach—both subject to more than a 100 years of critical review. Certainly, new moral thinking has emerged—for example, John Rawls's work on utilitarian theory (Chapter 6). But such work tends to build on rather than radically alter the moral theorizing that has gone before. This is not to assert that ethical philosophers do not have fundamental debates but rather to suggest that these debates have, in general, tended to deepen and enlarge previous insights rather than to "prove" them incorrect in some epistemological sense.

From this viewpoint, there is continuity in thinking about ethics that is lacking in the development of scientific thought. Further, thinking about ethics in a global way uncovers some striking areas of agreement. We are aware of no ethical system, for example, that argues that murder is an ethical behavior, or that lying, cheating and stealing are the sorts of activities that human beings ought to engage in on a regular basis. Applying the various ethical theories outlined in this chapter will deepen your understanding of these principles and the complexity of their application, but they are unlikely to change your views about the ethical correctness of murder or lying.

When the average person contrasts ethics with science, it is ethics that tends to be viewed as changeable, unsystematic and idiosyncratic. Science has rigor, proof and some relationship to an external reality. We would like to suggest that such characterizations arise from a short-term view of the history of science and ethics. In our view, ethics as a field has at least as much continuity of thought as developments in science. And while it cannot often be quantified, it has the rigor, the systematic quality, and the relationship to reality that moderns too often characterize as the exclusive domain of scientific thinking.

Suggested Readings

ARISTOTLE. *The Nicomachean ethics.*

BOK, SISSELA. 1978. *Lying: Moral choice in public and private life.* New York: Random House.

CHRISTIANS, CLIFFORD, JOHN FERRE, and MARK FACKLER. 1995. *Good news: Social ethics and the press.* New York: Oxford University Press.

GERT, BERNARD. 1988. *Morality: A new justification of the moral rules.* New York: Oxford University Press.

MILL, JOHN STUART. *On liberty.*

PETERS, JOHN D. 2000. *Speaking in the air: A history of the idea of communication.* Chicago: University of Chicago Press.

POJMAN, L. 1998. *Ethical theory: Classical and contemporary readings.* Belmont, CA: Wadsworth Publishing Co.

ROSS, W.D. 1930. *The right and the good.* Oxford, England: Clarendon Press.

CHAPTER 1 ESSAY

Cases and Moral Systems

DENI ELLIOTT
University of South Florida—St. Petersburg

Case studies are wonderful vehicles for ethics discussions. Some of their great strengths include helping discussants

1. appreciate the complexity of newsroom decision making;
2. understand the context within which difficult decisions are made;
3. track the consequences of choosing one action over another; and
4. learn both how and when to reconcile and how and when to tolerate divergent points of view.

However, when case studies are misused, these great strengths become their fundamental weaknesses. Case studies are vehicles for an ethics discussion, not its ultimate destination. The purpose of an ethics discussion is to teach discussants how to "do ethics"—that is, to teach them processes by which they can practice and improve their own critical decision-making abilities. Each discussant should, through the use of the case-study vehicle, reach the end point: a reasoned response to the issue at hand.

When the discussion stops short of this point, it is often because the destination has been fogged in by one or more myths of media case discussions:

Myth 1: Every opinion is equally valid.

Not true. The best opinion (conclusion) is the one that is best supported by judicious analysis of fact and theory. In an ethics discussion, it is the one that best addresses the morally relevant factors of the case. An action has morally relevant factors if it is likely to cause some individual to suffer an evil that any rational person would wish to avoid (such as death, disability, pain, loss of freedom or pleasure), or if it is the kind of action that generally causes evil (such as deception, breaking promises, cheating, disobedience of law, or neglect of duty) (see Gert 1988).

Myth 2: Since we can't agree on an answer, there is no right answer.

It's tough to take into account all of the various points of view when working through a case. One way people avoid doing this is to refuse to choose among the different perspectives. But this retreat to fatalistic subjectivism is not necessary. It may be that there are a number of acceptable answers. But there also will be many wrong answers—many approaches that the group can agree would be unacceptable. When discussants begin to despair of ever reaching any agreement on a right answer or answers, it is time to reflect on all of the agreement that exists within the group concerning the actions that would be out of bounds.

Myth 3: It hardly matters if you come up with the "ethical thing to do," since people ultimately act out of their own self-interest anyway.

The point of ethical reflection is to find and deal with those situations when one person should not simply do that which benefits oneself. Acting ethically means to refrain from causing unjustified harm, even when prudential concerns must be set aside.

Any institution supported by society, manufacturing firms or media corporations, as well as medical centers, provides some service that merits that support. No matter what the service, practitioners or companies that act only in the short-term interest, for instance to make money, will not last long. Free-market pragmatism, as well as ethics, dictates that it makes little sense to ignore the expectations of consumers and of the society at large.

The guidelines below can serve as a map for an ethics discussion. They are helpful to have when working through unfamiliar terrain toward individual end points. They also can help you detour around the myths discussed earlier. While discussing the case, check to see if these questions are being addressed:

1. What are the morally relevant factors of the case?
    (a) Will the proposed action cause an evil—such as death, disability, pain, loss of freedom or opportunity, or a loss of pleasure—that any rational person would wish to avoid?
    (b) Is the proposed action the sort of action —such as deception, breaking promises, cheating, disobedience of law, or disobedience of professional or role-defined duty—that generally causes evil?
2. If the proposed action is one described above, is a greater evil being prevented or punished?
3. If so, is the actor in a unique position to prevent or punish such an evil, or is that a more appropriate role for some other person or profession?
4. If the actor followed through on the action, would he be allowing himself to be an exception to a rule that he thinks everyone else should follow? If so, then the action is prudent, not moral. One way to test this out is for journalists to ask how they would react if a person in another profession did what they are thinking of doing. Would the journalists applaud the action, or would they write an exposé?
5. If, at this point, the proposed action still seems justified, consider if a rational, uninvolved person would appreciate the reason for causing harm. Are the journalists ready to state, explain and defend the proposed action in a public forum?

2

Information Ethics:
A Profession Seeks the Truth

By the end of this chapter, you should be familiar with:

- **both the Enlightenment and pragmatic constructions of truth.**
- **the development and several criticisms of objective news reporting as a professional ideal.**
- **why truth in "getting" the news may be as important as truth in reporting it.**
- **how to develop a personal list of ethical news values.**

INTRODUCTION

Each of the traditional professions has laid claims to one of the central tenets of philosophy. Law, ideally, is equated with justice; medicine with the duty to render aid. Journalism, too, has a lofty ideal: the communication of truth.

But the ideal of truth is problematic. In routine interaction we consider truth a stable commodity: it doesn't change much for us on a day-to-day basis, nor does it vary greatly among members of a community. While we are willing to accept some cultural "lies"—for example, the existence of Santa Claus—we stand ready to condemn others—for example, income tax evasion or fraud. Most of the time, we seem to know what the boundaries are, at least when we deal with one another face-to-face. However, the concept of truth has changed throughout human history. At one level or another, human beings since ancient times have acknowledged that truth may vary depending on individual points of view. Since Plato's analogy of life as shadows on the wall of a cave 3,000 years ago, people have grappled with the amorphous nature of truth.

Compounding the modern problem of the shifting nature of truth is the changing media audience. When a profession accepts the responsibility of printing and broadcasting the truth, facts that are apparent in face-to-face interaction become subject to different interpretations among geographically and culturally diverse viewers and readers. Ideas that were once readily accepted are open to debate. The whole concept of telling the truth becomes not merely a matter of possessing good moral character but something that requires learning how to recognize truth and how to convey it in the least distorted manner possible.

A CHANGING VIEW OF TRUTH

One pre-Socratic Greek tradition viewed truth—*alethea*—as encompassing all that humans remember, singled out through memory from everything that is destined for *Lethe,* the river of forgetfulness (Bok 1978). Linking truth and remembrance is essential in an oral culture, one that requires information be memorized and repeated so as not to be forgotten. Repeating the message, often in the form of songs or poetry, meant that the accumulated ideas and knowledge were kept alive or true for subsequent generations. Homer's *Iliad* and *Odyssey* or much of the Bible's Old Testament served this function.

This oral notion of truth, as noted in Table 2.1, was gradually discarded once words and ideas were written down. However, it has come to the fore again with the advent of television. Television allows viewers to hear the words of the president rather than wait for those words to be passed down orally or in writing. When we see something on television, we assume that it closely corresponds to reality—that it is in some sense true. The maxim "Seeing is believing" reminds us that truth has somehow become tangled up with pictures and presence. It is an oral concept of truth that has been a dormant form of knowledge for hundreds of years.

While the other ancient Greeks tied truth to human memory, Plato linked truth to human rationality and intellect. In *The Republic,* Plato equated truth with a world of pure form, a world to which human beings had only indirect access. In Plato's vision, there was an ideal notion of a chair—but that ideal chair did not exist in reality. What people thought of as a chair was as similar to the ideal chair as the shadows on the wall of the cave are to objects illuminated by the fire. Truth was knowable only to the human intellect—it could not be touched or verified.

Plato's metaphor has had a profound influence on Western thought. Not only did Plato link truth to rationality, as opposed to human experience, but his work implies that truth is something that can be captured only through the intellect. Platonic truth is implicit within a thing itself; truth defined the "perfect form." Plato's concept of

TABLE 2.1. A Philosophy of Truth Emerges

Source	Truth Equals
Ancient Greeks	What is memorable and is handed down
Plato	What abides in the world of perfect forms
Medieval	What the king, Church or God says
Milton	What emerges from the "marketplace of ideas"
Enlightenment	What is verifiable, replicable, universal
Pragmatists	What is filtered through individual perception

truth separated the notion of something as true from the external world in which that thing existed.

Subsequent centuries and thinkers adhered to Plato's view. Medieval theologians believed truth was revealed only by God or by the Church. The intellectual legacy of the Reformation centered on whether it is possible for the average person to ascertain truth without benefit of a priest or a king. About 200 years later, Milton suggested that competing notions of the truth should be allowed to coexist, with the ultimate truth eventually emerging (see Table 2.1).

Milton's assertions foreshadowed the philosophy of the Enlightenment, from which modern journalism borrows its notion of truth. The Enlightenment cast truth in secular terms and developed what is now called a "correspondence theory" of truth. The correspondence theory asserts that truth should correspond to some external set of facts or observations. The Enlightenment concept of truth was linked to what human beings could perceive with their senses harnessed through the intellect. Truth acquired substance. It was something that could be perceived, and ultimately perception of truth was something that could be replicated.

This Enlightenment notion of truth has remained with us and is essential to what contemporary scholars refer to as the scientific method. Truth has become increasingly tied to that which is written down, to that which can be empirically verified, to that which can be perceived by the human senses and to that which does not vary among people or among cultures. It is a truth uniquely suited to the written word, for it links what is written with what is factual, accurate and important in the most profound of senses.

This Enlightenment view of truth undergirds the journalistic ideal of objectivity. Objectivity has its intellectual roots in the previous 300 years. While objectivity has many definitions, it may be considered, most simply, a mechanism that allows journalists to divorce fact from opinion. Objectivity is a way of knowing, an episteme that connects human perception with facts and then knowledge. Objectivity is also a process of information collection (Ward 2004). Journalists view objectivity as refusing to allow individual bias to influence what they report or how they cover it. It is in journalism that all facts and people are regarded as equal and equally worthy of coverage. Culture, an individual sense of mission, and individual and organizational feelings and views do not belong in objective news accounts. An Enlightenment view of truth allowed objectivity to be considered an attainable ideal.

However, philosophy was not the only reason, and some scholars have argued not even the most important reason, that objectivity became a professional standard in the early 1900s. The libertarian press of the Enlightenment was not really a mass press, and it garnered most of its financial support from political advertising and most of its readers through partisan political reporting. As the United States became urban in the late 1800s, publishers realized that to reach this large urban audience, they needed more support from a wider variety of advertisers. To convince potential advertisers that their advertising would be seen and possibly acted upon by a large audience, publishers had to make certain their publications would be read. Partisan publications could not ensure that, for strong views offended potential readers. Interestingly, the Internet has removed the financial imperative of objectivity and made it once again financially viable to operate a partisan press, albeit a virtual one.

What publishers at the turn of the 20th century needed was a product that built on an Enlightenment philosophical construction that guaranteed that facts would be facts, no matter who was doing the reading. Opinion would be relegated to specific pages. Both facts and opinion could be wrapped around advertising (Schudson 1978).

Objectivity came along at an advantageous time for yet another reason. The mass press of the early 1900s was deeply and corruptly involved in yellow journalism. Fabricated stories were common; newspaper wars were close to the real thing. Although many of the specific events of the era (for example, the apocryphal story that William Randolph Hearst began the Spanish-American War so he would have something to photograph) have been exaggerated, the excesses in pursuit of circulation tarnished the profession's image.

Objectivity was a good way to clean up journalism's act with a set of standards where seemingly none had existed before. It fit the cultural expectations of the Enlightenment that truth was knowable and ascertainable. And it made sure that readers of news columns would remain unoffended long enough to glance at the ads.

The Enlightenment view of truth also was compatible with democracy and its emphasis on rational government. People who could reason together, who could arrive at some shared "truth" of how their political lives ought to function, could govern themselves. Information was essential to such a form of government, for it allowed citizens to scrutinize government. As long as truth was ascertainable by the rational being, government could function. Under this view, information—written, logical, linear—provided the social glue as well as the grease of such a society. Citizens and government need information in order to continue their rational function. Information, and the notion that it corresponded in some essential way with the truth, carried enormous promise.

Twentieth-century pragmatists—most notably Americans John Dewey, George Herbert Mead, Charles Sanders Pierce and William James—challenged the Enlightenment view of truth. They held that the perception of truth depended on how it was investigated and on who was doing the investigating. Further, they rejected the notion that there was only one proper method of investigation—that is, the scientific method. Borrowing from Einstein's insights, pragmatists argued that truth, like matter, was relative.

Specifically, the pragmatists proposed that knowledge and reality were not *fixed by,* but instead were the *result of,* an evolving stream of consciousness and learning. Reality itself varied based on psychological, social, historical or cultural contexts. Additionally, reality was defined as that which was probable, not as something intrinsic (the Platonic view) or something determined by only one method of observation (the Enlightenment view).

Pragmatism found a comfortable home in the 20th-century United States. Under pragmatism truth lost much of its universality, but it was in remarkable agreement with the American value of democratic individualism. Soon pragmatism filtered through literature, science and some professions, such as law.

Pragmatic notions of truth provided a philosophical basis to challenge objectivity. At roughly the same time that the journalistic community was embracing Enlightenment standards of objectivity, the culture itself was adopting more pragmatic notions of truth. That clash fueled criticism of objectivity on both a scholarly and a popular level. Several questions surfaced. If truth is subjective, can it be best obtained and reported by an impassive, objective and detached reporter? Does such a reporter exist? Is truth a construct that relies on the context of the source, the message and the receiver?

Postmodern philosophy (see *The Matrix* that follows) has taken these questions to their logical extension, suggesting that the concept of truth is devoid of meaning. Postmodernism asserts that context is literally everything, and that meaning cannot exist apart from contextual understanding. This philosophical approach is antithetical to fact-based journalism, but designers and other visual journalists have employed it in everything from layout to typography.

The last 30 years have added yet another level of complexity to the problem: the information explosion. Not only do we as a culture now question the meaning of the terms *fact* and *truth,* but we literally cannot sort them all out. Facts and truth come to us quickly from all over the globe. Our ability to attend to these various messages, let alone construct rational meaning from them, is on the verge of being overwhelmed.

In short, the concept of objectivity, which was once equated with printing the truth, has been deeply undermined by both philosophical shift and technological innovation (Christians, Ferré and Fackler 1993). Telling your readers and viewers the truth has become a complicated business.

> Telling the "truth" therefore is not solely a matter of moral character; it is also a matter of correct appreciation of real situations and of serious reflection upon them. . . . Telling the truth, therefore, is something which must be learnt. This will sound very shocking to anyone who thinks that it must all depend on moral character and that if this is blameless the rest is child's play. But the simple fact is that the ethics cannot be detached from reality, and consequently continual progress in learning to appreciate reality is a necessary ingredient in ethical action. (Bok 1978, 302–303)

It is to the issue of learning to appreciate reality that we will now turn. First, we will review some of the scholarly findings about news coverage and what the news does and does not reflect. Then we will ask you to apply these scholarly findings, as well as a question or two, to case studies that deal with the links between news and the truth.

WHO'S DOING THE TALKING ANYWAY?

The pragmatic's critique of objectivity has called attention to the question of who writes the news. Journalists—who themselves are primarily male, Caucasian, well educated, and middle to upper class—are often asked to cover issues and questions for which their life experiences have not prepared them. Stephen Hess (1981) noted that journalists, in terms of their socioeconomic status, look a great deal more like the people they cover than the people they are supposedly writing for. While the eastern elite press provides an extreme example of this tendency, other work on the national press corps has shown similar results (Weaver and Wilhoit 2007).

In the past 20 years, almost every professional journalistic organization has developed programs specifically to attract and retain women and minorities, many with limited success. Decades of programs to increase the minority presence in

The Matrix: A Postmodern Examination of Truth

"Do you ever have that feeling where you're not sure whether you are awake or still dreaming?"

"Yeah, all the time. . . . It just sounds to me like you might need to unplug, man . . . get some R&R?"

Thus begins Neo's journey down the rabbit hole (like Lewis Carroll's Alice) where reality literally turns inside out on itself. A computer wizard, and unknown genetic mutation, Neo—who is awakened to the possibilities courtesy of Morpheus—literally unplugs himself from the reality of a computer simulation where human beings serve as batteries for artificially intelligent machines that now run the world. The reality that most people know is nothing more than a computer code invented by the artificial intelligence and inserted electronically into billions of human neural systems from infancy onward. Neo, as his name suggests, is the person who has the capacity to crack and overcome the code.

The Matrix set the standard in the latter part of the last century for smart films about the potential of the computers that increasingly power, and in some subtle ways govern, the information age. The film was also stylish; in fact, the long, black trench coats Keanu Reeves and Carrie-Anne Moss wore were eerily predictive of the attire worn by the Columbine High School shooters. The special effects and set design, based as they were on a comic book reality, gave form to one vision of hyper-reality, as did the film's other-worldly and sometimes violent content.

More importantly for our purposes, the film provides an accessible discussion of the postmodern approach to truth.

Postmodernism is a logical outgrowth of pragmatism. Instead of suggesting that truth varies with receiver, or sender or context, postmodernism suggests that truth—if it exists at all—is unknowable. Those who believe they know the truth, like Neo at the beginning of the film, discover that their "reality" is merely false consciousness, founded on invalid assumptions that shift constantly in a chaotic environment.

Postmodernism rejects such concepts as the correspondence theory of truth, or even the Platonic ideal that truth is knowable only as an intellectual construct. In postmodernism, revealed truth, as medieval scholars understood it, does not exist, and the marketplace of ideas yields either false understandings or babble. In the film, dreams are real, reality shifts and absolutely nothing is what it seems. Control, in the form of computer programs (malleable by both the programmers and the programmed), and death, in the form of biological waste, remain.

Almost all journalistic endeavors by their very nature reject this postmodern way of thinking. Some philosophers, for example Clifford Christians, reject postmodernism on the grounds that the essence of humanity itself provides an irrefutable challenge to the postmodern premise. Others have noted that postmodernism too easily falls into the trap of solipsism—or the notion that it is impossible to know anything outside of one's individual thoughts and perceptions. Solipsism, of course, negates any attempt at social ethics where values, principles and other people exist independently of individual thought and biological function.

While traditional theory may reject postmodernism, contemporary culture itself sometimes embraces what Morpheus calls "the desert of the real." Magazine designers employ postmodern sensibilities to create designs that play with the entire concept of text. Media critics argue that a media-generated reality, subject to no counterargument from other messages or critical examination by audiences, is not so different from the matrix that Neo encounters. And, digitizing and editing visual images and sounds through sophisticated computer programs is the stuff of elementary school play.

So, if postmodernism is an appropriate worldview, does that mean journalists and persuasion professionals should abandon their jobs or their ancient foundations in the face of overwhelming information overload? We think not.

Neo and Morpheus still have to act. They learn to think in new ways, but their actions remain centered on their belief in human independence and the "rightness" of thinking about and connecting with others. Even in this postmodern vision, ethical thinking still has a place. Neo's goal, after all, is to dismantle one matrix so humanity can make its own choices.

newsrooms has met with only incremental and sporadic success. This lack of access to the engines of information has not been lost on a variety of minority groups—from religious fundamentalists, who have in some cases established their own broadcasting networks, to racial minorities, who fail to find themselves either as owners or managers of media outlets or in front of the cameras and with front-page bylines. They argue that the result is news about middle-class Caucasians, for middle-class Caucasians, about a political-economic system that systematically excludes everyone but middle-class Caucasians.

How individual journalists and the corporations they work for should remedy the situation is unclear. But many editors and publishers as well as their corporate bosses worry that as the demographics change us from a culture that is predominantly Caucasian to one that is not, the mass media, particularly newspapers, will play an increasingly minor role unless journalists find a way to report news that is of interest to the new majority of their readers. In the beginning of the 21st century, worldwide newspaper readership and broadcast viewership continued to decline. The winners: the Internet and magazines that focus on celebrity rather than public affairs (Thorson & Duffy 2006). Traditional journalists faced an audience in open rebellion with no clear strategy to regain the "eyeballs" advertisers desire or the public focus that civic engagement requires.

SEEING ISN'T BELIEVING

Another assumption embedded in the concept of objectivity centers on how the news is perceived. More than 80 years ago, journalist Walter Lippmann (1922) foreshadowed what modern psychology has now documented when he said, "For the most part, we do not first see, and then define, we define first and then see." He added that we tend to pick out what our culture has already defined for us, and then perceive it in the form stereotyped for us by our culture.

An example of this phenomenon is found in the study of a New York journalism professor, blind since birth, who could predict the race of football players being described in the play-by-play sports commentary by what was being said about them (Rainsville and McCormick 1977). Caucasian athletes were described as intellectually gifted while African-American athletes were described as physically gifted. In a culture that values brains over brawn, African-American football players were the subject of repeated stereotypical insults—all couched as praise in the play-by-play. And even though the professor's predictions and the study that validated them are now more than 30 years old, the tendency to go back to these stereotypes continues on sports broadcasts today.

Groups such as women, the elderly and the gay community have conducted studies with similar results. Their conclusion has been that while journalists maintain that they are objective, they (like their readers and viewers) bring something to the message that literally changes what they see and, hence, what they report (Lester 1996). What they bring, most often, is technology, and the technology of television has led scholars to question the role of objectivity in news reporting.

In a *Columbia Journalism Review* cover story in the summer of 2003 entitled "Rethinking Objectivity," author Brent Cunningham (2003) says that "our pursuit of objectivity can trip us up on the way to truth. Objectivity excuses lazy reporting. If you're on deadline and all you have is 'both sides of the story,' then that's often good enough." Cunningham cites numerous incidences of enterprising reporting spiked by editors who asked, "says who," when the facts went contrary to or beyond the conventional wisdom of the story based on the reporters' own work.

A slavish dedication to objectivity can keep reporters tethered to the government's version of the truth. Cunningham points to a study of 414 war stories on Iraq broadcast on ABC, CBS and NBC leading up to the 2003 conflict, where researcher Andrew Tyndall found that all but 34 originated from the White House, the Pentagon or the State Department. The result is that the "official truth" becomes the received truth, and only the bravest journalists dared depart from it, a trend that continued well into 2006 when investigative reporters finally began to acquire documents (such as the photographs of the torture at Abu Grieve) and human sources that contradicted the Bush administration's public pronouncements.

E. J. Dionne (1996) claims that the press is in internal contradiction. It must be neutral, yet investigative. It must be disengaged, but have an impact. It must be fair minded but have an edge. The conflicts make true objectivity in journalism virtually impossible to even define and even harder to practice.

DEFINING AND CONSTRUCTING THE NEWS

News reflects certain cultural values and professional norms. Those values and norms, often at odds with an Enlightenment concept of truth, lend themselves to a pragmatic version of the news, provided you remember who's doing the writing and story selection.

One professional norm that plays an important role in shaping the news is the journalistic imperative to tell a story to make a point. Often this leads to predictable narratives, many of them centering on crisis and politics (Nimmo and Combs 1985; Bennett 1988). Sociologist Herbert Gans (1979) studied how stories became news at *Newsweek* and CBS and found that almost all news stories reflected these six cultural values: ethnocentrism, altruistic democracy, responsible

1993, Washington Post Writers Group. Reprinted with permission.

capitalism, individualism, an emphasis on the need for and maintenance of social order and leadership. These dominant values helped to shape not only which stories were printed but also what they said. They are one basis for what communication scholars call "framing."

Gans called these values the "para-ideology" of the media, noting that "the news is not so much conservative or liberal as it is reformist." Researcher James Carey (quoted in Cunningham 2003) says that it is this para-ideology that is the source of charges of liberal bias against the media. "There is a bit of the reformer in anyone who enters journalism. And reformers are always going to make conservatives uncomfortable."

News stories about middle-class or upper-class people, those who tend to successfully adopt the culture's values, made the American news "budget," according to Gans, while stories about minorities, blue-collar Americans and those sharply critical of governmental policy got lost on the cutting-room floor. While Gans focused on journalism about the United States, other scholars have noted the same phenomenon, called *domesticating the foreign,* in international coverage (Gurevitch et al. 1991).

Journalists working for U.S. media outlets tell stories about international events in cultural terms Americans can readily understand but which also sacrifice accuracy and a non-American point of view. For example, routine coverage of elections in Britain or Israel is conveyed in horse-race metaphors even though both countries employ a parliamentary system where governing coalitions are common and who wins the horse race not nearly so important.

PACKAGING THE STORY: NEWS AS MANUFACTURED PRODUCT

The goal of telling a "good story" also raises other ethical questions, specifically those that focus on packaging to highlight drama and human interest. Ethical questions about packaging began with newspapers but have intensified with television. Television demands video, and television's video imperative has been found to dominate both story selection and placement (for example, Epstein 1974). If television arrives at a disaster before print journalists, it is television that frames the stories for the written word (Smith 1992).

Photo availability sometimes contradicts the classic notion of objectivity that each story should stand on its own merits, but it certainly reflects the professional norms of particular media. *USA Today's* graphic impact on the newspaper industry has not been applauded by everyone. Some see the paper as a further indication of the trivialization of news, with an emphasis on packaging. Political ads have helped journalists to frame news stories about the same issue (Jamieson 1992) to some extent because of compelling visuals in the ads.

Journalists also need something to package, which has led to a professional drive to find an "event" to report and to be there first. Few consumers realize it, but news is "manufactured" daily, just as surely as furniture, cars or the meal at your favorite fast food restaurant—and often the process can be as messy as these other manufacturing enterprises. Journalists start the day with a blank computer screen or blank video tape with press time or broadcast time looming. And adding to the built-in tension is the challenge to be fair, complete, accurate and, above all, interesting. The daily challenge leads to ethical problems as the temptation of the shortcut, when available, always beckons.

The need to find an event has meant journalists have missed some important stories because they were not events but rather historic developments with both a past and a future. For example, major social developments such as the women's movement (Mills 1989), the civil rights movement and the anti–Vietnam War movement were undercovered until their leaders created events such as sit-ins and demonstrations for the media to report. Director Michael Moore said he began his career with the 1989 film *Roger and Me* about the devastation of General Motors layoffs on his hometown of Flint, Michigan, because he "didn't see on the silver screen or the television screen what happened to people like us. It was a story then (in the mid 1980s) and it's a story now and that's part of the reason I did the movie" (Smith 1992).

This preoccupation with events affects coverage of several types of stories. Science is most frequently reported as a series of discoveries and "firsts" rather than as a process of discovery (Nelkin 1987). We are treated to stories about the next cancer or AIDS cure without the necessary context to interpret the latest research results. The twin dramas of "new hope" and "no hope" seem to drive most science reporting.

Stories are missed or misreported when they lack the easy "peg" editors look for. The socioeconomic, scientific and political causes of a disaster, such as the one that claimed thousands of lives in Bhopal, India, were seldom mentioned in news coverage that focused on the picture-friendly event (Wilkins 1987). Finally, phenomena not linked to specific events, such as the greenhouse effect or the growth of an American underclass, often go unreported or underreported until an appropriate news peg arrives to supply the needed event the coverage requires.

Elections become horse races with one candidate the "front-runner" and the "rest of the pack" struggling to narrow the gap with each new poll. But reporting an election as a contest fails to focus on the policy issues, which is what democratic elections are supposed to be about. The quintessential manifestation of this can be seen in the 2003 recall election of California's incumbent governor and the subsequent re-election of Arnold Schwarzenegger. And in a spectacular display of circular logic, many said they voted for the actor simply because they deemed him "electable."

The phenomenon of "pack journalism" has been chronicled in several films, dating back to the classic *The Front Page* and later recounted in Timothy Crouse's book *The Boys on the Bus* (1974) and Sabato's *Feeding Frenzy* (1992). All emphasize journalistic excesses and an unwillingness to engage in independent thought that would disturb enlightened and pragmatic philosophers alike. They also expose a system easily manipulated by politicians—particularly those in power on the highest levels—as editors remain skeptical of "scoops" that no other journalist has. This unwillingness to leave the "pack" with a break-out story led to many of the hottest political stories of the new century being reported first on the Web where such institutional pressures do not exist.

And just like the candidates they cover, journalists seek to break out of the "pack" and the ticket to front-runner status (and the front page) is the "scoop," a story no other journalist has or one no one else is willing to run. The twin problems of pack journalism and the scoop mentality still dominate much reporting and editing. Because of this, important stories have been killed, while some poorly researched stories have been aired or published.

Journalists have also been cowed by the threat of litigation. The film *The Insider* presents a fictionalized but nonetheless fact-based account about the impact of litigation on reporting stories critical of big tobacco. Seymour Hersh's original reporting of the My Lai massacre during the Vietnam War, which eventually appeared in the *New York Times,* was held up because no other reporter had a similar story and a particular media outlet was afraid to stick its neck out.

On the other hand, the *New York Times* resorted to quoting the supermarket tabloid the *National Enquirer* in its coverage of the O. J. Simpson case largely in an effort to keep up with media competition. Equally significant, the *Enquirer* had the story right. And, the entire Washington press corps was confounded when Internet gadfly Matt Drudge, who styles himself a political reporter, published what became the first mention of the President Bill Clinton/Monica Lewinsky scandal. Drudge has said that he prints rumor as well as fact; traditional journalists, who want to separate the two, remain deeply troubled by the impact of the speed of the Internet on the need to check facts before more traditional publication.

Truth is more than just a collection of facts. Facts have a relationship to one another and to other facts, forming a larger whole. Yet analytic coverage of American institutions, of science and technology, of politics, and of social movements is rare. If the role of the mass media is not only to detail events and issues, but to do so in a way that makes the relationships among them clear, is merely retelling a story sufficient? Or do we need to do it better?

Stephen Hess (1981) has argued that journalists need to engage in reporting that looks more like social science than storytelling. Gans argues for news that is labeled as originating from a particular point of view. If readers and viewers are alerted to the worldview of those who have selected the news, just as they were during the era of the partisan press, they would be better able to place news in context. Other scholars argue for news that is analytical rather than anecdotal, proactive rather than reactive and contextual rather than detached. And on a practical level, working reporters and editors insist that individual journalists need to do a better job of understanding their own biases and compensating for them.

These findings, from studies about how the media decide what is news to analyses of how individual audience members interpret the same news message, strike at the core of objectivity and its relationship to the complex truths of this century. Intellectually, we are living in a pragmatic era, but professionally we seem to be unable to develop a working alternative to the Enlightenment's view of truth.

DECEPTION: THE MEANS TO AN END

In a profession that values truth, is it ever ethical to lie? To editors? To readers? To sources, who may be liars themselves? Are there levels of lying? Is flattering someone to get an interview as serious a transgression as doctoring a quote or photograph? Is withholding information the same thing as lying? All of these questions plague the media in a day when "facts," verified or not, run rampant in blogs and on Web sites well before traditional media deadlines.

The *New York Times* faced a credibility crisis of its own in 2003 when a 27-year-old reporter, Jayson Blair, fabricated all or part of more than 40 stories he had written for the *Times*. After his May 1, 2003, resignation from the paper, the *Times* ran four full pages of corrections, including a front-page story, documenting every error discovered in Blair's reporting. The *Times'* correction, as well as subsequent reporting in other media outlets, made it clear that not only was Blair a person without a moral compass but that the newsroom organization at the *Times* had failed to correct the problem in earlier stages despite many opportunities to do so, an institutional failure of substantial proportions that toppled two *Times* editors as well.

Blair became a *Times* reporter after an internship with the newspaper. In a highly competitive reporting atmosphere, Blair rose through the ranks in part because of his interpersonal skills and hustle. The *Times* hired Blair based on his work at the paper and on the assumption that he had completed his college coursework. Had the editors investigated they would have learned that Blair never graduated from the University of Maryland. His editors found Blair's work fast but inaccurate. At one point, he was shifted to the sports desk, where he had similar problems, but he was returned to the regular newsroom to report on a series of sniper shootings in the Washington, D.C., area, in part because Blair's home was in northern Virginia, near where the shootings occurred.

Stephan Pastis reprinted by permission of United Feature Syndicate, Inc.

Throughout his brief *Times* career, Blair systematically deceived his bosses on many levels. He filed stories from locations where he had never traveled. He added detailed description to stories by electronically accessing photographs taken at the scene and writing about what he saw in the pictures. He plagiarized accounts published in other news organizations, among them the *Washington Post.* He doctored his expense accounts, and failed to document many expenses that he should have incurred had he been doing his job honestly.

Some of the errors were small—blue flowers in front of a house instead of pink; others were substantial—quotes from people he had never interviewed. Sometimes, Blair's sources complained to the *Times* about the inaccuracy of his coverage. Most telling are the ones who said they did not call because they assumed "that's the way things are done." The paper did publish some corrections. But it wasn't until a single editor served notice to his superiors that Blair did not "belong" at the paper that the organization decided it needed to look into a pattern of behavior that now stretched over more than 18 months of work.

In a subsequent analysis of the case, many at the *Times* and other places suggested that one reason Blair's actions had been unchecked for so long was because of his race. Blair was African-American, and he had been hired as part of the *Times'* diversity program. His mentors at the paper, Executive Editor Howell Raines and Managing Editor Gerald Boyd, who also is African-American, were among Blair's strongest supporters. Raines, who had been raised in the South, was particularly sensitive about racial issues. Boyd had personally mentored the young writer. While the *Times* denied that race was the reason that Blair had been promoted, Blair himself did not.

Errors in Journalism: Inevitability and Arrogance

Confounding truth and deception in journalism is the problem of errors. Inadvertent mistakes in stories are common. One freelance fact checker (Hart 2003) wrote in *Columbia Journalism Review* that she had not experienced an error-free story in three years of fact checking for *CJR,* one of journalism's leading watchdog publications. Her calls to fellow fact-checkers at other publications led her to believe that articles with errors are the rule, not the exception.

However, mistakes are different from fabrication (discussed more fully in Chapter 10) and do not indicate a lack of dedication to the truth. Some, if not most, mistakes are matters of interpretation, but others are outright errors of fact. In her article, "Delusions of Accuracy," Ariel Hart says that hearing journalists proudly claim to have had no errors or fewer errors than the *Times* found in Blair's writing is "scary, not the least because it encourages delusions of accuracy."

One problem seems to be audience members so disconnected from the media that they don't bother to correct our mistakes or, worse, assume as readers of the *Times* evidently did, that fabrication is *de rigueur* for journalists. "Journalists surely make mistakes often, but I think we don't— or can't—admit it to ourselves because the idea of a mistake is so stigmatized. . . . So mistakes need to be destigmatized or restigmatized and dealt with accordingly. They should be treated like language errors," Hart argues.

In interviews after his resignation, in which he was unrepentant for his actions, Blair said he believed that his race had had a great deal to do with why he had been hired and how he had been treated at the *Times.* "Anyone who tells you that my race didn't play a role in my career at the *New York Times* is lying to you," Blair told the *New York Observer.* "Both racial preferences and racism played a role. And I would argue that they didn't balance each other out. Racism had much more of an impact."

Other journalists reporting on the debacle noted that Blair's editors at the paper had been fearful of confronting the highest levels of management about the quality of Blair's work because they did not want to be perceived as racists. Other reporters had some indication about Blair's behavior but remained silent because he appeared to be close to the paper's top managers and because they did not want to be perceived as racists themselves. As Blair himself saw it, he had become the beneficiary of racial discrimination—in his favor. Many news organizations with diversity programs used the Blair case to examine how they were mentoring and overseeing young reporters of all races. The profession almost unanimously rejected any suggestion that diversity programs in and of themselves were somehow contributory to Blair's acts.

However, Blair wasn't the only bad news for the *Times* during those weeks. Pulitzer Prize–winning reporter Rick Bragg also resigned from the paper after it became public that he, too, had published stories based largely on the reporting of stringers who did not receive a byline in the *Times.* Furthermore, some of his stories filed with non–New York datelines had been written on airplanes and in hotel rooms where Bragg was functioning more as a rewrite editor rather than doing actual on-the-scene reporting. Bragg said his practices were known at the *Times* and common in the industry. Others vehemently disagreed. At the conclusion of this tumultuous six-week period, both Raines and Boyd resigned. In addition, the *Times* appointed an external review committee to examine the cases, and the organization's response to them, for the paper.

So, how do journalists feel about deception as an ethical problem? A 2002 survey of members of Investigative Reporters and Editors, perhaps journalism's most prestigious professional organization, provides some insight into the profession's thinking (Lee 2002). Journalists think about deception on a continuum. At one end, there is almost universal rejection of lying to readers, viewers and listeners. IRE members regard such lies as among the worst ethical professional breaches. At the other end, more than half of the IRE members surveyed said they approved of flattering a source to get an interview, even though that flattery could be considered deceptive and certainly was insincere. Lies of omission—such as withholding information from readers and viewers and also editors and bosses—were considered less of a problem than fabricating facts in a story or fabricating entire stories, which was almost universally condemned. IRE members were more willing to withhold information in instances when national security issues were involved. The journalists also said some lies were justified; they approved of lying if it would save a life or prevent injury to a source.

The journalists surveyed also noted that there were outside influences on these judgments. Broadcast journalists were more accepting of hidden cameras and altering video than were print journalists. And, those who worked in competitive markets were more willing to accept deception than were those who saw themselves in less competitive environments. Finally, the more experienced a journalist was, the less likely he or she was to accept any form of deception.

This recent history is only the latest chapter in journalists' challenging relationship with "the truth." (For a review of some of those historic cases, for example Nellie Bly, Janet Cooke and the Mirage Bar scam, see the Web site for this book.) While the Blair case illustrates that there are bad actors in any system, how organizations deal with those actors raises important questions. More important is the apparently fine-grained reasoning about ethics and the impact of professional circumstance on ethical thinking that the survey of Investigative Reporters and Editors reveals. In all these instances, what journalists worry about is the impact such reporting methods have on the believability of news accounts and on journalists' ability to cover subsequent stories.

Ethical theory suggests that many cases revolve around two issues: Is it ethical to lie to liars? Is withholding information the same thing as lying? If not, under what circumstances might it be appropriate? If it is, are there ethically based justifications for such an act?

Sissela Bok has written eloquently on lying to liars. She argues that such an act raises two questions. Will the lie serve a larger social good, and does the act of lying mean that we as professionals are willing to be lied to in return? Bok suggests that most of the time, when we lie we want "free rider" status—gaining the benefits of lying without incurring the risks of being lied to. In other words, some journalists may believe it's acceptable to lie to a crook to get a story, but they professionally resent being lied to by any source, regardless of motive.

Many philosophers have asserted that lying is a way to get and maintain power. Those in positions of power often believe they have the right to lie because they have a greater than ordinary understanding of what is at stake. Lying in a crisis (for instance, to prevent panic) and lying to enemies (for instance, to protect national security) are two examples. In both circumstances journalists can be, either actively or without their knowledge, involved in the deception. Do journalists have a right to counter this lying with lies of their own, told under the guise of the public's need to know?

Then there is the omission versus commission issue—a line professional journalists do appear willing to draw in some circumstances. Reporting via the Internet has given new urgency to the issue of lying by omission. In most instances failing to identify yourself as a reporter when collecting information electronically from news groups, chat rooms or other modes of public discussion the Internet makes possible is considered problematic. Journalists, when pressed, note that the U.S. Supreme Court has ruled Internet transmissions are public. The ethical issue emerges when most of those involved in the discussion are not aware of the legal standards and expect, instead, the more ethically based relations of face-to-face interactions. Ethical thought leaves journalists with difficult choices. Bok asserts that a genuinely white lie may be excusable on some grounds, but that all forms of lying must stand up to questions of fairness and mutuality. Even lying to liars can have its downside.

> In the end, the participants in deception they take to be mutually understood may end up with coarsened judgment and diminished credibility. But if, finally, the liar to whom one wishes to lie is also in a position to do one harm, then the balance may shift; not because he is a liar, but because of the threat he poses (Bok 1978, 140).

Since so many of the lies journalists are told emanate from powerful sources, the issue of telling some form of lie to report a socially beneficial story remains a troubling and important one. Another ethical issue centers on exactly how much truth journalists ought to tell. Completeness and accuracy are sometimes used synonymously with truthfulness and objectivity, but important ethical distinctions can be made among the concepts. If truth itself is relative, then how should a journalist balance getting the story against providing his or her readers with the essential information needed to evaluate it? Again, the issue becomes one of the means to a specific end, both now and in the long run.

ETHICAL NEWS VALUES

Most mass media courses present a list of qualities that, collectively, define news. Most such lists include proximity, timeliness, conflict, consequence, prominence, rarity, change, concreteness, action and personality. Additional elements may include notions of mystery, drama, adventure, celebration, self-improvement and even ethics. While these lists are helpful to beginning journalists, they probably will not help you decide how to recount the news ethically.

We suggest you expand your journalistic definitions of news to include a list of ethical news values. These values are intended to reflect the philosophic tensions inherent in a profession with a commitment to truth. If news values were constructed from ethical reasoning, we believe the following elements would be emphasized by both journalists and the organizations for which they work.

Accuracy—using the correct facts and the right words and putting things in context. Journalists need to be as independent as they can when framing stories. They need to be aware of their own biases, including those they "inherit" as social class, gender and ethnicity, as well as learned professional norms. Their news organizations need to trust journalists when they report independently rather than expect them to act as part of a pack.

Confirmation—writing articles that are able to withstand scrutiny inside and outside the newsroom. Media ethicist Sandy Borden (in press) refers to this as the "discipline of confirmation," a concept that reflects how difficult it can be to capture even a portion of the truth in sometimes complex news situations.

Tenacity—knowing when a story is important enough to require additional effort, both personal and institutional. Tenacity drives journalists to provide all the depth they can regardless of the individual assignment. It has institutional implications, too, for the individual cannot function well in an environment where resources are too scarce or the corporate bottom line too dominant.

Dignity—leaving the subject of a story as much self-respect as possible. Dignity values each person regardless of the particular story or the particular role the individual plays. Dignity allows the individual journalist to recognize that news gathering is a cooperative enterprise where each plays a role, including editors, videographers, designers and advertising sales staff.

Reciprocity—treating others as you wish to be treated. Too often, the journalistic enterprise is defined as "writing for the lowest common denominator." Reciprocity eschews the notion of journalism as a sort of benevolent paternalism—"We'll tell you what we think is good for you"—and recognizes that journalists and their viewers and readers are partners both in discovering what is important and in gleaning meaning from it.

Sufficiency—allocating adequate resources to important issues. On the individual level, sufficiency can mean thoroughness, for example, checking both people and documents for every scrap of fact before beginning to write. On an organizational level, it means allocating adequate resources to the newsgathering process.

Equity—seeking justice for all involved in controversial issues and treating all sources and subjects equally. Like the ethical news value of accuracy, equity assumes a complicated world with a variety of points of view. Equity demands that all points of view be considered, but that not all be framed as equally compelling. Equity expands the journalistic norms of "telling both sides of the story" to "telling all sides of the story."

Community—valuing social cohesion. On the organization level, a sense of community means that media outlets and the corporations that own them need to consider themselves as citizens rather than mere "profit centers." On the individual level, it means evaluating stories with an eye first to social good.

Diversity—covering all segments of the audience fairly and adequately. There appears to be almost overwhelming evidence that news organizations do not "look like" the society they cover. While management can remedy part of this problem by changing hiring patterns, individual journalists can learn to "think diversity" regardless of their individual heritages.

Like all lists, ours should not be considered inclusive or without some measure of internal contradiction. We believe those contradictions, however, provide an important continuum within which informed ethical choice can be made.

Suggested Readings

BENNETT, LANCE. 1988. *News: The politics of illusion.* Longman: New York.

BOK, SISSELA. 1978. *Lying: Moral choice in public and private life.* New York: Random House.

GANS, HERBERT. 1979. *Deciding what's news: A study of CBS Evening News, NBC Nightly News, Newsweek and Time.* New York: Vintage.

JAMIESON, KATHLEEN HALL. 1992. *Dirty politics.* New York: Oxford University Press.

LESTER, PAUL M. 2003. *Images that injure.* Westport, CT: Greenwood Press.

LIPPMANN, WALTER. 1922. *Public opinion.* New York: Free Press.

PLATO. *The republic.*

SABATO, LARRY. 1992. *Feeding frenzy: How attack journalism has transformed American politics.* New York: Free Press.

WEAVER, DAVID H., RANDAL A. BEAM, BONNIE J. BROWNLEE, PAUL S. VOAKES, & G. CLEVELAND WILHOIT. 2007. *The American journalist in the 21st century: U.S. news people at the dawn of a new millenium.* Mahwah, NJ: Lawrence Erlbaum & Associates.

Cases on the Web

"Columbine: News and community—A balancing act" by Lee Wilkins

"The doctor has AIDS" by Deni Elliott

"Taste in photojournalism: A question of ethics or aesthetics" by Lou Hodges

"Reporters and confidential sources" by Steve Weinberg

"Rodent wars and cultural battles: Reporting hantavirus" by JoAnn M. Valenti

"Too many bodies, too much blood: A case study of the 'family-sensitive newscast'" by Bill Babcock

"Nine days in Union: The Susan Smith case" by Sonya Forte Duhé

"SARS: The bug that would not go away" by Seow Ting Lee

CHAPTER 2 ESSAY

Informing the Public Must Come First

CHRISTOPHER HANSON
University of Maryland

Journalists who will stop at nothing to get a story—from paparazzi photographers pursuing Princess Diana, to TV crews shoving mikes into the faces of traumatized children—have given the news business a reputation for recklessness and cruelty. This might explain why many beginning journalism students believe avoiding harm should be the reporter's primary duty. Their strong inclination is to kill the story of the "family values" mayor downloading porn or the congresswoman who is drunk before noon in order to spare spouse, children and extended family the pain of disclosure.

Some would kill as "sensationalistic" any photograph that someone in the audience might find disturbing, from images of the World Trade Towers aflame to hospital scenes of Iraqi war victims to Enron executives in handcuffs.

Well intended though it may be, this approach cannot lead to sound journalism because its top priority is being kind and gentle, not informing the public. If minimizing harm were the universal threshold test for airing a story, we would have lots of blank pages and dead air, because stories of tragedy and wrongdoing tend to upset people.

Hence the responsible journalist leans strongly toward publication. Her imperative is not to kill that disturbing story or photo but to present it in a way that minimizes pain without holding back what the public needs to know.

This imperative to inform—and zeal in doing so—is essential if our system is to be open and democratic in practice and not just in principle. The most crucial role of journalists is to wrest "power from groups bent on retaining or accumulating it [and] redistribute power to the public by disseminating information." (Black, Steele, Barney, *Doing Ethics in Journalism,* 3rd ed., 20.) Consider these examples:

- In 1997, Sergeant Major Gene McKinney, the Army's most powerful noncommissioned officer, was appointed to a panel aimed at ferreting out sexual harassment in the military. Infuriated, former McKinney aide Brenda Hoster told the *New York Times* he had sexually harassed her, driving her to quit the service. The *Times'* front-page story led to McKinney's resignation from the panel, his court-martial and conviction for obstruction of justice. Using information as her lever, an obscure ex-soldier forced the mighty United States Army to act.
- Rep. Wes Cooley, R.-Ore., made much of his Korean War combat record. But the *Oregonian*'s revelation that the record was fabricated depleted his power to play the hero. It empowered voters, including many who had backed him, to make a more informed choice—thumbs down.
- When *Consumer Reports* rates a new model car a lemon or the *New York Times* pans a play, they shift power from producer to consumer.

There are cases, to be sure, when a news organization must withhold information. In the 2003 Iraq war, for instance, reporters refrained from disclosing advance knowledge of when and where U.S. military units would strike because a perishable scoop was not worth risking American lives.

Yet journalists who hold back information should always do so with uneasiness. The practice can be habit forming, especially for beat reporters who face the temptation to go soft on key sources. In 1972, Washington's seasoned political and White House correspondents had no stomach to investigate the Watergate break-in. It took two zealous but lowly metro reporters with no stake in coddling sources to crack the case and implicate Nixon's top lieutenants.

Information is power. Journalists perform a bold, even radical public service each time they break up an information monopoly that had allowed some politician, businessman or corrupt clergyman to operate unchecked.

Unfortunately, journalists do not perform the service enough. The powers that be spare no effort to rope journalists, break their zeal and filter their reports with offers of access, exclusive stories and high status, threats, complaints to the boss and hyped estimates of the damage a story would do. It works. As Black, Steele and Barney put it, "All too often, journalists 'wimp out.'"

Such choices have consequences. The less energy journalists throw into spreading information, the less power citizens have to choose the best leader, influence government policy, avoid shoddy or unsafe products, make the most of their money and otherwise control their own lives.

Zeal to inform the public is the paramount journalistic virtue. Sadly, it is in too short supply.

CHAPTER 2 CASES

CASE 2-A

Visualizing September 11th

SARA GETTYS
University of Missouri

The morning of Sept. 11, 2001, AP photographer Richard Drew was covering a fashion show in downtown Manhattan. When two planes slammed into the World Trade Towers, AP called Drew and sent him to the story (Cheney 2001). As people jumped, he photographed several of the jumpers, tracking one man in a white coat and dark pants in several frames. Drew remembers, "I've been at the AP for 32 years. I've covered my share of disasters and earthquakes and fires. . . . [So when], all of a sudden, people started falling out of the tower, I started photographing it" (Abransky 2002).

Papers across the country, including the *New York Times,* picked the photo to run as part of the coverage. The *Times* ran the photo above the fold on Page 7 of the A section in full color, the art for the lead story jump from Page A1. The photo ran alone surrounded by text that included a chronological accounting of the day's events.

That same morning, Milagros Hernandez received a frantic phone call from her brother Norberto Hernandez, who worked as a pastry chef at Windows on the World, a restaurant on the 107th floor of Number One World Trade Center. After speaking briefly with him, Milagros turned on her television set to watch coverage of the tragedy. She knew her brother worked above the burning floors, and she remembers her brother saying that if he ever were to be trapped, he would jump rather than burn to death.

Television coverage included pictures of people jumping, and one man in particular—wearing a white coat—caught her eye. But the fleeting image provided no clues as to the jumper's identity. When she opened the *New York Times* the next day, the victim's white jacket and dark complexion sent a shock of recognition through her. "Oh my God! That's my brother!" she remembers thinking.

Throughout the day on Sept. 11th, *Times* editors, along with their colleagues at other news organizations, worked to cover the attack. At the *Times,* staffers in the advertising and strategic planning departments worked the dictation desk, taking reports from reporters and eyewitness accounts (Tugend 2001). In an event where every aspect of coverage was graphic, violent and horrifying, the decisions about what to show to tell the totality of the story became the decisions that relied heavily on the standards of those working the desks. Stories from the Sept. 12th edition of the paper included photos of firefighters grieving for lost comrades, pictures and first-person accounts of the towers falling, and pictures of wounded victims waiting for help. There were no ads in the A section of the paper that day, with the exception of a full-page Verizon ad on the back cover.

When the photo ran, the *Times* started receiving calls from outraged readers who felt that this photo in particular was sensationalistic and exploited a man at the moment just before his death (Mitchell 2001). Papers nationwide that ran the photo received similar calls. In Allentown, Pennsylvania, more than 60 people called the

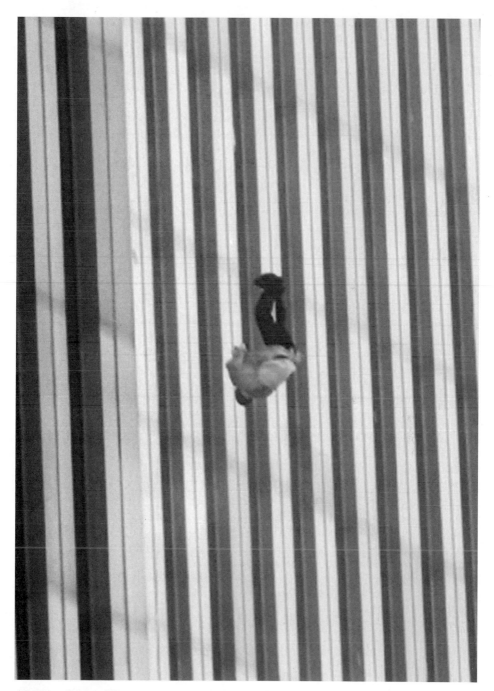

AP Photo/Richard Drew.

local paper to complain. The *Arizona Daily Star* posted the photo on its Web site but took it off in response to complaints.

In the midst of the tragedy and public outrage, Peter Cheney, a reporter for the *Toronto Globe and Mail,* was covering the attacks and cleanup and rescue attempts when he saw a missing person's poster of Norberto Hernandez and thought he might be the man in the photo. He contacted Milagros and decided to tell the story of the family who believed that the man pictured was their relative. In doing so, he addressed both the life of the victim the family believed was pictured and the grieving process of the survivors. He also included the family's response to the photo—from Milagros' belief that the man pictured was undeniably her brother, to Norberto's daughter, who didn't believe that the man in the photo was her father.

While the identity of the man in the photo remained uncertain, Cheney explored that possibility and allowed the family to express its grief and to celebrate the life of a loved one whose last moments may have been shared with millions of readers.

Micro Issues

1. Should AP photographer Drew have continued to "follow" the jumper once he realized what was happening?
2. Does it matter that it is difficult, some say impossible, to clearly identify the man in the photo?
3. Was it appropriate to place the photo on an inside page? Should it have run on Page A1? Should other publications in distant places have run the photo?
4. Was the story reporter Cheney wrote an invasion of privacy at this time of grief?
5. While Norberto Hernandez was included in a list of profiles that the *Times* ran on the victims, Hernandez's profile was only two paragraphs long and failed to mention the possibility that he was the man pictured on September 12th. Is this appropriate?

Midrange Issues

1. Does the placing of the photo on an inside page somehow mitigate what many concluded was an invasion of privacy?
2. How should the *Times'* editors have considered the fact that "the jumper" was alive when the photograph was taken?
3. Are the justifications for television running the video of the jumper somehow ethically distinct from those the *Times* adhered to? Should they be?
4. If the *Times* and other media outlets had failed to provide visual information about this element of the story, would those organizations have failed to recognize and report on the decisions these people made?
5. Compare this photo with the Pulitzer Prize–winning photo by Stanley Forman in Case 4-D of the girl falling to her death from a faulty fire escape in Boston. What are the differences? What are the similarities? Do you make the same decision for both photos? Justify your answer.

Macro Issues

1. Should the *Times* have altered the photo—or published a different one—where the individual jumper was less recognizable? Why or why not?

2. What values do you believe the *Times'* editors weighed as they arrived at their decision?
3. Because Sept. 11th was a horrific event, did coverage—in order to be accurate—have to picture some of the horror of that day? Would you apply the same reasoning to coverage of international events—say, conflict in the Middle East?
4. By publishing the photo, to whom or what is the *Times* being loyal?
5. Do the *Times* and other media outlets that published and broadcast such photos share any responsibility for the public emotion connected with the events of 9/11?

CASE 2-B

The Spouse Is Squeezed:
A South Carolina TV Reporter's Attempt to Conceal Her Source

SONYA FORTE DUHÉ
University of South Carolina

It seems like a typical news day.

A man telephones WIS-TV Senior Reporter Heather Hoopes, claiming to possess a "bombshell videotape" that she must see.

The source tells the Columbia, South Carolina, NBC affiliate reporter the tape is available to her only if she comes to his house to get it. He says he won't mail it or drop it off at the station. If she wants it, she *has* to come and get it.

Concerned for her safety, Hoopes asks her husband, Jim Matthews—who for more than 20 years has worked with the Department of Justice's Drug Enforcement Administration (DEA) and now heads the local Columbia office—to drive her to the caller's home. He agrees.

Matthews has no idea that the videotape contains a privileged conversation between a murder defendant and his lawyer, secretly videotaped by a local sheriff's deputy. Hoopes isn't exactly sure what she is getting either.

After reviewing the tape, she broadcasts a story about the videotaping of the privileged conversation. To Hoopes and colleagues, the tape is a clear violation of the prisoner's rights. Hoopes' move to have Matthews drive her to retrieve the videotape from this confidential source leads to numerous court battles and thousands of dollars in legal costs for her, her husband and her employer.

CONTEXT

In 1995, Lexington County sheriff's detectives arrested B. J. Quattlebaum and charged him with the murder of William Swartz. Quattlebaum was taken to the Lexington County Jail, where he called his attorney.

The men used a small room to talk. Unknown to them, a deputy sheriff was secretly and illegally videotaping their meeting.

At a later time, the same confidential source, who was subsequently identified as Columbia attorney Jack Duncan, called Hoopes at WIS to alert her to this alleged wrongdoing. Hoopes, her news director, and her editors decided to use a portion of the videotape to expose the illegal action. However, in an attempt to protect the arrested man's rights, the news team didn't use the audio portion of the tape.

The FBI attempted to obtain the name of Hoopes' confidential source but could not meet Justice Department protocol because of First Amendment questions. When the FBI's efforts to subpoena WIS ran into roadblocks, it attempted to make Matthews reveal the person's identity.

In a May 10, 1999, story in the *Washington Post,* Hoopes was quoted as saying, "I consider it a backdoor tactic. I don't understand why the Justice Department is doing this. It's very stressful for me and my husband. I carry an extra burden because I put him in the situation."

Prosecutors subpoenaed Matthews, and a federal grand jury demanded that the DEA agent testify about the case.

Matthews's lawyer, along with the WIS legal team, filed motions with U.S. District Court asking that Matthews not be forced to testify. Lawyers argued that forcing him to be a witness would violate his First Amendment rights. These motions were dismissed. Written pleas to Attorney General Janet Reno, FBI Director Louis Freeh and Justice Department official Beneva Weintraub also did not recuse Matthews from a court appearance.

The Radio Television News Director Association (RTNDA) is the world's largest professional organization devoted exclusively to electronic journalism. The organization represents local and network news executives in broadcasting, cable and other electronic media in more than 30 countries. In those letters, RTNDA President Barbara Cochran called on the Justice Department to end FBI attempts to force Matthews to testify. Cochran wrote:

> On behalf of the 3,400 members of the RTNDA, I am writing to express our grave concern about FBI attempts to force the husband of a South Carolina television station reporter to reveal to a grand jury what he knows about his wife's confidential source.
>
> Efforts to force Mr. Matthews to betray the confidence of his spouse not only raise compelling questions about marital privilege, but they represent a blatant attempt to circumvent the reporter's privilege recognized by the Constitution, the state, and the Justice Department.
>
> It is well recognized that news-gathering activities are protected under the First Amendment of the United States Constitution. This protection extends to information given in confidence to a reporter, including the source of that information. The South Carolina legislature has also expressed a strong public policy of protecting news-gathering activities, enacting a shield law whose aim is to protect the free flow of information to the public. Moreover, Department of Justice regulations expressly recognize that: Because freedom of the press can be no broader than the freedom of reporters to investigate and report the news, the prosecutorial power of the government should not be used in such a way that it impairs a reporter's responsibility to cover as broadly as possible controversial public issues.
>
> RTNDA is certainly aware of no case where a reporter's spouse has been ordered to disclose a confidential source. If prosecutors are allowed to obtain confidential news information from a third party where efforts to obtain the same information from the reporter have failed, then the protections afforded by the First Amendment and state press shield statutes would be meaningless.

Hoopes said, "I would have thought they [authorities] would have applauded the efforts of my source and WIS to bring this to light. Instead it seems like we're the criminals."

Quattlebaum was later convicted of first-degree murder and sentenced to death. In January 2000, the South Carolina Supreme Court overturned Quattlebaum's conviction, due in part to the videotape incident.

A federal judge ordered the deputy who videotaped the conversation to pay a $250 fine for civil rights violations. As for Hoopes' confidential source, he was sentenced to and spent several months in jail for lying to a federal grand jury and was disbarred.

Micro Issues

1. Should the reporter have taken the videotape? Why?
2. Should the reporter have asked someone to accompany her to pick up the videotape? If so, who?
3. Was it okay for the reporter to air the videotape?
4. Should the reporter have aired the audio from the videotape?

Midrange Issues

1. Does the reporter have the right to air videotape of an illegal act? When would it be inappropriate?
2. Was it the journalist's responsibility to expose this illegal taping of a privileged conversation?
3. Did the journalist breach her source's confidentiality by allowing her husband to accompany her to pick up the videotape?

Macro Issues

1. Should reporters be allowed to keep sources confidential if a criminal act has occurred?
2. What responsibilities do reporters have to law enforcement officials? Why?
3. Should spouses of reporters have the same First Amendment rights that reporters possess?
4. What role should nonjournalists play in the newsgathering process?

CASE 2-C

When Is Objective Reporting Irresponsible Reporting?

THEODORE L. GLASSER
Stanford University

Amanda Laurens, a reporter for a local daily newspaper, covers the city mayor's office, where yesterday she attended a 4:00 p.m. press conference. The mayor, Ben Adams, read a statement accusing Evan Michaels, a city council member, of being a "paid liar" for the pesticide industry. "Councilman Michaels," the mayor said at the press conference, "has intentionally distorted the facts about the effects of certain pesticides on birds indigenous to the local area." "Mr. Michaels," the mayor continued, "is on the payroll of a local pesticide manufacturer," and his views on the effects of pesticides on bird life "are necessarily tainted."

The press conference ended at about 5:15 p.m., less than an hour before her 6:00 p.m. deadline. Laurens quickly contacted Councilman Michaels for a quote in response to the mayor's statement. Michaels, however, refused to comment, except to say that Mayor Adams's accusations were "utter nonsense" and "politically motivated." Laurens filed her story, which included both the mayor's accusation and the councilman's denial. Laurens's editor thought the story was fair and balanced and ran it the following morning on the front page.

The mayor was pleased with the coverage he received. He thought Laurens had acted professionally and responsibly by reporting his accusation along with Michaels's denial. Anything else, the mayor thought, would have violated the principles of objective journalism. The mayor had always believed that one of the most important responsibilities of the press was to provide an impartial forum for public controversies, and the exchange between him and the councilman was certainly a bona fide public controversy. Deciding who's right and who's wrong is not the responsibility of journalists, the mayor believed, but a responsibility best left to readers.

Councilman Michaels, in contrast, was outraged. He wrote a scathing letter to the editor, chiding the newspaper for mindless, irresponsible journalism. "The story may have been fair, balanced and accurate," he wrote, "but it was not truthful." He had never lied about the effects of pesticides on bird life, and he had "never been on the payroll of any pesticide manufacturer," he wrote. "A responsible reporter would do more than report the facts truthfully; she would also report the truth about the facts." In this case, Michaels said, the reporter should have held off on the story until she had time to independently investigate the mayor's accusation; and if the accusation had proved to be of no merit, as Michaels insisted, then there shouldn't have been a story. Or if there had to be a story, Michaels added, "it should be a story about the *mayor* lying."

By way of background: The effects of pesticides on bird life had been a local issue for nearly a year. Part of the community backs Mayor Adams's position on the harmful effects of certain pesticides and supports local legislation that would limit or ban their use. Others in the community support Councilman Michaels's position that the evidence on the effects of pesticides on bird life is at best ambiguous and that more scientific study is needed before anyone proposes legislation. They argue that pesticides are useful, particularly to local farmers who need to protect crops, and because the available evidence about their deleterious effects is inconclusive, they believe that the city council should not seek to further restrict or prohibit their use. The exchange between Mayor Adams and Councilman Michaels is the latest in a series of verbal bouts on the subject of pesticides and the city's role in their regulation.

Micro Issues

1. Did Laurens do the right thing by submitting her story without the benefit of an independent investigation into the mayor's accusations about Councilman Michaels?
2. Is the mayor correct in arguing that Laurens acted responsibly by providing fair and balanced coverage of both sides of a public controversy without trying to judge whose side is right and whose side is wrong?
3. Is the councilman correct in arguing that Laurens acted irresponsibly by concerning herself only with reporting the facts truthfully and ignoring the "truth about the facts"?

Midrange Issues

1. Is it sufficient when covering public controversies to simply report the facts accurately and fairly? Does it matter that fair and accurate reporting of facts might not do justice to the truth about the facts?
2. Does the practice of objective reporting distance reporters from the substance of their stories in ways contrary to the ideals of responsible journalism?
3. If reporters serve as the eyes and ears of their readers, how can they be expected to report more than what they've heard or seen?

Macro Issues

1. What distinguishes fact from truth? For which should journalists accept responsibility?
2. If journalists know that a fact is not true, do they have an obligation to share that knowledge with their readers? And if they do share that knowledge, how can they claim to be objective in their reporting?
3. Justify or reject the role of objectivity in an era where more media outlets are available than ever before.

CASE 2-D

Monitoring *The Monitor:* Taste, Politics and an Explosive Photo

GINA BRAMUCCI
University of Missouri

The Monitor newspaper, launched in 1992, is the only independent paper in the small nation of Uganda in East Africa. The paper has an average daily circulation of 25,000, although it is estimated that at least 10 people read each paper in Uganda. Charles Onyango-Obbo, one of the paper's founding editors, is a high-profile critic of the government of President Yoweri Museveni. He has been imprisoned for what *The Monitor* has published, writes a weekly column for another paper, and is well known to the foreign media.

On April 28, 1999, an unnamed source brought a photo to *The Monitor*'s offices in Kampala, the Ugandan capital. The photo pictured a young woman, nude and pinned down by seven men. The men, wearing the uniforms of the Ugandan army, were shaving the woman's genital area with scissors. The photo is not printed in this book.

Deputy Editor David Ouma Balikowa received the photo, and shortly afterwards Ugandan security agents arrived to ensure that it would not be published. *The Monitor* editors wanted to talk with the security agents, but according to Ouma it was evident that if they shared the photo with the agents it would be confiscated. For the paper's editors, the attempt to suppress the photo was added incentive for publication. Gulu police confirmed that a case such as the one in the photo had been reported to them.

In his May 17, 1999, column on the incident Onyango-Obbo wrote: "The word was out that the paper had the picture. The paper's credibility as the country's only serious independent media voice was on the line. Here we were about to participate in what might seem like a cover up or take a risky plunge and get hurt."

The photo ran on May 11, 1999, on *The Monitor*'s back page with no accompanying story. The caption read:

> This picture was brought to *The Monitor* by someone who claimed to have taken it in Gulu barracks early this year without being noticed. Recent days have seen what locals say is renewed tension by state operatives to disrupt the calm that was returning to the region.

The northern barracks must be placed in context in order to grasp the significance of *The Monitor*'s claim. Since 1986, when Museveni first took power in Uganda, a small rebel insurgency in the north has plagued his presidency. The Lord's Resistance Army, or LRA, trumpets a pseudo-religious cause based on the premise of overthrowing Museveni and creating a utopian society that will be ruled by the Judeo-Christian Ten Commandments. To this end, the LRA targets its own people, the Acholi tribe, abducting children for soldiers, ambushing vehicles, and killing and maiming haphazardly.

The LRA is not the only threat to civilians in northern Uganda, however. The U.S. State Department and nongovernmental organizations such as Human Rights Watch and Amnesty International have regularly found government troops guilty of severe human rights abuses and have documented a pattern of looting, rape, torture and extrajudicial killings. The Gulu barracks, where *The Monitor* claimed the photo was taken, are the northern operational headquarters for these troops, the Ugandan People's Defense Force, or UPDF. It is in this context—a history of documented abuse—that *The Monitor*'s editors made the decision to publish the photo.

The publication of the photo caused immediate reaction from the media and civilians in Uganda. Reactions ranged from outrage to wholehearted support for *The Monitor.* Perhaps surprisingly, some of Uganda's women's rights groups criticized the paper's editors for their decision, as did Miria Matembe, the national minister of ethics and integrity. Matembe, who has been known for her advocacy on the part of women, felt that women and children would be disturbed by the graphic photo.

Arguments like Matembe's were countered forcefully by those in the media who felt that the photo's publication promoted basic equalities and liberties for women, the least advantaged party in Uganda's patriarchal society.

On the evening of May 12, with public discourse growing louder, Onyango-Obbo received a letter from the Criminal Investigation Department, or CID, of Uganda's police force. According to Onyango-Obbo, the editors spent six hours at CID before being taken to court. The state charged the men with sedition and publishing false news that could create "fear and alarm." The journalists pleaded not guilty of the charges and were released on bail of $63 each.

The UPDF released its own statement on May 12, denying that the photograph had been taken in Uganda and saying that "activities like rape as depicted in the picture cannot take place in any military barracks or for that matter in the UPDF operational zones." The army claimed that the fatigues worn by the soldiers pictured were not those used by the UPDF, and that the woman pictured has a West African hairstyle.

After a delay, the trial of *The Monitor* editors opened on Nov. 9, 1999, with Magistrate Pamela Mafabi hearing the case. In their testimony, UPDF officers repeated their claim that the uniforms of the soldiers pictured were not used in the Gulu barracks. But when presented with photos of well-known UPDF officers in uniforms similar to those pictured, one officer admitted that he wasn't familiar with all of the uniforms used. Although it's unclear when, at some point in 1999 northern UPDF officials also testified that women are regularly punished at army facilities by having their heads shaved with blunt razors.

After his first day in the courtroom, the defense lawyer for *The Monitor* editors, James Nangwala, was shot by unidentified gunmen in front of his home. He was hit in the shoulder, and Mafabi adjourned the trial until January 2000. The trial of 24-year-old Kandida Lakony, who came forward prior to the original trial and claimed to be the woman pictured in the photo, caused a further delay in *The Monitor* case. Lakony told officials the man shaving her was a former boyfriend and a soldier in the Gulu barracks. After a few days of protection in the state house of President Museveni, she was brought before a Ugandan court and accused of lying and giving misleading information to the police. The public was largely sympathetic to Lakony and her testimony was highly publicized, but the court found her guilty and she was sentenced to 12 months in prison. Lakony died shortly after her release.

Nearly two years after the photo's appearance in *The Monitor,* on March 6, 2001, Onyango-Obbo, Oguttu and Ouma were acquitted of the charges of sedition and publication of false statements. Another magistrate, Joshua Maruk, ruled that the state had failed to prove its case. "Looking at the caption of the photo, all that is indicated was a claim, the interpretation being that the publication was not vouching for the truth of the photo," Maruk wrote.

Micro Issues

1. Considering the circumstances, how should the paper have verified the photo's accuracy?
2. If it was impossible to verify the photo's accuracy, should the paper have published it?
3. Would your reasoning be different had the incident occurred in the United States?

Midrange Issues

1. Use utilitarian reasoning, and then the veil of ignorance, to analyze this case. How does the particular philosophical theory help you think through the issues?
2. How should journalists weigh their personal safety and well-being against their role as professionals?
3. Is this photo as described too offensive to be published in the United States? Are different standards appropriate in different cultures?

Macro Issues

1. What is the role of the media in developing nations? How might that role influence ethical decision making?
2. This case asks you to think about whether there is such a thing as universal ethical principles. Is there a universal standard you believe should be applied in this case?

CASE 2-E

Media on Trial: The Clash of Canadian Law and Cross-Border Crime Coverage

KANINA HOLMES
Carleton University, Ottawa, Canada

Until February 2002, Robert William Pickton was a small-time Canadian pig farmer in Port Coquitlam, a community in British Columbia on Canada's west coast. Pickton, also known to some as "Uncle Willy," had a reputation for holding wild parties on his property and, according to his friends, was a guy with a genuine desire to help prostitutes struggling on the hard streets of Vancouver's Downtown Eastside.

Pickton is now notorious, charged with murdering 26 women. If found guilty, he would become Canada's worst serial killer.

Pickton was initially charged by the Royal Canadian Mounted Police (RCMP) on weapons offenses. In the months after his arrest, following an extensive search of his property, a massive $63-million investigation, the charges grew, both in number and in gravity. Most of the alleged victims were among the estimated 70 drug addicts and sex-trade workers who have vanished from Vancouver's Downtown Eastside beginning in the 1980s. Many of the alleged victims disappeared since 1995.

The case has attracted national and worldwide attention, in part because of the number of victims, the sensational nature of the charges—including speculation of how the bodies were disposed of and even a health bulletin triggered by concern about the potential contents of the pork that came from the farm. RCMP officers and members of the city police force, assisted by archeology students at the University of British Columbia, spent almost two years sifting through dirt at the farm, in search of human remains and DNA. The search has generated more than 11,500 pieces of evidence.

To date, media from all over Canada, the United States and Europe have covered various stages of the proceedings. More than 200 journalists from media outlets including *Reuters, Agence France Presse, Associated Press,* the *British Broadcasting Corporation,* the *New York Times,* the *Washington Post* and the *Hollywood Reporter* have requested media accreditation to cover the trial.

After years of delays, in part due to the nature of the Canadian justice system, the complexity of the case, the sheer volume of evidence and wrangling between defense lawyers and the Crown (prosecution) about the admissibility of evidence and limits on pretrial publicity. A case on six counts of murder went before both a judge and jury in 2007, but no verdict had been rendered at press time.

The circumstances surrounding the deaths of these women are unusual, if not genuinely sensational. So far, reporters covering the case have likely heard some explosive evidence and grisly details about the women's deaths. But they're not supposed to publish or broadcast any of this information because of the rules governing media coverage of Canadian court proceedings.

Canadian reporters risk being charged with contempt of court—and up to two years in prison—if they do not respect these restrictions. If evidence that could arguably taint a jury is released by any member of media, Canadian or foreign, the accused could walk away without ever being tried, raising the specter of justice never being done.

The same limits apply to reporters from the United States. and other countries. The difference, however, is that charges laid against foreign media cannot be enforced. A judge could bar any journalist responsible for violating a ban from attending court but, by that point, the evidential cat could already be out of the bag, prompting calls by defense lawyers to abandon the case.

Because of the startling characteristics of the alleged crimes, the international media spotlight and technological advances in communication, some media law experts predict coverage of these proceedings will test the laws that protect fair trials in Canada more than any other case. Beyond these milestones, media coverage highlights what happens when different legal systems and different standards of reporting clash. When the law surrounding coverage falls into a grey zone, specifically, when a journalist is not governed by a sct of laws, his decision about how to cover a case is more dependent on ethical considerations.

Under Canadian law, a system inherited and adapted from Britain, the legal process from the time a person is charged and tried is dramatically different than the U.S. judicial process.

These differences have important implications for cross-border media coverage. For example, still and video cameras are not allowed in any Canadian courtrooms, regardless of the profile of or public interest in a case. TV reporters covering court cases must routinely rely on note taking, graphics and court artists to inform the public.

For more serious offences under Canada's Criminal Code, before a person can be tried, a preliminary hearing is usually held to determine if there is enough evidence to proceed with a trial. If an accused requests a ban on publication of the evidence presented, a judge must comply. In Canada, such bans are considered commonplace.

In upholding the right of an accused to a fair hearing, an untainted jury pool is seen as key. For that reason, several restrictions are often imposed on the Canadian media regarding what can be reported before a jury is selected. These rules are designed both to protect the accused and shelter potential jury members from hearing information that could be highly prejudicial and that, come trial, may not be permitted in court.

Members of the media are usually allowed to attend preliminary hearings, although under a publication ban, they cannot report on the evidence being presented until after a trial is over.

If a case moves forward, following a preliminary hearing, there can be weeks or months during which lawyers on both sides argue over the future admissibility of evidence. These proceedings can be included in most publication bans.

From the beginning of this case, Pickton's lead defense lawyer, Peter Ritchie, forcefully and colorfully argued for a rarely imposed (but not unprecedented) blanket ban on publication. He even asked the judge to close the courtroom to the general public—not just to reporters, but also to members of the alleged victims' families. Ritchie characterized the international media attention "as intense as it can be in our modern society."

Lawyers from various media outlets (Canadian and U.S.) argued against the ban on the grounds that Canadian laws restricting publication were sufficient and that blocking media from hearing the proceedings would prevent important information from reaching the public in the event of a mistrial or at the end of a trial, at which time publication restrictions are usually lifted entirely.

Ultimately, the judge rejected the defense team's request to close the court room and the proceedings continued under normal (at least customary to Canadian reporters) restrictions. Journalists were free to take notes in the court room, but they couldn't publish the information.

The terms of the judge's publication ban included "any submissions, representations or rulings respecting evidence or the nature of the evidence taken at the preliminary hearing of Robert William Pickton," and extended the restrictions to include "any publication in any newspaper, on the Internet or broadcast by any means."

The judge issued a stern warning that the media would be monitored closely and any breach of the ban would be prosecuted. Notably, the ban singled out Internet publication, including even the publication of Web site addresses directing audiences to additional coverage that overstepped the intent of the ban.

However, adding fuel to the defense's earlier fire, almost immediately after the preliminary hearing began, there were, in fact, a number of breaches. Crown lawyers said that some Canadian news outlets had violated the spirit of the ban by providing a roadmap to what others had published online. The judge also put two reporters from the *Seattle Times* and one from the Associated Press, on notice they could be barred from the hearing if they were responsible for any further violations of the ban.

The difficulty in enforcing such publication bans in the Internet age is shown by the fact that almost five years after his arrest, a simple Internet search engine query for "William Pickton" comes up with 20,000 hits, several of which include descriptions and comments on the case.

On the eve of Pickton's appearance before a judge and jury, Canadians are now bracing themselves for the hundreds of reporters and members of the public expected to attend. In addition to Robert William Pickton's fate and peace of mind for the victims' families, also at stake is the system Canadians use to protect the sanctity of the judicial process. The issue of how journalists do their jobs, what they or their employers choose to report and how this will affect the outcome of this case also will be put on trial.

Micro Issues

1. Is this case a matter of interest to U.S. audiences? If so, why?
2. Should members of the foreign media corps who covered the early stages of this case have respected the publication ban? Justify your decision.
3. TV stations in the state of Washington committed to blocking their cable signals to Canada during coverage of this case. Should they have done this? Justify your decision.

Midrange Issues

1. What steps, if any, should U.S. media outlets take to block coverage of this case that could be read, heard or seen in Canada and which violate the publication ban?

2. How realistic is it to expect that information won't leak out given widespread access to cable and satellite transmissions, not to mention Web sites and blogging?
3. In a highly competitive market, what would you do if one of your media rivals ignored the publication ban and published some of the evidence in this case?
4. Whose laws should govern American media covering the trial—Canadian or U.S? Does it matter to your answer if the information is not broadcast or published in Canada?

Macro Issues

1. While contempt of court charges are difficult to enforce on foreign media, do reporters from other countries—whose readers or audience members play no role in this trial—have an ethical obligation to respect publication bans on legal proceedings such as pretrial hearings?
2. Where does the American reporter's duty lie? With the accused? With the audience?

CASE 2-F

Rather Reckless: The Killian Memo Scandal

BLAKE JACKSON
Daily Oklahoman

RENITA COLEMAN
University of Texas–Austin

Dan Rather left the CBS News head anchor chair in March 2005, ending a 50-year career of unabashed reporting marred by *one* unforgivable error.

Rather, who reported on such historic and controversial events as the Kennedy assassination, the "Watergate" scandal in the Nixon presidency, the "Iran-Contra" scandal in the Reagan presidency and the impeachment of President Clinton, was known by both the public and his peers in the news industry as someone who was willing to take on any story (Miller and Marks 2005). Rather's tenacious reporting style won him the opportunity to replace Walter Cronkite as head anchor of the "CBS Evening News."

But that same tenacity, 24 years later, would cost Rather his anchor job and, to an extent, his reputation as a credible journalist.

The morning of Sept. 8, 2004, CBS Senior Vice President Betsy West and Executive Producer Josh Howard met with "60 Minutes" producers and lawyers to discuss the authenticity of documents alleging President George W. Bush disobeyed his commanding officer and received preferential treatment while a member of the Texas Air National Guard. Specifically, the document purported that Bush had ignored a direct order to receive a physical, had not flown with a Guard unit in a year, and that his superiors were pressured to "sugar coat" his evaluations (Ripley 2004). A report on the memos, signed by the late Lt. Colonel Jerry Killian, was set to air that night on CBS's "60 Minutes Wednesday."

When White House Communications Director Dan Bartlett heard that CBS was ready to run an exclusive on the documents, he contacted "60 Minutes." CBS staff read Bartlett the Killian documents over the phone, but Bartlett refused to comment on the air until he had physically seen them. The day of the broadcast, Bartlett was given three hours to peruse the memos. He showed them to the President, who said he didn't recall that specific documentation. Bartlett didn't deny the facts in the documents, but told CBS there was no way to verify the memos (Ripley 2004).

But Rather and producer Mary Mapes, who had recently garnered praise for her work in breaking the Abu Ghraib prison torture story, vouched for the authenticity of the memos, saying they had document experts and handwriting analysts who could support the signatures, typefaces, and typewriter characteristics of the Killian document, although the ink and paper could not be tested because they were not originals. They also pointed to numerous credible sources on and off the record, who verified the claims in the memos' content (Ripley 2004). Mapes and her team had compared the memos to Bush's official record—dates, names, addresses and other references with known official documents. They also looked for errors in wording, military jargon and format.

"From the moment we saw (them) our overriding concern was whether these . . . really represented the truth. . ." Mapes wrote (2005, 148). "We had all approached the new memos with the mindset that they could be frauds" (Mapes 2005, 154). The more the CBS team examined them, the more they were convinced of their authenticity. The report aired that night.

Later, Mapes would say one of the factors that contributed to the story not being ready to air was that it had been "crashed"—that is, those working on it did so in an unusually short amount of time, working nonstop, without sleep, right up to the moment of airtime. In the case of the Bush documents story, the team had only five days to pull it together. To put that in context, most "60 Minutes" reporting teams work on six or fewer stories in an entire year.

The day after Mapes and a colleague received the documents, an airdate was set. The team had asked for an airdate of a little more than four weeks away; instead, they were told it would air in five days. The reason? The date they asked for and the one in between had already been purchased for a Billy Graham Crusade and a Dr. Phil special. CBS also knew that other news organizations with more flexibility than their once-a-week time slot also were working on the story.

"The bottom line was that the story's airdate was determined not by its newsworthiness, (and) not by the amount of time we needed to get it ready," Mapes wrote (2005, 151). It was a tremendously controversial and complex story with an unbelievably short deadline. They tried to buy more time and air it on a different show but were "turned . . . down flatly" (Mapes 2005, 182).

Mapes would later write, "I was uncomfortable with the script and, in retrospect, I should have done something I'd never done at work before. I should have said 'No.' I should have said, 'You'll have to run some other story tonight. I'm not going to crash this'" (Mapes 2005, 189).

The morning after the story aired, the CBS team awoke to a storm of controversy on conservative Web sites including Little Green Footballs, Free Republic, and Powerline. The essence of the sites' and bloggers' claims was that the documents were forged because the typeface, superscripts and proportional spacing didn't exist on typewriters in the 1970s. After the fact, CBS found military documents dating back to 1968 that used these same characteristics, but the charges were picking up steam and mainstream news outlets also began to scrutinize the authenticity of the Killian memos.

The viewing public was inflamed by the time proximity of the unverified report, which aired just two months before the 2004 presidential election. At first, CBS stood firm behind the report. But as contradicting stories and analysis poured in from the *Washington Post, the New York Times* and ABC News, Rather and Mapes' case began to crumble.

Other discrepancies in the style and substance of the memos further discredited the CBS report's claims (D'Agostino 2004). The *Dallas Morning News* broke the story of Killian's former secretary, Marian Carr Knox, who said she did not type the documents and that she thought they were fake. She repeated her claims on CBS, adding that it was true that Bush had been admitted to the National Guard as a political favor and then shirked his duty for at least a year, angering his commanding officer Killian.

On Sept. 20, CBS officially withdrew its support from the "60 Minutes Wednesday" piece, apologizing to the viewing public and admitting it should not have used the Killian documents. Four days later, Rather announced that he would step down as anchor and managing editor of the "CBS Evening News." In January 2005, the network fired Mapes, and asked for the resignations of West, Howard and Howard's top deputy, Mary Murphy.

According to a CBS statement, an independent panel appointed by the network concluded that CBS News failed to follow basic journalistic principles in assembling the report on the Killian memos.

Micro Issues

1. Should the CBS team have accepted the Killian memo outright, despite its anonymous source? Is the team guilty of reckless disregard?
2. Over the course of his career, Rather had earned the reputation, deserving or undeserving, of being liberally biased. Understanding his public perception, should Rather have passed the story on to another reporter or anchor when it came across his desk?
3. Many, if not most, journalistic stories are made up entirely of human sources with no corroborating documents. For this story, the journalists had corroboration from numerous sources who knew of the situation including a first-hand witness who was there, as well as official records that corroborated the content of the memos. The controversy over this story turned on the authenticity of six documents. Would the story have been as strong without the documents? Does the need to have 100 percent proof of the authenticity of 30-year-old documents have a "chilling effect" on reporters? Does this cautionary tale discourage journalists from pursuing controversial stories about important and powerful people? What other steps could have been taken?
4. What role do you think "crashing" the story played? Should reporters have more courage to say no to bosses who want a story before it is ready? If the story was held, the next air date would have been after the election. Would it have been a disservice to the public to withhold this information? Or was the story so important that running a flawed piece was the better decision?

Midrange Issues

1. How ethical is the practice of releasing stories which, although not immediately newsworthy, could immediately and greatly influence the outcome of an election or political decision because of the air date?
2. What could CBS officials have done to prevent the airing of unauthenticated information? Should a story with significant social or political implications deserve more in-depth review from network executives before airing?
3. Did the fact that President Bush neither confirmed nor denied the claims of the Killian memo affect the relevance or immediacy of airing the story?

Macro Issues

1. How does the Killian memo issue, and its handling, affect the reputation or credibility of people in the news industry? How does the clarification of discrepancies by other news outlets affect the reputation or credibility of people in the industry?

2. Did the CBS team's actions ultimately affect the outcome of the 2004 election? Did the potential truth of the memo mar Bush's perceived character?
3. For CBS, Mary Mapes and Dan Rather, was the weight of the issue worth the risk of its consequences?
4. What steps could news media outlets take to prevent source accuracy and authenticity errors from recurring?

CASE 2-G

Opinionated or Offensive? Race and the *Daily Tar Heel*

MARK SLAGLE
University of North Carolina–Chapel Hill

The *Daily Tar Heel* (*DTH*) is the student newspaper of the University of North Carolina (UNC) at Chapel Hill. Published every weekday during the school year, the paper has a circulation of more than 30,000 and is funded entirely by advertising revenue. It receives no student fees, has no faculty advisors and operates almost entirely independently of the university. (Its offices are housed in the student union.) The paper has a reputation for excellence and has won the Pacemaker, one of college journalism's highest awards, several times in the past few years.

On Sept. 13, 2005, the *DTH* published an opinion piece by Jillian Bandes, an editorial columnist, entitled "It's Sad, but Racial Profiling Is Necessary for Our Safety." The column began with the sentence, "I want all Arabs to be stripped naked and cavity-searched if they get within 100 yards of an airport." Bandes then went on to argue that ethnic and racial profiling was the most efficient way to protect against future terrorist attacks. "And you can't debate that while most Arabs are not terrorists, sadly, most terrorists are indeed Arab," she wrote. To buttress her argument, Bandes quoted two undergraduates and a professor—all Arab—whose quotes suggested they agreed with Bandes. Bandes ended her column with the words "embrace the race."

The reaction at UNC, a school with a long tradition of liberal activism, was swift. Letters poured into the *DTH*'s offices and the paper's Web site was deluged with comments. Many thought Bandes' column was nothing more than a racist rant that should never have been published. Others applauded her for defying what they saw as a stifling atmosphere of political correctness. Still others deplored her message but supported the *DTH*'s right to publish it.

Opinion page editor Chris Coletta, the man who hired Bandes, initially defended Bandes' column. In a Sept. 13 posting on The Bullhorn, one of the blogs on the *DTH* Web site, Coletta wrote, "to cut an *opinion* [emphasis his] from our pages because a reader (or 10,000 readers) finds it offensive is to directly assault the marketplace of ideas that serves as the bedrock of the free press. It's also contrary to the mission of the University, which is to challenge conventional wisdom—and to defeat ideas whose time has passed."

The next day, however, the *DTH* published a letter from two members of the Muslim Students Association. The students objected to Bandes' column, calling it offensive, sensational and disrespectful. They also said Bandes had quoted the Arabic professor and one of the Arabic students out of context, distorting their opinions. Coletta and *DTH* editor Ryan Tuck spoke to the professor and the students quoted in the story. According to Coletta, all three told him that Bandes had described the article she was writing as a piece "about Arab-American relations in a post–9/11 world." Two of sources said they had been misquoted. However, Coletta said Bandes' notes of their meetings dispute this. In addition, all three sources agreed that their words had been taken out of context.

After meeting with Bandes and the three sources, Coletta and *DTH* editor Ryan Tuck fired Bandes from her position on the editorial page. In a posting on the *DTH*

Web site, Coletta said he did not fire Bandes because he thought her column was racist. "I fired her because she strung together quotes out of context," he wrote. "She took sources' words out of context. She misled those sources when she conducted interviews. In other words, she conducted journalistic malpractice, and that's simply not something I, or the *Daily Tar Heel,* will tolerate."

In a letter to the editor published on Sept. 16, Bandes took issue with Tuck and Coletta's public statements regarding her dismissal. She wrote:

> I was fired because my editors said that I implied that the three sources I quoted had agreed to be characterized as agreeing with the statement, "Yes, we want to be stripped naked and sexed up in an airport." When, in fact, they had not specifically condoned those exact actions. Those were my words, not theirs. My interview quotes were deliberately juxtaposed against the comment, "Arabs don't seem to think being sexed up is such a bad idea" in order to get the desired humorous effect. Was it taken humorously? No. Was it the best judgment call on my part? No. I offended people I truly respect and who have taught me valuable lessons of the problems with sensational journalism. But what I did was not journalistically out of bounds. My sources agreed with racial profiling, and I simply added my two cents.

Coletta, in a letter to the Romenesko blog on the Poynter Institute's Web site, maintained that Bandes had not been fired for her opinions but for misrepresenting herself to her sources and using their comments out of context. He also accepted responsibility for not vetting Bandes' quotes more carefully. Coletta took a leave of absence from the *DTH* for one week, for what Tuck described in a separate statement as time to reflect on the situation. On Nov. 3, Coletta resigned his position as opinion page editor. Tuck announced the resignation on a *DTH* blog, saying "it boiled down to a difference of philosophy and my goal to operate the smoothest and most efficient sailing ship possible."

The incident raised the question of the ethically acceptable limits for material disseminated under the heading of "opinion." Tuck and Coletta insist that the content of Bandes' column was not the reason she was fired and that the *DTH* places no limits on its columnists' subject material. In a statement released to the media, Tuck wrote:

> We at the *DTH* always have espoused the ideals of having a completely unfettered press and of giving columnists latitude to be able to express their own views. We ask only that they maintain the same journalistic standards that apply to the rest of the staff. We ask that they report fairly and accurately and that they gather information ethically.

Judging by many of the letters and e-mail comments the *DTH* received, however, a large number of its readers felt quite differently. The controversy surrounding Bandes' column and her subsequent dismissal raged for weeks, not only in the pages of the *DTH* but also on Web sites, radio shows and television programs across the country. People on every side of the issue weighed in with their opinions.

One interesting aspect of the affair is the role played by the blogs on the *DTH*'s Web site. A relatively recent addition, the blogs permitted the editors to communicate to their readers far more than just once a day. More importantly, the blogs allowed readers to instantly respond at length to the editors as well as to other readers.

Unhindered by space restrictions, readers were able to comment as much as they liked. The comments ran the gamut from well-reasoned and carefully written analyses of the situation to profane ranting. According to the *DTH* Web site, nothing posted on the blog was censored by the editorial staff. By permitting this robust (and occasionally infantile) discussion, the blogs became something most newspaper opinion pages have always aspired to be—an ongoing conversation between the newspaper and the community it serves.

Micro Issues

1. Discounting for the moment the problem with the quotes, was the subject of the column an acceptable one in a forum such as a college campus? Justify your decision.
2. Does the lead appear to be an inflammatory way to introduce the topic? Can you think of a better one?
3. Is this a firing offensive for the writer? For the editor who did not check the quotes? Why or why not?

Midrange Issues

1. Should the editors have used unofficial channels such as blogs to explain the newspaper's stance to its readers?
2. Does the use of blogs to explain the newspaper's actions bypass the normal gatekeeping function of the newspaper's editors?
3. Does the use of blogs disenfranchise newspaper readers who might not have access to the blogs or might not care to access the blogs?

Macro Issues

1. Should there be a limit on what an opinion columnist can write? Are certain opinions or ideas too dangerous or distasteful to be discussed in open forums?
2. What are the pros and cons of censoring or not censoring a campus newspaper's discussion boards? Are they a part of the "marketplace of ideas" or simply a forum for promoting bigotry or bias?
3. In an age of media ranging from traditional to virtual, where is the topic of race best discussed?

CASE 2-H

News as Persuasion: The *New York Times* vs. Wen Ho Lee

LEE WILKINS
University of Missouri—Columbia

On March 6, 1999, under the headline "Breach at Los Alamos: A Special Report; China Stole Nuclear Secrets for Bombs, U.S. Aides Say," the *New York Times* began a front-page, 4,000-word piece detailing how workers—specifically one worker—at the Los Alamos laboratory had leaked sensitive nuclear secrets to the People's Republic of China. The story, written by two of the *Times'* investigative reporters, James Risen and Jeff Garth, a Pulitzer Prize winner, linked the leaks with "breakthroughs" in Chinese weapons technology, posing a clear national security risk to the United States.

The reporters relied heavily on unnamed sources and one named source, Notra Trulock, a former Energy Department Director of Intelligence, who was described as a "star witness" in Congressional investigations. The story described Trulock as a "whistleblower," and said that the weapons leaks had become "one of the most damaging spy cases in recent history."

In the same story, the reporters said that the Clinton-administration Justice Department had failed to respond appropriately to the case. "A reconstruction by the *New York Times* reveals that throughout the Government, the response to the nuclear theft was plagued by delays, inaction and skepticism." The story also noted that while the investigation had continued for three years, no arrests have been made, and that the unnamed key suspect had been allowed to keep his high security clearance for more than a year after he had become the target of the investigation. "Only in the last several weeks, after prodding from Congress and the Secretary of Energy, have Government officials administered lie-detector tests to the main suspect, a Los Alamos computer scientist who is Chinese-American."

The unnamed, but clearly identified suspect, was 59-year-old Wen Ho Lee.

In an April 28, 1999, article written by the same reporters, the *Times* noted that Lee had improperly downloaded computer files containing nuclear codes. The lead on the story read: "A scientist suspected of spying for China improperly transferred huge amounts of secret data from a computer system at a government laboratory, compromising virtually every nuclear weapon in the United States arsenal, government and lab, officials say."

The government finally arrested Lee in December 1999—more than eight months after the *Times'* original story. By the time of the arrest, other reporters at the *Times* were questioning some conclusions in the original pieces. The *Times* reporter assigned the nuclear weapons beat, for example, reported five months after the original allegations that the information that Lee was supposed to have disseminated was widely available at the time the "leaks" supposedly occurred.

There were other problems with the *Times* original story. For example, the reporters never independently investigated Trulock. Had they done so, they might have uncovered other sources, equally expert, who would have told them that Trulock had been building a case against Lee for almost four years in some part because Lee was ethnic Chinese. That was the content of an affidavit filed with the court that ultimately released Lee.

"Based on my experience and my personal knowledge, I believe that Mr. Tru-lock improperly targeted Dr. Lee due to Dr. Lee's race and national origin," said Charles Washington, former acting director of counterintelligence at the Energy Department who filed an affidavit in the case. The two reporters also appeared to discount statements and sources that did not support their allegations against Lee. For example, the reporters either did not know and decided not to run information from the CIA that concluded the charges against Lee, which were based in an "intelligence windfall from Beijing," actually were the work of a double agent try-ing to impress the government of Taiwan with Beijing's nuclear weapons progress.

The reporters also apparently failed to check with, or discounted, other experts in the nuclear weapons field who asserted that the alleged massive "jump" in main-land China's nuclear capacity was really little more than minimal progress, readily accounted for by hard scientific work instead of spying. Perhaps most tellingly, the two reporters also failed to inform their readership that the original leak came from a Congressional Committee chaired by California Republican Christopher Cox.

There were other fact errors in the story: Lee had passed a lie detector test (the *Times* said he had not), he had not taken a secret trip to Hong Kong (the *Times* said he had) and the documents he was accused of downloading into his computer were not classified as "secret" until after formal charges were brought. The *Times* was silent on this last issue, which means the reporters either did not know, had been mis-led or did know but decided not to print the information. The *Times* coverage, of course, set the tone for much of the rest of the media reporting on the case, what some critics have described as a return to Cold War rhetoric and the most bogus set of spy charges since those that resulted in the deaths of Julius and Ethel Rosenberg at the height of the McCarthy era of American history.

Meanwhile, Lee, a cancer survivor, was placed in solitary confinement without bail for nine months. Judge James Parker, on the day Lee was released "for time served" with the government's agreement, told him: "I sincerely apologize to you, Dr. Lee, for the unfair manner you were held in custody by the executive branch."

When it became evident that the case against Lee was collapsing, the news organization did acknowledge that it had ignored problems with the government's case, failed to humanize Lee and discounted a political agenda that pushed to nar-row the pool of suspects prematurely. The September 26th article noted that a review of the totality of the paper's coverage, "found careful reporting that included exten-sive cross-checking and vetting of multiple sources, despite enormous obstacles. . . ." But . . . "In those instances where we fell short of our standards in our coverage of this story, the blame lies principally with those who directed the coverage, for not raising questions that occurred to us only later."

Other media critics were not nearly so kind. Bill Mesler, in an article entitled "The Spy Who Wasn't" accused the *Times* of launching a witch hunt that ended in Lee's incarceration. And Robert Scheer, who wrote more than 20 columns and arti-cles about the journalistic work in the case, called the *Times*' transgressions startling. "I don't know if it makes the all-time Top Ten list [of low points in the history of this nation's journalism], but the trial and conviction of Lee in the pages of the *Times* . . . is certainly right up there."

Micro Issues

1. What is the responsibility of journalists to investigate elements of their stories that run "counter" to their theories of events?
2. Evaluate the apology from the *Times* editors? Do you believe it was appropriate? What were the editors' responsibilities in relation to those of the reporters?
3. Should investigative reporters treat "whistleblowers" differently than other sorts of sources? How about those sources who wish to remain anonymous?

Midrange Issues

1. Should journalists include political context in stories? Can news reporters do this without making it seem like bias?
2. Should news organizations develop policies about how to handle leaks, particularly from political sources?
3. How much do you think Dr. Lee's ethnicity influenced the reporting in the case?

Macro Issues

1. The reporting in the Wen Ho Lee case came less than a year after the Monica Lewinsky story was broken by Matt Drudge on the Internet—without benefit of any official sources. Evaluate the impact of the journalism in the Lewinsky case on subsequent reporting, including the case of Wen Ho Lee.
2. How does the reporting of the *New York Times* in the Wen Ho Lee case compare with the reporting of Northwestern University journalism professor David Protess, whose students have unearthed evidence of innocent men on death row. Does either kind of story violate the tenants of journalistic objectivity? If so, is either story ethical? If not, why not?

Wen Ho Lee Part II: Don't Get Mad, Get Even

After his release from jail, the now exonerated scientist filed a civil suit claiming that government officials had smeared him through improper media leaks. Lee sued individual journalists as well as the government under provisions of the 1974 Privacy Act, with the goal of forcing the journalists who had written about him to disclose their confidential sources.

The journalists, Jeff Gerth and James Risen from the *New York Times*, Robert Drogin of the *Los Angeles Times,* H. Josef Herbert of the Associated Press and Pierre Thomas of CNN (later with ABC), lost every court decision as the suit moved through the legal system. Most troubling for journalists was an August 2004 decision by U.S. District Judge Thomas Penfield Jackson that fined the journalists $500 per day for every day they refused to provide the names to Lee through his attorneys.

The case, along with that of Valerie Plame (see Case 7-A), was the first of its kind to be decided in Washington D.C. since 1981. According to the suit, the case pitted the right of the media against Lee's right to obtain evidence that could prove his claims and hence his innocence.

Lee's attorney argued that the reporters involved were essentially government dupes. "What they were doing was not journalism it was a rush to judgment. We want accountability for the leakers," said Brian Sun, Lee's attorney. "The problem is journalists policing themselves. It's not wrong to listen when someone tells you that stuff. You're doing your job. But you run a risk to your paper and your source that you may not be able to protect the identity of your source if you got the information improperly, or if you print things that are just wrong." (Sterngold, 2005).

Although the district court agreed, the decision was not unanimous. Judge David S. Tatel stressed the importance of journalistic promises of confidentiality. "It's hard to imagine how his (Lee's) interest could outweigh the public's interest in protecting journalists' ability to report without reservation on sensitive issues of national security." Attorneys representing the journalists involved also accused Lee of greed, saying that by filing the suit under privacy law, rather than seeking a libel judgment, Lee was after money rather than principle.

However, others saw the case as raising important journalistic issues, eroding journalistic shield privileges and making it more difficult for journalists to obtain evidence of government malfeasance. "I see this as an even graver threat than the Plame (Valerie Wilson) case to a reporter's right to know," said Lucy Dalglish, executive director of the Reporters Committee for Freedom of the Press. "Really, the Plame case was almost a freak instance. The Lee case is far more of a problem in the long term because it is a civil suit and involves more routine reporting issues."

But, before it could reach the U.S. Supreme Court, the news organizations and the federal government settled. The June 2006 agreement stipulated that Lee would receive $1.6 million, $895,000 from the federal government and the remaining $750,000 from the five news organizations for which the journalists worked. None of the news organizations had been named in Lee's suit.

"Unfortunately, the journalists in this case . . . reluctantly concluded that the only way they could continue to protect the bond with their sources and sidestep increasing punishment, including possible jail time, was to contribute to the settlement with the government and Wen Ho Lee," said Henry Hoberman, senior vice president of ABC. "It was not a decision that any of the journalists came to easily or happily" (Farhi 2006).

The payments from news organizations were the only money that Lee would be able to retain. The rest—the government's portion of the settlement—went to pay attorney's fees and income taxes on the settlement. Government attorneys insisted that the government not pay anything that would be perceived as damages to Lee.

Micro Issues

1. In the journalist/source relationship, what is the ethical obligation of the source, if any?
2. Evaluate the assertion that the journalists were essentially government dupes. What specific actions could the journalists have taken to avoid this perception? How might it be justified ethically?

Midrange Issues

1. By paying the settlement, do you think the news organizations admitted that they had some culpability in the Lee matter?

2. Evaluate the statement by Judge Tatel in light of Kantian theory and utilitarian theory.
3. Evaluate Lee's attorney's statement in light of Kantian and utilitarian theory.

Macro Issues

1. Should states and the federal government enact shield laws for reporters?
2. What is an appropriate recourse for a person who has been admittedly wronged by the news media short of a civil suit?
3. Compare this case with that of Valerie Plame (Case 7-A). What are the morally relevant differences?

3

Advertising Ethics: From Buyer Beware to Empowerment

By the end of this chapter, you should be familiar with:

- **why both advertising and news can be evaluated as symbol formation.**
- **the balance and cognitive dissonance persuasion theories and their role in advertising.**
- **the issues surrounding the interaction between ads and vulnerable audiences.**
- **the TARES test for evaluating the ethics of individual ads.**

INTRODUCTION

Since the days of ancient Greece, a major function of communication has been to persuade. Greek citizens used the art of rhetoric to their advantage in the Greek city-states where democracy was practiced through an elaborate court system. Eventually, the courts of Athens became crowded with those who sought to use their persuasive powers for gain. Today's airwaves and printing presses are likewise filled with messages designed to increase the influence and wealth of their sponsors.

But ancient Athens has morphed into a 21st-century democracy that runs on the engines of capitalism, fueled in large part by advertising. While the ancient Greeks overtly attempted to persuade, contemporary advertising employs elements that act on the human psyche in more subtle ways. Indeed, communication theory has evolved in an attempt to discover how it is that some messages persuade and others do not. And, although the ancient Greeks accepted all speech as persuasion, contemporary understandings have separated advertising from news.

We think the Greeks had the right idea some 3,000 years ago. We suggest that both advertising and news be understood as elements of the same activity: symbol formation (Wilkins and Christians 2001). Both news and advertising are rooted in culture. Both make some assumptions about the relationship between mediated messages and the individuals who receive them. Most important, if news and advertising really are different parts of the same process, then the same ethical tools—and standards—can be applied.

The similarities between advertising and news are particularly important when the lines between the activities blur (as they do in advertorials) or when advertising about newsworthy issues, such as who should be elected president, becomes an important way people learn about those questions. A set of ethical standards shared between both activities will give contemporary practitioners a better chance at "doing the right thing" in an increasingly competitive media environment.

But before we talk theory, let's talk some economic fact.

YOU PAY WHEN YOU WASH, NOT WHEN YOU WATCH

Anyone in the management end of a media business understands this truth: the role of programming on television (either news or entertainment), the role of copy (news, features or editorials) in newspapers or the role of click to a specific screen is to deliver an audience to advertisers.

The United States is the only country in the world that has chosen to fund its media system almost exclusively through private dollars. The public broadcasting system receives a tiny fraction of 1 percent of the U.S. budget; requirements for the publication of legal advertising may keep weekly newspapers alive, but those revenues are insignificant to such media behemoths as the *New York Times.* While Americans may find advertising intrusive, seriously misleading and environmentally unfriendly (think of the trees we could save if McDonald's didn't have to package every burger and fry with its own logo), it funds the world's most robust media system. As George Gerbner (1987) says, "You pay when you wash, not when you watch."

Contrary to what news journalists believe, most people regard advertising as another form of information. Experiments have shown that people prefer newspapers with advertising to newspapers that lack ads. Auction sites on the Web, such as ebay, are one of the most popular kinds of Internet activity and provide further evidence that an audience with a purpose will seek out advertising to help make an informed choice.

These facts of media life do not blunt some of the deepest criticisms of advertising. The nature of the advertising message itself—short, highly visual and intentionally vague—supports criticism about advertising's reliance on stereotypes, its glorification of consumerism at the expense of community and its apparent willingness to indulge in any excess to "make a buck." Indeed, some of the most compelling evidence that advertising works has arisen from studies of the impact of tobacco advertising on children under 18. The United States—and the rest of the world—have the cancer rates to prove it.

As a nation, the United States has chosen to regulate some of advertising's most egregious excesses, but we also have chosen to continue this method of paying for news and information. If advertising practitioners are ever to be ranked above the bottom of the occupational trustworthiness scale, then ethical thinking needs to become every bit as much a part of the advertising process as market research and strategic communication plans.

THINKING ABOUT THE AUDIENCE:
FROM PERSUASION THEORY TO PHILOSOPHICAL
ANTHROPOLOGY

Psychologists first began to try to understand persuasion by working with a stimulus–response model. This early behaviorist approach led many to believe that the media could act as a "hypodermic needle" or a "magic bullet," sending a stimulus/message to an unresisting audience. These researchers, called "powerful effects theorists," found examples to support their theory in the public panic after Orson Welles's *War of the Worlds* broadcast on Oct. 30, 1938, and in the success of propaganda during both world wars.

But, the stimulus–response model proved a poor predictor of much human behavior. By the 1940s, most researchers were concluding that media effects were limited or nonexistent. However, by studying only behavior change (i.e., changing my vote), the researchers overlooked the true power of the media in the cognitive (knowledge) and affective (emotional) realms.

Later, communication theorists focused on cognitive psychology. Rather than analyzing persuasion as a simple behavioral reaction to a sufficient stimulus, these scholars theorized that how people think helped to explain persuasion. According to these theories, people strain toward cognitive balance. Simply put, we are most comfortable when all of our beliefs, actions, attitudes and relationships are in harmony, a state theorists called "symmetry."

Doonesbury Copyright 1988 G. B. Trudeau. Reprinted with permission of Universal Press Syndicate. All rights reserved.

Such theories have become known as "balance theories," since they stress the tendency of people to strive for cognitive balance in their lives. A person achieves balance only when his or her attitudes, information and actions are in harmony. Leon Festinger (1957) coined the term *cognitive dissonance* to describe the state where a message and an action give conflicting and uncomfortable signals. The desire to eliminate that dissonance is a strong one, strong enough to influence purchasing behavior and voting habits or opinions—at least some of the time.

Advertisers use this theory. A frequent scenario in advertising copy is to knock a consumer off balance early and to promise restoration of that balance through the purchase of a product. For instance, the headline of an ad might suggest that your dandruff is making you a social outcast, and the subsequent copy promises you social approval if you use the correct shampoo. A television ad might suggest that the wrong choice of tires means you don't care about your family's safety, while the correct choice of tires restores peace of mind by providing needed protection.

This social science–based approach to understanding advertising helped in creating ads and, to a more limited extent, explained their effectiveness. However, the social science approach makes some assumptions about the nature of people that advertising itself calls into question. For example, advertising scholars have tried to outline how people cognitively "process" or think about ads. Yet the same studies indicate that people are often irrational, emotional and not necessarily well informed about the various claims made in ads.

Despite the equivocal findings of social science based research, the ultimate practical justification for advertising was summed up in the ancient Roman phrase *caveat emptor,* "Let the buyer beware." In other words, the creators of the ads were willing to assume little responsibility for the impact of their work, and academic studies gave them partial cover: if you can't prove that something's been effective, then it's unreasonable to suggest you take some responsibility for it.

Philosophical anthropologists assert that human rationality exists on equal footing with human beings who explain themselves through daily experience, language and symbols. Culture and our personal experience balance rationality (Wilkins and Christians 2001). If philosophical anthropology is correct, then ethical analysis of advertising founded in "Let the buyer beware" is morally untenable. Instead, the ethical goal of advertising should be the empowerment of multiple stakeholders—from those who need to buy, those who need to sell and those who need to live in a community fueled by commerce and tax dollars. If the concept of human being as creator of culture and dynamic user of symbols becomes an ethical foundation for thinking about the audience, then advertising practitioners could be expected to operate within the following framework:

- Clients and the public need information that gives them "a good reason to adopt a course of action" (Koehn 1998, 106). The reason needs to be nonarbitrary and capable of helping people support one action instead of others.
- Rather than offering only expert opinion, advertising should foster ongoing discussion so that people can explore when options are sound and when practical knowledge (common sense) is superior.
- Advertising, just like news, can help foster reflective community, including the community of consumers.

- Advertising needs to take seriously the role of culture in our lives. That means that advertising must authentically reflect the diverse voices that comprise our culture.
- Advertising will speak to the role of organizations in our lives. Questions of history and background can be conveyed in ads, but that must be done accurately and in context.

Given these general guidelines, let's explore a specific framework that puts ads to an ethical test.

THINKING ABOUT THE MESSAGE: THE TARES TEST

Baker and Martinson (2001) have suggested a set of questions called the TARES test that the creators of every ad should ask themselves to determine the ethical worthiness of the ad. If the answers are "yes," the ad passes the test. If the answers to some or all of the questions are "no," then the creator must justify—in the sense that Bok discusses—the ad content decisions. While the TARES test will not solve all ethical problems in creating ads, it does give creative people, marketing directors and strategic communication planners a tool.

The first element of the test—**T**—stands for **truthfulness.** Are the ad claims, both verbal and visual, truthful? If the message communicates only part of the truth (and many ads do this), are the omissions deceptive? Conversely, an ad would pass the test if it meets a genuine human need to provide truthful information, even if some facts are omitted.

The Cheerios television ads that emphasize eating Cheerios as part of a heart-healthy lifestyle could easily pass the first element of the TARES test. People do have to eat, and the ads provide needed information. The ads also omit some information—for example, the other components of a heart-healthy lifestyle or the fact that other breakfast cereals also meet these requirements. But the omitted information does not lead the mature consumer to make false assumptions and bad choices.

Step two in the TARES test—**A** for **authenticity**—is closely linked to step one. Authenticity suggests that it's important not only to do the right thing, but also "to do it with the right attitude" (Pojman 1999, 158). We link this notion to the concept of sincerity. First, is there a sincere need for this product within the range of products and services available? Second, are the reasons given the consumer purchasing the product presented in such a way that they also would motivate the person who developed and wrote the ad?

Let's take a set of ads about products designed to help elderly or infirm people live more independently. Although some of these products—for example, devices that turn on lights in response to a hand clap—may seem little more than high-tech toys, anyone with a grandparent in a wheelchair, a sibling crippled by an illness like rheumatoid arthritis, or even a young person suffering from the imposed immobility of a broken leg can readily understand the need for such devices. But in making this point, if the ads stereotype elderly people as frail, helpless, weak or easily panicked, they do not authentically reflect the reality of life beyond age 65. Indeed, such

The TARES Test of Ethical Advertising

T   Are the ad claims **Truthful?**

A   Is the claim an **Authentic** one?

R   Does the ad treat the receiver with **Respect?**

E   Is there **Equity** between the sender and the receiver?

S   Is the ad **Socially** responsible?

stereotypical and fear-filled appeals omit a substantial number of consumers who might benefit from the product. The ad lacks authenticity. Thus, the TARES test would suggest rethinking the specific appeal in the ad to one that scares and stereotypes less and informs more. For creative people, such a switch is readily accomplished. Just as important, a fresher approach might well sell more.

The **R** in the TARES test stands for **respect,** in this case, respect for the person who will receive the persuasive message. However, as a shorthand way of thinking through this element of the test, it might be appropriate for advertising practitioners to ask themselves, "Am I willing to take full, open, public and personal responsibility for the content of this ad?"

Take the recent car insurance campaign that began with an ad of an actual car crash filmed from inside the car. Even though the ad itself was filmed in a single take, the company received a great deal of criticism for developing an ad that "scared" consumers into considering its product. The company took the criticism to heart and produced a second set of ads that reminded consumers how frequently and unexpectedly serious auto accidents occur. Although the ads relied on fear as a primary emotional tactic, they also provided rational reasons to purchase their product and took consumer response seriously.

The **E** in the TARES test stands for **equity.** We conceptualize mutuality as follows: is the recipient of the message on the same level playing field as the ad's creator? Or, to correctly interpret the ad, must that person be abnormally well informed, unusually bright or quick-witted and completely without prejudice? Advertising copy that takes advantage of these common human frailties would not pass the equity portion of the TARES test. Phrased another way, the ad would fare well behind John Rawls's veil of ignorance (see Chapter 6).

Think about this corporate image ad for Mobil Oil—the one with the pristine scenery, glorious sunset and an oil tanker. The ad claims that Mobil has the best interest of the environment at heart by building tankers with double hulls. While Mobil's claim—that it builds double-hulled tankers—is literally true, correctly interpreting the ad requires a rapid and thorough recall of recent legislative history. Mobil, and all other oil companies, were required by Congress to build double-hulled tankers after the single-hulled tanker, the *Exxon Valdez,* ran aground and spilled an enormous amount of oil in Alaska, an environmental disaster of the first magnitude. (For more on this episode, see the Exxon case on the Web site for this book.) For the image ad to work, it counts on the average person not knowing—or not being able to connect—legislative requirements with corporate behavior. In fact, the ad assumes an unequal relationship between the knowledge of the person who created the ad and the consumer. It flunks the concept of equity.

Finally, the **S** in the TARES test. Is the ad **socially responsible?** This is perhaps the most difficult element of the test for the simple reason that advertising practitioners have duties to many groups, among them their clients, the agencies for which they work, consumers, people who see the advertising but do not buy a particular product and society at large. Because this text emphasizes social ethics, we suggest interpreting this portion of the TARES test in the following fashion:

- If everyone who is financially able to purchase this product or service did so and used it, would society as a whole be improved, keeping in mind that recreation and self-improvement are worthy societal goals?
- If there are some groups in society that would benefit from using this product as advertised, are there others that could be significantly harmed by it? Are there ways to protect them?
- Does this ad increase or decrease the trust the average person has for persuasive messages?
- Does this ad take the notion of corporate responsibility, both to make money and to improve human life and welfare, seriously and truthfully?

Using this concept of social responsibility should enable you to think ethically about television's decisions to air condom advertising. MTV, the network targeted at teenagers, chose to air such ads in 2000. More traditional network television outlets did not. Which decision do you believe is more ethically justified? Why? Does the notion of social responsibility have any place in your analysis?

The TARES test is a demanding one. But asking these questions, particularly during the process of creating an ad, can also be a spur to better, more creative execution and can be rewarded in the capitalistic marketplace. The TARES test may help advertising practitioners warn their corporate clients about the kind of advertising that could do them, as well as society at large, great long-term harm.

ADVERTISING'S SPECIAL PROBLEMS: VULNERABLE AUDIENCES

Advertising in a mass medium reaches large, heterogeneous audiences. Sometimes, advertising intended for one group is seen by another. Sometimes the results are humorous, and maybe even a little embarrassing, as when ads for contraception or personal hygiene products make their way into prime-time programming.

However, in the case of Camel cigarettes, this "confusion" of intended audience with actual recipients appears quite deliberate. A few years ago, Camel agreed to withdraw its cartoon spokesperson "Joe Camel" from magazines and billboards after internal documents revealed the industry targeted underage smokers. In other cases—for example, the beer industry—no such ban exists. Advertising intended for adults is often seen by those who cannot legally drink but do remember the catchy commercials and the presentation of drinking as something connected with fun and good times. Even young children remembered the recently used Budweiser talking bullfrogs and other creative beer ads. These ads air in a time when most adult alcoholics report having had their first drink when they were underage.

These examples revolve around the same ethical question: are there certain types of audiences who deserve special protection from advertising messages? In keeping with thousands of years of ethical thinking, U.S. law has answered this question in the affirmative, particularly in the case of children. Thus, there are a number of legal restrictions on advertising targeted at children, in everything from Saturday-morning television programming to the sorts of messages and characters that advertisers may employ. The reason is that children, unlike adults, are not assumed to be autonomous moral actors. They reason about advertising imperfectly, and in an attempt to protect them, American society has accepted some regulation of commercial speech.

However, the issue gets murkier when the target audience is formed of adults—for example, ethnic consumers. Exactly when advertisers began to actively court ethnic consumers is uncertain. Brooks (1992) quotes a 1940 *BusinessWeek* article that reported an organization was established in Los Angeles to help guide advertisers who wished to garner the patronage of African-American consumers. The businesses were cautioned against using words such as "boss," "boy," and "darkey" in their advertisements. Instead, the advertisers were urged to refer to African-American consumers as "Negroes" who want the same things as other shoppers.

The real attempt to court ethnic audiences began when those audiences acquired buying power. Hispanics are now the largest minority in the United States. The buying power of African-American consumers now tops more than $300 billion. The Asian-American market has also increased substantially. Yet, a relative handful of advertisements reflect this emerging demographic reality, and commercials designed to appeal to this market segment sometimes employ troubling stereotypes or encounter other difficulties. For example, R. J. Reynolds Tobacco Company spent millions developing a cigarette aimed at African-Americans and putting billboards in African-American neighborhoods to announce it, only to pull the product when consumer outrage over the impact of tobacco on the health of the target market became public.

Other tendencies in advertising combine, in troubling ways, cultural understandings and product sales. Magazines pointed at teenage girls seldom reflect the reality of teenage bodies. Scholarly studies have shown that women, when exposed to advertising images, find their own bodies less acceptable. The same goes for facial features. Scholars have noted that the ideal image of beauty, even in magazines targeted at African-Americans, is a Caucasian one of small noses, thin lips and lighter skin tones. African-American women simply don't see themselves in these advertisements. Scholars in the cultural studies tradition argue that the impact of these repeated images is cumulative—the culture itself comes to accept without question what is, in reality, nothing more than a gender or a racial stereotype.

Few scholars have suggested that adults who are members of minority communities need special protection from advertising. What they have noted is that ads that abuse the trust between consumer and product have both short-term and long-term consequences. In the short term, products may not sell or may find themselves the target of regulation. In the long term, the load of cynicism and societal distrust increases.

People sense they are being used, even if they can't explain precisely how. The buyer may learn to beware of advertising itself rather than to use advertising to help make better-informed decisions.

Suggested Readings

BAKER, S. and MARTINSON, D. 2001. "The TARES test: Five principles of ethical persuasion." *Journal of Mass Media Ethics* Vol. 16, Nos. 2 & 3.

FESTINGER, L. 1957. *A theory of cognitive dissonance.* Stanford, CA: Stanford University Press.

KOEHN, D. 1998. *Rethinking feminist ethics.* New York: Routledge.

LEISS, WILLIAM, STEPHEN KLINE, and SUT JHALLY. 1986. *Social communication in advertising: Person, products and images of well being.* New York: Methuen Publications.

O'TOOLE, JOHN. 1985. *The trouble with advertising.* New York: Times Books.

PATTERSON, THOMAS E., and ROBERT D. MCCLURE. 1972. *The unseeing eye.* New York: G. P. Putnam's Sons.

SCHUDSON, MICHAEL. 1984. *Advertising: The uneasy persuasion.* New York: Basic Books.

Cases on the Web

"A case of need" by Deni Elliott

"Exxon's whipping cream on a pile of manure" by JoAnn M. Valenti

"A sobering dilemma" by Beverly Horvit

"Superman's Super Bowl Miracle" by Renita Coleman

"The Plagiarism Factory" by John P. Ferré

CHAPTER 3 CASES

CASE 3-A

Daisy Girl Redux: Using Fear as a Political Weapon

ANDREA MILLER
Louisiana State University

In the 21st century, an old fear, one that many felt came tumbling down with the Berlin Wall, has been rekindled. The fear of nuclear war appears as real now as it was when people built concrete bunkers back in the 1960s. In 2003, the saying "everything old becomes new again" was manifested in the controversial "Daisy Girl" anti–nuclear war ad.

Broadcast a single time on television in 1964, the Daisy Girl political advertisement showed a little blonde girl picking the petals off a daisy. As the petals are plucked one by one, a voice counts down to a nuclear bomb blast. The ad was originally created by legendary adman Tony Schwartz for Lyndon Johnson's presidential campaign against conservative Barry Goldwater. The implied message was that a vote for Goldwater was a vote for nuclear war. The Republican Party claimed the ad slandered Goldwater. In the fearful Cold War climate, the advertisement aired once before viewer protests forced it to be pulled.

In January 2003, a group with another agenda attempted to replant the seeds of fear. The grass-roots organization MoveOn.org had a new version of the "Daisy Nuke" ad created to protest the United States' seemingly inevitable path to war with Iraq. The reincarnation's message was less subtle this time. As the young girl picked the petals, the voiceover said: "War with Iraq. Maybe it will end quickly. Maybe not. Maybe it will spread. Maybe extremists will take over countries with nuclear weapons."

Images of wounded soldiers and burning oils wells appeared on the screen. The nuclear explosion and mushroom cloud appeared with the final message: "Let the inspections work." The group spent $400,000 for the ad to air on local stations in 13 major cities, including New York, Chicago and Miami.

The organization behind the ad's revival, MoveOn.org, was formed in the 1990s to oppose the impeachment of former President Bill Clinton. Prior to the airing of "Daisy 2," the group also had spent more than $300,000 on newspaper ads urging President Bush to avoid war with Iraq. Eli Pariser, MoveOn.org's international campaign director, told the Associated Press that the goal of "Daisy 2" was to encourage a national discussion. But critics argued that, just as the original did 40 years ago, the ad stirred more fear than debate.

Two network-affiliated television stations decided not to run the ads.: KNBC-TV in Los Angeles and WRC-TV in Washington, D.C. Both are owned by NBC. NBC's owner, General Electric, released the following statement concerning the ad's "non-acceptance": "We prefer to handle controversial issues in our news and public affairs programming, where we can be fair and balanced." Responses from the individual stations mirrored the parent company's statement.

Four decades after the first Daisy Girl ad, Daisy 2 was less controversial than historically and psychologically significant. The ad was reincarnated hoping to capitalize on its familiarity and the emotion the ad evokes: fear. In the post 9/11 world, Americans have an unprecedented level of fear for safety—physical and economic. Because a person's fears can shape their perception of the facts (Jamieson 1983), the ad could cause people to believe in the reality of the worst case scenario it represents. The link that was created was tenuous, but not improbable, especially after millions watched the impossible crash of a passenger jet into the World Trade Center.

The ad's history garnered more attention than the ad itself. Because of the ad's historical significance, the news media covered the release of the ad extensively. The ad was scheduled to air for only five days and in just over a dozen large television markets. However, MoveOn.org released the ad to the media prior to its broadcast. Most Americans saw the ad in the television coverage of the ad or read about its contents in the newspapers. As with the original Daisy Girl ad, MoveOn.org got its money's worth in free publicity.

Micro Issues

1. Was the decision by the two NBC affiliates not to air the Daisy Girl ad an appropriate one?
2. Should other stations have joined in the decision? Defend your answer.
3. What were some possible positive and negative consequences of the ad?

Midrange Issues

1. How was the agenda behind the ad different between the 1964 and 2003 versions? Does that make a difference in the appropriateness of the ad?
2. Fear of nuclear war? Fear of no future for your children or grandchildren? Fear of another Vietnam-like conflict? This ad evoked a strong negative emotion that is usually associated with the primal instinct to flight. Is that what MoveOn.org hoped to accomplish?
3. Did the media play an additional role in the controversy by covering the story of the ad itself? Does the story have news value from an ethical standpoint?

Macro Issues

1. Advertisers play on the emotions of viewers all the time to sell products. How is the use of fear different? Is the use of fear to sell an idea different than using fear to sell a product?
2. Images and ideas that question patriotism also evoke a visceral response. What role does or should war play in patriotism? Does duty ethics come into play in the issues of war, patriotism, and safety?
3. Conflict is a necessary part of ethical decision making. What ethical theory could MoveOn.org have used to justify their decision to reincarnate this ad? What ethical theory could television stations have used to justify their decision not to air the ad?

CASE 3-B

Was That an Apple Computer I Just Saw? A Comparison of Product Placement in U.S. Network Television and Abroad

PHILIP PATTERSON
Oklahoma Christian University

Michael Scott, the buffoonlike office manager in the Emmy-award winning NBC comedy "The Office," shows up at casual Friday encouraging his shocked employees to check out his backside in his new Levi's jeans. In the wildly popular ABC drama/comedy "Desperate Housewives," Gabrielle (played by Eva Longoria) gets desperate enough for cash to model beside a Buick LaCrosse at a car show and for a mattress firm. In the now-cancelled "American Dreams," which portrayed American life in the 1960s, such American icons as Campbell's Soup and Ford Mustang were woven into the show.

Hollywood calls it "brand integration." Its critics—some of them the very writers for shows using product placement—call it much worse. But by any name, the phenomenon is growing. During the 2004–2005 television season, more than 100,000 actual products appeared in American network television (up 28 percent in one year) according to Nielsen Media Research, generating $1.88 billion (up 46 percent in a year) according to PQ Media (Manly 2005). Advertising agencies have set up product placement divisions. Research organizations have cropped up to take on the task of measuring the effectiveness of product placement. And television shows in the United States seem to have an insatiable appetite for what they offer.

"The fact is, these brands are part of our lives, and brands exist in these television environments, so why not showcase them," said Ben Silverman, chief executive of the firm that produces "The Office" (Manly 2005, A14).

However, not everyone is pleased. In a 2005 meeting in New York during "Advertising Week," television writers protested outside a panel discussing the state of brand integration in television programming. Among their gripes: they want more of a say in how products will be placed and, inevitably, a share of the profits generated from writing a product into the script.

Most see the move as one of survival. Taking a cue from radio and its "soap operas," the original television shows were named for the sponsors ("The Colgate Comedy Hour" and "Texaco Star Theater"), and the audience had little option but to watch the ads. But while commercials undergirded the television industry for the first 50 years, the advent of the remote, and more recently TiVo have allowed consumers to avoid the very commercials that make the programming free.

"The advertising model of 10 years ago is not applicable today," according to Bruce Rosenblum, president of Warner Bros. Television Group. "At the end of the day, if we are unable to satisfy advertisers' appetites to deliver messages in new ways to the viewer, then we're destined to have a broken model" (Manly 2005, A14).

However, for government sponsored television in Europe, the practice of product placement remains a sticky issue.

In a 2005 edition of "Spooks," a BBC drama, a logo for an Apple computer appeared in early airings of the show and then was removed in subsequent showings after

British print media alleged that the Apple logo and others had slipped into BBC programming in exchange for cash and favors, which violates BBC rules. In Germany, firings occurred after public broadcaster ARD was found to have shows full of illegal product placements for years (Pfanner 2005).

Not every European country has such a ban. In Austria, public broadcaster ORF airs more than 1,000 product placements a year on its shows and provides the ORF with about $24 million in funds to supplement its budget of approximately $1 billion. The ORF says that allowing the placements actually regulates what happens anyway. "If you don't regulate it, it exists anyway, in a gray zone," said Alexander Wrabetz, chief financial officer for ORF (Pfanner 2005, A15).

And even within the BBC, which has not announced any intent to change its ban on product placement, there are differing opinions. One BBC executive, speaking to the *International Herald Tribune* off the record said, "Back in the '50s, everything was called Acme, or we stuck stickers over all the brand names. There isn't a TV company in the world that does that now. Viewers don't find it convincing" (Pfanner 2005, A15).

Ultimately, success in product placement still comes down to whether the placement fits the plot. "The needle we have to thread," according to Johnathan Prince, creator of "American Dreams" and now working on Madison Avenue, "is to have brand integration that is effective enough to have resonance, but . . . subtle enough so that it doesn't offend" (Manly 2005, A16).

Micro Issues

1. Would you personally prefer to go back to the days where made up names like "Acme" were placed on products to conceal the true brand names of the products?
2. Does the authenticity that real products such as name brand computers bring to a television show outweigh the intrusiveness of inserting a product into the plot of a show?
3. Are products placed into television shows the "price" you pay for free television, just as watching 30-second commercials were the "price" your parents and grandparents paid?

Midrange Issues

1. News magazines such as *Newsweek* will often run multi-page special sections on issues such as "Women's Health," and all of the ads within the section will be for products promoting women's health. What do you see as the difference between this practice and product placement on television shows?
2. Do you see a difference in whether product placement should occur in scripted dramas and comedies as opposed to reality television?
3. How does product placement in television shows differ from naming sports stadiums or college bowl games after corporate sponsors where presumably they will be mentioned on air for free during newscasts? Should newscasters avoid the corporate names of these places and events?
4. When a news show ends with rolling credits that attribute the wardrobe of the anchor to a certain store, is that product placement? Is that an intrusion on the objectivity of the news? Justify your answers.

Macro Issues

1. If consumers are "zapping" and "TiVo-ing" through commercials in free television, what will happen to the medium if product placement fails to deliver the needed revenue to keep the programming free? What will happen to the United States if free television is eliminated?
2. In trying to "thread the needle" between effectiveness and offensiveness, what are some of the guidelines you would write for product placement?
3. Is the argument made by Wrabetz in this case an ethical one? Compare the argument to the five standards of the TARES test found in this chapter and see how it measures up.

CASE 3-C

Breaking Through the Clutter: Ads That Make You Think Twice

FRITZ CROPP IV
University of Missouri

Controversial advertising campaigns were nothing new for Benetton when it un-veiled its spring–summer 2000 worldwide communication campaign. In January 2000, "We, on Death Row," a statement against the death penalty featuring U.S. death row convicts, brought Benetton an unprecedented level of criticism, complete with an apology from its president and the loss of a potentially lucrative contract with a mainstream American retailer.

Benetton, the Italian clothing company, had a 15-year record of concerning itself with social issues, including peace, war, AIDS awareness and multicultural-ism. Previous imagery featured a dying AIDS patient surrounded by his anguished family, a picture of a black horse and a white horse copulating, an unwashed new-born baby with an uncut umbilical cord, a buttock branded with an HIV-positive stamp, a priest and a nun kissing, the blood-soaked uniform of a dead Bosnian sniper, a white baby nursing at a black breast and the like.

Such ads invite controversy. The Vatican criticized the ad featuring a nun and priest kissing, and a French court ruled that the company had exploited human suffering in a campaign depicting dying AIDS patients and ordered it to pay damages to French citi-zens infected with the HIV virus. Yet Benetton seemed to invite the controversy, pro-claiming its approach "looks reality in the face" (http://www.benneton.com) by tackling social issues. Company President Luciano Benetton said 10 years ago that "Our campaigns are an attempt to get away from traditional advertising in the belief that it has no power and no value any more." Adds Oliviero Toscani, Benetton's photogra-pher and creative director, "My brief is not to concern myself with commercial images to sell more T-shirts but rather to create an image for the company that touches people in all of the countries in which Benetton is present" (Mundow 2000, 61).

While one cannot directly or singularly credit the advertising, Toscani's work has coincided with Benetton's worldwide growth. While critics decry the seeming vacuum between the provocative campaigns and the relatively mainstream Benet-ton stores and products, the company enjoyed a steady increase in worldwide sales and net profits through the 1990s. Benetton now sells clothes, accessories, and sporting goods in more than 7,000 stores in 120 countries, with 70 percent of its sales originating in Europe (Conley 2000).

"We, on Death Row" began when Toscani began working with freelance jour-nalist Ken Shulman to photograph and interview 26 U.S. prisoners on death row. The work culminated in a 96-page supplement in the January 11, 2000, edition of *Talk* magazine, followed by a series of individual pictures of the prisoners in se-lected U.S. magazines and on billboards in major U.S. cities.

"The campaign is about the death penalty," proclaims the Benetton press re-lease on the company's Web site. "Leaving aside any social, political, judicial or moral consideration, this project aims at showing the public the realities of capital punishment, so that no one around the world will consider the death penalty neither as a distant problem nor as news that occasionally appear [sic] on TV." The *Talk* magazine supplement included pictures and comments from the prisoners, along with quotes from Pope John Paul II and the Dalai Lama. Questions were decidedly soft. Shulman asked inmates about their families, prison food, what they dream and what they miss, with no mention of the victims, no discussion of current feelings of remorse.

Given space limitations, the advertisements, which Benetton claims were decided upon after the pictures and interviews had been taken and completed, were limited to a picture of an inmate, a description of his crime, the method by which he would be killed, the words "Sentenced to Death," and the "United Colors of Benetton" logo. Seven inmates agreed to allow their photographs to be used for this campaign. Even less context is provided in this format. There was no warning for the victims' families that the pictures were about to appear.

When they did, criticism came from many angles.

Sears, Roebuck and Company canceled a franchising contract it had recently signed with Benetton. The contract was forged to help Sears with its declining clothing sales and help Benetton reestablish itself in the United States, which accounts for just 5 percent of the company's business. Further, Sears pulled from its shelves all brands owned by the global parent company.

California House leader Scott Baugh drafted a resolution urging all California residents to boycott Benetton until the campaign disappeared. The bill passed 59 to 8. Pennsylvania Attorney General Lynne Abraham called for a nationwide boycott. Activists from Parents of Murdered Children staged a protest outside Benetton's U.S. office in New York City. The company also was targeted in Texas by Justice for All, the New York group Center for the Community Interest and the International Union of Police Associations. Missouri Attorney General Jay Nixon filed a circuit court suit, saying that representatives from Benetton tricked their way into Missouri's jails by pretending to be journalists. "Selling sweaters on the backs of death row inmates is sick and wrong," he said.

Advertising critics were equally appalled. Bob Garfield, a columnist at *Advertising Age,* wrote, "There is no brand—not a single one—that has the right to increase its sales on the backs, on the misery, on the fates of condemned men and women, much less their slaughtered victims" (Steuver 2000, C01).

In April 2000, Benetton announced that Toscani, who once said there is no such thing as going too far (Hughes 2000), was leaving after 18 years. The company did not address whether the "We, on Death Row" campaign was a factor.

In the end, it is difficult to assess the cost or benefits to Benetton of "We, on Death Row." The $1.8 million in royalties to have been generated by the Sears deal represents a fraction of the company's $2 billion in annual sales. Similarly, the $15 million the company said it spent on global distribution, combined with the undisclosed production costs, may be balanced by the resulting publicity, which continues to build upon Benetton's edgy image among its young target as a socially conscious company. "A substantial number of consumers seem to sense genuine integrity and principle behind Benetton's actions," notes Patrick Allossery of the *Financial Post* (2000, C3).

Micro Issues

1. The 26 prisoners interviewed by Toscani and Shulman were convicted of 37 murders. Should Benetton have considered the victims' families before running its campaign? Should the company have given them advance warning that the images would appear?
2. Responding to 144 consumer complaints, the British Advertising Standards Authority accepted Benetton's explanation that the campaign was intended to encourage debate and remind people that even death row prisoners have human rights. Thus, it ruled that its duty was to uphold an advertiser's freedom of speech. When a clothing company exploits shocking issues in its advertising, is it an abuse of that freedom?
3. Was it okay for Benetton to expand its campaign to print advertisements and billboards without seeking the same type of permission it was granted prior to interviewing the prisoners for the *Talk* magazine insert?

Midrange Issues

1. It's been said that there's no such thing as bad publicity. Does the end of free publicity justify the means?
2. Does this type of campaign illuminate the issues or potentially trivialize them?
3. If the point of "We, on Death Row" was to raise awareness of issues surrounding the death penalty, is a one-sided approach appropriate? Should Benetton have sought opinions from people in favor of the death penalty?

Macro Issues

1. Should the definition of advertising be altered to include efforts such as "We, on Death Row," or should such campaigns be considered differently by review boards and by the media outlets that sell time and space?
2. Should standards be developed to prevent advertisers from insensitive or potentially irresponsible actions, or does paying for space or time supersede the need for balance, fairness or objectivity?
3. Benetton claims to "tear down the wall of indifference, contributing to raising the awareness of universal problems among the world's citizens." However, there are cultural chasms to be addressed. In this case, the company's belief that the death penalty is inherently wrong is consistent with European opinion on the issue but inconsistent with what many Americans believe. Should advertisers—or companies paying for space to espouse their own commentary—be sensitive to cultural differences? If so, what guidance should be provided for them?
4. Jim Faulds, an advertising executive in Edinburgh, says ads that go beyond the boundaries of good taste also push back those boundaries. People become numbed to the shock tactics, and the only recourse is to shock further. Asks *Scotsman* reporter Michael Kerrigan (2000, 22), "As we recall the outrage that greeted those late 1990s campaigns we do indeed seem to be harking back to an age of innocence, long gone by. Have we, too, been implicated in Benetton's little habit?"

CASE 3-D

If You Let Nike Play . . .

RENITA COLEMAN
University of Texas

It takes you by surprise. A television commercial without a product. Just a half dozen or so preteen girls of various ethnic backgrounds in a working-class playground. With the rhythm and cadence of a song, they voice the refrain "If you let me play; if you let me play sports." The verse goes like this:

> I will like myself more.
> I will have more self-confidence.
> I will be 60 percent less likely to get breast cancer.
> I will suffer less depression.
> I will be more likely to leave a man who beats me.
> I will be less likely to get pregnant before I want to.
> I will learn what it means to be strong.

At the end of 30 seconds, the screen goes black and the familiar Nike logo appears with the slogan "Just Do It."

Unusual, certainly. Only a few advertisements have departed so radically from standard practice. Is this commercial socially responsible or ethically questionable? Is its audience children or their parents? This 30-second commercial is startlingly effective precisely because of its ambiguity. It grabs your attention with its rapid fire visuals; it makes you sit up and pay attention with its hard-hitting issues; and it makes you curious to know what this unusual ad is all about. The net effect is that this subtle pitch of a sportswear company becomes all the more memorable.

The Nike "If you let me play" ad makes unique use of the time-honored advertising technique of cognitive dissonance. It knocks the viewer off balance with the incongruous image of preteen girls discussing such adult subjects as spouse abuse, breast cancer, and depression. It is emotionally and cognitively unsettling to hear children discussing such things because we assume youth equals innocence. We would rather not have to face the fact that many children today are intimately acquainted with such topics. Perhaps a mother or other family member has battled depression or even lost a fight with breast cancer. More unsettling yet, perhaps children have seen daddy hitting mommy.

Even absent firsthand knowledge, children today are subjected to such situations via the news and entertainment media. Who really thinks children have been shielded from the facts of O. J. Simpson's battering of his ex-wife Nicole? From Columbine High School? And the trend is for family secrets to be less concealed than they once were. Children today are not the innocents of the past or the innocents we would still like to believe they are. This Nike ad is an in-your-face testimonial to that. And true to the formula of ads that use cognitive dissonance as a tool, Nike proposes a solution to restore the viewer to balance: let me play, and inferentially, let me do so in Nike apparel.

"Our goal wasn't to be alarmist, just direct," said Andrea Bonner, who helped create the "If you let me play" commercial. "We just wanted to be real." She acknowledges that this issue-oriented commercial is "a different kind of animal for Nike." In fact, she says, it "borders on being a pro bono message."

Nike has been questioned on ethical grounds in the past. In 1994, a commercial featuring basketball's bad boy, Dennis Rodman, was criticized for reinforcing an ends-justifies-the-means mentality when Santa Claus grants Rodman his Christmas wish of expensive new shoes despite his unsportsmanlike conduct. African-Americans criticized the company for using Rodman as a role model when other, more positive African-American role models were available. Nike has similarly been criticized for advertising its shoes on billboards located in poor, inner-city neighborhoods where parents can ill-afford $100 shoes.

The company was even accused of helping to cause thefts and violence in ghettos where the apparent reason for the assault was the victim's expensive sports shoes. The children in the "If you let me play" ad appear to be from working-class families. While it is rather ambiguous, the appearance of the playground and the children's clothes provide visual cues to suggest this. Perhaps Nike tried to avoid being accused of marketing expensive products to socioeconomic groups that either cannot afford them or would do without necessities in order to purchase them.

The subject of target markets also brings up the issue of advertising to children. The poor and elderly as well as the young have often been singled out as audiences deserving special sensitivity and responsibility from advertisers. Because they are potentially more vulnerable, less experienced and adept at sorting out product claims and more subject to peer pressure and advertising's influence, children's advertising must assume a greater sensitivity than advertising to the general population, an audience considered to be active and autonomous.

Research by Carol Gilligan and others has shown that adolescence is a particularly formative time for a girl's self-esteem. Adolescence is a time for issues of attachment for girls, and identity formation takes place within relationships. There is special vulnerability for girls in finding a way of caring for themselves while maintaining connections to others. The topics in this commercial are all of a connective nature—pregnancy involves a male and a child; domestic violence involves a relationship with a male, at least; strength, self-confidence, depression and even breast cancer, with its strong ties to feminist issues, are all issues of self-caring and identity formation.

Another controversy centers on the source of the statistics in the ad. In "If you let me play," Nike claims it got its statistical information from the Women's Sports Foundation (WSF), a nonprofit organization that collects studies regarding athletics and women and girls. However, a representative of the WSF said the foundation would never knowingly provide its research to Nike because it is sponsored by Reebok, Nike's chief competitor. The advertising agency that created the commercial also claims that the information was obtained from WSF.

Micro Issues

1. Is Nike guilty of using "scare tactics" to sell its clothing line?
2. Nike claims the message borders on being a pro bono message, in other words a free public service ad for a worthy cause. Critique that claim.

Midrange Issues

1. Would the same commercial have been any less arresting had it featured adult women? Would it be less effective?
2. Nike never produced a similar ad for boys, although there are documented health and social benefits for males who play sports. Why do you think there was not an "If you let me play" ad made featuring young boys?

Macro Issues

1. The Women's Sports Foundation gets its research data from a variety of academic and not-for-profit sources. Given its goals of promoting fitness through sports for women, why would it consider the statistics in the Nike ad to be proprietary information? Shouldn't the foundation be pleased at the larger audience generated by the Nike ad?
2. Obviously many girls who do not play sports do not suffer any of the maladies mentioned in the ad later in life either. Is Nike guilty of portraying women as more vulnerable than they are in order to sell clothing?

CASE 3-E

Fried Chicken as Health Food? The FTC Cries Foul

PHILIP PATTERSON
Oklahoma Christian University

Say "fried chicken" to the typical consumer and many images come to mind. The image of fried chicken as health food is not near the top of the list, or even on the list. But according to commercials aired in the fall of 2003 by KFC (the former Kentucky Fried Chicken), their signature product, Original Recipe fried chicken, can be a part of a balanced diet, and may even help you lose weight.

First came consumer skepticism and the late-night comedians' jokes. Then came action by the Federal Trade Commission (FTC), which sent a civil subpoena asking the franchise chain to justify the health claims made in two television ads that debuted in November of 2003. The action was another attempt by government to manage weight-loss products and weight-loss claims, all while the growing obesity problem in the United States threatens to overwhelm the nation's health care system.

The two ads in question were developed for KFC by the advertising agency Foote, Cone and Belding. In a press release announcing the campaign, a KFC executive was quoted as saying that "consumers should no longer feel guilty about eating fried chicken" (Matthews and Steinberg 2003, B-1).

In one television ad a man notices a slimmer appearance in one of his friends. "Is that you, man? You look fantastic," he says. When asked what he had done, the friend announces (through a mouthful of food) "Eatin' chicken." An off-camera announcer claims that one Original Recipe chicken breast has 11 grams of carbohydrate and 40 grams of protein and implies that fried chicken fits neatly in low-carbohydrate, high protein diets that have been popular in the United States in the past decade.

In the second ad, a woman arrives home where her husband is watching television. "Remember when we talked about eating better? Well, it starts today," she says as she sets down a KFC bucket. The off-screen announcer claims that two Original Recipe chicken breasts have fewer fat grams than a Burger King Whopper sandwich (the difference later revealed in small print to be only five grams). The spot goes on to say that you could "go skinless for just three grams of fat per piece," even though decades of KFC advertising has touted the formula of spices in its chicken breading.

Both commercials contained a small disclaimer on the bottom of the screen urging viewers to eat the chicken as part of a balanced diet and exercise. Other disclaimers were also necessary, including one that admits that the bucket of chicken shown in the ad typically contains pieces other than breasts and that KFC chicken is not a low sodium product—something obvious to anyone who has ever tasted the product. Consumer reaction ranged from skepticism to outrage. The Center for Science in the Public Interest sent a letter to the FTC calling the ads "outrageous" and urged government action. Their complaint included the charge that basing the numbers on single-piece servings simply was not realistic for many consumers.

In previous cases, the FTC has used the "net impression" test to determine if the totality of the ad—words, pictures and disclaimers—is misleading to the consumer. While the FTC allows "puffery" in advertising (such as ads claiming that KFC tastes "best" even in the absence of empirical evidence), ads may not be misleading.

Early indications were that the FTC would focus on the disclaimers and whether they could be easily read. At least one partner in a New York law firm specializing in advertising law told *The Wall Street Journal* that because the health claims are intentionally vague, it might be difficult to prove that they were misleading.

Micro Issues

1. Given the fact that these ads fly in the face of all conventional dieting wisdom, is it plausible that the average American would be convinced by these ads to begin eating KFC's Original Recipe fried chicken to lose weight? Should the government have to prove that in order to make KFC stop the ads?
2. By comparing one poor dietary choice—fried chicken—favorably to a poorer dietary choice—a Burger King Whopper—which parts of the TARES test, if any, are being violated?
3. Is the standard for an "ethical ad" simply one that doesn't mislead or should there be a higher standard? If so, what would that standard be?

Midrange Issues

1. These ads featured models as regular people—two friends, a couple—who are discussing chicken in a living room setting. If the ads had featured actors as doctors, pharmacists, or some other trusted health care authority, possibly wearing lab coats, would that have crossed any legal or ethical line?
2. Does the inclusion of small printed disclaimers about the spoken and visual claims absolve the company from charges of misleading consumers?
3. Does the fact that few consumers eat only one piece of chicken at a sitting and virtually none peel the skin off before eating prevent KFC from ethically basing its health claims on those serving choices?
4. Many advertising critics argue that it's the total number of messages—rather than individual messages—that matter. Should ethical thinking on this issue consider the totality of the messages rather than individual ads?

Macro Issues

1. The ads featured normal-sized models. Given the percentage of Americans who are overweight, and especially the percentage of fast-food patrons who are overweight, should at least one of the four actors have been overweight? Would that have detracted from the message KFC was trying to send? What does this casting decision say about our nation's thinking on body image?
2. Advertising deals in "strategic ambiguity." By being less than specific about health claims or individual results, is KFC being cautious or being purposely ambiguous to stay out of court, or both?

3. Fast food has its place in American culture. In a time-starved culture, franchises such as KFC sell a product that is equal parts convenience and nutrition. It can be argued that in these ads, KFC simply wants people to feel good about choices they are already inclined to make. Should the FTC be using the finite resources of government to police these kinds of ads, especially when products such as dietary supplements have the potential to do real harm? Or should the FTC try to tackle both with equal vigor, even if one drains resources from the other? Justify your answer.

CASE 3-F

In the Eye of the Beholder: Dove's Campaign for Real Beauty

BRANDI HERMAN-ROSE
University of Missouri-Columbia

In the summer of 2005, Dove, a division of Unilever Corporation, launched its campaign for real beauty in the U.K. (see www.campaignforrealbeauty.com). This marketing campaign—initially to promote skincare products such as a firming lotion—has expanded to include public services ads and promotions that simply question what constitutes real beauty.

Dove's campaign has drawn extensive media attention because it features six very unconventional models. They range in dress size from 6 to 14 and have different body types. Some have tattoos. Others have larger thighs. Dove touts these models as "real women" with "real beauty."

To view a number of the ads that have run as part of this continuing campaign, go to the following Web sites: **www.Dove.com** or **www.Campaignforrealbeauty.com.**

These ads feature six women in no-frills white bras and panties. All six are in their 20s. They are of different races, sizes and shapes. One has a large tattoo on her thigh. They vary in height. One is lily white, others have curly hair.

Women are pictured large on billboards and print ads that ask about each woman's characteristics. One 95-year-old woman is pictured with the two words "Wrinkled or wonderful?" Another larger-than-average woman is pictured smiling broadly at the camera with the words "Overweight or outstanding?" Each ad features women who are outside the conventional modeling stereotype. Each image also asks whether the model should be described with a positive or negative word or phrase.

In an advertisement featured on TV for Dove's hair care products, women are seen walking the streets with identical blonde coifs. At a given point, these women pull off their wigs to reveal curly-, straight-, blonde-, brown- and black-haired women. This ad ran in multiple countries and emphasized the beauty found in each woman's unique hair type.

Other companies have tried to showcase real women in their ads without boosting sales or receiving the same recognition as Dove's real beauty campaign. So, how did Dove come up with this campaign idea? Did Dove push for this creative direction or was the idea the work of Ogilvy and Mather, Dove's advertising agency?

Dove's campaign for "real beauty" was the result of an extensive research initiative that studied 3,200 women in Argentina, Brazil, Canada, France, Italy, Japan, the Netherlands, Portugal, Britain and the United States. Of the women sampled, only 2 percent considered themselves "beautiful." Another 5 percent described themselves as "pretty" and only 9 percent described themselves as "attractive."

For the survey, Dove commissioned the services of StrategyOne and MORI International to ensure that the study met criteria and codes of conduct established by global research associations. In addition, Dove utilized leading independent thinkers and academic institutions for research design and data analysis. Finally, Dove ensured that the study itself contained no reference to the brand or its parent, Unilever, and participants remained unaware of their sponsorship of the study (Lagnado 2004).

Dove, a company whose entire success is tied up in the actions and beliefs of women, is highly invested in research about women's belief systems. In a report entitled "The Real Truth about Beauty," the researchers (Entcoff et al. 2004) claim:

> Women's interest in and preoccupation with beauty, is not some easily dismissed concern. This study shows conclusively that women now judge beauty as important and even crucial as they navigate today's world. In attempting to democratize and make accessible to all the idea of beauty, women are eager to see a redefinition and expansion of the ideals, along the lines they see it and away from the limiting, narrowed and restricted body shapes and sizes we see in moving images and in print.

The campaign for real beauty launched in the summer of 2005 in the U.K. to wide acclaim in the British press, and that same media attention spread throughout the United States and worldwide. This global campaign has received a mixture of praise and ridicule.

Alicia Cregg, a writer for www.brandchannel.com, wrote about the real beauty campaign after its launch in the U.K. "By showing a wider range of skin types and body shapes, Dove's advertising offers a democratized view of beauty to which all can aspire. The campaign also has an implied moral purpose, one that takes on the ethical issues of consumerism" (Cregg 2005).

Despite the positive comments that Dove received, still others felt that the methods of marketing used for this campaign was nothing more than a veiled attempt to convince women of their imperfections. "Some people think that the ads were just a ploy for Dove to make money by trying to boost a woman's confidence, while at the same time catering to her insecurities by selling her a firming cream" (Marchese 2005). Still others (Gogoi 2005) have suggested that the only reason that this campaign showcasing "real women" works well at this time is because of the prevalence of reality television within the past few years.

When held up against other campaigns for beauty products, Dove is doing something considerably different. Campaigns for brands like Olay and Jergens, two of Dove's main competitors, feature long-legged, very thin women in sexy poses, choices that Ogilvy, with Dove's direction, avoided.

Dove's campaign has received more positive reception in the U.K. Citizens of the United States responded well to the ads for hair products, but getting U.S. women to see overweight women as beautiful has been a more difficult task.

Micro Issues

1. What about this ad represents an attempt to "cut through the clutter."
2. Using the TARES test outlined in the chapter, how would you evaluate this ad?
3. What is the role of authenticity is getting consumers to buy products that make them look "better" than they really do?

Midrange Issues

1. The Dove campaign has been praised as an example of ethical advertising. Evaluate this statement.

2. What role does stereotyping—specifically about beautiful women—play in the creation of this ad? Is that use of stereotyping ethically distinct from ads that feature more traditional models?
3. To whom or what have the ads' creators been loyal?

Macro Issues

1. Examine the literature on eating disorders. What role do you believe ads play in the development of those disorders? How important is advertising compared to some other influences?
2. Since the population of the planet is aging, is what Dove is doing really just smart marketing? What role do you believe ethical thinking played in the campaign?

4

Loyalty: Choosing Between Competing Allegiances

By the end of this chapter, you should:

- **understand why the articulation of loyalties is important in professional ethics.**
- **know Royce's definition of loyalty and at least one of the major problems with that conceptualization.**
- **understand how journalists' role in society provides them with an additional set of loyalties to consider.**
- **be familiar with and able to use the Potter Box as a justification model for ethical decision making.**

LOYALTY AS PART OF THE SOCIAL CONTRACT

Decisions involving loyalty occur routinely for media professionals. When journalists make a decision to air or not to air a story, they have decided to whom they will be loyal. When recording executives cancel the contract of a controversial artist to avoid a boycott, they have chosen a loyalty. Most ethical decisions come down to the question "To whom (or what) will I be loyal?"

The original discussion of loyalty in Western culture was written by Plato in *The Trial and Death of Socrates* (see Russell 1967). In Plato's *Phaedo,* Socrates bases his defense against the charges brought against him on his unwavering adherence, or loyalty, to divinely inspired truth. When asked by his accusers if he will stop teaching philosophy, Socrates responds:

> Men of Athens, I honor and love you: but I shall obey God rather than you, and while I have life and strength I shall never cease from the practice and teaching of philosophy, exhorting any one whom I meet. . . . For know that this is the command of God; and I believe that no greater good has ever happened in the State than my service to God.

While the word *loyalty* is not present in English translations of the *Phaedo,* the overall tone of the work is a tribute to loyalty, in this case a willingness to die for a cause. This willingness to make one of the ultimate sacrifices has troubled those who wrote about loyalty in subsequent centuries.

Social contract theorist Thomas Hobbes was the first major Western philosopher to assert that God did not have to be the focus of loyalty and that people could have competing loyalties. In his historic work on the theory of the state, *The Leviathan,* Hobbes asserted loyalty is a social act, that it is the core of the agreement that allows people to form the social contract that is the basis of political society. However, Hobbes, unlike Socrates, admitted loyalty has its limits. Loyalty to the ruler stops when continued loyalty would result in a subject's death. One has a higher loyalty to self-preservation in this instance than to the ruler. The turmoil surrounding U.S. involvement in the Vietnam War is a classic example of this type of conflict of loyalties.

Hobbes made two central alterations in the Socratic notion of loyalty. First, he emphasized its social nature. Second, he acknowledged that people could have more than one loyalty and might, at certain times, be forced to choose among them. These two elements, in addition to the original insights of Socrates and Plato, provide the basis of contemporary philosophical discussion of the concept.

THE CONTRIBUTIONS OF JOSIAH ROYCE

American theologian Josiah Royce, who taught at Harvard in the early 1900s, believed that loyalty could become the single guiding ethical principle. In *The Philosophy of Loyalty* (1908), Royce wrote, "My theory is that the whole moral law is implicitly bound up in one precept: 'Be loyal.'" Royce defined loyalty as a social act: "The willing and practical and thoroughgoing devotion of a person to a cause." Royce would be critical, therefore, of the stereotypical journalist found in Ben Hecht's *The Front Page*—a cynic of everything and everyone, a professional who gets a story at all costs and whose only loyalty is to himself. In Royce's view, loyalty is an act of choice. A loyal person, Royce asserted, does not have "Hamlet's option"—or the leisure not to decide. For in the act of not deciding, that person has essentially cast his loyalty.

Loyalty also promotes self-realization. Royce spent much of his academic career fascinated with what were then the new insights of Freudian psychology, and he viewed loyalty in a psychological and developmental light. As a person continued to exercise loyalty, Royce believed, he or she would develop habits of character that would result in systematic ethical action. Like other aspects of moral development, loyalty can be learned and honed, Royce believed.

Loyalty as a single ethical guide has problems. *First,* loyalty, incompletely conceived, can be bias or prejudice cloaked in misleading language. *Second,* few people maintain merely a single loyalty, and if loyalty is to become a guiding ethical principle, we need to develop a way to help distinguish among competing loyalties. *Third,* with the advent of a mass society, the entire concept of face-to-face loyalty has lost much of its power to compel ethical action. *Finally,* one of the most troubling questions arising from the concept of loyalty is whether an ethical person can be loyal to an unethical cause, for example racism or gender discrimination.

However, Royce suggested a way to determine whether a specific cause was worthy of loyalty. A worthy cause should harmonize with the loyalties of others within the community, which can be defined in a number of ways. For instance, the loyalty of the journalist should be in harmony with the loyalty of the reader. The loyalty of the advertising agency should not conflict with the loyalty of either its client or the consumer. Surely, loyalty to the concept of free and unfettered political discussion— the basis of modern democracy and journalism—would meet Royce's test of loyalty.

A true understanding of loyalty allows people to reject unethical causes, Royce believed. The true problem was not a poor choice of loyalties but failure to adhere to chosen loyalties: "The ills of mankind are largely the consequence of disloyalty rather than wrong-headed loyalty" (Royce 1908). The cause that is capable of sustaining loyalty, Royce noted, has a "super-individual" quality, one that is apparent when people become part of a community. A spirit of democratic cooperation is needed for Royce's view of loyalty to result in ethical action. For instance, advertising agencies are demonstrating an ethical loyalty when they view their role as providing needed information for intelligent consumer choice, but more often they opt for loyalty to the bottom line.

Royce's thought has been criticized on a number of grounds. First, some philosophers assert that Royce's concept of loyalty is simplistic and that the adoption of loyalty as a moral principle may lead to allegiance to troubling causes. For instance, the advertising copywriter who scripts distorted television spots about an opponent in the belief that she must get her candidate elected is demonstrating a troubling allegiance to a politician over the democratic process. Similarly, a reporter who must get the story first, regardless of its completeness or accuracy, would be demonstrating a misplaced loyalty to the professional ideal of the scoop.

Second, others have noted that Royce provides no way to balance among conflicting loyalties other than his assertion that loyalty to a particular cause should evoke a similar response in others. Who the others are, in this case, becomes an important question. The executive producer who relegates all but the most important foreign news to the end of the broadcast because Americans aren't interested in hearing about activities in other nations may have an excessively narrow definition of whom the viewers are concerned about.

Third, it is unclear how Royce's ethical thinking would balance majority notions against minority views. Royce's notion of loyalty could inspire adherence to the status quo or strict majority rule. For instance, advertisements that stereotype groups of people despite evidence to the contrary help perpetuate incorrect images. The ads work because they appeal to the majority, but by stereotyping, they have crowded out more accurate impressions.

Yet despite these criticisms, Royce's thought has much to recommend it. First, Royce speaks to the development of ethical habits, something most modern ethical theorists believe is necessary for continuing ethical behavior. Second, Royce reminds us that the basis of loyalty is social, and loyalty requires we put others on an equal footing with ourselves. In this sense, his view of ethics is not a purely rational one, but one that is founded in a concept of relationships. When you acknowledge loyalties, you also are acknowledging that things could have been otherwise. Most important is the overriding message of Royce's work: *when making ethical choices, it is important to consider what your loyalties are and how you arrived at those loyalties.* We believe this is particularly pertinent when people are acting in a professional role in a society that has given the profession both rights and responsibilities.

JOURNALISM AS A PROFESSION

Loyalty is not a fixed point but a range within a continuum. In *Loyalty: An Essay on the Morality of Relationships,* George Fletcher (1993) identifies two types of loyalty. The first is minimal loyalty: "Do not betray me." The second is maximum loyalty: "Be one with me." Between these two poles is a range of possibilities for allegiance and for corresponding media behavior. The location on the continuum for *YouTube* will differ from that of *The Nation* magazine.

One of the problems modern news media face is that a large percentage of the U.S. public subscribes to the notion that if the media are not maximally loyal—that is, one with government, the military and so forth—then they are traitorous. The media have been called disloyal by more than one politician, often for no greater sin than fulfilling the watchdog role. Fulfilling this role puts the journalist, and their media outlets by extension, on trial in the court of public opinion. For instance, in the summer of 2003, as journalists called for the Bush administration to provide proof that Iraqi dictator Saddam Hussein had possessed weapons of mass destruction, polls showed that Americans were willing to give the president the benefit of the doubt in the absence of the weapons, even though their supposed existence was one of the primary reasons Americans went to war with Iraq.

Loyalty can be linked to one's role. A role is a capacity in which we act toward others. It provides others with information about how we will act in a structured situation. Some roles are occupationally defined—account executive, screenwriter, editor. Others are not: mother, spouse, daughter. We all play multiple roles, and they help us sort out situations and know what to expect from others.

When the role you assume is a professional one, you add ethical responsibilities. Philosophers claim that "to belong to a profession is traditionally to be held to certain standards of conduct that go beyond the norm for others" (Lebacqz 1985, 32), and journalism qualifies as one of those professions with a higher expected norm of conduct.

However, not all journalists agree in practice. Hodges (1986) makes the distinction in this manner: when asked what she does for a living, one journalist says, "I am a journalist" while another says "I work for the *Gazette.*" Hodges claims the first speaker is a journalist who recognizes her responsibility as a professional while the latter merely acknowledges her loyalty to a paycheck. The first would be expected to be loyal to societal expectations of a journalist, the second may or may not.

Journalists and their employers have debated whether journalism should be considered a profession. For some, the concept of professionalism itself is not inherently positive. Advocates of professionalism assert that professionalism among journalists will provide them with greater autonomy, prestige and financial rewards. Critics see the process of professionalization as one that distances readers and viewers from the institutions that journalists often represent.

Despite these debates, we intuitively sense that journalists have two central responsibilities that are distinct because of the role journalists play in modern society. First, they have a greater responsibility to tell the truth than members of most professions. Second, journalists also seem to carry a somewhat greater obligation to foster political activity than the average person.

Philosophers note that while specific ethical dilemmas are transitory, roles endure. Role expectations carry over from one situation to another. Most of the time, loyalty to the profession means loyalty to the *ideals* of the profession. To Aristotle, loyalty to a profession also would mean being loyal to and maintaining high professional standards. The Aristotelian notion of virtue means being the best television producer or advertising executive you can be in the belief that you are being loyal to the profession and its abstract ideals.

CONFLICTING LOYALTIES

As the foregoing discussion indicates, we are no longer talking about merely a single loyalty. We live in an age of layers of loyalties, creating added problems and complications.

Sorting through competing personal and professional loyalties can be difficult, particularly when loyalties in one role appear to conflict with the loyalties of another. However, those concerned with professional roles and the loyalties they generate have done some thinking about this issue. We have adapted one such framework from William F. May (2001), who outlined these layers of loyalties for college professors. We suggest a similar approach for those who work in the media.

1. Loyalties arising from shared humanity:

   - demonstrate respect for each person as an individual.
   - communicate honestly and truthfully with all persons.
   - build a fair and compassionate social and cultural environment that promotes the common good.

2. Loyalties arising from professional practice:

   - fulfill the informational and entertainment mission of the media.
   - understand your audience's needs.
   - strive to enhance professional development of self and others.
   - avoid the abuse of power and position.
   - conduct professional activities in ways that uphold or surpass the ideals of virtue and competence.

3. Loyalties arising from employment:

   - keep agreements and promises, operate within the framework of the law and extend due process to all persons.

- do not squander your organization's resources or your public trust.
- promote compassionate and humane professional relationships.
- foster policies that build a community of ethnic, gender and socioeconomic diversity.
- promote the right of all to be heard.

4. Loyalties arising from the media's role in public life:

- serve as examples of open institutions where truth is required.
- foster open discussion and debate.
- interpret your professional actions to readers and viewers.
- serve as a voice for the voiceless.
- serve as a mirror of society.

The problem of conflicting loyalties is evident in the media employment reality of today. Most media practitioners work for a corporation. They owe at least some loyalty to their corporate employers. However, such loyalty is tenuous because it seldom involves a face-to-face relationship. Modern corporations often demand employee loyalty but are much less willing to tell employees their corporate loyalties or responsibilities. These mutually understood promises are essential to corporate loyalty, where the fear is that one's allegiance to the organization will advance the interest of the organization without reciprocal loyalty to the employee.

In the final analysis, most ethical decisions are not about loyalties to corporations or abstract concepts such as freedom of the press. They are about how you treat the subject of your interview or the consumer of your advertising. An element that is essential in such ethical decisions is the notion of *reciprocity*. Simply articulated, reciprocity requires that loyalty should not work against the interest of either party.

Copyright © Ed Stein. Reprinted with permission of Rocky Mountain News.

Even in an era of sometimes shifting loyalties, there are some loyalties that should only be most reluctantly abandoned. We recommend you give further consideration to two of them: loyalty to humanity and loyalty to truth. *Virtually no situation in media ethics calls for inhumane treatment or withholding the truth.* Maybe you can think of other loyalties you would rarely, if ever, break. Even if you can't devise a list of every conceivable conflict of loyalties, knowing where your ultimate loyalties lie isn't a bad place to start.

THE POTTER BOX

In Chapter 1, you learned an ethical decision-making model developed by Sissela Bok, one that could help you make an ethical choice. In this chapter, you will learn a second decision-making model, one that incorporates articulation of loyalties into the reasoning process. The model was developed by Harvard theologian Ralph Potter and is called the Potter Box. Its initial use requires that you go through four steps to arrive at an ethical judgment. The case below will help familiarize you with the model.

> You are the assistant city editor for a newspaper of about 30,000 circulation in a western city of about 80,000. Your police reporter regularly reports on sexual assaults in the community.
>
> While the newspaper has a policy of not revealing the names of rape victims, it does routinely report where such assaults occurred, the circumstances surrounding the attack and a description of the assailant, if police can provide it.
>
> Tonight the police reporter is preparing to write a story about a rape that occurred in the early-morning hours yesterday on the roof of the downtown bus station.
>
> Police report that the young woman who was raped went willingly to the roof of the bus station with her attacker. Although she is 25, she lives in a group home for the educable mentally handicapped in the city. She is one of seven women living in the facility.
>
> She could not describe her assailant, and police have no suspects.
>
> Your reporter asks you for advice about how much detail, and what detail, he should include in the story.

The Potter Box has four steps (see Figure 4.1) that should be taken in order. They are (1) understanding the facts, (2) outlining the values inherent in the decision, (3) applying relevant philosophical principles and (4) articulating a loyalty.

Facts	**Loyalties**
Values	**Principles**

FIGURE 4.1. **The four steps of the Potter Box**

You proceed through the four steps in a counterclockwise fashion, beginning with the factual situation. We will examine each step individually.

Step One: Understanding the facts of the case. In the scenario, the facts are straightforward. You, the newspaper editor, have the information. Your ethical choice rests with how much of it you are going to print.

Step Two: Outlining values. Values is a much abused word in modern English. People can value everything from their loved ones to making fashion statements. In ethics, however, values takes on a more precise meaning. In this sense, when you value something—an idea or a principle—it means you are willing to give up other things for it. If, as a journalist, you value truth above all things, then you must sometimes be willing to give up privacy in favor of it. In the foregoing case, such a value system would mean that you would print every detail, because you value truth, and would risk invading the privacy of a person who is in some important ways unable to defend herself. If, as a journalist, you value both truth and privacy, then you may be willing to give up some truth, the printing of every detail, to attempt to preserve the victim's privacy.

Values often compete, and an important element of using the Potter Box is to be honest about what you really do value. Both truth and privacy are lofty ideals. A less lofty ideal that most of us value keeping our jobs. Journalists often value getting the story first. A forthright articulation of all the values wrapped up in any particular ethical situation will help you see more clearly the choices that you face and the potential compromises you may or may not have to make.

Step Three: Application of philosophical principles. Once you have decided what you value, you need to apply the philosophical principles outlined in the first chapter. For example, in the previous scenario, a utilitarian might argue that the greatest good is served by printing a story that alerts the community to the fact that some creep who rapes women who cannot defend themselves mentally or physically is still out there. Ross would argue that a journalist has duties both to the readers and to the victim, and they must be weighed before making a decision.

Aristotle's golden mean would counsel a middle ground that balances printing every detail against printing no story at all. Kant would suggest that the maxim of protecting someone who cannot protect herself is a maxim that could be universalized, making a decision to omit some information justifiable.

In this case, application of several ethical principles leads to the same general conclusion: the newspaper should print some story, but not one that inadvertently reveals the victim's identity or that makes her out to be hopelessly naive in her trust of strangers.

However, you should be alert that while application of different ethical principles in this scenario leads to the same conclusion, other ethical dilemmas may not produce such a happy result. This is precisely why use of the Potter Box demands the application of more than one ethical principle, for if ultimate judgments may vary, you need to be able to explain why.

Step Four: Articulation of loyalties. Potter viewed loyalty as a social commitment, and use of the Potter Box will reflect that sort of ethic. In the fourth step, you need to articulate your loyalties—and to decide whether any of them conflict. In the foregoing case, you may have a loyalty to telling the truth, to alerting the community to a potential danger, to protecting individual privacy, or to doing your job well. Again, in this case, your loyalties are not in severe conflict with one another unless you adopt an absolutist view of the truth the community needs to know. It is possible to counsel your reporter to write a story that tells the truth but omits some facts (for example, the woman's residence in a group home and her mental retardation), alerts the community to a danger (there's a creep out there who police haven't caught), protects the victim's privacy (you won't print her name or where she lives), and allows you to take pride in the job you've done (you've told the truth and not harmed anyone).

However, use of the Potter Box often highlights a conflict between loyalties. In these instances, we refer you to Royce's conception of loyalty itself. What you choose to be loyal to should be capable of inspiring a similar loyalty in others who are both like and unlike you. Journalists are often accused of being "out of touch" with their viewers or readers, and it is at precisely this point of idiosyncratic loyalties that the profession is most highly criticized.

Our experience with the Potter Box has been that the vast majority of ethical decisions will allow you to sustain a variety of loyalties. Those decisions that are truly most troubling are ones in which loyalty to one particular cause or principle becomes so dominant in your reasoning process that you are forced to abandon a variety of other loyalties that once seemed quite essential to you.

While you may initially find the stepwise process of the Potter Box somewhat cumbersome, as you learn to use it you will become fluent in its application. You also may discover that you can go through the Potter Box on different levels of abstraction.

The following case study, "The Pimp, the Prostitute and the Preacher," illustrates how you might use the Potter Box when making an ethical decision.

The Pimp, the Prostitute and the Preacher

You are the court reporter for a daily newspaper in a city of about 150,000 in the Pacific Northwest. About a year ago, the local police force began to crack down on prostitutes working the downtown mall. However, the stated goal of the department's activities was to limit prostitution by arresting pimps—men who make money from prostitutes—rather than by arresting either the prostitutes or their customers. The first of those arrests has now come to trial, and your paper has assigned you to cover the story on a daily basis.

In his opening statement, the local assistant district attorney tells the jury that in order to convict a person of pimping under state law, the state must prove first that money was exchanged for sexual favors, and second that the money was then given to a third party, the pimp, in return for protection, continued work, etc. During the first two days of the trial, he calls as witnesses four young women, ages 14 to 16, who admit they have worked as prostitutes in the city but are a great deal less clear on the disposal of their earnings. Your story after the first day of the trial encapsulates the police activities, the prosecutor's goals in the case and the public testimony of two of the young women without disclosing their names.

Near the end of the second day in the trial, the prosecuting attorney begins to call as witnesses men who say they paid one or more of the four young women to have sex with them. Among those who testify is a middle-aged man who in an almost inaudible response to a question lists his occupation as a minister at one of the more conservative Protestant churches in the city. He admits to having paid one of the young women for sex, and that day's portion of the trial ends soon after his testimony is complete.

About 45 minutes later you are back in the office to write the story of that day's testimony when the newsroom secretary asks you if you have a few minutes to speak with "Reverend Jones." The name itself doesn't register, but you look up and realize you are facing the minister who testified earlier in the day. In the open newsroom he begs you, often in tears and at one point on his knees, not to print his name in your story. He even holds out a copy of the story you wrote, which appeared on page one of this morning's paper, outlining why the names of the prostitutes had not been used. He asserts that, should a story with his name appear, his marriage will crumble, his children will no longer respect him and he will lose his job.

After a few minutes and a whispered conversation with the newsroom secretary, the paper's managing editor realizes what is happening and calls you, the minister and the news editor into his office for a conference. What do you say?

Using the Potter Box, determine how you would report this story. Your decision will reflect a set of loyalties as well as the values and principles you have chosen. Others may choose differently. A justification model such as Potter's or Bok's (introduced in Chapter 1) does not eliminate differences. What it will do, ideally, is ensure that your choices are grounded in sound ethical reasoning.

When you are finished, the final casting of loyalties will inevitably create another fact for the first quadrant of the box. For instance, in this case, if the decision is to run the name, anything that might subsequently happen to the minister as a result—firing, divorce, even possible suicide—is now an additional "fact" for the first quadrant of the Potter Box. If you decide not to run the minister's name and his parishioners discover his indiscretion anyway, the loss of credibility the newspaper suffers from those who find out the name was withheld is also a "fact" to be entered into the first quadrant of the Potter Box. Considering these additional "facts" (even though they are at present hypothetical), you may want to go through the process again to see if your decision will remain the same.

For a concrete example of how to do this, consider the fate of Tami Silicio, the photographer in Case 9-G, who lost her job as a result of the publication of her photograph of the flag-draped coffins. If you knew this fact beforehand, would it make a difference in your final loyalty and therefore your final decision?

Now that you've made a decision about revealing the name of the minister based on the facts, we'd like to introduce you to additional facts. After you read them, go through the Potter Box again while focusing less on the minister and more on larger issues that affect how the story is written and how it is run in the newspaper. This time, think about the notions of stereotyping, how members of minority communities are portrayed in news reports and the idea of what exactly we mean by the journalistic watchwords "objectivity" and "truth."

> As the trial continues, it becomes increasingly clear to you that there are other factors at work. In your largely Caucasian community, the only people arrested for pimping have been African-American. All the young women who work as prostitutes are Caucasian, as are the customers who testify. As far as prostitution goes, your Pacific Northwest version is relatively mild. There are no reports of drug use among the prostitutes and their customers, and none of the prostitutes has complained of physical violence. Further, the prosecuting attorney cannot make any of the young women admit under oath that they ever gave the pimps any money. The jury verdict in this case is not guilty.

Do the new facts change your loyalties articulated in the first application of the model to the facts? If so, in what ways?

We recommend that you try using both the Bok and Potter justification models at various times in your ethical decision making. Becoming a competent practitioner of both methods will provide you with greater flexibility and explanatory power. We also recommend, regardless of the approach you use, that an unvarnished and critical discussion of loyalty becomes part of your ethical dialogue. We believe it will enable you to anticipate situations as well as react to them.

Suggested Readings

FLETCHER, GEORGE P. 1993. *Loyalty: An essay on the morality of relationships.* New York: Oxford University Press.

FUSS, PETER. 1965. *The moral philosophy of Josiah Royce.* Cambridge, MA: Harvard University Press.

HANSON, KAREN. 1986. "The demands of loyalty." *Idealistic Studies,* 16, pp. 195–204.

HOBBES, THOMAS. 1958. *Leviathan.* New York: Bobbs-Merrill.

OLDENQUIST, ANDREW. 1982. "Loyalties." *Journal of Philosophy,* 79, pp. 73–93.

POWELL, THOMAS F. 1967. *Josiah Royce.* New York: Washington Square Press, Inc.

Cases on the Web

"She chose before losing the choice" by Tom Lyons
"Standing behind a reporter: The CBS/*News Journal* Controversy" by John Sweeney
"The anchor as activist" by Fred Bales
"The wonderful world of junkets" by Ralph Barney

CHAPTER 4 CASES

CASE 4-A

Where Everybody Knows Your Name: Reporting and Relationships in a Small Market

GINNY WHITEHOUSE
Whitworth College

Everybody is a source when you're covering an agricultural town with a population under 12,000.

But Sunnyside Police Sergeant Phil Schenck had not been a source for Jessica Luce when he asked her out for a date during a Halloween party in 1999. Luce had worked as a general assignment reporter at the *Yakima Herald-Republic* for almost a year. Sunnyside, Washington, was one of four communities she covered in this first job out of college. The two spent time together infrequently over the next two months.

"I was interested in him, we had fun, but if I had been asked what was going on I would have said we were friends," Luce said.

Nonetheless, a co-worker was incredulous. Luce remembers him saying, "You can't go out on a date with a source. It's one of the biggest taboos in journalism!"

The *Herald-Republic*'s four-page code of ethics advises staff to avoid conflicts of interest and to disclose those that are unavoidable. Prohibition of gifts and free travel is clearly explained. However, no specifics are given describing personal relationships that might cause conflicts of interest.

Luce decided to keep her relationship with Schenck, however it might be defined, quiet. Even with all the police stories she had written, she had never needed Schenck as a source and never thought the occasion would arise.

Schenck's boss, however, was another matter. Sunnyside Police Chief Wallace Anderson had been accused of shooting a great blue heron outside the police station, storing explosives at the station house and of having a threatening temper. Following a lengthy and expensive investigation, Anderson resigned in November.

By New Year's Day, Luce and Schenck decided they were definitely dating. "I kept my relationship under wraps save for a few confidants at work. I felt the relationship would be perceived as something wrong," Luce said. "But I didn't see it interfering with my job. Phil and I didn't talk about work as much as normal couples might. We knew it wasn't fair to either one of us."

In mid-February, Schenck was named acting captain, giving him the number two position in the Sunnyside police department and making him the official media spokesman. Luce realized she needed to be pulled off the Sunnyside police beat immediately. Her editors agreed.

"It was hard to talk with them about my private relationship, and I was forced to define things about the relationship that I hadn't even done for myself," Luce said.

Craig Troianello, her city editor, sat her down for a long conversation. "Jessica made it easy because she was straightforward. We didn't ask intimate questions—

that's irrelevant in this case," Troianello said. "By taking the proactive ethical stand that she did, it was easy for us to deal with this."

Luce said Troianello emphasized that his concern did not mean he was questioning her integrity. However, he had to make sure he hadn't overlooked something that could be perceived as a conflict by readers.

"This was a lesson on perception versus reality," Luce said. Luce's reporting did not affect Schenck's promotion, nor had Schenck ever implied that a story should or should not have been covered. Nonetheless, Schenck benefited from the chief's departure.

Troianello said he was never worried that Luce's reporting was compromised, but he wanted to make sure the newspaper was above suspicion. "Issues involving the police department were in the forefront of the news," Troianello said. "People could read anything into it—that she was protecting the chief, that she was trying to bring the chief down. Those kinds of spins drove my concern."

On the other hand, Schenck questions whether a strict conflict-of-interest standard is realistic in a small town. "Everybody is a potential source—even the clerk at the grocery store. We eat food. If her husband or boyfriend is a farmer, you could say she is promoting eating. This is an ideal that might be somewhat impractical," Schenck said. "If you can't be a real person, how can you report on real people?"

Luce says if she had to do it all over again she would not have kept the relationship a secret as long as she did. Nonetheless, it would still be hard to talk to a supervisor about dating. Troianello said he understands the complexities of a journalist's personal life but would rather Luce had brought the relationship to the newspaper's attention by New Year's Day when the two began dating.

However, he understands the dynamic of the situation. "She's in a small town where the number of people with four-year degrees and professionals is small," Troianello said. "It seems like there will be some mixing at some point. Relationships could occur as naturally as it does in the newsroom. I married a copy editor."

Once their relationship went public (they were later engaged), Luce was surprised at how supportive the community and city officials were, including the new police chief (someone other than Schenck). "What we as journalists see as an ethical problem and conflict of interest isn't necessarily going to be seen as an ethical problem by the public."

However, Luce never heard comments one way or another from the former chief or his supporters. On several occasions, city officials have questioned whether Schenck leaked information to Luce or *Herald-Republic* reporters. Schenck simply explained that he had not. "I deal with stuff every day that Jessica would love to get her hands on," Schenck said. "But we just don't talk about it."

Luce now covers education in the city of Yakima.

Micro Issues

1. Did Luce have a responsibility to tell her editors about her relationship with Schenck? If so, when should Luce have informed them?
2. What responsibility did the *Yakima Herald-Republic* editors have to explain expectations on conflicts of interest? Is spelling out those expectations necessary or appropriate in a code of ethics?

3. How would the ethical questions have changed if Schenck worked in another capacity for the city, such as being a teacher?
4. How would the ethical questions have changed if Luce and Schenck had remained only friends?

Midrange Issues

1. What aspects of their lives should journalists be able to keep private?
2. Is public perception of an ethical problem truly relevant?
3. Journalists spend most of their time with two groups: their sources and their co-workers. Considering those limitations, is dating possible or advisable?
4. Recently, NBC "Dateline" correspondent Maria Shriver took a leave of absence as her husband, Arnold Schwarzenegger, ran a successful race for governor of California. As she returns to her duties, what limitations, if any, should be imposed on her reporting? Justify your decision.

Macro Issues

1. Can journalists cover communities effectively if they are expected to remain remote and removed?
2. How specific should codes of ethics be on conflicts of interest?

CASE 4-B

A Question of Role: Is a Documentary Filmmaker a Friend, a Journalist or an Entertainer?

NANCY MITCHELL
University of Nebraska–Lincoln

In 1998 independent filmmaker David Sutherland wrote, produced, directed and edited a story about a young Nebraska farm couple, Juanita and Darrel Buschkoetter, and their three daughters. It is a riveting story of the family facing the dual hardships of trying to keep the family farm and the family intact. Taken from more than 200 hours of film shot in rural Nebraska over a period of three years, Sutherland painted a portrait of the impact of the economic struggles of family life.

Sutherland interviewed 40 families before he decided on featuring the Buschkoetters. During his initial stay with the couple, Sutherland said he showed the couple examples of his work so they knew what they were getting into. During the making of the film, neither Sutherland nor his crew ever became friends with the family. However, he said he did develop a friendship after the project wrapped up.

The series won much critical acclaim. The documentary was nominated for four Television Critics Association awards, including Program of the Year. The project also was included in many critics' list for Best of TV for 1998, including the *Chicago Tribune, TV Guide* and the *Boston Globe* (David Sutherland Web site). Steve Johnson, critic for the *Chicago Tribune,* said: "One of the extraordinary television events of the decade. 'The Farmer's Wife' is a breathtaking piece of work, a harrowing intimate love story set against an unforgiving physical and cultural landscape . . . [it] is bigger than just a farm story, offering lessons for a culture that acts as if poverty only occurs in inner cities, that piles up debt and ducks out by declaring bankruptcy, or that hits a rough patch in a marriage and scurries off to see a divorce lawyer."

Another rave came from David Bianculli, *New York Daily News,* who said: "It's a heavy viewing load, but certainly nothing compared to the trials and troubles, on the farm and in the home, thrown at Juanita and Darrel Buschkoetter. And watching 'The Farmer's Wife' is time very well spent: This is an honest, haunting, unflinching instructive and intimate study of a family that seems doomed to fail, but refuses to give up easily. 'The Farmer's Wife' has a coherent and compelling story worthy of a classic novel. (Four stars)."

Ron Miller of *The Oregonian,* wrote, "Not until this week's 'The Farmer's Wife' has any filmmaker probed so deeply into the heart of an American family with such gut wrenching results. Sutherland's film ultimately gets at a truth about human relationships that surely will resonate through every household that tunes into 'The Farmer's Wife.'" And tune in they did. The film attracted 18 million PBS viewers when it first aired in September 1998, according to Sutherland's Web site, making it one of the most watched series in PBS history. The six and one-half hour documentary aired in three segments. The first segment introduced viewers to the Buschkoetters, who tell the story (without the intrusion of a narrator) of the troubles they face both in their marriage and the risk of losing the farm after years of drought.

The second segment chronicles family life and the relentless challenge to make ends meet. At this point, the family is in danger of losing its farm. The loan officer, Hoy Bailey of the USDA, tells the Buschkoetters that they need to ask all the creditors for an extension. In one compelling scene Juanita drives at night to the office of one of the creditors, where she asks for a two-year extension. The creditor, Rich Kucera, listens to her and eventually agrees. The next scene finds Darrel in the kitchen of their home and Juanita arrives home to tell Darrel that Kucera has agreed, even if reluctantly, to extend their agreement. Darrel comments that he can't believe that Kucera was nice:

DARREL: "He wasn't even nasty?"
JUANITA: "No."
DARREL: "Richard, not nasty? That's a first. . . . I couldn't even imagine that guy being nice."

In the ensuing scene, Darrel calls Hoy Bailey. The loan officer tells Darrel that all of the extensions have been granted except for one for $100, and without that, they'll lose the farm in a buyout.

DARREL: "You mean $100 would cause a buyout?"
HOY: "Yep."
DARREL: "Don't you think that's a little bit ridiculous? I mean, if it had to be, I could go out and sweep a street and make $100 and eliminate a buyout."

In the next scene, the couple is working with Hoy and is apparently not in danger of losing the farm anymore. The second segment ends without the viewer knowing how the Buschkoetters resolved the financial questions.

The last episode depicts the resolution of their problems. Darrel harvests a bumper crop but suffers the stress of working his farm and another to make enough money to feed the family. After Darrel lashes out at his wife, Juanita takes their girls to her sister and leaves him. Juanita and the girls return after a week or so. Darrel seeks counseling, and the couple seems to be working things out. The Buschkoetters save their farm and their relationship through their hard work and commitment.

Sutherland describes himself as "a portraitist, not an investigative reporter. I'm not driven by the spectacular, the sensational, but I am interested in all the nuances of personality in making the portrait."

Sutherland said he crafted the film in such a way as to let family interactions and the family's interactions with outsiders tell the story. A narrator was never involved. Sutherland described the approach as "third person, close up, not first person, not omniscient." Sutherland said he had no agenda for the film but was concerned about the agendas those he interviewed might bring to the project. Sutherland said he is as concerned about those being filmed trying to use him to promote their agenda as he is with filmmakers' potential to use the subjects for their selfish gain.

Just how far would Sutherland go to observe a journalistic convention of not interfering with the subjects because that might change the story? "If someone's life were in the balance, I'd have come up with the money [to save the farm]." Sutherland saw himself in Juanita and Darrel; he said their dream of saving the family farm was parallel with his own dreams of creating a documentary that was not just a story about a farm family, but an intimate portrait with a social issue as a backdrop. To Sutherland, it was important to "talk to them [the subjects] from your heart, being an outsider and not taking advantage of them."

In the final episode, when Juanita left Darrel, Sutherland chose not to follow her even though Juanita gave him permission. Sutherland trusted the story could be told in another way at another time, and he eventually captured a summary of the event after the family was reunited.

Response to the series and the publicity led to opportunities for the Buschkoetters. They testified before Congress on the plight of the family farm; they traveled on publicity tours and gained experience from speaking engagements. Sutherland believes that the Buschkoetters' girls gained more self-esteem. Sutherland said he, too, was changed. He said the project "made me fall in love with America again. It was about people who tried their best. What more could you ask for?"

Micro Issues

1. If you were the producer, would you have lent the Buschkoetters the $100 if doing so meant they wouldn't lose the farm? What does it do to the story if you lend the money? What does it do to the story if you don't lend the money? What does it do to the family?
2. Would you answer the question differently if you were a news journalist working on an in-depth piece on the same subject?
3. Did Sutherland make the right decision about filming the marital breakup? How would you explain his decision to an editor, using concepts of professional excellence and the philosophy surrounding the issue of privacy?

Midrange Issues

1. When asked if he thought the personal rewards of creating a documentary might be construed as using people for personal gain, Sutherland responded: "I'm as uptight about them [subjects of his documentaries] using me." Evaluate this statement. Is this same tension prevalent in news journalism?
2. Sutherland describes himself as a portraitist, not an investigative reporter (e-mail, September 7, 2003). Do you think this gives him freedom to make different choices than he would had he claimed to be an investigative reporter?
3. Does having a camera present change the story? Do you think filming the meeting when Juanita asks the creditor for the extension on the loan changed the creditor's behavior? Does that matter?
4. When, if ever, can a journalist or documentarian become friends with those he has written about? What do you think a philosopher such as Kant or Ross would say about your response?

Macro Issues

1. Is it possible to produce a documentary from an objective point of view? What should be a guiding principle in creating this type of work?
2. Does a documentary need to conform to different ethical understandings than other entertainment forms—for example, reality television or a prime-time magazine show? Why?

CASE 4-C

Conflicted Interests, Contested Terrain: The *New York Times* Code of Ethics

BONNIE BRENNEN
Temple University

In January 2003 the *New York Times* broke a lengthy tradition and published its new ethics code on the Web. The *Times* decision was an important one, for ethics codes are often controversial in both their creation and their application. However, ethics codes can be an important marker of specific social practices created under particular social, economic and political conditions at distinct times in history.

For example, members of the American Newspaper Guild in 1933 crafted one of the first ethics codes developed by journalists rather than managers. That code suggested the "high calling" of journalism had been tarnished because news workers had been pressured by their employers to serve special interests rather than the public good. Conflict of interest was centered on the relationship between reporters and sources, and the code made a particular point that business pressures were putting undue stress on newsrooms, specifically the suppression of sensitive news and the "suppression of legitimate news concerning 'privileged' persons or groups, including advertisers, commercial powers and friends of newspapermen." The code recommended that to combat business pressures the news should be edited "exclusively in newsrooms."

Ethics codes in general are controversial among professionals and scholars. Some maintain that ethics codes are nothing more than generalized aspirations—too vague to be of any use when specific decisions must be made. Others insist codes can be helpful to beginning journalists, photographers and public relations practitioners; they provide some guidance in the form of rules that can be internalized as professional expertise and experience deepen. And still others agree with Williams; codes are a manifestation of the ideology of an era. They are more about power and politics than they are about ethics.

The new *Times* code linked its creation to the public perception of the "professional reputations of its staff member(s)." The code was directed to "all members of the news and editorial departments whose work directly affects the content of the paper."

The code focused primarily on issues of conflict of interest. In fact, the code did not mention accuracy and fairness and devoted only a single sentence to issues of privacy. However, when addressing the issue of conflict of interest, the code was both specific and detailed. The *Times* code considered the impact that spousal relationships might have on news coverage. The *Times'* willingness to consider spousal relationships was an acknowledgment of the changing role of women in the workforce and the ethical issues that this social change raises. It also addressed whether journalists working abroad should abide by the ethics and mores of the countries in which they are stationed, most of which do not provide the equivalent of First Amendment protections.

The code required staff members to disclose yearly speaking fees in excess of $5,000 and prohibited staff members from accepting gifts, tickets, discounts or other "inducements" from organizations the *Times* covered. Staff members could not invest in companies they covered, and payment for favorable or altered coverage was specifically forbidden.

However, staff members were allowed to do certain sorts of unpaid work—for example, public relations for a child's school fund-raising event. But *Times* staffers were forbidden from giving money to candidates or causes, marching in support of public movements or appearing on radio and television shows to voice views that went beyond those of the paper. When family members, such as spouses, participated in such activities, *Times* staffers were required to disclose those activities to management and recuse themselves from certain sorts of coverage.

The *Times* code also was protective of the newspaper's place in the marketplace. Staffers were prohibited from disclosing confidential information about the operations, plans or policies of the newspaper to other journalists. Such questions were to be referred to management. If readers asked such questions, *Times* staffers were encouraged to respond "openly and honestly." *Times* staff members also were prohibited from doing freelance work for any media outlet that competed with the *Times.* "Staff members may not appear on broadcasts that compete directly with the *Times'* own offerings on television or the Internet. . . . As the paper moves further into these new fields, its direct competitors and clients or potential clients will undoubtedly grow in number."

Like the earlier American Newspaper Guild code, the new *Times* code reflects the ongoing tension between economic realities and a social responsibility philosophical framework of traditional American journalistic issues. It may also be useful to consider Williams's notion that codes ironically suggest that a more complete understanding of the relationship between journalism practices and societies exists apart from the actual codes. The *New York Times'* attempt to codify specific relationships may actually work to obscure them.

Micro Issues

1. Should managers and owners be subject to a code of ethics, particularly for publications as influential as the *Times*?
2. Why is the notion of perception—as opposed to action—important in considering the issue of conflict of interest?
3. Should the *Times* code have addressed a variety of common journalistic issues—such as accuracy, fairness and privacy?
4. Evaluate the code of the American Newspaper Guild on these issues.

Midrange Issues

1. Disclosure is often suggested as a remedy for conflict of interest. Evaluate this remedy.
2. Should conflict of interest rules be different at a small newspaper or television station as opposed to the *Times*?
3. Does the *Times* code infringe on staffers' First Amendment rights? Do journalists give up some of their rights as citizens in order to do the work of journalism?
4. Are there instances when recusing oneself from an assignment is unsatisfactory? What should journalists do if such a case arises?
5. Should a conflict of interest extend as far as prohibitions against a journalist being an officer in the parent-teacher association (i.e., PTA or PTO) of his or her child's school?

An officer in your local homeowners association? Does the potential for those organizations to get involved in the news pages (i.e., teacher problems, zoning protests) influence your decision?

Macro Issues

1. What are the specific historical developments in the field of journalism that may have promoted the development of this particular version of the *New York Times* code?

2. Research indicates that codes that are developed by the newsroom have a much better chance of influencing behavior than codes that are superimposed by management. If the *Times* had used this approach, would it have "discovered" the actions of reporters such as Jayson Blair (details of the Blair case may be found in Chapter 2)? Should the development of codes include the potential for discovering wrongdoing?

3. Does the *Times* code place the organization's financial health on equal footing with the public trust? Is that appropriate?

CASE 4-D

One Person's Tragedy, Another Person's Prize

PHILIP PATTERSON
Oklahoma Christian University

July 22, 1975, was a busy day for *Boston Herald* photographer Stanley Forman. Early in the day he climbed towers and rode elevators all over Boston to get pictures of the city's skyline for a Sunday magazine feature. During that time, he remained on call for other daily assignments.

After returning his film to the newspaper, he was hoping to leave for the day when a call came about a fire in one of the city's older sections of Victorian row houses. The dispatcher mentioned that some people might be trapped in the burning structure. Forman followed the fire engine to the scene and heard on his scanner an SOS ordering a ladder truck to the scene. When he arrived, he followed a hunch and ran down the alley to the back of the row of houses.

There he saw firefighter Bob O'Neil and two people, a 2-year-old girl and her 19-year-old godmother, on the fifth-floor fire escape. The fireman was calling for help from a fire truck below. The truck raised its aerial ladder to the trio. Forman climbed aboard the bed of the truck to get a better angle on what he anticipated would be a routine rescue.

Meanwhile the WBZ radio traffic helicopter had landed on the next roof, and the pilot was offering to take the child. Though he is visible in most of the photos, he never got a chance to help.

As Fireman O'Neil reached for the ladder of the fire truck below, there was a loud noise—either the sound of a scream or the shriek of metal bending. The fire escape gave way, sending the two victims falling and leaving O'Neil clinging for his life to the ladder. Forman saw it all through his 135 mm lens and took four photos as the two were falling, before turning away to avoid seeing them hit the ground. The woman, Diana Bryant, broke the fall of the girl, Tiare Jones, who survived. Bryant sustained multiple head and body injuries and died hours later.

O'Neil was shaken by the experience. "Just two more seconds. I would have had them," he said repeatedly. Though Forman took a few more pictures, he was shaking too much to hold the camera still.

Returning to the newspaper, he waited anxiously to see if he had the photos that he thought he had. When it was obvious he did, he stayed to help with some of the prints and went home, exhausted. At 8:00 p.m. he learned that Bryant had died. He wondered if the newspaper would still run the photos.

He saw the first morning edition of the paper shortly after 2:00 a.m. and was surprised to see that the key photo in the sequence (the one reprinted here) was printed on Page 1 and measured $11^1/_{12}$ inches by $16^1/_{12}$ inches—virtually the entire tabloid page. A full sequence of the four photos ran on Page 3.

By 4:00 a.m., Forman had made a set of prints for the Associated Press, which gave the pictures worldwide distribution that same day. Tearsheets on the photos came from 128 U.S. papers and several foreign countries.

Stanley J. Forman, Pulitzer Prize 1977. Used with permission.

Within 24 hours, action was taken in Boston to improve the inspection and maintenance of all existing fire escapes in the city. Fire-safety groups around the country used the photos to promote similar efforts in other cities.

Numerous awards came as well. The Pulitzer Prize committee gave Forman its 1976 news photo prize. The National Press Photographers Association named the photo Picture of the Year. Several other groups, including the Society of Professional Journalists, honored the photo as well. Forman went on to win the Pulitzer Prize again the following year, making him the only photographer to win consecutive Pulitzer Prizes for news photography. His awards earned him a Nieman Fellowship at Harvard and lecture engagements around the world.

Micro Issues

1. What are the rights of victims of a tragedy such as this one? Should they have protection from being photographed? Being interviewed?
2. Forman's instincts and resourcefulness enabled him to capture photos that no other photographer got. Is the exclusive nature of the photos a factor in whether to run them?
3. Forman said that when he heard Bryant had died, he assumed that the photos would not run. Should the death of one of the girls have affected the treatment of the photos?
4. Did the newspaper sensationalize the photo shown in this case by its size or placement?
5. Do the rights of the other people pictured—O'Neil and the helicopter pilot—enter into the decision of whether to use the photos?

Midrange Issues

1. Is the repair of aging fire escapes a morally justifiable reason for running the photos?
2. Many newspapers outside of Boston ran the photos as well. When the local news peg (the fire) is absent, what is the ethical reasoning for running the photos?

Macro Issues

1. Photos such as Forman's are often singled out for awards within the industry. In fact, more than half of all photos that have won the two major prizes in photojournalism have involved tragedy. Should one person's calamity be a photojournalist's good fortune?
2. Are prizes too important to the profession of journalism? Are they ethical in a field such as journalism?

CASE 4-E

Freebies and the Houston Rodeo

JIM MATHENY
University of Missouri–Columbia

The annual Livestock Show and Rodeo is a long-time civic tradition in Houston, Texas. Since the rodeo's inception in 1931, organizers have seen their project grow into the largest livestock show and rodeo competition in the world. The three-week event showcases steers, roping and riding as championship athletes compete for some of the largest cash prizes in the sport. Furthermore, the rodeo features performances from some of the nation's most popular singers and entertainers.

Tickets to the various shows range in price from $16 to $77. Expenditures on the rodeo approached $220 million annually in 2005, but show officials say the return on investment is even more immense with an overall financial impact of $345 million (http://www.hlrs.com, Economic Impact 2005). A portion of the revenue goes to the rodeo's philanthropic efforts, such as their scholarship program. In 2004, the rodeo spent 17 percent of its revenues on youth programs and scholarships for Texas high school students to attend in-state colleges and universities (Feldstein 2005a).

Scholarships are awarded based on a variety of criteria, including a large allocation of need-based financial assistance for students who would otherwise struggle to afford higher education (http://www.hlrs.com, FAQ Scholarships 2005). While all proceeds are not used solely for philanthropic purposes, emphasis on the altruistic acts is ubiquitous in promotional material for the event. The Web site for the Houston Livestock Show and Rodeo (HLSR) prominently displays the phrase "Benefiting Youth and Supporting Education" at the top of the page (http://www.hlrs.com, (HLSR Homepage 2005).

The 2005 edition of the Houston Livestock Show and Rodeo was considered by many to be the most successful in history, breaking prior records for attendance and revenue thanks to good weather and performances by superstar entertainers including Hillary Duff, Alicia Keyes and Gretchen Wilson. Paid attendance for all shows totaled $1,127,239 and topped 1 million patrons for the 11th consecutive year (Chow 2005). The festivities are hosted in several large venues within Houston's Reliant Park, a property featuring several facilities with a combined capacity of more than 150,000 seats, so there are still many empty chairs during the 21 days of rodeo and music. Only the most popular individual performances sell out Reliant Stadium, a massive structure with a retractable roof that is home to the city's NFL franchise. With lots of leftover tickets in the "nosebleed" sections unlikely to be sold, rodeo organizers have routinely donated these less-desirable tickets to other organizations in the community.

Recipients of free tickets included media and news organizations. A spokesperson for the rodeo told this author that virtually every news organization in Houston received free tickets to the 2005 Livestock Show and Rodeo. The rodeo has been in the practice of donating tickets to the press for more than 40 years. According to the *Houston Chronicle,* 1,700 free tickets were distributed to television stations and the *Chronicle* itself received 1,200 free tickets (Feldstein 2005b). Dan Feldstein, the author of the *Houston*

Chronicle news article about the "freebies," says his paper's relatively new editor was actually unaware that the tickets were free and assumed the donated seats were somehow part of a "trade-out" for advertising space.

In addition to new organizations habitually accepting the donated tickets, reporters assigned to cover the event were able to take advantage of other complimentary goods. According to Feldstein, those "covering the event could ask for up to 10 'free alcoholic drink' coupons." Camera operators and on-air talent from local television stations, as well as photographers from the *Chronicle,* reportedly redeemed the coupons. The television station accepting the most alcoholic drinks free-of-charge was KTRK Channel 13, the local ABC affiliate that televises the Houston Livestock Show and Rodeo Parade on the opening day of the three-week event. KTRK has been broadcasting the parade live since 1959.

KTRK ABC 13 added an additional twist to the story of the 2005 Houston Livestock Show and Rodeo. Wayne Dolcefino, one of the station's investigative journalists, has developed a reputation for his flamboyant and sensational style of reporting. One of his reports was scheduled to coincide with the Houston Livestock Show and Rodeo and focused on the nonprofit's questionable spending habits (Feldstein 2005b). Editors at KTRK killed the story, and Dolcefino protested the decision by refusing to work for two weeks.

While no one other than employees of KTRK had seen Dolcefino's story, Feldstein's article in the *Chronicle* said it apparently implied that the nonprofit spent funds on items such as unusually expensive office furniture and other aesthetics seemingly unrelated to their philanthropic mission. Feldstein also said Dolcefino inquired about the nonprofit's distribution of free tickets, alcoholic beverages and catering services to event volunteers and news organizations. Dolcefino's inquiries into the amounts paid to entertainers resulted in a lawsuit by the rodeo against KTRK. The rodeo requested an injunction against such requests because payment amounts are considered to be trade secrets. The rodeo stated that to publicize such details would provide valuable information to competing national events wishing to bid for the services of entertainers sought by the rodeo.

In an interview with Dan Feldstein, the *Chronicle* writer conveyed his interpretation of the prevailing attitudes among news organizations covering the Houston Rodeo. With regard to freebies, Feldstein said, "I don't think most people thought about it, or, they figured nobody ever covered the rodeo like a news event anyway" (Dan Feldstein, personal communication, November 4, 2005). Feldstein acknowledged the problems associated with rodeo freebies and believes the practice should be eliminated. But most of his concerns relate to potential damage to the news organization's reputation due to negative public perceptions.

Feldstein does not believe the gifts influenced news coverage. "Although the public perception of freebies is bad, a few cameramen having free drinks or staffers going to the shows is not going to influence an editor's decision," said Feldstein. He added, "For one thing, the tickets just aren't that valuable. Nobody in the media is falling over themselves to see Clay Walker perform in a cavernous football stadium for the 10th year in a row" (personal communication, November 4, 2005). Some members of the media may indeed lack enthusiasm for such a performance, but the rodeo's Web site reports 56,023 in paid attendance for the March 20, 2005, Clay Walker concert on the event's final night (http://www.hlrs.com, Ticket Availability 2005).

Sports journalists are routinely offered, and sometimes come to expect, free food in the press box. Team owners and athletic directors across the country have engaged in a virtual arms race to build the most luxurious press facilities in an effort to pamper and favorably impress members of the media. The office spaces of many sports journalists are littered with freebies from prominent events covered by the reporters. Freebie memorabilia is proudly displayed as a badge of honor touting prior work experience without considering the possible implication of unethical behavior.

The problem is not exclusive to sports reporters. Entertainment features writers are frequently sent free CDs and DVDs from entertainment companies hoping to provide exposure for their product via the media. The Houston rodeo is simply an extreme example, considering the massive quantities of free booze available to on-duty reporters.

In the wake of Dan Feldstein's article explaining the problematic nature of freebies and the livestock show, the rodeo's organizers said free tickets would not be distributed to the media in the future.

Micro Issues

1. Should newspaper and television reporters and crews covering the rodeo accept free tickets to the event?
2. Should media employees who are not covering the rodeo accept free tickets to the event?
3. What might be the motivation of the Houston Rodeo to give free tickets to the media? Do sports or entertainment outlets that give tickets to the media have a right to expect publicity in return? Do they have a right to expect *favorable* publicity?

Midrange Issues

1. Do you see a difference between free tickets to a sporting event where news will be generated and a resort or theme park where presumably the only reason for the junket would be free publicity?
2. Is there a different standard for accepting freebies in news as opposed to sports? Entertainment? Travel?
3. Do you see a difference in accepting tickets to an event that might help you cover a story and accepting memorabilia from that event? In accepting alcoholic drinks from the event?

Macro Issues

1. Is this a credibility issue? Do you agree with Feldstein's statement that none of the freebies influenced coverage? Justify your answer.
2. Does the benefit to your audience from the coverage that freebies allow—especially for far-flung trips your budget would not allow—overcome the question of credibility if the subject of the story pays a significant amount for you to be there?

CASE 4-F

Can You Relate: Cross-Cultural Sensitivity and Reporting

ISABEL ORDOÑÉZ
University of Missouri–Columbia

Author's Note: *Sources used in this case study are personal, phone and e-mail interviews with Christina Tercero, Jim Larsen and Macarena Hernandez and a content analysis of stories in the Whidbey* News-Times.

"I want to see you in my office now," was the order that Jim Larsen, editor of the Whidbey *News-Times,* gave two hectic reporters arriving in the newsroom.

He wanted to speak with Jessie Stensland, a veteran police reporter, and Christina Tercero, a general-assignment reporter and photographer for the Oak Harbor-based newspaper, which covers Whidbey Island, Washington. They knew Larsen's request was related to the recent encounter they had with the family of Elaine Sepulveda, 15, who vanished on the morning of Nov. 6, 2004. During the visit to the Sepulveda's house, Tercero had been expected to take some photos and learn from the experienced Stensland, but it had developed into more than that.

"The family said they want to talk just with you," Larsen told Tercero following a call from a spokeswoman for the Sepulveda family.

Tercero, 24, was born to Hispanic parents in Portsmouth, Virginia. She graduated from Western Washington University's with a degree in journalism in 2003 and interned at the *News-Times* that summer. Tercero had worked for the Whibey *News-Times* since September of 2004 and, like the rest of the staff, she had to write stories, take photos and even help with the page layout. But she had not yet covered the police crime or court beats.

When both reporters arrived at the home of the Sepulveda, a Hispanic family from Texas, Stensland immediately began asking cold and direct questions that made the family feel pressured. They soon asked the journalists to leave. Soon after, however, Stensland and Tercero decided to return and, through Tercero, the journalists apologized. After Tercero offered their apology, the family told her that they would be willing to talk, but just with her. During the conversation Tercero spoke Spanish and explained that she understood the pain this tragic event brought to the entire family.

The Sepulveda family's request put Larsen in an unexpected situation. How would the newspaper provide the best possible coverage if the family was only willing to talk with a reporter with no experience covering crime? Larsen decided that Tercero would cover the family side of the story and Stensland would follow the investigation. The family accepted the decision.

During the next few weeks Tercero wrote two stories about a candlelight vigil in which the family and other members of the Oak Harbor community prayed to find the girl. The first one published on November 20 was a short story in which Tercero reported the family's plans to hold a vigil and included information about the fruitless police search for Sepulveda.

"Elaine Sepulveda used to kiss her mother on the cheek every day before she would leave to school. That kiss has not come to her mother's cheek for two weeks, since Elaine's disappearance," wrote Tercero in her lead graphs, highlighting the Latino tradition of kissing among family members.

Meanwhile, Stensland wrote four stories on the search. Tercero's role was limited to contacting the family when Stensland needed comment or information from them. "Because I had the link with the family they asked me to call," Tercero said. However, she didn't receive credit in the stories for her help.

But things changed radically for Tercero after police discovered Elaine Sepulveda's body on January 16 in a grave under a compost heap and arrested Sepulveda's 18-year-old boyfriend.

In a feature story published on Jan. 19, Tercero painted a portrait of Sepulveda's life in a sensitive manner, loaded with details she gathered through interviews in Spanish with the family. She had been collecting information about Sepulveda for more than two months and wrote a profile about her life within a Latino family. The purpose of the story was to show the victim's human side.

"Elaine's mother said, often, when they would watch scary movies together, Meagan (Sepulveda's youngest sister of 7 years old) would say, 'Hold my hand. I'm scared,' and Elaine would tease her that she wasn't going to, but would in the end," Tercero wrote in the front-page article.

Tercero's piece gained the respect of Larsen, who assigned her a beat. She also gained the family's gratitude.

Did Tercero succeed in her coverage thanks to her Hispanic background and fluency in Spanish or was it due to her personality? Was Stensland's problem one of her ethnicity or her approach to the story?

Those questions are floating not only at the Whidbey *News-Times* newsroom but also in many U.S. newsrooms where editors often make assignments based on reporters' ethnic or religious backgrounds. And as even more minorities continue to populate all corners of the United States and newsrooms compete to hire minority reporters, the assignments these reporters are given will come under even more scrutiny.

For Larsen, using ethnic criteria in deciding who covers what in a newspaper "seems like a bad idea. An outsider might bring a different perspective to the assignment and take fewer things for granted. Besides, any journalist should be able to cover any assignment in a small community such as the one this newspaper covers. I can see an exception for language, if there is a language barrier."

In the case of Elaine Sepulveda, Larsen believes Tercero succeeded due to her empathy and because she is a person with whom people are comfortable talking. "Our more seasoned 'hard nosed' reporter had trouble getting access to the family, but Christina quickly established a trusting relationship with them. I think it's more a personality issue. She did an outstanding job bringing the human element to the crime story," he said.

Macarena Hernandez is an opinion columnist for the *Dallas Morning News,* where she writes about Hispanic issues and is an advocate for diversity in newsrooms. She agrees that the relevant criterion should be the reporter's ability to get information and communicate with sources, not their ethnic origin. "I don't agree with the idea of hiring journalists just because they are minorities," she said. "There are people who apparently belong to a minority, but they don't speak the language or understand the culture of the group they supposedly represent."

Hernandez described her experience working for the San Antonio *Express-News* where she was assigned the minority beat, including the Muslim community. "More than once, I felt that I was doing a bad job with them because I don't speak their language," Hernandez said.

Larsen and Hernandez agree that the principles that should guide every reporter's behavior are professionalism and responsibility. "A reporter's responsibility is to the facts and fairness; if both are achieved, any community should feel well served," Larsen said. "First I am a journalist and second, Latina," Hernandez said.

Micro Issues

1. Should Larsen honor the request of the Sepulveda family? Does this threaten the editorial independence of the *News-Times* to be told by the family which reporter to send?
2. Should Tercero decline the offer and return to the family explaining that the community would be better served if the regular crime reporter handled the story?
3. Should Stensland agree to the arrangement?

Midrange Issues

1. Critique the final statement of Hernandez above. Do you agree that one can be a journalist "first" and a member of an ethnic community "second" or is it impossible to separate the two?
2. Critique the statement of Larsen that using ethnicity to determine who covers a story "seems like a bad idea." Is it always a bad idea? When, if ever, could it be a "good idea?"

Macro Issues

1. Hernandez says that she disagrees with hiring journalists "just because they are minorities." What role, if any, should race play in hiring journalists? What role, if any, should race play in assigning beats?
2. Does a diverse news staff ensure diversity of coverage in the pages of the newspaper or the minutes of a newscast? If not, what else must happen?
3. What other ways should the media employ to ensure diversity in news coverage other than hiring practices?

5

Public Relations: Standards of Advocacy

By the end of this chapter, you should be familiar with:

- why the relationship between the media and public relations is both symbiotic and strained.
- how the concept of advocacy can provide an ethical justification for public relations.
- four ethically based criteria for evaluating public relations messages.

JOURNALISM AND PUBLIC RELATIONS: THE QUINTESSENTIAL STRUGGLE

Public relations began as a profession in the late 19th century when newsmakers sought to find a way to get past journalism's gatekeepers to get their stories told. From simple press releases to elaborate publicity stunts (such as the "torches of freedom" march for women smokers envisioned by Edward L. Bernays in the early years of the 20th century), PR practitioners offered a way to unlock the gate and get stories into the newspapers for their clients. At the same time they offered "free" news to publishers. Consequently, any controversy surrounding public relations as a profession must be viewed in light of the alternative. If the more than 200,000 public relations professionals in the United States did not exist, many stories would go unreported.

Despite the occasional animosity between journalists and public relations practitioners, the relationship is truly symbiotic—they simply could not live without each other. No news organization is large enough to gather all the day's news without several public relations sources. Business pages are full of press releases on earnings, new product lines and personnel changes, all supplied by writers not paid by the media. Travel, entertainment and food sections of newspapers would be virtually nonexistent if not for press releases. On the other hand, media outlets provide the all-important audience for an institution wanting the publicity.

With this common need, why are the two professions sometimes at odds? Much of the problem stems from how each of the two professions defines news. To the public relations professional, the lack of breaking news is newsworthy. Plants that operate safely and are not laying off any employees, nonprofit organizations that operate within budget and provide needed services, companies that pay a dividend for the 50th consecutive quarter are all signs that things are operating smoothly and make for a story that the public should hear.

However, to the journalist, news is a change in the status quo: a plant that pollutes, employees who embezzle, firms that go bankrupt—all are worthwhile news stories. Caught in the middle, the news consumer probably prefers a choice of both stories. However, shrinking "newsholes" (the amount of space available for news copy) and static amounts of airtime won't allow both, and the editorial bias is toward disruption more often than efficiency.

CREATING ETHICAL MESSAGES: A FOUR-PART APPROACH

In 2000, for the first time, the Public Relations Society of America (PRSA), public relations' major professional organization, acknowledged advocacy as a core value in the field. Advocacy means "understanding and valuing the perception of publics inside and outside organizations," (Grunig, Toth & Hon 2000). Advocacy also means communicating those perceptions to other publics, an effort that has become more complex because it involves relationships with multiple stakeholders "in a world of increasingly diverse and more active publics who are empowered by and connected through the Internet" (Fitzpatrick 2006, x). Scholars in the field suggest that there is a direct relationship between effective advocacy and ethical advocacy in this demanding environment.

The justice system has long recognized the need for each side to have an advocate to navigate the adversarial system of the courts. Landsman (1984) says the system requires a "zealous advocate." According to adversary theory, "when each actor performs only a single function the dispute before the court will be resolved in the fairest and most efficient way" (pp. 45–46). In the system, each advocate must find and present the most persuasive evidence and downplay that evidence that might be harmful to the client.

Those who support the advocacy model argue that any misleading information put out by public relations professionals will be somehow "self-corrected" by the gatekeepers of the media or by the self-righting "marketplace of ideas." Those who reject the advocacy model do so on two grounds. First, they assert that advocacy too easily morphs into distortion and lies. Second they argue that the long-term health of many enterprises, from business to government programs, is ill-served by "spin" and better served by honest, timely communication—even at the expense of short-term losses.

Kathy Fitzpatrick and her colleagues in *Ethics in Public Relations: Responsible Advocacy* (2006), suggest that individual messages be constructed and evaluated on four criteria, principles they suggest are the heart of responsible advocacy. If such principles are not applied, Fitzpatrick suggests that government regulation may be the only reasonable alternative.

> Of course, public relations professionals do not enjoy the special status of the 'Fourth Estate.' Indeed, as representatives of *special* interests—as compared to the *public* interest—they and their clients and employers may have less protection from judicial forays into questions of ethics. Public relations professionals must consider both whether the special obligations associated with the freedom to communicate are being met and whether, in the absence of effective *self*-regulation, the government might step in to hold practitioners accountable for irresponsible behavior," (Fitzpatrick 2006, 16). [italics in the original]

The first of those principles is **access,** and it takes its ethical power from the role of free speech in a democratic society. Free people are the autonomous moral actors philosophers insist must be the foundation of ethical choice. Access, then, equalizes an individual's ability to participate in the marketplace of ideas. "Actions intended to monopolize the marketplace freeze out other voices and violate fundamental democratic principles" (Fitzpatrick 2006, 9). There are some important assumptions that undergird this principle. One is that others will have what is required to gain access to the marketplace. Another is that unpopular ideas deserve a forthright presentation (Martinson 1999). The PRSA code, and the industry more generally, have remained almost silent on this issue which is, nonetheless, at the core of democratic functioning.

The second principle is **disclosure**—the provision of complete information about who is paying for the message and whether the message itself provides enough information to allow a reasonable person to make an informed and rational choice based on it. Under this concept of disclosure, lying by omission is unethical. The ethical end of disclosure is equally important: the generation of trust among and between various publics. "Ethical public relations professionals are forthright and honest and counsel clients and employers to adopt responsible communication policies built on principles of openness and transparency," (Fitzpatrick 2006, 13).

The third, and perhaps most important principle, is **truthfulness.** As you know from the discussion in Chapter 2, truth is an elusive concept. However, its demanding meaning for public relations practitioners might begin with meeting the strict legal standards for truth outlined in U.S. law and by the Federal Trade Commission. In addition, practitioners should be able to verify with clients the truthfulness of client claims, and they should provide information to their audiences that will allow them to verify the truthfulness of claims in messages aimed at the public.

This concept of telling the truth in times of crisis, or becoming an advocate for the long-term health of a particular client, has become one of the foremost professional principles for public relations practitioners engaged in crisis communication. The history of the field would suggest that businesses and agencies whose actions demonstrate that public health and safety are more important than short-term profits—in sum, telling the truth even when it hurts—are quite likely to profit substantially in the long term. That was the lesson that public relations practitioners learned a generation ago from Johnson & Johnson's handling of the Tylenol scare, when seven people in the Chicago area died as a result of taking Tylenol capsules laced with cyanide. Johnson & Johnson voluntarily pulled the product off the shelves,

Message	Intent
TRUTH/truth facts and information journalistic news	to inform accurately and with no apparent bias
PR copy editorials/columns advertising copy propaganda	an intent to persuade by using selective information; the truth but not the whole truth
parables and allegories fiction honest error	nontruths told with no intent to deceive
deceit "white lies" BLATANT LIES	intent to deceive, even if for a purpose claimed to be justifiable

FIGURE 5.1. The continuum of truth

reimbursed consumers who had purchased it but could no longer use it and cooperated completely and openly with both government investigators and the media.

Less than two years after the incident, the result was that Tylenol's market share had increased and the corporation itself was trusted by the public. Contrast these actions with those of Firestone/Bridgestone's stonewalling over the recall of faulty tires on sport utility vehicles and the long-term impact of those actions on corporate health. Public relations practitioners who advocate telling the truth in times of crisis can serve both their clients and the public without fear of compromising professional or personal ethics.

Deaver (1990) provides a useful tool (see Figure 5.1.) in which he identifies four layers in a continuum of truth and the intent of those who practice it. At the top are those intending to inform, followed by those intending to persuade, followed by those who often intend to entertain, and finally by those who intend to deceive.

It is interesting to note that Deaver distinguishes between "TRUTH," which is absolute and usually derived from an ultimate source of authority, and "truth," which is the documentable facts and information we deal with every day. Deaver's configuration puts public relations and advertising safely within the realm of what society deems acceptable behavior. Their purposes are distinct from those of their journalistic peers but well above the level of deceit.

The final principle is **process,** defined as whether public relations advocacy impedes or contributes to the robust functioning of the marketplace of ideas. An evenhanded process encourages both the journalists who use PR-generated information for news stories and various audiences who must rely on those stories as part of their decision making to use the information provided. Indeed, public relations that interferes with the integrity of political or judicial systems, such as the Hill & Knowlton firm's manufactured accounts of injured Kuwaiti newborns in testimony before the U.S. Congress (Safer 1992), corrodes the workings of democracy itself.

Public relations professionals also are encouraged to apply these values within their own organizations. This has become particularly important as more women than men enter the field, although men still retain their dominance in management. Research suggests that women balance the dual demands of work and home somewhat differently than men, a reality that makes creating and maintaining a collaborative environment a challenge for all those involved. Some scholars have gone so far as to suggest that women in the field are oppressed because they do not have the benefit of a direct relationship with top managers or client CEOs (Gruning, Toth & Hon, 2000). At least some practitioners have met this challenge by creating their own firms—agencies that specialize in working with specific subsets of clients that have been the historic targets of discrimination.

PUBLIC RELATIONS AND RESPONSIBILITY

Hodges (1986) says that the notion of professional responsibility can be summed up in a single question: For what am I prepared to respond ably? In other words, what have my education and my experience equipped me to do and to assume responsibility for? Ask a public relations practitioner, "To what are you ably equipped to respond?" and he or she might answer, "To respond to a crisis for a client" or "To generate favorable media attention for a client." However, there are greater responsibilities.

Hodges further states that responsibilities come from three sources. First there are those that are *assigned,* such as employee to employer. Second there are those that are *contracted,* where each party agrees to assume responsibilities and fulfill them. Third there are the *self-imposed* responsibilities, where the individual moral actor takes on responsibilities for reasons indigenous to each individual. It is our contention that public relations, practiced ethically, will not only fulfill the assigned or contracted responsibilities with the employer or the paying client but also take on the greater calling of self-imposed responsibilities. These self-imposed responsibilities could include such constructs as duty to the truth and fidelity to the public good. The more self-imposed responsibilities the PR professional assumes, the more ethical the profession will become as practitioners see their personal good as being synonymous with the public good.

CONCLUSION

The founding of the Public Relations Society of America (PRSA) in 1948 was a major step in the professionalization of the field. Today its ethics code is the professional standard. By the end of the 20th century, more than 2,000 PR firms operated in the United States, with many more around the world. The scope of public relations today is hard, if not impossible, to define, with no simple, uniformly accepted definition of the craft or art of public relations. At the individual level, the goal of the profession is information acquisition, opinion change and often behavioral change. At the system level, public relations provides the media and the public with necessary assistance in the information and newsgathering process.

While the proliferation of news releases is a source of mild irritation between the professions of journalism and public relations, it is a minor nuisance compared to the differences in how the two sides approach "hard" news stories. Unfortunately, some public relations practitioners see their jobs not only as telling the good news about their company but also as keeping the bad news from being told. This stand-off results in the perpetuation of a vicious cycle. Business executives perceive that the press is out to "get" them, so they refuse to speak, while the press perceives that a corporation has something to hide by its silence.

Public relations began as a profession when certain newsmakers wanted more media coverage. Today because of what business perceives as a negative bias, many public relations professionals are used as dissemblers of legitimate stories. Some businesses have found it expedient to refuse to cooperate with the media, and some have extended the policy to all employees. For instance, one major retailer does not even allow its managers to grant interviews about the expected best-selling toys for the upcoming Christmas season. Though this policy seems a bit extreme in a Christmas feature story, it is based on the assumption that most of the time the media will want information that will harm a business.

The average news consumer rarely observes this constant struggle for control over the content of the news, yet he or she is affected by it. How should we evaluate a profession with the goal of persuading in a manner that does not look like traditional persuasion or the goal of preventing the dissemination of information that might harm the illusion that has been created?

Practitioners in the field justify their profession with the following arguments: First, the stories they attempt to tell are the unreported or the underreported stories of products that work, employees who are honest and corporations that are good community citizens. Second, the rules are set by the other players in the game—the media. Finally, if the media would ever agree that good news *is* news, the animosity and duplicity might diminish.

Suggested Readings

CUTLIP, SCOTT. 1994. *The unseen power: Public relations—a history.* Hillsdale, NJ: Lawrence Erlbaum Assoc.

FITZPATRICK, K. & BRONSTEIN, C., eds. 2006. *Ethics in public relations: Responsible advocacy.* Thousand Oaks, CA.: Sage Publications.

HODGES, LOUIS. 1986. "Defining press responsibility: A functional approach." In D. Elliott (ed.), *Responsible journalism.* (pp. 13–31). Newbury Park, CA: Sage Publications, Inc.

VONNEGUT, KURT. 1952. *Player piano.* New York: Dell Publishing Co.

Cases on the Web

"Handling the media in times of crisis: Lessons from the Oklahoma City bombing" by Jon Hansen

"Public relations role in the Alar scare" by Philip Patterson

"A case of need" by Deni Elliott

"Endowment or escarpment: The case of the faculty chair" by Ginny Whitehouse

"The gym shoe phenomenon: Social values vs. marketability" by Gail Baker

CHAPTER 5 CASES

CASE 5-A

Quit, Blow the Whistle or Go With the Flow?

ROBERT D. WAKEFIELD
Brigham Young University

Anyone who spends sufficient years in public relations will face a crisis of conscience. Practitioners are trained for the tenuous task of balancing institutional advocacy with the "public interest" (Newsom, Turk and Kruckeberg 1996). Yet this role can lead to personal conflict, as it did in my case.

The setting was an urban school district with about 40 schools and more than 35,000 students. Its superintendent had a national reputation for innovative community outreach, and he was a media favorite. I worked with him for five years before he accepted a statewide position. His replacement was a quiet man with conservative views who, along with the administrative team he brought with him, believed that educators were trained to run the schools and could do so best with minimal interference.

Like most inner-city school districts, the system was losing students as people moved to the suburbs. In the previous decade, a student population that once filled four high schools could now fill only three.

The seven-member school board had approached—and then abandoned—the question of closing one of the schools because the proposal aroused such strong feelings among students, faculty and parents. However, the new administration, trying to balance those responses against the financial drain of supporting an additional high school on taxpayer dollars, decided to broach the question again.

Promised a tumultuous situation, the new administrators aggravated the problem by how they handled it. Rather than sharing the issue with the community or with school faculties to seek a mutually agreeable solution, they tried to resolve the entire problem behind closed doors.

I first learned about the closed-door approach at a "study meeting" with the school board. The new superintendent held these informal meetings during his earliest days in the district; they tended to be so boring and ambiguous that journalists seldom attended.

Before the meeting in question, the superintendent asked me whether any media would be present. I told him one reporter might come late. As the meeting began, I was surprised to hear him tell the board and the few staff members, "If any reporter shows up, I will change the subject—but today we're going to talk about closing a high school." He then outlined the results of meetings he had already held on the issue, discussed a proposal from a local community college to buy the building so it would not be abandoned and sought the support of the four high school principals.

Thus began my ethical conundrum. I agreed that the enrollment problem was serious and that closing a school was probably the best alternative, but I opposed the administration's method of resolving the issue. As public relations officer, I believed that public institutions must be open and that involving those affected by the closure in the actual decision-making process would eventually generate long-term support for whatever decision was made. I was appalled at the attempts to exclude the public; but I said nothing.

Closed doors can quickly swing ajar, and it took less than one day for news of the decision to leak. The school targeted for closure was one of the oldest in the state. It had recently received a U.S. Department of Education award as an exemplary inner-city school, but its community was the least affluent and arguably the least politically powerful.

The day after the "study session," and with a regular board meeting scheduled for the same evening, reporters called to verify what they were hearing. (Chief executives often forget that supervisors of individual units within the system have their own allegiances. In this case, one of the high school principals left the "study meeting" and informed his teaching staff that they would be receiving transfer students "from that inner-city school." The rumors began.)

After the phone calls, I asked the superintendent what he planned to say at the board meeting and was told, "We will discuss space utilization needs." I told him about the calls and that our jobs would be threatened if we were not truthful with the community. To his credit, he responded quickly and openly. The evening meeting unfolded as expected. The room was jammed with district patrons and with the media. The expected lines were drawn. Underlying the fervor was a common theme: closing a traditional high school was awful enough, but the secretive way in which the administration had reached its conclusions was unforgivable.

The next several weeks were an intense period of work for a young public relations officer. I did media interviews, talk shows, and forums to explain the situation. I also met with dozens of teachers, parents and citizens, both to hear their comments and to take their suggestions. I had to be careful that my words represented the district instead of myself. I had worked with some local reporters for several years and felt comfortable giving them background so they could seek additional materials without revealing me as the original source. It was a personal risk, but the reporters never betrayed my trust.

Two additional incidents epitomized my ethical struggles. The first occurred after the initial board meeting, when a top administrator said the community misunderstood why decisions were made behind closed doors. I lobbied for openness. The administrator admonished me to remember who paid my salary, a rebuke that confirmed the new administration did not share my own values.

The second incident occurred when I was asked to meet with a man who had been chosen to speak on behalf of the community. I had taken only a few steps into his office when he said to me, "You don't agree with your administration, do you?" My response was silence while he explained his position.

For some reason, it was this encounter that forced my crisis of conscience: do I quit, blow the whistle or keep quiet? I had a wife and child to support; the employment picture at the time was not robust. Right or wrong, I surmised that the various relationships I had developed could appease many angry feelings. I also believed in the importance of education. So, I decided to stay through the crisis, then seek new employment.

About one month into the crisis, the board retained a consultant who, like me, believed in open communication. Two weeks later, four board members came to my office and requested a meeting. Because this constituted a majority of the board, such an assembly violated the law requiring the meeting be made public. I violated the law and invited them to stay. They said they were worn down by the constant tension and asked what I, as a public relations practitioner, thought they should do.

To me, the answer was straightforward. Relying on basic public relations formulas and common sense, I suggested that they could diffuse the tension by reverting to what should have been done in the first place: announce that selected representatives from throughout the city would form a committee to help review the situation and come to a decision that would then be discussed by the board.

To my surprise, the board members took this advice to the administration, and much of what I recommended was done. A few months later, the school was closed in a tearful farewell. And, five weeks after the school closed, I accepted a job with a local public relations firm.

Micro Issues

1. What sort of press releases or other talking points should Wakefield have prepared once the rumors began?
2. Should Wakefield have gone off the record with reporters he trusted?
3. Are there some sorts of decisions governmental bodies make that really should be kept from the media and hence the public? Is this one of them?
4. How should Wakefield have responded to the racial subtext of some of the protests about the closing of the school?

Midrange Issues

1. Should Wakefield have "blown the whistle" on the board members who requested an illegal meeting?
2. Was it appropriate for Wakefield to advise the board to take an approach different from that suggested by the superintendent?
3. How much does Wakefield's previous experience with a different superintendent influence his understanding of how the district works? How did this "workplace" socialization influence his ethical thinking?

Macro Issues

1. To whom should Wakefield be loyal?
2. Should he ever have told members of the community of his own personal views?
3. How does Wakefield's job compare with that of a press secretary for a political figure?
4. Is it ever appropriate to keep journalists in the dark about how political decisions are made?

CASE 5-B

Getting the Story, Getting Arrested: Photojournalism and Activism

LEE WILKINS
University of Missouri

British photojournalist Steve Morgan had worked as a freelancer for more than 20 years. Among his repeat clients was Greenpeace, an environmental organization that some characterize as radical, in part for tactics designed to stop various sorts of activities the group feels will degrade the environment. Supporters note that Greenpeace uses peaceful means to promote environmental change. However, the organization and its members have not shied away from direct confrontation, for example, attempting to physically prevent the killing of whales, when the environmental group and its members believe such action is warranted. All would agree that Greenpeace has a point of view.

On July 14, 2001, Morgan, along with Spanish videographer Jorge Torres, accompanied a group of 15 Greenpeace members as they protested a missile test off the coast of California, near Vandenberg Air Force Base. The protest involved boarding boats and sailing into the test path, an action that potentially could have stopped such a test. There had been previous protests at Vandenberg, but of the 50 people arrested as part of them, all had been charged with misdemeanors, which usually lead to a fine and probation.

Morgan's assignment from Greenpeace was to take pictures of the protest and to make certain those photos were circulated internationally by news services such as Reuters and Agence France-Presse (AFP). Greenpeace often employed the news media in this way to publicize its views. Morgan took a boat to the site of the protest, shot his photos and returned to shore. There he was arrested by the FBI, which charged him with trespassing, disobeying the orders of a federal officer and conspiracy—a felony.

Morgan's press credentials were examined and discarded by the FBI, Morgan said. He spent six days in the county jail, and then was allowed to fly home to Great Britain upon posting $20,000 bond, over protests of the prosecutor. About six months later Morgan returned to California with his wife and two children, where he was given probation by a U.S. court. The charges the journalists faced, and their sentences, were the same as those given to the protestors. "It was never my intention to go to the U.S. to break any laws," Morgan said. "I was attempting to document a protest, rather as I would if I were working for AP, Reuters, *The Guardian* or the *Independent,* and, as far as it's possible to be, I was there to be objective. As far as I was concerned, I was doing my job."

At the time of his sentencing, Morgan told the British newspaper *The Guardian* (which is considered the most left-of-center of the elite British print media), "As a photojournalist, my interpretation of events is shaped by my personal views and not by the persons or organizations who commission the assignments." A few months earlier, soon after his arrest, Morgan said, that he would agree to work for Greenpeace again. "I would have no qualms about working for Greenpeace again—it would be determined by the kind of assignment offered. Greenpeace is an organization that in general I believe has done a lot of good. I may not agree with everything that they do, but agree in general as do most people that we all want to live on a clean and peaceful planet. But if I was asked to cover a demo involving the U.S., inflatables and the military, I think the answer would be pretty clearly: 'no, thanks.'"

Greenpeace saw the arrest as politically motivated and capable of setting precedent for other photojournalists. "There is no question that there's some political motivation behind these charges," said Aaron Dyer, the group's lead attorney. "It doesn't appear to be related to Sept. 11, because it predates the attacks, but it does appear to be based on the desire of the Air Force to make a statement about these protests; and the government, the U.S. attorney general's office, seems to be assisting their efforts, It's inappropriate and it's unprecedented in U.S. jurisprudence."

Micro Issues

1. Should Morgan and the other journalist have been in the same boat as the protestors?
2. Does getting close enough to get a good picture—a professional necessity—lend some notion of support to the group?
3. Does the fact that Greenpeace hired Morgan constitute a real or potential conflict of interest for Morgan?
4. Should Morgan tell international news agencies that he is being paid by Greenpeace when he offers his work for sale?

Midrange Issues

1. How are freelance journalists like or unlike their salaried counterparts in terms of loyalty to their employers?
2. If you were a public relations professional, would you suggest that your organization hire its own photographer to cover events and provide the local media with the images? Does the kind of event matter?
3. Is Greenpeace's action in hiring a photographer ethically distinctive from political candidates who provide "photo ops"?

Macro Issues

1. In Europe, and in much of the rest of the world, news organizations are expected to have a point of view. How might that expectation change how editors would evaluate the newsworthiness of Morgan's pictures?
2. Was Morgan, a British citizen, ethically justified in relying on the U.S. First Amendment in his work? Should American journalists working in other nations rely on U.S. understandings of ethics and law, or should they adopt the local standards?

CASE 5-C

Selling Brand America

PATRICK LEE PLAISANCE
Colorado State University

Less than a month after the terrorist attacks of Sept. 11, 2001, Charlotte Beers was given what many described as the toughest public relations challenge ever: selling the idea of a benevolent, moral America to a hostile and embittered Arab world.

In a high-profile advertising career, Beers built a reputation on Madison Avenue as a shrewd and tireless generator of Big Ideas That Worked. The "Queen of Branding," *BusinessWeek* once crowned her. She capped her career by heading Ogilvy & Mather and later J. Walter Thompson, two of the world's advertising behemoths. She quickly was recruited by Bush administration officials eager to launch a public relations front in the war on terror. Her work generated a wave of commentary and triggered fits of soul-searching among many media practitioners. Was her work misguided propaganda or admirable outreach?

Countering misperceptions with assertive dialogue, Beers argued, is critical—especially in the Middle East. "We have all been made aware of the polls which report our eroding goodwill with the rest of the world," Beers said during a December 2002 speech at the National Press Club. "But it's considerably more intense and more deliberately manipulated by extremist factions in the Middle East. It serves their purpose, you understand, to paint us as decadent and faithless; a place and a people who are inimical to the tenets of Islam. These distortions happen every day in their press, in their magazines and from their pulpits. Our share of the mainstream voices is at an all-time low in terms of being heard. Our silence, I believe, is dangerous."

Beers received credit for helping to jump-start the long-dormant "public diplomacy" arm of the State Department, persuading the foreign-service corps that devising strategies to get the U.S. message out should be a critical part of foreign-policy decisions. One of her first moves as Undersecretary of State for Public Diplomacy and Public Affairs was to produce a glossy brochure that detailed, with grisly photos, the human carnage of Sept. 11. The brochure, called "The Network of Terrorism," was distributed in Middle East countries as a newspaper supplement. And at her behest, the State Department Web site aimed at foreigners added a feature on "Muslim life in America," illustrated with pictures of mosques and smiling Muslim families.

The centerpiece of her campaign became a series of short video presentations of Muslims describing their lives in the United States. The video campaign was called "Shared Values." In one of four video segments that government officials in Indonesia, Kuwait and Morocco allowed to air in late 2002, a Muslim family in Toledo, Ohio, is shown at a school softball game extolling American virtues. "I didn't see any prejudice anywhere in my neighborhood after Sept. 11," says Rawia Ismail, a Lebanese-born mother, who also is a schoolteacher. The other videos tell the stories of a prominent Arab doctor, the Algerian-born director of the National Institutes of Health, a Libyan-born baker, and a medic with the New York Fire Department.

Also in 2002, Beers launched a new campaign, reminiscent of the Cold War cultural exchanges of the 1960s, in which 15 American writers such as Richard Ford and Michael Chabon were recruited to write essays answering the question, "In what sense do you see yourself as an American writer?"

For Beers and other officials involved with the information campaign, the mission was clear: to get the word out that America was a badly misunderstood place and that many Muslims live here happily and safely and interact with people of other faiths. "The whole idea of building a brand is to create a relationship between the product and its user," Beers said in an interview during her first month on the job. "We're going to have to communicate the intangible assets of the United States—things like our belief system and our values."

The State Department spent about $15 million on the "Shared Values" videos, which were produced by the advertising company McCann-Erickson using State Department research. The videos were targeted to run in Muslim countries through Ramadan, the traditional period of fasting and reflecting that lasts from early November to early December.

The campaign also featured junkets to show America to Arab journalists, government-published books such as *Iraq: From Fear to Freedom,* and a new radio station, Radio Sawa, that broadcasts in the Arab world, playing pop music in Arabic and English and providing top-of-the-hour news from an American point of view.

Renowned "brand consultant" Wally Olins, who has worked with Spain and several central European countries in image-building projects, said marketing strategy, directly and indirectly, has always been part of national diplomacy. " Historically, nations have always used powerful and consistent ways of branding themselves—the issue is whether it is done consciously. For example, nations emerged as powerful entities during the late 18th-century French Revolution and later on with the German idea of *die Volk.* People think of this as sociocultural political history—not branding. But that's what it was." Rance Crain, editor of *Advertising Age,* praised Beers. "Charlotte Beers knows how to crystallize that message and drum it home to her target audience," Crain said. "That's what advertising can do."

Beers dismissed charges that launching an advertising campaign to "sell America" was misguided. "Just because I'm from Madison Avenue doesn't mean I think I'm selling," she told the National Press Club. "There is not an assumption that we have a ready buyer out there. So please believe me when I say that these mini-documentaries are presented as offering to create a dialogue, which is a really different starting point than a pitch."

When he appointed Beers, Secretary of State Colin Powell was unapologetic. "We are selling a product," Powell said. "We need someone who can rebrand American policy, rebrand diplomacy."

But from the outset, questions and doubters proliferated. Could the same strategies that Beers used to sell Craftsman power tools, Hoover vacuums and Uncle Ben's rice also sell Uncle Sam? How was a slick veneer of marketing going to change hostile attitudes without any changes in the largely pro-Israeli policies, at which the hostility is directed? Was a $30 million propaganda campaign the best way to address anti-American sentiment? Crafting an effective message was one thing; getting it out to Arab populations was another. The vast majority of the media outlets in Muslim countries are state controlled, and many eventually refused to broadcast Beers's campaign packages. Saudi Arabia and Egypt, among other countries, refused to air the

"Shared Values" video packages; Egyptian broadcast officials said they don't accept "propaganda from a foreign country."

It also didn't help Beers's efforts when, just before launching the Muslim ad campaign, news of plans for a Pentagon "disinformation" office leaked. In February 2002, the Defense Department announced plans for an Office of Strategic Influence, which would plant false or misleading stories in foreign media outlets and would hire people to organize pro-American rallies. Defense Secretary Donald Rumsfeld quickly called a halt to the office once it was publicized.

Combating deeply entrenched hostility to U.S. policy with feel-good ads is a dubious endeavor, critics said. "The problem is that America isn't a product and Brand America isn't necessarily a good analogy for what public diplomacy is all about," said Martin Kaplan of the Annenberg School of Communication at the University of Southern California. "For one thing, public diplomacy is a two-way street. It's not, 'We sell, you buy.' It's rather, 'We have to listen to each other. We have to demonstrate some mutual respect.' Unfortunately, in our country, we are notorious for not being interested in other nations."

No amount of public diplomacy spin will "make a dent in the public opinion in the Arab world, that largely opposes American policies toward Israel and Palestine," Kim Andrew Elliott, a broadcast veteran and an analyst in the Office of Research at the U.S. International Broadcasting Bureau, wrote in a *New York Times* opinion column. Rather than propaganda, Elliott said the United States should promote independent broadcasting.

In the middle of Beers's speech to the National Press Club, protesters interrupted her by chanting, "You're selling war but we're not buying!" Such U.S. protesters, however, weren't the only ones not buying Beers's message. The ad campaign was regularly mocked and derided in the Arab media. Mohamad Wahbi, a prominent Egyptian journalist, said Beers's strategy was simplistic. "They're not going to sell America to the Arab world the way you would sell any commodity," he said.

Christopher Simpson, a communications professor at American University and author of *Science of Coercion: Communication Research and Psychological Warfare, 1945–1960,* said Beers's campaign was based on two fundamental misconceptions. The first was that selling a product simply is not the same as promoting a belief. "Advertising and propaganda is well known to have an impact on short-term decisions—are they going to buy Tide detergent or Cheer, vote Gore or Bush," Simpson said. "It's also well known to have very little impact on more fundamental beliefs."

The second problem is that Beers operated on the belief that anti-American sentiment is based on a misunderstanding of America—that to know America is to love it. "The central illusion here is that the U.S. is somehow not getting its message across," Simpson said. "The large majority of people in the Middle East understand pretty well what the United States is actually saying and doing, and no amount of propaganda is really going to change that."

Others agreed that a major flaw in the strategy was that Beers and her team insisted that the problem of anti-American sentiment was really a "communication" problem. "The ads were extremely poor," said Youssef Ibrahim, a senior fellow at the Council on Foreign Relations. "It was like this was the 1930s and the government was running commercials showing happy blacks in America. It is the policy itself we have to explain."

But Beers defended the "Shared Values" campaign and suggested it was the kind of strategy that the United States needed to do more of. The advertising-oriented strategies didn't seem to take. In late 2002, the White House took over the job of selling Brand America from Beers's State Department office. Beers's "Shared Values" television campaign was abandoned in January 2003 after it met with stiff resistance from some crucial allied nations.

Beers resigned in March 2003 at age 67, after 17 months in office.

Micro Issues

1. Research by the British Council has shown that while people may love the American way of life represented by the films of Hollywood, they hate American foreign policy and diplomacy, which many perceive as self-serving, arrogant and insensitive to other cultures. How might you argue that Beers's campaign was a positive effort to address this dichotomy?
2. What other kinds of media messages might Beers have constructed to counter anti-American sentiment among Muslim populations?

Midrange Issues

1. Some have said the Muslim-friendly video ads that Beers produced suffered from an inherent contradiction: They were slickly produced TV ads designed to convince Arab audiences that America was not all slick TV. How might PR practitioners view the relationship between their message and the methods through which it is presented or delivered?
2. Can advertising campaigns such as the "Shared Values" videos be considered a "dialogue," as Beers suggested?
3. Foreign protests against America are largely "pseudo-events" staged for the media. Does that fact carry any "moral relevance" in whether the Pentagon could organize pro-American rallies? Defend your answer.

Macro Issues

1. What would be some key features of a public-diplomacy campaign that treated audiences as means rather than as ends?
2. Nancy Snow, a professor at California State University–Fullerton and author of *Propaganda Incorporated: Selling America's Culture to the World,* argues that propaganda is not necessarily evil, but *how* groups or governments engage in propaganda can raise serious ethical questions. When can propaganda serve as an effective and ethical tool?

CASE 5-D

The *New York Times* Sudan "Advertorial": Blood Money or the Marketplace of Ideas?

HEATHER HOLLOWAY
University of Texas

The conflict in western Sudan began in February of 2003 when the Justice and Equality Movement (JEM) and the Sudan Liberation Movement (SLM), two local rebel groups, attacked government installations. The government was unprepared and responded with aerial attacks in Darfur. The attacks were carried out by Janjaweed, a militia group that recruited its members from local Arab tribes. According to the Save Darfur Coalition, the Janjaweed "received government support to clear civilians from areas considered disloyal to the Sudanese government." For its part, the government denies any connection to the militia group and issued statements calling them "thieves, gangs and crooks."

The conflict quickly took on ethnic dimensions based not only on race but also on economics due to the clash between farmers (primarily non-Arabs) and herdsman (generally Arabs) for land and water. There are not any significant ethnic or religious differences between the two groups; both include Muslims, blacks and Arabs.

The tactics of the Janjaweed include indiscriminate killing and dismemberment of noncombatants, even young children and babies; systematically gang raping women; organized starvation and burning entire villages (Kristof 2005, Nov. 22). The people of Darfur live in fear of their village being attacked, their wives being raped, their children being brutally beaten to death or kidnapped and their homes and property being burned, leaving them to seek refuge in a nearby village where a similar fate may await them.

U.S. Secretary of State, Colin Powell, visited refugee camps of Darfur with the Sudanese foreign minister in the summer of 2004. He later testified before Congress that what was happening was genocide. The government of Sudan denied claims of their involvement, but Powell and his team of investigators "found that the government is clearly and directly involved in committing the genocide." Later, Congress, the Bush Administration and many others denounced it as genocide (Costello 2006).

Following Powell's visit, the conflict continued with failed attempts at compromise and a death toll that continued to rise. Save Darfur, a group organized to raise awareness of the conflict and to lobby for U.S. and U.N. intervention, claims that no one has been charged with any crime, and there remains a state of total impunity towards human rights violations. They compare Darfur to the Rwanda genocide of 1994.

According to reports by the World Food Program, the United Nations and the Coalition for International Justice, 3.5 million people are now hungry, 2.5 million have been displaced due to violence and 400,000 people have died in Darfur thus far. On April 30, 2006, Save Darfur led a rally in Washington, D.C. to raise awareness of the genocide in Darfur and to encourage the Senate to act.

As the conflict continued to escalate, militia attacks followed refugees over the border into neighboring Chad (Kristof 2006, March 7). The United States has had sanctions against Sudan since 1997. Initially the sanctions were because of Sudan's "support for international terrorism, efforts to destabilize neighboring governments and violation of human rights." More recently they are due to "allegedly encouraging genocide" (Weiss 2006).

Once the United States labeled the conflict in Darfur as genocide, the *New York Times* has been covering the conflict intensely and has also covered groups like Save Darfur. Nicholas Kristof, a columnist at the *Times,* won the 2006 Pulitzer Prize for his commentary on the Darfur conflict. The Pulitzer board states he won Note: "for his graphic, deeply reported columns that, at personal risk, focused attention on genocide in Darfur and that gave voice to the voiceless in other parts of the world."

Kristof spent a month in Sudan visiting refugee camps and destroyed villages and speaking with many who had suffered losses due to attacks by the Janjaweed. His reporting raised the public's awareness of the situation, and in later columns he urged the U.S. government and the United Nations to resolve the conflict. His proposals include sending troops and enforcing a no-fly zone from a French airbase in Chad (Kristof 2005, Nov. 22). Kristof has had the support of the *New York Times,* as evidenced by the editorials supporting his claims.

On March 20, 2006, the *New York Times* ran an eight-page "advertorial" supplement promoting the country of Sudan. The "Special Advertising Section" was written by Summit Communications, a public relations company that claims to hold an exclusive agreement with the *New York Times* to run ads for foreign governments (Salmon 2006). The advertorial looks more like a news page than an ad page, but it meets the requirements for advertorials set by the *Times* by being labeled as an "Advertising Supplement to the *New York Times*" in all caps and in an acceptable size. In addition, the insert does not use any style, layout or font of the *New York Times.* The cost of the insert was almost $1 million (Salmon 2006).

The lead story on the front page of the supplement was titled "The Peace Dividend" and promised that prosperity could lie ahead after years of conflict. The article quoted the Sudanese minister of investment saying, "The images that are being projected in the media do not present a coherent picture of Sudan in any way. Sudan is not only Darfur." The tone of the stories in the supplement was that the conflict in Darfur is minor compared to the prosperity of the rest of the country and that international media was blowing things out of proportion.

But the story reported in the editorial pages of the *New York Times* paints a different picture. According to Kristof, even getting an exact count of the number killed is impossible because of the government's attempt to cover up the atrocities.

There was an immediate reaction against the *Times* for accepting the advertorial. Activist groups claimed that the publication made the *Times* complicit in genocide. According to an article on the Pulitzer Prize Web site, Nicholas Kristof released a statement claiming that it "represents blood money" and "tarnishes a newspaper I love" (Chaffee 2006).

Catherine J. Mathis, spokeswoman for the *New York Times,* released this statement:

> The *Times* has vigorously reported on Sudan and our editorials have condemned the actions the Sudanese government has taken against its citizens. We accepted this special advertising section, however, in our strong belief that all pages of the paper's news, editorial and advertising must remain open to the free flow of ideas.

In accepting it, we do not endorse the politics, trade practices or character in its leaders. Just as we print advertisements that rebut *New York Times* editorials, news articles or critical reviews, we print ads that differ from our editorial position. We do so in the belief that it is in the best interests of our readers for our pages to be as open as possible (quoted in Salmon 2006).

Because of the sanctions against Sudan, the State Department investigated the *Times* for publishing an advertisement encouraging investment there. This investigation focused on financial transactions between Sudan, Summit Communications and the *New York Times,* not on the content of the advertorial. According to a spokesperson from the Treasury Department, since the advertisement was published but not written by the *New York Times,* it is permissible under the sanctions (Weiss 2006).

During the controversy, Allen Siegel, the standards editor at the *Times,* claimed that "news and ads occupy opposite sides of a church-state wall. Newsroom editors don't approve or disapprove advertising, just as ad sales people don't pass upon the news content." However, the *Times'* relationship with Summit is an ongoing one. On their Web site (www.summitreports.com) Summit Communications states *(italics added)*:

Summit Communications is dedicated to raising the profile of the world's most dynamic emerging markets. *Through an exclusive arrangement with the* New York Times *Advertising Department, Summit Communications has published over 112 reports since 1999, reaching the most influential decision-makers in the American political, financial, and economic communities.*

The *Times'* argument for running the ads has been questioned by many. "In the face of genocide that has been documented, the defense of 'free flow of ideas' doesn't hold water," said Cheri Hadley (2006), Chairwoman of Sudan Peace and Justice Committee of Dallas in a personal interview with the author. "I believe that this being published in the *New York Times* makes this complicit with the whole genocide campaign. I know those are strong words, but I truly believe that. They need to do something to ameliorate being bought off."

Micro Issues

1. Should the *New York Times* have accepted the ad? Does it matter if the "facts" of the ad do not match those being reported by the news department?
2. Is the *Times* "complicit" in the genocide by deciding to run the advertorial?
3. Should Summit Communications have taken Sudan as a client?

Midrange Issues

1. If the advertorial had been written from the Janjaweed perspective, praising the work of the killers in driving undesirables out of the country, should the *New York Times* have rejected that ad? If so, who decides what views are acceptable in advertorials?
2. If Summit Communications had released the video on its Web site as a video news release (VNR) with similar content to the advertorial, should television stations have run it in their newscasts? Why or why not?
3. Does your answer change if the VNR is labeled as such? If Summit pays to have it run during commercial time?

Macro Issues

1. Are the advertising pages of a newspaper a part of the "marketplace of ideas?" Should they be reflective in any way of the editorial stances of the paper?
2. Should advertorials be subjected to the same standards of truth as a newspaper's editorial copy?
3. If you were one of the "reporters" for Summit, how important would it have been for you that you agree with the policies of the government you are touting in the pages of the advertorial? Could you have done the job regardless of whether you thought government-aided genocide had occurred?

CASE 5-E

Whose Opinion Is It Anyway?

LEE WILKINS
University of Missouri

Drumming up public support for a controversial piece of legislation is standard operating procedure in Washington, D.C. Leaks, laudatory statements in Congress and gathering favorable responses from a variety of constituencies are the norm.

But when *USA Today* reported on its front page that television commentator and newspaper columnist Armstrong Williams had been paid $240,000 to promote the Bush administration's education initiative entitled the "No Child Left Behind Act," both journalists and members of Congress were outraged (Toppo 2005).

The matter was made all the more complicated because Williams is African-American and the No Child Left Behind Act specifically targeted the often-failing inner-city schools populated by ethnic minorities and demanded that their test scores be equal to those of schools containing primarily Caucasian students.

USA Today found out about the contract through a Freedom of Information Act request. That request turned up an agreement between the U.S. Department of Education and the Ketchum public relations firm to promote the Bush initiative. Part of the agreement stipulated that Williams would use his contacts with America's Black Forum, a group of African-American broadcasters, to urge others in the media to periodically address the proposed legislation. According to their Web site on tvimedia.com, America's Black Forum is "the only program in national television that provides news and opinion targeted to the fast-growing and increasingly influential ethnic market."

Williams, a former aide to U.S. Supreme Court Justice Clarence Thomas, hosts "The Right Side," a nationally syndicated television commentary show, writes op-ed pieces for a number of newspapers and runs the public relations firm Graham Williams Group. As part of this agreement, Williams had twice interviewed then-Secretary of Education Rod Paige on Graham's television show. Williams also persuaded television personality Steve Harvey to invite Paige onto his show (Toppo 2005).

Williams did not disclose the contract or its terms in any of his columns or during any of his television broadcasts. As part of the *USA Today* story, Williams was quoted, saying: "I wanted to do it because it's something I believe in" (Toppo 2005).

The day after the *USA Today* story broke, Williams' newspaper syndicate, Tribune Media Services, canceled his column. One television network dropped his television program, pending the outcome of an investigation.

In a *Washington Post* story that appeared the next day, Williams characterized the agreement as "bad judgment" on his part (Kurtz 2005). Williams said he understood "why some people think it's unethical," and in response to a question about whether he was willing to sell his opinions to the government, Williams responded, "It's fair for someone to make that assessment" (Kurtz 2005).

In addition to the Williams' agreement, the contract between Ketchum and the education department included a $700,000 payment for the public relations firm to rate journalists on how positively or negatively they reported on the No Child Left

Behind Act and to produce a VNR on the education bill that was aired as news by some television stations.

A spokesperson for the Department of Education said, "Our contract was for advertising. Our intent was to reach out to minority audiences. Armstrong went out and talked about it—we didn't have anything to do with that. Our objective was to put out basic information to audiences. . . . We certainly had no intention to do it in an underhanded way."

Micro Issues

1. Should Williams have disclosed the agreement? If so, to whom?
2. Since Williams said he believed in the law, does the agreement really constitute buying his opinion?
3. Does Williams, as a columnist and a television commentator, work under a different set of rules than news journalists?
4. Should the Ketchum firm have accepted the contract in the first place? Would you recommend changes before accepting such a contract? Why?

Midrange Issues

1. Does Williams' race make a difference? If so, in what ways?
2. Should the journalists whose work the Ketchum firm rated ask to see it? Why might the government request such an analysis?
3. Evaluate the statement by the Department of Education spokesperson. Based on the contract with Ketchum and how it played out through the use of Williams, does it seem accurate?
4. Are the television stations that ran the VNR without divulging the source ethically culpable in any way?

Macro Issues

1. Evaluate this case using the four principles outlined by Fitzpatrick earlier in this chapter.
2. Rep. George Mill, the ranking Democrat on the house education committee, called the agreement "propaganda." Evaluate this statement.

CASE 5-F

Looking for Truth Behind the Wal-Mart Blogs

PHILIP PATTERSON
Oklahoma Christian University

When you think of blogging, the image of a lone person passionately pounding out a late-night journal hoping to gain a few loyal readers comes to mind. But if you're Wal-Mart, the largest retailing chain in the world, you can afford a little professional help, and that's precisely what the corporation did on at least two blogs until Wal-Mart's public relations firm was forced to reveal the ruse.

Before the admission, rumors had been circulating about the authenticity of the blogs. In an article on www.cnnmoney.com entitled "Corporate Blogging: Wal-Mart's Fumbles," *Fortune* senior writer Marc Gunther (2006) broke the story in the mainstream press with this posting:

> A blog praising Wal-Mart called "Wal-Marting Across America," ostensibly created by a man and a woman traveling the country in an RV and staying in Wal-Mart parking lots, turned out to be underwritten by Working Families for Wal-Mart, a company-sponsored group organized by the Edelman public relations firm. Not cool.

The couple, it turns out, were Laura St. Claire, a freelance writer and an employee at the U.S. Treasury Department and Jim Thresher, a staff photographer at the *Washington Post.* And Wal-Mart, far from being the lucky beneficiary of a blog that found happy Wal-Mart employees at every stop, was shown to be behind the trip and was paying for the couple's support, including money for renting the RV, gas and fees for writing the blog (Gogoi 2006). And behind Wal-Mart was Edelman, a nationally-recognized PR firm as a part of their "Working Families for Wal-Mart" campaign.

As bloggers expressed their outrage at the ruse, Edleman CEO Richard Edelman issued an apology on his personal blog. "I want to acknowledge our error in failing to be transparent about the identity of the two bloggers from the outset. This is 100 percent our responsibility and our error, not the client" he wrote (Gogoi 2006).

But the happy RVing couple was not the only phony Wal-Mart blog. Two days after Gunther's article, cnnmoney.com exposed the practice on their Web site, in an unsigned article entitled "PR Firm Admits It's Behind PR Blogs." In that article, the following information was posted:

> A public relations firm has revealed that it is behind two blogs that previously appeared to be created by independent supporters of Wal-Mart. The blogs Working Families for Wal-Mart and subsidiary site Paid Critics are written by three employees of PR firm Edelman, for whom Wal-Mart is a paid client, according to information posted on the sites Thursday. Before Thursday, the authors of the blogs were not disclosed. But Web critics had been skeptical of claims that the blogs were grass-roots efforts, and pushed for greater transparency.

Employees of the Edelman public relations firm were eventually revealed as the source of blogs on two more sites that produced favorable stories about Wal-Mart and sought to debunk its critics. In mid-October of 2006, the following message appeared on www.forwalmart.com:

In response to comments and emails, we've added author bylines to blog posts here at forwalmart.com. The site has been updated, but readers may have to refresh the page for the new information.

By clicking on the single name byline of "Miranda," the reader would find the following information: "Miranda Grill works for Edelman. One of her clients is Working Families for Wal-Mart." The same message appeared on the www.paidcritics.com site, whose tagline is ironically, "Exposing the Paid Critics" in a posting entitled "A CHANGE TO PAIDCRITICS.COM" written by "Brian." A click on Brian's byline yielded the following information: "Brian McNeill works for Edelman. One of his clients is Working Families for Wal-Mart."

According to their Web site (www.edelman.com), the Edelman public relations firm claims 2,220 employees in 46 offices worldwide and billed $305 million in fees in fiscal year 2006. They were named "Large PR Agency of the Year" by *PR Week US* in 2006. The "welcome" page on the Edelman Web site contains the following description over the signature of Daniel J. Edelman, Founder and Chairman, and Richard Edelman, President and CEO:

> We were the first firm to apply public relations to building consumer brands. We invented the media tour, created litigation and environmental PR, were the first to use a toll-free consumer hotline and the first to employ the Web in crisis management. That's just the beginning. Today we're on a mission: to make public relations the lead discipline in the communications mix, because only public relations has the immediacy and transparency to build credibility and trust.

There was no mention of the Wal-Mart incident under "Latest Headlines" on the Edelman Web site in the week after the story broke.

Micro Issues

1. Should Edelman have acknowledged the problem on their Web site before the *Fortune* magazine reporter broke the story? Should they have responded afterwards?
2. How common do you think Wal-Mart's actions are? Is it possible that "grassroots" fan sites are actually paid for by celebrities or their publicists, for instance?
3. If Wal-Mart is right that its critics are "paid," does that justify paying a public relations firm to say good things about Wal-Mart?

Midrange Issue

1. In the "marketplace of ideas" is there any place for this type of "stealth" public relations?
2. How does this differ from "viral marketing," where companies try to generate "buzz" about products to bypass traditional advertising media to reach the public with a message, often paying agents in the process?
3. How does this differ from "product placement" in television or movies where the audience is not informed if a product manufacturer paid to be on the screen?

Macro Issues

1. Upon hearing of Thresher's involvement, the *Post*'s executive editor demanded that he pay back any money he received for the trip and remove his photographs from the blog

(Gogoi 2006). Should there be any other penalties for his actions? Does it make a difference if he is on his own time during the trip? Does it make any difference if every posting represents his true opinion?

2. Critics called for greater transparency in the blogs. Edelman claims to use "transparency to build credibility and trust." What does transparency mean in public relations? Is it different from transparency in journalism? Was Edelman transparent in its dealings on these two Web sites?

3. Barbara Ehrenreich in her book *Nickel and Dimed* writes a very different story about the plight of Wal-Mart workers. To get the story, she took a job in a Wal-Mart and attempted to live on the income they paid. Her bestselling book was highly critical of the way Wal-Mart treats its employees. Is her work, for which she received royalties, any different than the paid Wal-Mart bloggers? If so, in what way? Is Ehrenreich a journalist? Is it the role of journalism to put pressure on corporations such as Wal-Mart?

6

Privacy:
Looking for Solitude
in the Global Village

By the end of this chapter, you should be able to:

- **appreciate the difference between the right to privacy and a need for privacy.**
- **distinguish between the law and ethics of privacy.**
- **understand the concepts of discretion, right to know, need to know, want to know, and circles of intimacy.**
- **understand and apply Rawls's veil of ignorance as a tool for ethical decision making.**

WHY PRIVACY IN THE NEW MILLENNIUM?

If there is one area in media ethics that was stretched almost beyond recognition during the early years of this new century, it is privacy. The rapid pace of change has highlighted one of the most enduring understandings of philosophy: new technologies sometimes raise old questions in novel ways. Consider the case of the social-networking site Facebook.

For most college students, on most college campuses, Facebook has become what is euphemistically referred to as *the* "social networking site." In other words, it's a place to virtually meet people, talk to friends, form groups around various interests where geography—and the prying eyes of parents, teachers and others—don't matter. Better yet, it is "in." Most college students report accessing Facebook at least once a week, and many report accessing it multiple times per day.

Facebook also has rules, which is one of the reasons it is more popular than some other sites. Facebook members can build a personal profile, and then control electronic access to it in various ways and at various levels. If a member wishes to join another member's network, they must be granted permission by that Facebook member. It is a good example of control over circles of intimacy—a concept you'll learn more about in this chapter.

But in September 2006, owner Mark Zuckerberg made some changes, specifically News Feed and Mini-Feed, that automatically alerted everyone in a user's network any time any other member of that person's network updated anything—from a personal profile to a posting on someone's wall. Students with hundreds of Facebook connections were flooded with minutia. What many found even more objectionable was that messages intended for one person, or one part of an individual's network, were directed to *everyone* in a network (Stanard, 2006). And, in the ways of the Web, the reaction was vociferous and instantaneous. A sampling of postings follows:

"If you don't want this information to be out there, don't put it on Facebook. How did the news feed work any differently than the real-world gossip chain? . . . Eh, maybe this will convince people that they shouldn't put their whole lives on the Internet."

"It's not the fact that they can see it, it is the fact that it is 'broadcast' that makes it bad. I don't care that people I know find out that I break up with a girl, but I don't want it to be sent RSS style to everyone I know."

"How information is accessible is sometimes just as important as what information is accessible. . . . Stop acting as though privacy is a binary proposition: either top-secret or totally public with no differences in between."

One Facebook user even attempted to organize an in-person demonstration to protest the changes. It's important to note that Zuckerberg both apologized to Facebook users and relented on the changes to the site.

These comments, and their consequences in terms of actions, make some important points. First, privacy on the Web is still important—even though the law considers Web content quite public. Just because there's a new technology doesn't mean the questions have changed. Second, the previous individual comments above reflect some sophisticated thinking about privacy—thinking that is deeply philosophical even though the language of philosophy is never used. Much of that thinking has already been applied to the more traditional media, and the debate was as contentious then as it is now. Third, these comments remind us that privacy isn't just about sex, it's about much that we do and are as human beings.

The Facebook flap occurred on the Web, out of view of many in the mainstream media. But, when former President Bill Clinton was discovered to be having oral sex with White House intern Monica Lewinsky, the mainstream media were deeply involved. The Clinton-Lewinsky affair came to symbolize the media's apparent inability to make distinctions between news and what one scholar has characterized as "mediated voyeurism," described as "the consumption of revealing images of and information about others' apparently real and unguarded lives, often yet not always for purposes of entertainment but frequently at the expense of privacy and discourse, through the means of the mass media and the Internet" (Calvert 2000, 23). Calvert lists such diverse activities as hidden camera reports, the paparazzi phenomenon and video surveillance in businesses as well as private homes and suggests that such technology-based media content has forever changed journalism. "Our notions of news and human interest stories have shifted over time. Today, voyeurism passes as news" (Calvert 2000, 29).

The nation's capital is not the only place an overheated press can pursue a story, trampling on the rights of victims and families in the process. In 2006, the CEO of Hewlett-Packard attempted to spy on members of her governing board, including having private investigators pose as journalists and surreptitiously collect phone records—an investigative method called "pretexting." The corporate spying, of course, made national news, provoked a Congressional hearing, and resulted in the CEO's resignation. It was just one more indication that, in many ways, voyeurism has become an element of news made particularly disturbing because private investigators had been masquerading as journalists.

Yet some stories that might be considered voyeuristic can have an important purpose. In early 2000, former NBC "Today Show" host (now "CBS Evening News" anchor) Katie Couric, whose husband had died about two years earlier from colon cancer, had her own colonoscopy broadcast on national television. Several months before that, talk-show host Oprah Winfrey videotaped women having mammograms— although visual images of the women's breasts never aired due to carefully selected camera angles. The goal in both cases was a worthy one: protecting the public health by demonstrating that routine medical screening exams don't hurt and can save a life. In these instances, Couric and the women in Winfrey's report gave up some element of privacy that most Americans continue to cherish.

Not everyone is so open. After the 2000 presidential election, NBC's highly regarded political correspondent Tim Russert noted in an interview with Vice President-elect Richard Cheney that for months he had asked for specific information regarding the health of Cheney's heart only to be stonewalled with generalities. It was only after Cheney had a mild heart attack that the public got an accurate and detailed response to Russert's questions and learned that Russert had asked them in the first place.

Domestic politics are not the only place where the lines between what is private and what is public seem to have disappeared. Reality television treats us to "Survivor" and "Temptation Island" and the Internet brings us images of journalists and civilians being beheaded during the Iraq war. We watch in horror as the victims of Hurricane Katrina emerge and then flip the channel to "Real World" and "Road Rules." The travails of O. J. Simpson (accused of murder) or Mel Gibson (accused of driving under the influence whose arrest included an anti-Semitic diatribe) or Brooke Shields (whose book on her battle with post-partum depression provoked an angry, televised rejoinder from actor Tom Cruise, who was later released from his studio contract for this and other questionable public behaviors) become a sort of reality television for the all-news set. Through it all we remain confused about whether we are responding as normally curious human beings, citizens who need information or journalists doing important work in a democratic society.

THE NEED FOR PRIVACY

Much has been written on the "right to privacy," a right made problematic by the fact that the term never appears in the U.S. Constitution. Relatively little, however, has been written about the "need for privacy." Philosopher Louis W. Hodges has attempted to focus attention on the need for privacy. He says that "without some degree of privacy, civilized life would be impossible" (Hodges 1983). Both a personal and societal need for privacy exists, Hodges claims.

First, we personally need privacy to develop a sense of self. Constance T. Fischer (1980) states that people need privacy to "try out" new poses, future selves and so on, without fear of ridicule by outsiders. If we are to become the person we wish to be, a certain degree of privacy is needed to develop that person apart from observation. Religious cults that seek cognitive control over their members do so in part by depriving the members of any real degree of privacy, restricting both growth and reflection.

Second, society needs privacy as a shield against the power of the state. As the state gains more information about its citizens, it is increasingly easy to influence, manipulate or control each one.

Precisely because the state is seen as the agency of the citizens' own authority, its independent power is feared, and limitations on the power of the state, such as the Bill of Rights, were established to protect private life (Neville 1980). Throughout history, totalitarian regimes have used extensive government surveillance—the near absence of privacy—as a major component of any attempt to create a uniformly subservient citizenry, a subject that dominates Orwell's *1984.*

Therefore, while much of the debate focuses on the *right* to privacy, an equally compelling argument must be made for the *need* for privacy. Privacy is not to be viewed as a luxury or as an option or even a gift of a benevolent government. It is a necessary component of a democracy upon which many of its values, such as freedom, individual dignity and autonomy, rest.

Perhaps no issue in contemporary journalistic ethics has been as troubling as invasions of privacy. That trouble exists for at least two specific reasons. First, community and national standards are changing. What was once strictly private, for instance the mention of breast surgery in the newspaper or on television, is not only common but also is credited with saving lives. Second, privacy is both a legal concept in the domain of the courts and an ethical concept debated by philosophers. Confusion over which analysis is appropriate confounds our thinking.

The result is that journalists have been caught between what the law allows and what their consciences will permit. This confusion has led to ethical bungling on a scale that has probably undermined the entire profession's credibility and fed two stereotypical notions: first, that journalists will do anything to get a story, and second, that audiences will willingly consume anything the journalist delivers. These images not only are at odds with reality but also make getting and understanding legitimate stories even more difficult.

LEGAL AND ETHICAL DEFINITIONS

The legal notion of privacy began in 1890 with a *Harvard Law Review* article, written by lawyers Samuel Warren and Louis D. Brandeis (who eventually became a U.S. Supreme Court justice), calling for a constitutional right to privacy. Today privacy is guarded legally in four distinct ways:

1. Intrusion upon a person's seclusion or solitude, or into private affairs, such as invading one's home or personal papers to get a story.

2. Public disclosure of embarrassing private facts, such as revealing someone's notorious past when it has no bearing on that person's present status.
3. Publicity that places a person in a false light, such as enhancing a subject's biography to sell additional books.
4. Misappropriation of a person's name or likeness for personal advantage, such as using Hollywood megastar Julia Roberts' image to sell a product without her permission.

While this four-part list is straightforward, the court's interpretation of it is not, placing privacy among the least satisfactory areas of constitutional law. Not only are decisions themselves contradictory, but also some of the concepts themselves are open to question or change. What once might have been an embarrassing, private fact—for example, that an unmarried woman is pregnant—is now commonplace knowledge and, quite often cause for celebration. In recent years, one's sexual orientation has increasingly moved toward this same level of commonplace knowledge. But at the same time, information once available for the asking, such as a student's telephone number or the address of an individual based on driver's license registration, is now closed by a maze of privacy legislation enacted in the 1970s and 1980s.

To further cloud the issue, the claim to privacy is different for different categories of people. Public figures, for example, are subject to a different standard than are others, as are "limited" public figures and even "accidental" public figures thrown into the spotlight by chance. Just exactly who the courts will consider a public figure fluctuates. When the media invade privacy, the legal remedies occur after the fact. A huge monetary award can make a plaintiff rich, but it cannot return that sense of control the initial invasion takes away. For this reason alone, the law provides an unsatisfactory solution. Ethical thinking prior to broadcast or publication is preferable to a court battle.

The ethical basis for privacy is much older than the legal one and appears throughout literature. The bulk of this work asserts that privacy is something we all possess by being human. Modern philosophical interpretations make the assumption that privacy is considered a need, a way of protecting oneself against the actions of other people and institutions. Privacy carries with it the connotation of control and limited access. The individual should be allowed to control who may have certain sorts of information and, sometimes, the context within which that information is presented.

Part of what is confusing about the concept of privacy is that, as a concept, it cannot stand apart from community. Responsibility for keeping things private is shared: individuals have to learn when to withhold information, the community has to learn when to avert its eyes completely or to narrow its gaze. Legal scholar Jeffrey Rosen notes that this attention to the role of the community in avoiding the unwanted gaze stems from Talmudic law. He writes:

> Jewish law, for example, has developed a remarkable body of doctrine around the concept of *hezzek re'iyyah,* which means 'the injury caused by seeing' or 'the injury caused by being seen.' This doctrine expands the right of privacy to protect individuals not only from physical intrusions into the home but also from surveillance

by a neighbor who is outside the home, peering through a window in a common courtyard. Jewish law protects neighbors not only from unwanted observation, but also from the possibility of being observed. . . . From its earliest days, Jewish law has recognized that it is the uncertainty about whether or not we are being observed that forces us to lead more constricted lives and inhibits us from speaking and acting freely in public (Rosen 2000, 18–19).

Part of the problem with a "shoot first, edit later" philosophy for photographers and videographers at the scene of a tragedy is that the "injury caused by being seen" has already been exacerbated by the camera. The injury caused by being seen is something many of those who wrote protesting the Facebook changes understood intuitively. Like the philosophical approach developed by the Greeks, in both these instances privacy is linked to our ability to "become" human and retain some element of dignity while doing it. "Only citizens who respect one another's privacy are themselves dignified with divine respect" (Rosen 2000, 19).

THE CONTINUING CONFLICTS

Most would agree with Grcic (1986) that while privacy is a prima facie right, it sometimes can be negated by other, more compelling rights. In simpler times, the right to invade privacy belonged almost exclusively to the government. The government can demand, for example, that an individual relinquish control of a substantial amount of private information to complete federal and state income tax forms. Further, failure to provide such information makes one legally liable. For the survival of the entire political community, the government demands that its citizens provide it with certain information that is otherwise private. However, specific rules govern such disclosure. The government cannot legally give your tax return information to other interested parties. Such a check on government power theoretically allows the maintenance of some level of individual privacy.

However, the government is not the only institution today that can demand and receive private information. Banks, credit companies, doctors and attorneys all can request (and usually receive) a variety of highly private information, the bulk of it willingly disclosed. Inevitably, such disclosure is one-directional. While you are required to provide your physician with your medical history to ensure proper treatment, your physician might be surprised if you inquired about her success rate with a particular surgical procedure, and she certainly is not required to give it to you. Doctors in Massachusetts were uncomfortable and protested when the state passed a law requiring such information be made available to patients.

Computers and databases have become tools for gathering and repositories for storing private information. Huge industries have cropped up selling a single commodity: private information. When you buy a house or apply for a job, you will watch as the information industry disgorges huge amounts of legal and financial information about you with about a 40 percent chance of some error, according to industry figures. The tensions over what should or should not remain private are not resolved; they are merely accounted for and debated in today's complex society.

However, Warren and Brandeis had the press, not the government or financial institutions, in mind when they wrote their precedent-inspiring article. The pair developed their novel legal argument after a breakfast in celebration of Mr. Warren's wedding was covered by the press, an article that would be a benign social mention today if it made the press at all. Offended by this "outrage," Warren and Brandeis could not have anticipated trash television, "kiss-and-tell" books, computerized databases, or the myriad other ways the mass media disseminate private information about people who are more or less willing to disclose it. The issue is not more complex today than it was during the country's formative years, but the ways privacy is violated are substantially different, and perhaps more threatening.

DISTINGUISHING BETWEEN SECRECY AND PRIVACY

People tend to think of private information as something they would like to keep secret, but such thinking confounds these two related but separable concepts.

Secrecy can be defined as blocking information intentionally to prevent others from learning, possessing, using or revealing it (Bok 1983). Secrecy ensures that information is kept from *any* public view. Privacy, however, is concerned with determining who will obtain access to the information. Privacy does not imply that information will never reach public view, but rather that an individual has control over what information becomes public and to whom.

Secrecy often carries a negative connotation. However, we agree with Bok in asserting that secrecy itself is neither morally good nor bad. Privacy and secrecy can overlap but are not identical. "Privacy need not hide; and secrecy hides far more than what is private. A private garden need not be a secret garden, a private life is rarely a secret life" (Bok 1983, 11). Privacy can and should be balanced against other considerations; secrets are something an individual decides to keep.

The law has given us an interesting metaphor for the ethics of privacy. In *Dietemann v. Time,* jurist Alan F. Westin viewed privacy as the ability to control one's own "circles of intimacy." In the case, two reporters for the former *Life* magazine lied to Dietemann to enter his California home and later expose him as a medical quack practicing medicine without a license. While the courts saw some social utility in exposing such behavior, Dietemann, they ruled, had a reasonable expectation of privacy in his own home.

Philosopher Louis W. Hodges has used the concept of circles of intimacy to develop a working concept of privacy for journalists and other professionals. If you conceive of privacy as a series of concentric circles, as Figure 6.1 illustrates, in the innermost circle you are alone with your secrets, fantasies, hopes, reconstructed memories and the rest of the unique psychological "furniture" we bring to our lives.

The second circle you probably occupy with one other person, perhaps a sibling, a spouse, a parent, roommate, or loved one—a person who might change at various times in your development. In that circle, you share private information. In order for that relationship to work well, it needs to be reciprocal, and it should be based primarily on trust.

PUBLIC   PUBLIC

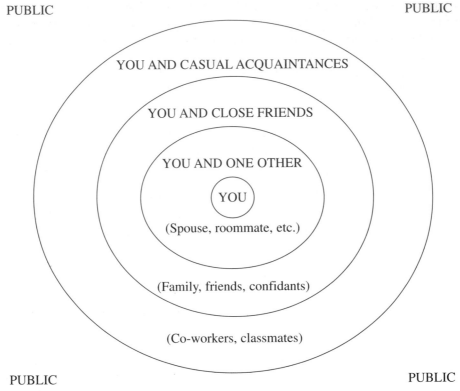

PUBLIC   PUBLIC

FIGURE 6.1. The concept of circles of intimacy

The third circle contains others to whom you are very close—probably family or friends, perhaps a lawyer or clergy member. Here, the basis of relationships is still one of trust, but some communications can be primarily one way—and you do not expect to have complete control over them. As the ripples in the pond of intimacy continue to spread, what you reveal about yourself becomes progressively more public and less intimate, and you lose progressively more control over information about you.

Using this model of expanding circles, privacy can be considered individual control over who has access to your various circles of intimacy. Invasion of privacy occurs when your control over your own circles of intimacy is wrestled from you by people or institutions. Rape victims who unwillingly see their names in print or their pictures broadcast frequently speak of the loss of control they felt during the experience as being similar to the loss of control during the rape itself.

Journalists, both as individuals and as representatives of powerful institutions, can and sometimes do invade circles of intimacy. Awareness of the concept will allow you to consider the rights of others as well as balance the needs of society in critical ways, particularly when the issue is newsworthy. Under at least some circumstances, invasion can be justified, but under other circumstances invading privacy constitutes usurping an individual's control and stripping him or her of individuality and human dignity. Part of the ethical growth of a journalist is to know when the rule applies and when the exceptions should occur.

DISCRETION: WHETHER TO REVEAL PRIVATE INFORMATION

With the distinction between privacy and secrecy in mind, the next problem confronting the ethical journalist is "discretion"—a word not usually associated with journalism. Bok (1983, 41) defines discretion as "the intuitive ability to discern what is and is not intrusive and injurious."

We all decide at times to reveal private information, and doing so wisely is a mark of moral growth. Discretion demands moral reasoning where the interests of more than one party are balanced. Once a source decides to reveal private information, a reporter's discretion remains the sole gatekeeper between that information and a public that might need the information or might merely want the information. The journalist is forced to rely on moral reasoning to decide if he is feeding the voyeur or the citizen in each of us.

What is a journalist to do with information resulting from another's indiscretion? Kantian theory would suggest that the journalist treat even the indiscreet source as the journalist herself would wish to be treated, making publication of the indiscretion less likely. Yet many journalists claim that, in practice, everything is "on-the-record" unless otherwise specified. In situations like these, a return to Ross's list of prima facie duties could be helpful. What is my duty to an often vulnerable and sometimes unwitting source? To a curious readership or viewership? To a media owner who wants (and pays for) my story? Which duties emerge as foremost to the journalist who should make such decisions more consistently?

Returning to the issue of Facebook, it seems that many 18- to 22-year-olds have yet to learn discretion in their postings. And the problem is even greater on the social networking site MySpace which draws an even younger crowd. Indiscreet postings have led to numerous problems including sexualy predatory behavior on the parts of some adults who read the posts.

WHEN THE RIGHT TO KNOW IS NOT ENOUGH

Just as the distinction between secrecy and privacy is easily confused, there is also a misconception on the part of both journalists and the public among the concepts of "right to know," "need to know" and "want to know." However, the three concepts are distinct and not interchangeable.

Right to know is a legal term often associated with open-meeting statutes and based on the philosophy that government runs more honestly in the open. Right to know is a way to counterbalance government power. In recent years both federal and state governments have passed right-to-know laws. These laws are a legal, not ethical, construct. Journalists have a legal right to the same information that other members of the public may obtain—for example, the transportation of hazardous materials through their communities.

Ethical problems can emerge from right-to-know information. Is it ethical to print everything a journalist has a legal right to know? For instance, police reports routinely carry the names of suspects, victims and witnesses to a variety of crimes. Does the journalist publish such information, even though it has been legally obtained? If a reporter has information that might harm national security if printed, should it be withheld? Clearly, even right to know carries with it ethical considerations.

Need to know originates in the realm of philosophy. Media ethicists such as Deni Elliott (1986) have argued that one of the functions of the mass media is to provide information to citizens that will allow them to go about their daily lives in society, regardless of political outlook. Citizens may have a legal right to much of this information, but perhaps not all of it. In this view, providing information the public needs to know includes within it the concept of journalistic tenacity and responsibility.

Too often, when journalists assert that the public has the "right to know" a fact, what they mean is that citizens "need" such information to get along in their daily lives. For example, the average citizen cannot examine bank records. That duty is left to auditors and the government. But with the recent turmoil in the financial sector, journalists could reasonably argue that at least some information about the health of financial institutions and the character of those who run them is needed by the public to make informed economic decisions. Need to know often requires a tenacious journalist, as the law is not a tool to access information for such stories.

Need to know is the most ethically compelling argument of the three. Need to know demands that an ethical case be constructed for making known information that others wish to keep private. Need to know also demands that journalists present the information in a manner that will make its importance evident to a sometimes lazy citizenry.

When an argument is framed in terms of right to know, it reduces the journalist to ethical legalism: I will do precisely what the law allows. When an argument is framed in terms of need to know, however, it means that counterbalancing forces have been weighed and that bringing the information to light is still the most ethical act. Asserting your right to know may be the best way to get the facts regarding a crime, but only by weighing the public's need to know will you be satisfied with the decisions you make in airing the story.

Finally, there is the issue of want to know, which speaks to the curiosity in all of us. Want to know is the least ethically compelling rationale for acquiring information and disseminating it. We all want to know a lot of things—what our neighbors do in the evening hours, how much money other people earn and who in Hollywood is sleeping with whom. While we may want that information, however, we don't really need it and most certainly have no right to it. It serves the function of gossip, providing us with small talk or a smile.

By nature of their occupation, journalists often become repositories for much "want to know" information. A number of media outlets have been founded on the public's desire to know about celebrities, criminals and even common folk. More than half a century ago, *Police Gazette* titillated its readers with information they wanted to know that no other media outlet provided, and today "want to know" magazines are the only growing area in the entire industry.

Consider the wonderful world of YouTube, where anything you "want to know" is probably available. Have a blooper at your wedding? There's an entire category for that. Getting irritated at the end of a bad day? You just might become as famous as Chan Yuet-tung, known to four million (and counting) viewers on YouTube as "Bus Uncle" (Boulware 2006).

The Bus Uncle phenomenon started when Elvis Ho Yui Hei, a 23-year-old rider on a Hong Kong motor bus, tapped Yuet-tung on the shoulder and asked him to please speak more softly on his cell phone, addressing him with the culturally-respectful term of "Uncle." The request prompted a six-minute, sometimes profane and always loud verbal harangue by the 51-year-old Yuet-tung while Hei sat mostly silent. Across the aisle, however, a student held up his camera phone to capture the moment. After he uploaded the video to a Hong Kong Internet forum, it quickly made its way to YouTube—the 13th most visited site on the Web—where millions saw the meltdown that only a few had witnessed on the bus. In an article about YouTube entitled "Everybody's Watching," author Jack Boulware (2006, 100) stated:

> We've all been privy to a moment like this at one time or another—a rare window of real life that you might see and tell your friends afterward; another little anecdote from the daily pageant of human beings trying to share space on the planet. . . . What began as a simple, weird altercation on a Hong Kong bus has turned into a worldwide phenomenon. And all because of a small company in an office above a pizza parlor in San Mateo, California.

"Bus Uncle" was eventually subtitled in English and Chinese (from Cantonese) and spawned everything from T-shirts ("I have pressure. You have pressure. Why did you provoke me?" a repeated phrase from the video) to a world wide search by journalists to find the man (they eventually did). Many even used the video to make social statements about the pressures of living in a densely populated area such as Hong Kong.

In the world of YouTube and its competitors, everyone can get the 15 minutes of fame predicted by pop artist Andy Warhol whether you want it or not. One person who did is comedian Judson Laipply whose six-minute video tape of a live performance of his "Evolution of Dance" drew more than 30 million viewers in the first six months it was posted in 2006. But for every Judson Laipply there is a Chan Yuet-tung and YouTube, even with its editors screening content, cannot or will not always differentiate between a lust for publicity and an invasion of privacy.

Today, providing "want to know" information is an entire industry. In the fall of 2006, Google purchased YouTube for $1.6 billion. Yesterday's *Police Gazette* is today's *America's Most Wanted,* or any other number of reality based television shows, some of them focusing on the work of police, but all designed to garner ratings and profits. Reality television (and its Internet permutations) provides evidence that U.S. culture itself is shifting the concept of privacy more toward "want to know." That shift raises an important professional issue: when "want to know" becomes enmeshed in the profit motive, what is the long-term result for journalism?

JOHN RAWLS AND THE VEIL OF IGNORANCE

Preserving human dignity in times of crisis is a difficult task. Political philosopher John Rawls, considered this century's most articulate proponent of the social contract theory of government, has provided a helpful exercise to help make decisions about particularly thorny privacy issues (Rawls 1971).

Rawls's theory of "distributive justice" is designed to take the best from utilitarian theory while avoiding some of its more fundamental problems. It begins with the premise that justice should be equated with fairness. In order to achieve "justice as fairness," Rawls suggests an exercise he calls the "veil of ignorance." In the exercise, before any member of a community can make an ethical decision affecting others, he or she must consider the options behind a veil of ignorance.

Behind the veil, everyone starts out in an "original position" as equals who do not know whether they will be powerful or powerless when they emerge into the community from behind the veil. Rawls suggests that rational people would be willing to make and to follow those decisions when individual distinctions such as gender or socioeconomic status are laid aside.

For example, if the issue is whether to photograph or interview survivors at the scene of an airline crash, you could gather many people with diverse views behind the veil. Among them could be a reporter, a photographer, a survivor, a victim's family, an average reader or viewer, the management or owner of the media outlet, the owner of the airline, paramedics at the scene, the flying public and others. Behind the veil, in the original position, none of the participants would know what their status would be when they emerged. Their arguments would then be free of bias that comes from points of view. The participants would argue the pros and cons of the public's need to know and the victim's right to privacy without knowing whether they would emerge as a reporter, a reader, or a victim.

Rawls's veil of ignorance provides journalists with an important tool to use when they begin an ethical dialogue with the stakeholders in your decision much like the one Bok recommends (see Chapter I). Behind the veil of ignorance it is possible to walk in the shoes of the stakeholders, to air various views and then to make a reasoned choice.

When people begin their deliberations behind such a veil, Rawls suggests that two values emerge: we will act so that *individual liberty is maximized; however, weaker parties will be protected.* We will look at each concept separately.

First, Rawls suggests the liberty of all will be valued equally. Behind the veil, freedom of the press (a liberty journalists cherish) becomes equal to freedom from unwarranted intrusion into private life (a liberty readers cherish). How you retain both becomes a debate to be argued from all points of view without the bias of status since each participant is in the original position, ignorant of personal position or status.

Second, under the framework the weaker party is usually protected. Few participants would make an ethical decision that might not be in the interest of the weaker party unless the evidence was overwhelming that it would better the lot of the entire group. Behind the veil participants would be forced to weigh the actual and potential harm that journalists, as powerful people representing powerful institutions, could inflict on people who are less powerful.

It is important to note that consensus is not required, and maybe even not expected, behind the veil. The veil of ignorance is designed to facilitate ethical discussions, not stymie them from lack of unanimity. Using the veil of ignorance, the ethical decision maker arrives at what Rawls calls "reflective equilibrium." In the state of reflective equilibrium some inequalities are allowed. However, they will be the inequalities that contribute in some significant way to the betterment of most individuals in the social situation. For instance, the consensus of the group behind the veil might be to run a photo of a victim of tragedy if it might prevent a similar tragedy from occurring.

Reflective equilibrium summons what Rawls calls our "considered moral judgment." Decisions would be based on the principles we would be most unwilling to give up because we believe doing so would result in a grave wrongdoing for all. Balancing the liberties of various stakeholders, while protecting the weaker party, allows for a thorough exploration of all of the issues involved, which utilitarianism sometimes fails to address.

Using the concepts of right to know, need to know, discretion and circles of intimacy, along with Rawls's concept of distributive justice, will provide you with the ethical tools to begin the work of balancing conflicting claims of privacy. These tools will enable you to better justify your choices, to make decisions systematically and to understand what went wrong when mistakes occur.

Selected Readings

ALDERMAN, ELLEN, and CAROLINE KENNEDY. 1995. *The right to privacy.* New York: Alfred A. Knopf, Inc.

BOK, SISSELA. 1983. *Secrets: On the ethics of concealment and revelation.* New York: Vintage.

GRCIC, JOSEPH M. 1986. "The right to privacy: Behavior as property." *Journal of Values Inquiry* 20, 137–44.

HIXSON, RICHARD F. 1987. *Privacy in a public society.* New York: Oxford University Press.

HODGES, LOUIS W. 1983. "The journalist and privacy." *Social Responsibility: Journalism, Law, Medicine* 9, 5–19.

ORWELL, GEORGE. 1949. *1984.* San Diego: Harcourt, Brace, Jovanovich.

RAWLS, JOHN. 1971. *A theory of justice.* Cambridge, MA: Harvard University Press.

ROSEN, JEFFREY. 2000. *The unwanted gaze: The destruction of privacy in America.* New York: Random House.

SCHOEMAN, FERDINAND D., ed. 1984. *Philosophical dimensions of privacy: An anthology.* New York: Cambridge University Press.

Cases on the Web

"Naming names: Privacy and the public's right to know" by John B. Webster

"Public grief and the right to be left alone" by Philip Patterson

"A reporter's question: Propriety and punishment" by Stanley Cunningham

"Computers and the news: A complicated challenge" by Karon Reinboth Speckman

"Honor to die for: *Newsweek* and the Admiral Boorda case" by Philip Patterson

"Culture, law and privacy: Should ethics change in a cultural context" by Lee Wilkins

"Arthur Ashe and the right to privacy" by Carol Oukrop

CHAPTER 6 CASES

CASE 6-A

Funeral Photos of Fallen Soldiers: Public Interest or Public Outrage?

PENNY COCKERELL
Daily Oklahoman

PHILIP PATTERSON
Oklahoma Christian University

On May 11, 2004, an improvised explosive device struck the vehicle in which Army Spc. Kyle Adam Brinlee, 21, was riding in Iraq. He was killed in the explosion, the first combat-related death of an Oklahoma National Guard member since the Korean War. On May 19, more than 1,000 people gathered in the Pryor (OK) High School Auditorium for his funeral. Guests included the governor of Oklahoma, who spoke at the ceremony. Members of the media were allowed to attend but confined to a sectioned-off area. Most of the media were reporters from Oklahoma City and Tulsa media outlets.

In attendance also was photographer Peter Turnley who was shooting a photo essay for *Harper's Magazine*. It was to be the first of four "major eight-page photo essays" of Turnley's work that *Harper's Magazine* would showcase in the coming year (2004), according to a press release on the National Press Photographers Web site (**www.npp.org).** Turnley was a well-known photographer whose work had been on the cover of *Newsweek* more than 40 times, according to Turnley's own Web site (**www.peterturnley.com).** He also had had photos appear in such publications as *Life, National Geographic, Le Monde* and *The London Sunday Times,* among others. He also had covered wars in such locations as Rwanda, South Africa, Chechnya, Haiti, Afghanistan and Iraq.

In August 2004, three photos from Brinlee's funeral appeared in *Harper's* in a photo essay entitled "The Bereaved: Mourning the Dead in America and Iraq." The essay focused on both American and Iraqi funerals with several pictures of grieving families, a photo of doctors unable to save a 10-year-old Iraqi boy and a stark scene of Iraqis passing by a corpse lying on the street in Baghdad. In an interview given before the essay was published (Winslow 2004), Turnley said, "This first essay speaks in images about a very important theme touching our world today in a way that I don't think has been seen much before elsewhere."

One of the photos shows Brinlee in an open casket at the rear of the auditorium with several mourners still seated in the background. As of the spring of 2007, this photo does not appear on a Web site of all the Turnley photo essays for *Harper's Magazine*. It was not available for printing in this book, but can be found on page 47 of the August 2004 edition of the magazine.

Brinlee's family filed suit against Turnley and the magazine claiming a variety of torts including intentional infliction of emotional distress, invasion of privacy and unjustly profiting from the photos. In their filing, the family claims that despite the large crowds in a public school, the funeral was a "private religious ceremony." They added that the photos went "beyond all bounds of decency."

The family claimed that Turnley had been told by the funeral director to abstain from photographing the body of the soldier. In a response to the court, Turnley denied he had received the instructions, and claimed the body was placed near the media section for access. In a later interview with CNN, Turnley claimed: "It seems to me that the responsibility of a journalist today is to tell as much as possible about the true realities of what is taking place in the world. My desire is to simply try to dignify the reality of what people experience in war by showing the public what does happen there."

"The casket was open for friends and family—not to gawk at and take pictures and publish them. Not for economic gain," the lawyer for the family argued in an interview with the Associated Press.

The family sought $75,000 in actual damages on complaints including publication of private facts, appropriation of Brinlee's photo for commercial purposes and intrusion. In December 2005 a federal judge ruled that the family privacy was not invaded by the photos. "[P]laintiffs appear to have put the death of their loved one in the public eye intentionally to draw attention to his death and burial," Judge Frank Seay ruled in granting summary judgment to the media defendants. Elsewhere in the ruling, Seay pointed out that the plaintiffs lost their right to privacy during the funeral by choosing to publicize the event.

Harper's Magazine publisher John R. MacArthur echoed the ruling of the judge. "For me, from the beginning, it was a First Amendment issue and it was also a matter of our integrity. I have not met anyone yet who thought that photograph was disrespectful in any way."

Micro Issues

1. Can a funeral that is held in a public place be considered a private event?
2. Does it make a difference that Turnley and other media were given permission to attend the funeral?
3. Does it make a difference that the photos taken were of images in plain view of those attending the funeral?

Midrange Issues

1. Is newsworthiness a legal defense to the claim of invasion of privacy? Is it an ethical defense?
2. Does the fact that the family allowed media coverage of the funeral prevent them from suing for the distress that the Turnley photos allegedly caused? If the family had not allowed media coverage of the funeral, would your opinion of Turnley's photos be different?
3. In what way, if any, would video of the funeral differ from the still photographs of Turnley?
4. Are open-casket photos of soldiers a reality that journalists should be covering as Turnley contends or "beyond all bounds of decency" as the family contends? Can the two sides be reconciled?

Macro Issues

1. Is this a First Amendment issue as the judge and the media maintain? When other rights, such as the right to privacy, come into conflict with the First Amendment, how is the conflict best resolved?
2. What is the role of the media in covering conflicts such as the war in Iraq? Do wounded soldiers or those attending them have any privacy rights that trump the public's right to know?

CASE 6-B

A Person of Interest

CARA DeMICHELE
University of Missouri

Scarcely a week after America was attacked on Sept. 11, 2001, terrorism took a different twist—letters tainted with deadly anthrax. The first such letters were postmarked from Trenton, New Jersey, on Sept. 19, 2001, and sent to the *New York Post* and "NBC Nightly News" anchor Tom Brokaw. A New Jersey letter carrier began to show symptoms of an unusual illness on September 27, but it wouldn't be identified as anthrax exposure until after the death of Bob Stevens, a photo editor at American Media, Inc., in Boca Raton, Florida. Stevens died of inhalation anthrax. By the end of November, five people would die from the disease, and 17 more would be infected, while nearly 30,000 others would be given antibiotics. Congress shut down for two days after contaminated letters were mailed to Senators Tom Daschle and Patrick Leahy.

Multiple agencies tried to trace the infection, and by October 2001 it became clear that the anthrax had originated in the United States, from a strain grown at Iowa State University in Ames. Tests also showed not only that some of the anthrax was very refined but also that some had been "weaponized," making it more likely to be inhaled. There were at least 200 people in the United States who were thought to have the expertise to be capable of such a crime, but only 30 to 40 of them had access to the Ames anthrax strain.

Careful not to label anyone a "suspect" prematurely, the FBI spent months repeatedly interviewing and investigating 20 to 30 "persons of interest" who had worked or did work for federal laboratories on contract. Media outlets worldwide followed the investigation. Part of that reporting process demanded that journalists keep an eye on discussion boards and statements coming from the Federation of American Scientists (FAS) on the Web. Dr. Barbara Hatch Rosenberg, a molecular biologist at the University of New York at Purchase and chairwoman of a biological weapons panel at FAS, is familiar with the work of scientists in the close-knit biological weapons community and had been acting as advisor to the FBI.

On Feb. 19, 2002, Rosenberg made a statement at Princeton University claiming that the FBI had identified and twice questioned the man responsible for the anthrax attacks but was "dragging its feet" because the man was a former government scientist. In her comments, which also had been the subject of discussion at the FAS Web site for months, Rosenberg stated that many scientists in the field knew of the suspect who may have formerly worked at the U.S. Army Medical Research Institute of Infectious Diseases at Fort Derick, Maryland, and was currently working as a contractor in the Washington, D.C., area. Her comments were first reported in the *Trenton Times* newspaper and then were slowly picked up by other U.S. media outlets.

The news coverage died down in the ensuing month until early June, when news organizations were tipped that the FBI would be searching the Maryland apartment and Florida storage locker of a bioweapons expert on June 25, 2001. Dr. Steven J. Hatfill, a former Fort Derick scientist, was first interviewed by the FBI in December 2001. Like some of the other 20 to 30 scientists who were deemed "persons of interest," Hatfill consented to the searches. At that time, the agency had searched the homes and offices of 25 other scientists with little to no media coverage. Just like the other searches, the FBI found nothing in the Hatfill searches but chose to keep him as a "person of interest." And, unlike the other searches, the Hatfill investigation received extensive and ongoing media coverage.

It is likely that some news organizations had been aware that Hatfill was a possible target since December 2001 because his name and gossip about him had appeared on the FAS Web site. According to the articles and transcripts that covered the Hatfill case, there was plenty about his past that made him a likely suspect. ABC News, among others, reported that the FBI was interested in Hatfill partly because in the late 1970s Hatfill attended medical school in Zimbabwe near a Greendale elementary school. "Greendale School" appeared as the phony return address on one of the tainted letters sent to the Senate. In the early 1990s, Hatfill worked as a researcher for the National Institutes of Health (NIH). During this time he was widely quoted in newspaper articles as a bioterrorism expert and often gave lectures on the dangers of biowarfare.

After leaving the NIH, Hatfill had worked in the virology division of the Army's biodefense laboratory at Fort Derick from 1997 to September 1999. A Fort Derick spokesman told the Associated Press that the virology division studies how to protect military personnel from biological weapons. The spokesman stated that while Hatfill probably had access to labs that contained the Ames anthrax strain, it wasn't part of his primary duties. In 1999, however, Hatfill commissioned a report that describes placing 2.5 grams of a simulated form of anthrax into a business envelope, which has only fueled speculation.

On March 4, 2002, Hatfill was fired from his job at Science Applications International Corporation, a Pentagon and CIA contractor that helps the government with biological defenses. Hatfill told the *Baltimore Sun* that he had been fired because journalists were constantly pursuing him. Most recently, Hatfill lost his research job at Louisiana State University as a result of the investigation.

On Aug. 1, 2002, the FBI performed a second search of Hatfill's apartment and again found nothing. By the time of Hatfill's Aug. 11 press conference to again deny any involvement with the anthrax attacks, the FBI had searched his home twice, his car, his storage facility in Florida and his girlfriend's apartment with no success. Despite not being able to place Hatfill in New Jersey when the letters were sent, the FBI decided not to change Hatfill's "person of interest" status. Now years later, out of about 20 to 30 "persons of interest" investigated by the FBI, Hatfill's name was the only one to have been released publicly. He was never formally charged with any crime or officially named a "suspect."

Micro Issues

1. When, if ever, did Hatfill become news? When, if ever, did the case cease to be newsworthy?
2. When the original allegations surfaced, what sort of questions, if any, should journalists have asked Dr. Rosenberg, who made the original allegations?

3. When should Hatfill have been contacted to respond to the suspicions? How should his responses have been reported?
4. Would legal action on Hatfill's behalf be a better remedy than an ethical one? Why or why not?

Midrange Issues

1. Journalists covering this beat almost certainly knew about Hatfill but did not report what was being said about him until Dr. Rosenberg's comments were made in public. Evaluate this news judgment.
2. Should journalists have attempted to obtain the names of other "persons of interest"? Should they have published those names?
3. Are journalists responsible for Hatfill losing his job?
4. Do you think the FBI used the news media to try to pressure Hatfill? If you do, how should the journalists have responded?

Macro Issues

1. When, if ever, did the FBI's failure to solve the anthrax case become news?
2. How do you think the fact that journalists themselves were the targets of some of the anthrax letters figures into the media accounts of the investigation?
3. Using both utilitarian theory and Kant's categorical imperative, develop a newsroom policy that provides guidelines for covering "persons of interest."

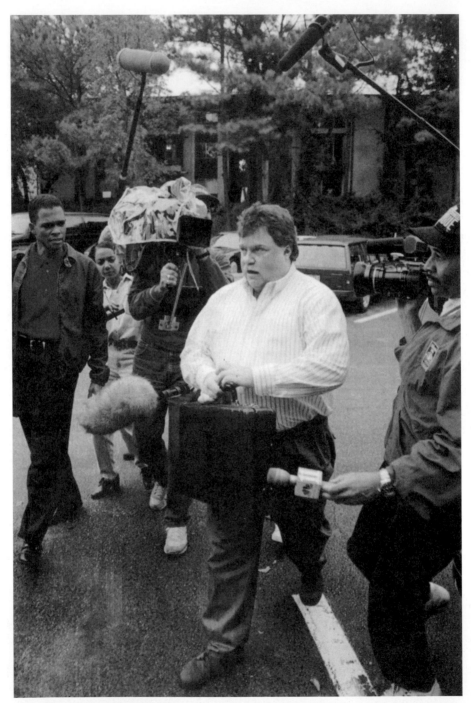

AP/WIDE WORLD PHOTOS. Used with permission.

CASE 6-C

Old Story/Fresh Wounds: Media Mistreatment of Richard Jewell 10 Years Out

GREG LISBY
Georgia State University

Author's note: *The summer of 2006 marked the 10th anniversary of the story below. At that time, Richard Jewell, the subject of this case, granted an exclusive interview to the Associated Press. His comments are at the end of this case. Now 43, Jewell works as a sheriff's deputy in a rural Georgia county and occasionally talks with journalism classes about his experience with the media.*

On July 27, 1996, at around 12:45 a.m., Richard Jewell, a security guard employed to protect AT&T's interests and property in Atlanta's Centennial Olympic Park during the Summer Olympic Games, showed an agent with the Georgia Bureau of Investigation an unattended green knapsack lying beneath a bench outside a sound and light tower that was being used for a performance at the AT&T Global Olympic Village stage. Federal agents called to the scene determined that the knapsack contained a bomb, and Jewell and other law enforcement officers quietly began evacuating the area.

At 12:58 a.m., a bomb threat was called in to law enforcement officials from a pay phone three blocks from the scene. The tower and most of the immediate area surrounding the bomb had been cleared by the time it exploded at approximately 1:20 a.m., killing one visitor, leading to a fatal heart attack for a foreign journalist on the scene and injuring 111 others.

For the next two days, the 33-year-old Jewell was hailed as a hero. He was interviewed by several major newspapers and television networks, including NBC's "Today" show, about his role in spotting the knapsack, alerting authorities, evacuating the area and helping the injured.

On Tuesday, July 30, however, FBI agents interviewed Jewell about the bombing while telling him he was participating in a training film on how to investigate suspicious packages. When agents asked Jewell to "pretend" to waive his right to an attorney, he called his lawyer and ended the meeting.

That same day, the *Atlanta Journal-Constitution* learned of police suspicions and revamped the front page of its special afternoon Olympics "Extra" supplement to spotlight Richard Jewell as "the focus of the federal investigation." Although the story was not attributed to any source, the paper has since said that three of its employees independently confirmed the investigation. The newspaper was distributed around 4:30 that afternoon, and a CNN anchor read the story verbatim on the air shortly afterward.

That night each of the three major networks' newscasts picked up the story, and the next day virtually every one of the country's major newspapers gave the story front-page billing. An exception was the *New York Times,* which ran a piece inside its "B" section, focusing more on the media than on Richard Jewell. Many news organizations later cited not wanting to "appear foolish" by not running a story or the suspect's name when so many other organizations were. Many also were careful to point out that Jewell had not been charged, or even officially named as a suspect. Investigators had been discovered staking out Jewell's apartment, and by late afternoon, the media, led by CNN and local Atlanta television stations, joined them.

By midday Wednesday, an estimated 200 national and international journalists were on the scene as federal investigators, including agents from the FBI and the Bureau of Alcohol, Tobacco and Firearms, searched the apartment Jewell shared with his mother, and took away boxes of belongings and Jewell's pickup truck. In one of the few statements he made to the media at the time, Jewell "categorically" denied being the Centennial Olympic Park bomber in response to a reporter's question, an exchange that also was shown on CNN and NBC.

NBC also reported on July 31 that agents that day had searched the shed near a cabin Jewell had rented in northeast Georgia before he had moved to Atlanta in May. ABC and CBS, however, reported that the FBI's suspicions of Jewell might be diminishing, with ABC citing the lack of evidence—of fingerprints at the phone from which the 911 call originated, of a voice match and of the short time span between the 911 call and the explosion.

On Thursday, Aug. 1, the front page of the *Atlanta Journal-Constitution* detailed the search in an article that included the name and location of Richard Jewell's apartment complex. The apartment number, its address and a map detailing its location were included in an inside story. According to the *Journal-Constitution,* Jewell became a suspect after the president of Piedmont College, a small campus in north Georgia, contacted authorities after seeing Jewell interviewed on television. He said that Jewell, who had once worked as a security guard for the college, had been "overzealous" in the pursuit of his duties there, harassing students and asking to work undercover.

Prior to his job at the college, Jewell had been a deputy for the Habersham County Sheriff's Department until he wrecked his patrol car, was demoted to jailer and subsequently resigned. His 1990 arrest for impersonating a police officer in DeKalb County in metropolitan Atlanta also was widely reported. Media organizations stated that the FBI was looking at whether Jewell fit the "profile" of a loner who might have planted the bomb in order to draw attention to his heroism; indeed, some said he had sought out interviews after the bombing. (It was later revealed that an AT&T spokesperson, not Jewell, had solicited interviews on his behalf.)

On Friday, Aug. 2, two of the bombing victims filed suit against Richard Jewell. They alleged that he failed to clear the area around the bomb before it exploded.

On Aug. 3, the FBI returned to Jewell's apartment with a subpoena for hair samples and fingerprints. Jewell and his lawyer, G. Watson Bryant Jr., refused to allow more voice samples or a polygraph test. About two weeks later, Jewell passed a lie detector test administered by an expert his legal team hired because they "didn't trust" the FBI to conduct the exam. In an article detailing the results, the *Atlanta Journal-Constitution* quoted several people extolling the expert's integrity, but the next day reported that the expert had also "cleared" two other men subsequently convicted as felons. Richard Jewell left his apartment for the first time in five days on Sunday, Aug. 4, when Bryant spirited him past law enforcement officers and the media still keeping vigil in the parking lot. He met with criminal lawyer Jack Martin, who with Bryant on Monday tried without success to unseal the affidavits filed by the FBI to obtain its search warrants.

During the next week the *Journal-Constitution* reported on Bryant's assertion that a piece of bomb shrapnel recovered by the FBI from the apartment was a "souvenir" given to Jewell by other guards at the park, and on Martin's demonstration, by walking the route involved with a reporter, that Jewell didn't have the time to make the 911 call.

The role and behavior of the media during the investigation were examined on ABC's "Viewpoint" on Aug. 22. Discussing "The Bizarre Case of Richard Jewell" were Martin and Bryant, along with representatives from CNN, ABC, CBS, NBC and NBC's Atlanta affiliate. The FBI, the Georgia Bureau of Investigation and the *Journal-Constitution* declined to attend.

Four days later, at a news conference called by Jewell's lawyers, Richard Jewell's mother made an emotional appeal to President Bill Clinton, asking him to direct the Justice Department and the FBI to state whether or not they intended to charge her son. She also asked the media to leave them alone, stating that their life was a "nightmare." The White House did not comment, but a few days later Attorney General Janet Reno declined to exonerate Jewell, saying that she understood the Jewells' feelings but that the investigation had to be pursued. The *Journal-Constitution* commented that the exchange was part of a public relations campaign mounted by Jewell's lawyers—by then four in number—to get the FBI and the Justice Department to clear and apologize to their client.

A federal magistrate ruled on Sept. 14 that the lawyers would be permitted to see portions of the FBI affidavits submitted to justify the search warrants. On Sept. 22, Richard Jewell gave his first public interview since coming under investigation, appearing on CBS's "60 Minutes." The discussion with correspondent Mike Wallace focused on whom he would sue if he were not charged.

By the end of September, the FBI agreed to "less obtrusive" surveillance of the Jewell apartment, and on Saturday, Oct. 5, returned most of the property it had seized from the apartment and the north Georgia sites, including Mrs. Jewell's collection of Tupperware. The following day, in lieu of taking an FBI polygraph, Jewell submitted to a six-hour interview in what the *New York Times* called a deal approved by the Justice Department in which Jewell would receive within six weeks of the interview a letter clearing him if no damaging information was revealed during the questioning. Attorney Lin Wood later told the *Journal-Constitution* there was no guarantee of such a letter.

In a court hearing on Oct. 8, U.S. District Judge J. Owen Forrester rebuked the media for "the worst example of media coverage I've ever seen since watching 'La Dolce Vita'" (Federico Fellini's 1960 film depicting journalists as vultures). Forrester cited published reports of material in the sealed affidavits for search warrants as evidence of a probable leak by law enforcement officials and was assured by U.S. Attorney Kent Alexander that a Justice Department and FBI investigation into the leaks was under way.

Fourteen guns were returned to Richard Jewell that day. Two days later, the *Journal-Constitution* published a "letter to the editor" from Alexander that defended the FBI's conduct in the investigation.

On Saturday, Oct. 12, the *Journal-Constitution* reported "little progress" in the bombing investigation "as the FBI turns its attention away from Richard Jewell." The next day, it reprinted an *American Journalism Review* article critical of the media coverage the Jewell story had received.

Less than two weeks later, on October 24, Judge Forrester ordered public disclosure of the affidavits in response to a motion filed by the *Journal-Constitution* and the Atlanta ABC affiliate, WSB-TV, saying he believed Jewell was no longer the focus of the investigation. Although the affidavits had already been released to Jewell's legal team, and the disclosure of such documents during a criminal investigation was unusual, Forrester called the situation "unique."

On Saturday, Oct. 26, Alexander issued a letter to Richard Jewell's lawyers notifying them that Jewell was no longer considered by the Justice Department to be a target of the investigation. The letter expressed regret that "the Jewells have endured highly unusual and intense publicity that was neither designed nor desired by the FBI." The absolution received front-page treatment in the *Journal-Constitution* and the *New York Times* the next day.

Richard Jewell held a news conference on Monday, Oct. 28, which was carried live by CNN and all three network affiliates in Atlanta. Introduced by his lawyer as the "114th victim" of the Olympic bombing, Jewell characterized press coverage of him as "all lies," said he had never asked for media attention before that day, and declared the day the start of "the other part of my nightmare—trying to restore my reputation and good name."

Postscript from the 10th anniversary interview with the Associated Press (Weber 2006)

On his brief stint as a hero:

"The heroes are soon forgotten. The villains last a lifetime. I dare say more people know I was called a suspect than know I was the one who found the package and know I was cleared."

On the effect of the investigation on his mother:

"For that two days, my mother had a great deal of pride in me—that I had done something good and that she was my mother, and that was taken away from her. She'll never get that back, and there's no way I can give that back to her."

On his life now:

"I can tell you for sure I'm a different person. I'm paranoid. I'm cynical. I'm not rich by any means monetarily. I'm rich because of my family."

Micro Issues

1. In the days following Jewell's press conference, media organizations defended the manner in which they had reported the story, saying they were following "common procedures."

Identify the "common procedures" of reporting a news story such as the one described here. Discuss the ethics of each procedure.

2. Richard Jewell's attorneys indicated that he was planning to sue several news organizations, including the *Journal-Constitution,* NBC News, and NBC anchorman Tom Brokaw. However, many people don't sue to win; instead they win by suing. What are the ethical issues involved in Richard Jewell's attempt to restore his reputation by threatening a lawsuit for libel, when—as a public figure—he would have an extremely difficult time establishing the necessary legal standard of fault required to collect monetary damages?

Midrange Issues

1. The results of an ABC News poll conducted at the time of Jewell's exoneration revealed that 69 percent of Americans thought Jewell had been unfairly treated by the media; 82 percent said it was not acceptable for the media to identify a suspect before he or she was charged. Under what circumstances, if any, is it ethically permissible for the media to identify a suspect before he or she is charged with a criminal offense?
2. Justify your answer to the previous question using ethical reasoning and principles.
3. In late 1996, NBC agreed to pay Jewell more than $500,000 to avert a lawsuit over comments made by Tom Brokaw. In your opinion will the threat of lawsuits "chill" the media from reporting on suspects in the future?

Macro Issues

1. Deadline pressure, the competition for news and "pack journalism"—the individual assignments of a number of reporters to follow a single person or issue for weeks or months at a time "like a pack of hounds sicked on a fox" (Crouse 1974, 7)—all contributed to the media's coverage of Richard Jewell's heroics at the Olympics. How might deadline pressure have been handled differently yet within an ethical framework? How might the journalists have competed for news differently in this situation?
2. How is the journalistic standard of objectivity twisted by "pack journalism"?
3. How did the concept of authority as an accepted source of information affect the media's attitude toward Richard Jewell? Under what circumstances, if any, is it ethically permissible for the media to allow themselves to be used as either an investigative or surveillance arm of the police? Do they have any different ethical obligations than do ordinary citizens witnessing a similar situation?

CASE 6-D

Blind Justice? On Naming Kobe Bryant's Accuser After the Rape Charge is Dropped

PATRICK LEE PLAISANCE
Colorado State University

In June 2003, Los Angeles Lakers star Kobe Bryant was recovering from medical treatment at the exclusive Lodge and Spa at Cordilera in Colorado. Bryant asked the resort's 19-year-old concierge, whom he had met earlier, up to his room, and the two had intercourse. Bryant insisted the sex was consensual, but the woman claimed she was forced against her will. After a weeklong investigation, Bryant was arrested and prosecutors filed a rape charge against him. A national media frenzy ensued.

Mainstream news outlets, however, scrupulously avoided identifying the woman in their coverage—even when Eagle County court officials mistakenly released documents containing some of her personal information. Colorado is one of several states with so-called rape shield laws, which prohibit authorities from disclosing the identity of victims in rape cases to spare them the additional trauma of public—and possibly unfair—scrutiny. Most news organizations themselves also have policies against naming assault victims on the theory that the social stigma that continues to be attached to sexual assault merits special treatment in coverage. So these mainstream news organizations never disclosed the woman's name to their audiences.

But anyone with Internet access and a few minutes to spare could quickly learn quite a bit about her. Her name, photos, e-mail address, cell phone number and even details about rumors surrounding her sexual and mental history were instantly made available—mostly on Internet sites created by fans of Bryant. A Los Angeles-based sports radio talk-show host, Tom Leykis, began referring to her by name on the air soon after the rape case was filed. His show is heard on 60 stations across the country.

Fifteen months later, the high-profile case presented a second ethical challenge for journalists. Just as a jury was being selected for the trial, the woman decided to back out as a witness for the state prosecution's case. The criminal case against Bryant was dropped. But at the same time, his accuser filed a civil lawsuit against him in federal court in Denver. The switch in courts posed the question of whether the playing field had changed for journalists who, since that point, had protected her identity in their coverage. Denver's two competing metropolitan daily newspapers, the *Rocky Mountain News* and the *Denver Post,* reacted in diametrically opposite ways.

John Temple, editor and publisher of the *Rocky Mountain News,* said the paper decided to reverse its policy and name the woman once she filed her civil suit because the issue changed. It was no longer a story about the state pursuing a sex-assault charge based on her evidence and testimony. By continuing to press her case on her own in civil court to seek monetary damages, the notion of fairness obligated journalists to treat all civil plaintiffs the same, Temple said—especially after a federal judge denied the woman's request to file her civil suit anonymously. "In the criminal case, we did not name the accuser because it was the state of Colorado prosecuting the case. The state . . . was attempting to vindicate a state interest," Temple said in an interview. "In the civil matter, the woman is pursuing an individual monetary interest. She is using the public courts in what is essentially a personal injury case.

"She had the choice not to go forward after Judge Matsch said she couldn't proceed anonymously. As a general rule, the *News* names plaintiffs in civil suits. Here, both sides' personal integrity and credibility are at issue and the *News* believes fairness requires that both parties be named in reporting on this civil suit. . . . In a case where there is no state interest involved and the complaint doesn't address a larger public interest, it's unfair for the accused to be treated differently from the accuser."

The *Denver Post* editors, however, reached the opposite decision and argued that naming her in coverage of her civil suit would be unethical. In a letter published for readers explaining their decision to continue to withhold the woman's name, *Post* editor Gregory L. Moore and managing editor Gary R. Clark argued that the potential harm to the woman created by naming her far outweighed any disadvantage for Bryant in granting her anonymity. "It is clear from the Bryant case—and from similar cases—that a stigma remains and that rape provokes a unique set of questions and blame that does not apply to victims of other crimes," Moore and Clark wrote. "It is our hope that societal attitudes toward alleged rape victims would mirror the treatment afforded alleged victims of other violent crimes. But judging from the reaction to the accuser of the Kobe Bryant case, whose life has been threatened, we don't believe that to be the case just yet. Though her identity will be available to anyone who attends the federal trial or reads court documents, and many in her community know her name, it is not the same as publishing her name and photograph day after day in hundreds of thousands of newspapers."

In March 2005, six months after Bryant's accuser initiated her civil suit, she and Bryant reached a monetary settlement involving a payment to her of an undisclosed amount, and the suit was dismissed.

Micro Issues

1. Is rape just like any other crime, or should it be treated differently by the news media?
2. The name of the alleged victim is not used in this case study. Should her name be used in the context of a robust ethics debate?

Midrange Issues

1. Temple of the *Rocky Mountain News* relies on claims of "fairness" to make his case for publishing her name. How might this notion of fairness be considered differently to argue that it would serve "fairness" *not* to name her?
2. Moore and Clark of the *Denver Post* rely on claims of minimizing harm to defend their decision to withhold her name. How might you argue that potential "harm" to Bryant may be as great or greater than the harm to the woman in allowing her to maintain anonymity?

Macro Issues

1. How would you say the two decisions of both newspapers reflect philosophical principles? In what ways do either draw from a Kantian notion of *duty* to respect human dignity in all our dealings? How do they draw from utilitarian thought in their assessment of the consequences of naming or not naming the woman?

2. In 1991, the *Des Moines Register* won a Pulitzer Prize for a series that documented one woman's journey through the court system after her rape, and she consented to be named throughout the stories. Geneva Overholser, editor of the *Register* at the time, has since argued that the journalistic practice of withholding the names of rape accusers and victims actually reinforces the social stigmatization of rape victims that editors and reporters claim to be fighting. Is she correct?

3. Should this perceived stigma be considered a factor in the decision whether to name the woman in this case?

7

Mass Media in a Democratic Society: Keeping a Promise

By the end of this chapter, you should be familiar with:

- **many of the criticisms leveled at the way the U.S. media cover government and elections.**
- **the special problems of reporting on terrorism and hate.**
- **why the media should be concerned with social justice for the powerful and the powerless alike.**
- **evaluating all forms of political communication through a single, ethically based framework.**

INTRODUCTION

Americans view the written word as essential to political society. The First Amendment to the U.S. Constitution states:

> Congress shall make no law respecting an establishment of religion, or prohibiting the free exercise thereof; or abridging the freedom of speech, or of the press; or the right of the people peaceably to assemble, and to petition the government for a redress of grievances.

Scholars such as John C. Merrill (1974) assert that the First Amendment should be interpreted purely as a restriction on government. This view emphasizes the role of freedom of expression and downplays assertions of journalistic responsibility. But others, including Alex deToqueville (1835), who studied the experimental democracy about 150 years ago, viewed the press of the day (or the mass media now) as an essential antidote to a culture that valued liberty over community. The press, deToqueville said, was an incubator of civilization in such a society. About 75 years later, political philosopher John Dewey asserted much the same role for the mass media.

We prefer this second view, one shared by founders Madison, Hamilton and Jay in the *Federalist Papers,* which asserted that communication among the citizens serves an important political purpose. The Founders expected citizens to be informed and then to participate in politics. They expected that political debate, including what was printed in the press of the day, would be partisan and biased rather than objective, but they also believed that from this cacophony of information the rational being would be able to discern the truth. Unfettered communication was essential to building a new nation.

As the authors made clear by circulating those documents as a series of newspaper articles, one way to enhance political learning was publication in the media of the time. Citizens had an obligation to read such information; the press had an obligation to provide it. Tucked within all of this, we believe, is a promise that the mass media, both in 1791 and more than 200 years later, will provide citizens with what they need to know to get along in political society. Scholars have labeled this analysis of the media's role in a democratic society the "social responsibility theory" of the press. However, assuming such a responsibility is becoming progressively more difficult. Some of the difficulties emanate from the structure of the contemporary American political system and, hence, are appropriately the subject for political reform. Others reflect the ethical choices contemporary journalists are making. After providing some historic context, it is to those issues we will turn.

EVALUATING POLITICAL COMMUNICATION

Many Americans, especially in the eight weeks before any election, might well wish they were in ancient Greece. For the Greeks, the art of politics was a gift from the gods, who provided men with *adios,* a sense of concern for the good opinion of others, and *dike,* a sense of justice, or that which makes civic peace possible through the adjudication of disputes. In the ancient myth, these gifts were bestowed on everyone, not just on some ruling economic or social elite. All men were able to exercise the art of politics through rhetoric and argument in the assembly, a form of direct democracy that survived for only a few years in Athens. No newspapers, no television, just a good, in-person debate. The Greeks called it *polity* which translates as community—the highest, most ethical of human activities. Ancient Greece was the first—and last—place it was seriously attempted.

Considering the contemporary cacophony, that's not such a big surprise. It's not just the negative campaign commercials. It's the barrage of opinion masquerading as analysis on cable television, the thousands of blogs available on the Internet, the candidate campaign Web sites—including entries into domains such as Facebook—the late night comedians, Comedy Central and all the rest. One study by the Pew Charitable Trusts in 2004 found that more than 50 percent of Americans under the age of 50 get their news about politics "regularly" or "sometimes" from late-night comedians. However, Pew research showed those respondents who regularly tuned in to late-night comedians for information were among the least likely to know basic facts about candidates.

Evaluating this plethora of political information is a problem—for media consumers and for journalists. The first task is to decide what is politically relevant information. Political scientist Bruce A. Williams (in press) has an answer to that question: a four-part test.

First, is the information **useful**—does it provide citizens with the kind of information that helps individual and collective decision making? Second, is the information **sufficient**—is there enough of it and at enough depth to allow people to make informed choices? Third, is the information **trustworthy?** Fourth, **who is the "audience"**—the "we" of the polity on which the ancient Greeks placed so much emphasis? Information that meets, at least in part, these criteria can be, and Williams argues ought to be, considered politically relevant, mediated information:

> In a democracy, politically relevant communications shape opportunities for understanding, deliberating about, and action on the relationships among: 1. The conditions of one's day-to-day life; 2. The day-to-day life of fellow members of the community; and 3. The norms and structures of power that shape these relationships. It is the connection among these three elements that constitute the inevitably contested, but nonetheless central definition of politically relevant truth.

Note that under this definition, a Jon Stewart show or a Stephen Colbert monologue would be considered politically relevant communication every bit as much as a campaign ad or an investigative piece. In fact, some elements of comedy—because they play on the uneven impact of power on our daily lives or the daily lives of our neighbors, may be more informative about what's really at issue than the traditional news story. Under this sort of analysis, cable news programming, which features dueling opinions unsubstantiated by evidence, would fare less well. Putting all kinds of political communication into the same arena also has other virtues. It means every message can be evaluated along the same standard. Here, again, Williams (in press) suggests four criteria.

- **Transparency**—Does the audience accurately know who is speaking?
- **Pluralism**—Does the media environment provide an opportunity for diverse points of view, either in different messages that are equally accessible or within a single message?
- **Verisimilitude**—Do the sources of the messages take responsibility for the truth claims they explicitly and implicitly make, even if these claims are not strictly verifiable in any formal sense?

- **Practice**—Does the message encourage modeling, rehearsing, preparing and learning for civic engagement and actual engagement and participation, like voting or less direct forms of political activity like thinking about issues, looking at Web sites, blogging or talking to neighbors face-to-face?

Political journalists could do well to evaluate their own reporting according to these standards, particularly considering the highly contentious nature of politics in the early 21st century.

GETTING ELECTED

For any politician to enact change, he or she must first be elected, and in our mass society, that means turning to the mass media to reach the electorate. Scholars agree on this starting point: political advertising is unique (Kaid 1992). It's also important. Voters sometimes learn more about candidates' stands on issues from advertising than they do from news (Patterson 1980). Factual accuracy, therefore, must be the starting point for ethical political advertising. As philosopher Hannah Arendt has noted, "Freedom of information is a farce unless factual information is guaranteed and the facts themselves are not in dispute" (Arendt 1970).

Other scholarly studies have found that news stories about elections emphasize strategy and tactics rather than stands on issues (Sheehan and Robinson 1983). This forces voters who want to become informed about the candidate's policy choices to get their information from ads, many of them "negative" or "attack" ads. They do this in part because policy information is missing from news stories.

Negative political ads are literally as old as the republic. One early patriot, Yale President Reverend Timothy Dwight, claimed that if Thomas Jefferson were elected, the Bible would be burned, the French national anthem sung in Christian churches and women dishonored in the most biblical of senses. The majority of voters obviously didn't believe him.

Contemporary voters are providing scholars with evidence that they, too, can discern among the various types of political ads. Comparative ads, ones that contrast candidate positions on specific issues, are viewed as information rich, and voters view them as an appropriate part of political discourse. Attack ads, ones that are personal and negative, that contain no "positive" or "issue-oriented" information, are disliked and distrusted. Voters appear to be able to distinguish between negative, comparative and positive or biographical ads (Jamieson 2000). Furthermore, recent analysis indicates that the majority of political ads fall into the positive or contrast categories (Benoit 1999), providing ample evidence that it is possible to create ethical political advertising on the local, state and national levels.

Journalists are deciding that covering the advertising a campaign produces can result in legitimate news stories focused on policy issues. These news stories, often called "ad watches," appear in both broadcast and print and have the goal of putting the claims in political ads to the tests of truthfulness and context. While the scholarly findings are not conclusive, anecdotal evidence from states as diverse as Colorado, California and North Carolina suggests that aggressive news journalism focusing on attack ads and negative campaigning can have an impact on the voters'

SOUND BITES AND PHOTO OPS EMERGED AS THE FRONT-RUNNERS IN YESTERDAY'S VOTING. THE ISSUES FINISHED A DISAPPOINTING THIRD, AND MAY DROP OUT OF THE CAMPAIGN.

Copyright © Ed Stein. Reprinted with permission of Rocky Mountain News.

knowledge of particular candidates and their evaluation of those candidates. In addition, we would suggest that it is the responsibility of journalists to evaluate political advertising as legitimate news and to hold candidates publicly accountable for the advertising sponsored by a campaign or, in the grayer areas, advertising paid for by political action groups in favor of a particular candidate and which that same candidate refuses to disavow.

Ideally, the same standards that apply to other kinds of political communication should be applied to political advertising as well. Further, many philosophers link facts with rationality, particularly in the area of political debate. The use of emotional arguments designed to stir listeners or viewers "to set aside reason" has been characterized as a "violation of democratic ethics" (Haiman 1958, 388). There may, however, be times when valid issues have strong emotional content, such as the ongoing debate over abortion. At those times, the melding of emotion with issue content in such cases is not prima facie unethical.

Students of history will realize that many totalitarian regimes have used emotional appeals to either gain or retain power. However, such ads usually lack any public revelation of evidence to support the claims. Making the evidence behind political assertions public—what Kant called the "transcendental principle of publicness"—has historically been the role of the news media. We believe such reporting stands on firm ethical ground. The lack of this sort of journalism was foreseen by Lippmann: "In the absence of debate, restricted utterance leads to the degradation of opinion. By a kind of Gresham's law the more rational is overcome by the less rational, and the opinions that will prevail will be those which are held most ardently by those with the most passionate will" (Lippmann 1982, 196).

If political advertising is indeed a special case, then journalists and their audiences should demand higher standards, more regulations or both. While some of the solutions to the current problems have First Amendment ramifications, they are worthy of discussion. They include the following:

- Allot limited amounts of free time to qualified candidates for major office to level the playing field for candidates without destroying the bottom line at already strapped broadcast outlets.
- Strengthen state regulations against corrupt campaign practices and find ways to enforce those regulations.
- Encourage journalists to stop covering the "horse race" aspect of campaigns and focus on problem and policy solutions.
- Hold candidates accountable for their ads, not only in verbal terms but in visual and audio terms as well. Do the same for political action committees or other groups such as **Moveon.org.**
- Teach journalists to read and report on the visual imagery of a campaign, and to ask candidates questions about it.
- Allow attack ads only if they include the image of the candidate directing the attack.
- Reject unfair or inaccurate ads created by political action committees.
- Conduct ad watches as part of media coverage of a campaign, analyzing the ads for omissions, inconsistencies and inaccuracies.

It takes money to buy ads, and in contemporary democratic societies that means the candidate with the most money often has the loudest voice. Many of those in public life, such as former New Jersey Senator Bill Bradley or Arizona Senator John McCain, argue the influence of money in the political system is pervasive and corrosive, and many bills have been introduced to limit the power of money in politics only to die in the political process or be ignored in the real world by substituting "soft money" for restricted money.

How to deal with the money that finances political advertising is an important policy question, one with significant ethical overtones, but there seem to be no good candidates for conducting an investigation. Politicians are too entrenched in the existing system to be objective, and the media that could presumably investigate political money and its negative influence are compromised by the act of receiving so much of the cash. The problem cannot be "solved" in this brief chapter, but it is worth considering whether a highly profitable media system such as the one in the United States might not be able to find a way to "give back" access to political candidates who cannot raise enormous sums to purchase newspaper space and broadcast airtime.

LEARNING ABOUT LEADERS AND THEIR CHARACTER

In the 21st century, perhaps the most pressing political issue is: can people become acquainted well enough and deeply enough with any candidate to acquire an opinion? After all, a representative democracy rests on what the Greeks called *adios*, a concern for the good opinion of others. Except for a small group of government and corporate insiders, the mass media have become the primary mode of receiving political discourse. In addition to providing voters with facts, something that is generally assumed to be the role of news, the media also provide citizens with a framework to understand those facts, the realm of culture and myth that is the role not only of news but also of entertainment and advertising.

Candidates have been quick to learn that the public uses a variety of media sources to get to know their candidates. California Governor Arnold Schwarzenegger announced his candidacy on the "Tonight Show With Jay Leno." Studies of news reporting of political campaigns have uncovered some disturbing trends. Journalists function as a pack; there is seldom any really distinctive political reporting during elections (Crouse 1974; Sabato 1992). However, campaign assignments remain sought after by members of the national press corps for reasons of personal prestige. The person who covers the winning candidate for the network will almost assuredly become the White House correspondent for the next four years, a guarantee of celebrity status, increased income and, many would argue, real political power. Because of the financial ramifications, journalists covering a national election have almost as much at stake as the candidates they cover.

Further, journalists treat front-runners differently than they do the remainder of the candidate pack (Robinson and Sheehan 1984). Front-runners are the subject of closer scrutiny, but those examinations are seldom about issues, even though it is issue-oriented reporting that tends to provoke political interest and public participation. Candidates and their paid consultants seem to have intuitively understood what academic research has shown. They've developed strategies that will allow them either to capitalize on front-runner status and image or to compensate for a lack of it. Free media—synonymous with a positive story on the 5:00 p.m. news—has become the watchword of most state and national political campaigns. Candidates have mastered the "photo opportunity" and the "Rose Garden strategy"—although in 2004 the Rose Garden was replaced by the battlefield in Iraq and such "backdrops" as President Bush landing on an Air Force carrier with "Mission Accomplished" in the background. All seem designed to thwart anything but the most carefully scripted candidate contact with the voting public.

At the same time candidates try to script their every move, the media have the right, and some would say even the responsibility, to get "behind the curtain" (Molotch and Lester 1974) to the real candidate. What happens after the curtain is down often makes news in ways the candidates could not have foreseen. Journalists face a number of questions in cases such as these. Just because the information is available and even accurate does not automatically mean that it is relevant.

Conceptualizations of character have changed significantly since the founding of the republic, when character was defined in Aristotelian terms—an observable collection of habits, virtues and vices. Freudian psychology has altered that definition to include motivation, the subconscious and relationships that help to form all of us as people. What journalists cover is "political character," that is, the intersection of personality and public performance within a cultural and historical context. Character is dynamic; it represents a synergistic interaction of a person within an environment (Davies 1963). Journalists who explore character often do so for an ethical reason, despite apparent invasions of privacy.

Political figures are powerful people. Ethicist Sissela Bok (1978) has noted that when an unequal power relationship is involved, it is possible to justify what would otherwise be considered an unethical act. To paraphrase Bok, at the core of any serious investigation of the private character of public people is the notion that if the person one wishes to investigate is also in the position to do one harm, then invading privacy in an attempt to counter that threat is justified. However, that invasion also needs to meet some tests (Schoeman 1984):

- The invasion must be placed in a larger context of facts and history and must include enough context to provide meaning.
- The revelation of private facts about political figures should meet the traditional tests of journalism and needs to be linked to public, political behaviors before publication or broadcast becomes ethically justifiable.
- The invasion of privacy must further the larger political discourse and must meet the most demanding ethical test: the "need to know."

Careful reporting on character can pass these tests. However, journalists also must be willing to weigh the harm done to others, particularly those, such as family members, who have not sought the public limelight. Even reporting that passes these three tests must be filtered through discretion. Merely publishing private information without this tie to a more public role is a form of "tabloid journalism" that casts doubt on journalistic motives and credibility. More seriously, such publication denigrates politicians in such a way that every official becomes a "crook," "liar" or "philanderer" without some larger understanding of why those character traits may or may not be important in doing the public's business.

Reporters covering political character should be aware of some or all of the following building blocks of character:

- The politician's development of a sense of trust.
- A politician's own sense of self-worth and self-esteem.
- The development of a politician's relationship to power and authority.
- Early influences on adult policy outlook.
- How a politician establishes contact with people.
- The flexibility, adaptability and purposefulness of mature adulthood.
- The historical moment.

The media's current emphasis on covering political character provides the best illustration of the need to balance the demands of governing with privacy considerations. No culture has ever expected its leaders to be saints; in fact, some cultures have prized leadership that is decidedly unsaintly. In fact, in American culture, the concept of public servant—which is the work of politics—has been replaced by the epithet "politician"—synonymous with "crook," or "liar," a caricature reinforced in popular culture by historic films such as "Mr. Smith Goes to Washington" or the contemporary remaking of "All the King's Men." However, Americans were reminded that public service can be a high calling indeed, as shown by the first responders to the 9/11 tragedy, many of whom lost their lives.

THE PROPER ROLE OF THE MEDIA—GUARD DOG OR LAP DOG?

As we stated before, one of the ironies of democratic politics is that, in order to accomplish something, you first have to get elected. But accomplishing something, not getting elected, is the major work of politics. Many inches of newspaper space are devoted to the process on the local level. Local television news provides much less attention to policy making. Regulatory agencies, the courts and even Congress are not considered glamour beats by the national press corps, and annual surveys by journalism watchdog groups show a dwindling number of reporters on the regulatory beat.

Yet the national press corps, particularly, has changed how the policy process operates. No one is quite certain when the "media leak" originated, certainly back in the last century and quite likely as early as the founding of the country. Not only has a leak to a reporter become a fact of political life; it appears to alter how policymakers, and sometimes policy itself, work.

Political scientist Martin Linsky (1986) describes how leaks have become part of the Washington policy-making process. Government officials, both elected and appointed, use the mass media to help make policy in a variety of ways, he says. Sometimes they leak a story to find out how others will react to an idea, a practice known as floating a "trial balloon" in the press. Other times, policy-makers will leak a story because they wish to mount either public or bureaucratic support for or opposition to a set of options.

Sometimes leaks take the form of whistle-blowing when a government employee honestly believes the public good is not being served by working through the system. Watergate's famed and now named source, "Deep Throat," apparently was motivated by such a belief when he leaked parts of the government investigation into the break-in to *Washington Post* reporters Bob Woodward and Carl Bernstein. Much of the initial information about the Abu Ghraib scandal in Iraq came to journalists such as Seymour Hersh in the form of e-mails from service men and women who were alarmed at the treatment of Iraqis held at the prison and of the military command's unwillingness or inability to change the system.

Still other times, government officials leak a story to put a particular reporter or publication on notice about who really holds the power in a particular situation. Network news correspondent Bill Moyers was taught that lesson by Lyndon Johnson, who told him that he planned to fire J. Edgar Hoover, a scoop Moyers reported. The very next day Johnson appointed Hoover director of the FBI for life. Moyers was stuck with a story that was accurate but not true. Worse, he had become the subject of Johnson's well-known propensity for power plays. It was a lesson in trust and political power Moyers never forgot.

More than two decades ago, Linsky (1986) wrote about the role of the media in the policy-making process and raised two important points regarding ethical journalistic practice still relevant today. First, leaks are an acceptable way of doing government business, and policy-makers are using them skillfully. In the summer of 1989, when terrorist groups in the Middle East threatened to kill one or more of the Americans they held hostage, then-President George H. W. Bush allowed a staff member to leak a story to a trusted *New York Times* reporter that the United States would retaliate militarily if hostages were killed. Bush's message was sent to the terrorists not through diplomatic back channels but on the paper's front page.

Second, leaks can alter the outcome of the policy process itself. President Bill Clinton's 1993 trial balloon about the potential of freezing the Social Security cost-of-living allowance provoked immediate congressional opposition. But it enlarged the range of politically acceptable options—including taxing a larger percentage of some Social Security benefits—to reduce the nation's deficit.

Of fundamental importance for journalists is the question of whether reporters, editors and their news organizations should become consciously involved in the process of governing, and in what manner? The Valerie Plame case, at the end of this chapter, will ask you to respond to such questions.

Although the evolving role of the mass media in a democratic society has been widely analyzed, most ethicists agree that the media's primary function is to provide citizens with information that will allow them to make informed political choices (Hodges 1986; Elliott 1986). As part of performing that job, the media are expected to act as a watchdog on government. This concept of the media as the "fourth estate" was originally suggested by Edmund Burke, in a speech in the House of Commons during the late 1700s. (Ward 2004). The Founders tried to guard against any single check fundamentally undermining the American experiment. The watchdog media— examined from this perspective—also have a "guide dog" function. Their goal is to help citizens make their way through the political process, not to immobilize them with a series of false trails or a sense that all political activity is futile.

However, many contemporary media critics argue that a particular style of covering politics, one emphasizing conflict and wrongdoing, has soured both journalists and citizens on American democracy. Political reporter E. J. Dionne in *Why Americans Hate Politics* (1991) argues that definitions of news that emphasize conflict inevitably help to degenerate political debate into a shouting match between diametrically opposed factions that have no reason to compromise. Others have argued that, particularly since 9/11, individual journalists and media institutions have been far too willing to kowtow to powerful political interests for fear of being characterized as unpatriotic.

This is not a problem exclusively confined to the U.S. system, as documentaries such as "Control Room"—in an in-depth look at Al Jazeera—make clear. Dionne adds that politics without government, a concept that seems to have rhetorical support across the U.S. political continuum, is an oxymoron. While he does not blame the mass media for creating these sorts of false rhetorical divisions, he does hold those in his own profession accountable for failing to point out what they mean in the context of a democratic form of government. In this, Dionne agrees with Plato, who said that democratic politics, while a "degenerative" form of government, was probably the best available system considering that human beings were its primary components.

Media critic James Fallows goes one step further. He holds a journalism permeated by a cynical and conflict-laden view of politics directly responsible for voter apathy, congressional gridlock and government via opinion polls rather than political leadership (Fallows 1996, 7):

> The harm actually goes much further than that, to threaten the long-term health of our political system. Step by step, mainstream journalism has fallen into the habit of portraying public life in America as a race to the bottom, in which one group of conniving, insincere politicians ceaselessly tries to outmaneuver another. The great problem for American democracy in the 1990s is that people barely trust elected leaders or the entire legislative system to accomplish anything of value. . . . Deep forces in America's political, social and economic structures account for most of the frustration of today's politics, but the media's attitudes have played a surprisingly important and destructive role.

In fact, media critic Katherine Hall Jamieson (1992) has suggested that, when it comes to politics, journalists should get themselves a new definition of news. Instead of emphasizing events and conflict, Jamieson believes news stories could equally revolve around issues and multiple policy perspectives. This suggestion even has some support in academic research; readers are more interested in coverage that emphasizes policy issues than fights and horse races (Sheehan and Robinson 1983). Fallows and others insist that journalists have a right to report on government. But implicit in that right is the sense that successful governing is a political outcome for which the media are partially responsible. The cynical assumption that government can never act for the public good, and the arrogant stance that journalists and the media are somehow outside the political system, are almost nihilistic in this view. Conscientious ethical practice will allow journalists and media consumers to begin the work of carving out new understandings of our *responsibilities and rights* when the mass media become involved in the American democratic political system.

MODERN PROBLEMS: TERRORISM AND HATE

Terrorism is, at its most fundamental, an act of communication. In fact, scholars suggest that terrorism was not possible before the advent of the mass media. Terrorists and the media have a symbiotic relationship: terrorists need the media to communicate their messages, and the media garner ratings and increased readership when terrorism is in the news, even while deploring the violence. At the same time, the media perform an essential role: acting as a filter on the terrorists' message and as a watchdog on government response.

Terrorism presents journalists with what philosophers call "hard questions." Terrorism is news, but news coverage furthers terrorists' ends and makes more terrorism likely. How to break that cycle has been the subject of much professional anguish throughout the world, beginning in the Middle East (soon after Israel became a state and Palestine did not), continuing with the troubles in Northern Ireland that intensified after 1972 (which provoked the British government to censor the BBC) and culminating in the images of New York's twin towers (and the resulting war that included the military takeover of Iraq).

Cartoon by Walt Handlesman. Copyright © 2003 Tribune Media Services. Reprinted with permission.

In the face of some forms of terrorism such as genocide, journalists must take the side of humanity, even if it means abandoning objectivity. CNN correspondent Christiane Amanpour did this when she argued on air with former President Bill Clinton about America's reluctance to involve itself in the racial and civil war that developed after the former Yugoslavia disintegrated. Amanpour was not alone in her views, and it should be noted that after extensive debate the United States and NATO did engage in the conflict.

Despite instances where journalists drop their objectivity in favor of advocacy, the more general journalistic understanding is that coverage of terrorism must avoid partisanship and must include the depth needed to place the act in its historical context. In the long run only this sort of news coverage will make reasoned debate and response possible. However, the reality of more than half a century of war in the Middle East, and the continuing struggles by those who employ terrorist methods to gain power, provides a discouraging reminder that a free media system is an inadequate solution to solve the problems caused by deep-seated hatred and ill-conceived national self-interest.

Terrorism also presents nation-states with hard problems. Nations under attack almost reflexively clamp down on their citizens—particularly those who question or dissent—because leaders believe diplomacy will be ineffective. Democracies pass laws, for example the PATRIOT Act, that enhance government's powers over its citizens. In the case of the PATRIOT Act, not only did the law increase the government's powers of search and seizure unchecked by the courts, but it also made possible incarceration of suspected terrorists without bail or public notification. What made the act more devastating, from the journalists' perspective, was the inclusion of a provision that made it impossible for journalists to get information needed to evaluate the effectiveness of the PATRIOT Act.

Cases about the media and coverage of terrorism can be found throughout this book, and we urge you to revisit them in light of the tension between a government under stress and news media that inevitably will be used by terrorists as news organizations perform their journalistic, institutional role. If truth is the first casualty of war, then independence of thought and action is the first casualty of terrorism.

Journalists perform another role in such historic times—that of moral witness. Ethicist Patrick Plaisance (2002) suggests that when journalists report on such events as terrorism, its causes, its execution and its results, the journalist functions as a "moral witness" because such news stories cannot be understood or reported outside of a moral framework. Plaisance and others assert that to be detached and objective about genocide and hate is to condone it. When journalists write the first draft of history of the early part of this century, they must deal with competing claims about justice, community, truth and power. Such reporting requires excellence in both ethical reflection and professional technique. It has seldom been more difficult—or more important—to do both well.

SOCIAL JUSTICE IN A DEMOCRATIC SOCIETY

Just as there are members of a power elite, there also are those who feel excluded from political society. While some scholars have argued that one interpretation of U.S. history has been the gradual extension of the franchise to ever more diverse publics, that extension of basic rights has been uneven and contentious. All of these minority groups seek access to the political process and, since the mass media have become major institutional forces in that process, they seek access to media as well.

Media ethicists suggest these political and social outgroups provide the mass media with a further set of responsibilities. For instance, they assert that the mass media, and individual journalists, need to become advocates for the politically homeless. Media ethicist Clifford Christians suggests that "justice for the powerless stands at the centerpiece of a socially responsible press. Or, in other terms, the litmus test of whether or not the news profession fulfills its mission over the long term is its advocacy for those outside the socioeconomic establishment" (Christians 1986, 110). This socially responsible view of the media suggests that journalists have a duty both to promote community and to promote the individuals within it. Those who are in significant ways outside the community—economically, socially or culturally different—need a voice.

By advocacy, Christians does not mean reporting that espouses only one sort of political or social agenda. Rather, he insists:

> Press portrayals feed into public discourse and play a portentous role in the shape our culture and the sociopolitical realm ultimately take. In its loftiest sense, the press ought to amplify public debate and reconstitute the argument so that it becomes an important public forum where significant issues of social justice are fruitfully raised and resolved. (Christians 1986, 123)

Christians' argument can be amplified beyond democracy's racial, ethnic and economic outgroups. In contemporary democratic society, clearly some "things" also are without political voice. The environment, racial equality and events beyond American shores all have difficulty finding a powerful domestic spokesperson. These issues cross traditional political boundaries. Those who will be affected by them also seem to be without a voice.

Communitarian thinking takes social responsibility to the next level. It urges that justice, rather than truth, become the ethical linchpin of journalistic decision making. If justice becomes the fundamental value of American journalism, then the media—functioning at institutional level—have the goal of transforming society, of empowering individual citizens to act in ways that promote political discussion, debate and change (Christians et al. 1993).

What makes journalists uneasy about either the communitarian or social responsibility approaches is that they smack of a kind of benevolent paternalism. If individual human beings carry moral stature, then assigning one institution—in this case the mass media—the role of social and political arbiter diminishes the moral worth of the individual citizen. The mass media become a kind parent and the citizen a sort of wayward child in need of guidance. Such a relationship does not promote political maturity.

While the weight of recent scholarly opinion sides with Christians, such a view is not without risk. If accepted, it means a thoroughgoing change for the mass media in the U.S. political system. That change would bring about other changes, some of them not easy to anticipate. But whether change is what's needed, or merely a return to the strict libertarian view, both call for some sophisticated ethical reasoning. As Thomas Jefferson said, being a citizen of a democracy is not easy—to which journalists might well add, neither is covering one.

Suggested Readings

DIONNE, E. J., JR. 1992. *Why Americans hate politics.* New York: Touchtone.

FALLOWS, JAMES. 1996. *Breaking the news: How the media undermine American democracy.* New York: Pantheon.

FRY, DON, ed. 1983. *The adversary press.* St. Petersburg, FL: The Modern Media Institute.

JAMIESON, K. H. 2000. *Everything you think you know about politics . . . and why you're wrong.* New York: Basic Books.

LINSKY, MARTIN. 1986. *Impact: How the press affects federal policymaking.* New York: W. W. Norton.

MADISON, JAMES S., ALEXANDER HAMILTON, and JOHN JAY. *The Federalist papers.*

WARD, STEPHEN. 2004. *The invention of journalism ethics.* Montreal: McGill-Queen's University Press.

Cases on the Web

"The David Duke candidacy: Fairness and the Klansman" by Keith Woods
"Whose abuse of power: The *Seattle Times* and Brock Adams" by Lee Wilkins
"Denver's Rocky Flats: The role of the alternative press" by Lee Wilkins
"Terrorist use of the news media: News media use of terrorists" by Jack Lule
"Singapore: Balancing democracy, globalization and the Internet" by Seow Ting Lee.

CHAPTER 7 CASES

CASE 7-A

The *New York Times* and Judith Miller: When a Reporter Becomes the Story

KARON REINBOTH SPECKMAN
Truman State University

In 2005, *New York Times* reporter Judith Miller became the story rather than just a reporter covering the story. The Miller narrative has all the makings of a best-selling journalistic mystery—anonymous sources, charges of shoddy reporting, leaked identities of CIA agents, national security concerns and jail sentences.

To supporters, Miller is a press hero for going to jail for 85 days rather than revealing her sources to a grand jury. However, others called her a shill for two reasons. First, critics charged that top Bush officials used her to spread the belief that Iraq had weapons of mass destruction (WMDs) in the buildup to the March 2003 U.S. invasion. Second, critics charged that Bush officials then used her and other reporters as part of a conspiracy to discredit WMD critics—even by outing a covert CIA agent.

The Miller story is especially important because journalists value the principle of source confidentiality to maintain the trust of sources and to serve the public interest. Yet, as is often the case, defenders and prosecutors don't always get to choose the ideal client or circumstances in court cases. Miller—a Pulitzer-prize winner for her 2001 series on Osama bin Laden and Al Qaeda—became a press hero with baggage.

Miller started reporting for the *Times* about WMDs in December 2001. The U.S. invasion of Iraq began March 20, 2003. Whether the *Times*' stories were accurate or not was relevant because the Bush administration used Iraq's alleged possession of WMDs as a major justification for the invasion.

Her stories relied on defectors who claimed to have worked on Iraqi weapon facilities—nuclear, chemical and biological—and on unnamed administration sources. For example, her Dec. 20, 2001, story focused on a named defector who gave "an extensive interview" claiming to have "personally worked on renovations of secret facilities for biological, chemical and nuclear weapons. . . ." Miller's 2002 stories continued the theme. A June 29 story by James Dao and Miller told of the Bush administration's concern about liquid anthrax and added that "some administration officials said they could not rule out such attacks in the United States."

A Sept. 8 story by Michael Gordon and Miller turned up the heat with discussion that Iraq was trying to buy aluminum tubes to use as centrifuge components. According to the lead, "More than a decade after Saddam Hussein agreed to give up weapons of mass destruction, Iraq has stepped up its quest for nuclear weapons and has embarked on a worldwide hunt for materials to make an atomic bomb, Bush administration officials said today." The authors identified sources as "a senior administration official" and "Bush administration officials."

The day after that story ran, Tim Russert interviewed Vice President Dick Cheney on "Meet the Press." Cheney cited the *Times* story as corroboration of the administration's assertion that Saddam was attempting to acquire the bomb materials. But critics suggested the administration leaked the story to Miller and the *Times* and then went on Sunday talk shows as part of a plan to make it appear that there was evidence supporting their assertion.

As more stories followed in 2002 and 2003, critics identified various problems with Miller's stories: sources were not verified independently, no other reporter was writing the same type of stories and the Bush administration was providing the unnamed sources. Also, Miller was the only journalist granted the right to be embedded with the Mobile Exploitation Team Bravo, whose task was to find the WMDs in Iraq. She signed an agreement that all articles would be censored.

After the March 2003 invasion, those troops found no WMDs. An April 2, 2003, article with the dateline of northern Kuwait, concluded that weapons weren't found in southern Iraq because experts believed they were closer to Bagdad. Miller's April 5 article again said they hoped to find WMDs closer to Bagdad but also said that defense secretary Donald Rumsfeld was asserting that toppling the government was the first priority over finding WMDs. Miller wrote articles in April and May 2003 that tried to rationalize why troops found no WMDs.

In 2005, Miller responded to charges that she was misled by her administration sources and said: "The analysts, the experts and the journalists who covered them—we were all wrong. If your sources are wrong, you are wrong. I did the best job that I could."

Another part of the Miller story began in 2002 when conflicting intelligence reports suggested that Niger had sold uranium, a material needed for nuclear weapons, to Iraq. In February 2002, CIA officials asked Joseph Wilson, a career foreign service officer and former ambassador to Gabon, to take a fact-finding trip to Niger. Wilson went to Niger and reported that it was highly unlikely Iraq had made that purchase. Thus, when the Bush administration continued to assert Saddam Hussein's purchase of uranium from Niger as a rationale for an Iraqi invasion, Wilson wrote a July 6, 2003, op-ed piece in the *Times* criticizing the administration's decision to go to war with Iraq. He said, "Based on my experience with the administration in the months leading up to the war, I have little choice but to conclude that some of the intelligence related to Iraq's nuclear weapons program was twisted to exaggerate the Iraqi threat."

Syndicated columnist Robert Novak followed eight days later with a column that criticized Wilson and identified Wilson's wife, Valerie Plame, as a CIA agent. Novak used unnamed administration sources who said that Plame had suggested sending Wilson on the trip. *Time* magazine writer Matthew Cooper also followed with a story that identified her as a "CIA official." Although Miller didn't write an article about the CIA agent, an administration source also had given her Plame's name.

Knowingly revealing the name of a covert CIA agent violates the federal Intelligence Identities Protection Act. In December 2003, the Justice Department appointed special prosecutor Patrick Fitzgerald to investigate who revealed Plame's CIA status to journalists. When a federal judge found Miller in civil contempt for not revealing her sources to the special prosecutor and a grand jury, she chose to go to jail rather than reveal those sources. Miller stayed in jail from July 6 to Sept. 30, 2005. She was released when she asked for, and received, a letter from the vice president's chief of staff, I. "Scooter" Lewis Libby, who was her source, releasing her from the confidentiality promise. In a later attempt to justify his role in the leak, Libby said that the president had authorized the leaking of sensitive intelligence and thus the information he leaked was declassified and not illegal. Libby was found guilty of perjury after a two-week trial. Plame filed a lawsuit in July 2006 against the vice president, Libby and Karl Rove, Bush's White House political strategist. Plame's lawsuit contends that the administrators set out to ruin her career because of her husband's criticism of the administration.

Source protection is an important issue for reporters because no federal law exists even though 31 states have some type of shield law. The dissenting opinion in the narrow 1972 Supreme Court ruling in *Branzburg v. Hayes* said there are times when not revealing sources is either an absolute or qualified privilege. However, *In Re: Grand Jury Subpoena, Judith Miller, 387 F. 3rd 964, 2005,* a lower federal court upheld the *Branzburg* majority ruling that said there is no reporter privilege. Thus, it would appear that Miller took a heroic stand on the principle of not revealing her sources.

But some critics countered that the circumstances sullied the principle. For example, Pulitzer-prize winning investigative reporter Seymour Hersh told the *Toronto Star* in a 2005 interview that Miller was wrong because she was protecting someone who she knew used and abused her. He said: "You got reporters saying they're willing to go to jail to defend the right of somebody to lie to them about something that leads to the deaths of thousands of people. Do you understand the crazy value system? It's pretty bad."

In spite of her critics, Miller received many accolades for her refusal to name sources and the subsequent jail term. For example, the Society of Professional Journalists (SPJ) awarded her a First Amendment Award, sparking a controversy from many SPJ members.

Although Miller received most of the criticism, the *Times* was not blameless in both the reporting of the WMDs stories and the Wilson-Plame source controversy. In late 2005, the *Times'* editors handling—or nonhandling—of their star reporter became another part of the story. Critics from within and outside the *Times* said the paper had too little oversight over her reporting. An Oct. 16, 2005, *Times* article of more than 6,200 words laid out to the public what problems the paper had with her coverage of WMDs, what the editors regretted about the handling of the Miller and Plame-Wilson source and a discussion that Libby had given her permission to testify much earlier than she claimed.

Executive Editor Bill Keller accused Miller of not being totally truthful about the Plame-Wilson leak. In an e-mail response, Miller denied that charge. Finally, Miller reached an agreement with the *Times* and retired from the paper in November 2005. Part of the agreement was the publication of a letter to the paper giving her side of the controversy. In that letter she said, "I have chosen to resign because over the last few months, "I have become the news, something a *New York Times* reporter never wants to be."

Micro Issues

1. Did Judith Miller violate any journalistic principles with her use of anonymous administration sources for her reporting on WMDs? Is she responsible in any way for the nation going to war with Iraq?

2. Should Judith Miller have given the grand jury the name of her source?
3. Does imbedding of journalists with troops improve war coverage? What are the advantages and disadvantages of the practice?

Midrange Issues

1. What do you think about Miller's explanation that her sources were wrong and thus she shouldn't be blamed?
2. Should journalists and editors consider it their responsibility to "judge" anonymous sources?
3. Is there a difference between a source who is revealing crime and a source who wants protection for political reasons? How do journalists tell the difference?
4. Should the *New York Times* more closely supervise reporters? Should the *Times* have "come clean" or published an article about the Miller controversy earlier?

Macro Issues

1. Often "star" reporters who have won prizes are given free reign in their reporting. What problems can this practice create and what are some other examples in which this practice created problems?
2. Does immunity from testifying about sources serve the public good? Why or why not?
3. How should professional organizations decide who will receive awards? Does the giving of awards (Pulitzer, etc.) bolster strong journalism or encourage reporting for the sake of winning awards?
4. When reporting ideas contrary to the administration's position is labeled "unpatriotic," what responsibility do reporters and editors have to covering both sides of an issue?

CASE 7-B

Victims and the Press

ROBERT LOGAN
National Institute of Medicine, Washington, D.C.

Alice Waters' daughter, Julie, seven, has leukemia. Her illness was diagnosed in its early stages in March 2000. Julie's physicians believe her condition can be success-fully treated.

Ms. Waters, 37, lives in a mobile home in an unincorporated area a few miles from Metroplex, a city of 1.5 million. Ms. Waters' street is the only residential sec-tion in the area. At the north end of the street—which has 12 mobile homes on each side facing one another—are four large gas stations that catch traffic off the inter-state that runs a quarter mile away to the west. At the south end of the street (about a quarter mile away) are two large tanks that are a relatively small storage facility for Big Oil, Inc. Next to this—starting almost in her backyard—is the boundary of a successful, 700-acre grapefruit orchard, which borders on a municipal landfill. About a quarter mile away are large well fields that are the principal source of drink-ing water for Metroplex.

In July 1999, a 6-year-old boy in the household two doors down from Ms. Waters was diagnosed as having leukemia. He was not as lucky as Julie; his diagnosis was late in the progression of his disease, and he died in December 2000. In 2001, an in-fant girl became the second baby born with birth defects in the neighborhood within seven years. Both families moved before Ms. Waters came to the neighborhood in 1999. Internal medicine specialists Dr. Earnest and Dr. Sincere met Julie soon after she was admitted to the hospital in October 2000. They were instrumental in getting funding for Julie's care when her mother was unable to pay. They are members of Worried M.D's for Social Responsibility, a self-proclaimed liberal, national public interest group that gets actively involved in national political issues.

The physicians told Ms. Waters that they were suspicious about the causes of Julie's illness. Three cancer and birth-defect incidents on the same street, the physi-cians said, were not a coincidence.

In November 2001, they began to collect water samples from the wellhead at Ms. Waters's house. They sent the samples to a well-regarded testing lab in another city. Since then, they have tested the water at a professional lab every four months. Every test revealed traces of more than 10 human-made and natural chemicals often associated with oil storage tanks, pesticides, grapefruit orchards, gas station leaks, lead from automobile emissions and a large landfill.

However, each chemical occurs consistently at 6 to 15 parts per billion, which is considered safe for drinking water based on standards set by the U.S. Environ-mental Protection Agency (EPA). At higher levels these chemicals are associated with carcinogenic risks or increases in birth defects, but the levels found at Ms. Waters' wellhead are within safety thresholds set by the EPA. There is no evidence the chemicals are associated directly with the health problems found in Ms. Waters' neighborhood.

At a fund-raising party last night for mayoral candidate Sam Clean, Drs. Earnest and Sincere privately told Clean what they had found. Clean is a well-known public figure, has a reputation as an environmentalist, owns a successful health food restaurant chain, is media wise and looks good on television. He is a long shot to become mayor and needs fresh issues to draw attention to his candidacy.

At 11:00 a.m. today, KAOS news radio begins running as the top story in its 20-minute news rotation "Clean Attacks City Lack of Cleanup." In the story, Clean gives a sound bite attacking city officials for "ignoring cancer-causing agents in water in a neighborhood where children have died, which is next door to the city's water supply." He describes the neighborhood's medical problems and describes (without naming) Julie and Alice Waters. The news report explains that water from the neighborhood has several "toxic agents believed to cause cancer at higher levels" and points out that the city's water wells are within a quarter-mile of oil tanks, gas stations, a grapefruit orchard, a landfill and septic tanks. County officials are said to be unavailable for comment. The report runs throughout the day at 20-minute intervals.

By 2:30 p.m., calls to the switchboard have jammed the newsroom. The callers who get through are frightened about their drinking water. City Hall's switchboards are jammed. The callers sound upset and ask whether their water is safe to drink.

By 4:00 p.m., reporters from the local ABC affiliate are already knocking on doors in the trailer park and sending live reports from the scene. Neighbors tell them where Alice and Julie Waters live.

At 4:15 p.m., your managing editor gives you the story. You are an ambitious reporter for *Metroplex Today,* the only morning newspaper in Metroplex. Both of you realize this is clearly Page 1 potential, but you have only a few hours before deadline for the next morning's edition. After a few phone calls, you discover that the mayor, the city council and most city and county officials are all out of town at a retreat and are unavailable for comment. The regional EPA office is not answering the phone.

A trusted spokesperson for Regional Hospital tells you that Drs. Sincere and Earnest are furious at Clean for releasing the story and have no comment. She fills you in with all of the above information. The same Regional Hospital spokesperson says Ms. Waters does not want to be interviewed. She suddenly realizes that her husband, whom she walked out on several years before, might see the story and return to town.

Sam Clean is more than happy to talk to you.

Micro Issues

1. Is Clean a reliable enough source for KAOS radio to base its reports on?
2. Should KAOS have broadcast the story?
3. Should you respect Ms. Waters' wishes and leave her and her daughter out of the story?
4. Are Dr. Earnest and Dr. Sincere reliable sources?
5. What do you tell the public about whether the water supply is safe?

Midrange Issues

1. Would you be working on the story if KAOS and ABC had ignored it?
2. Would you be working on the story if there was little public reaction after the KAOS broadcast?

3. If Ms. Waters decides to do an interview on ABC later today, do you then include her in your story?
4. If city and county officials remain unavailable, how do you handle their side of the story? Does that delay publication until you can get more information, or do you go with what is available?
5. Are there unbiased sources you can contact about risk assessment? Who?

Macro Issues

1. How do you handle the discrepancy between the information from the EPA and the skeptical scientists and environmentalists?
2. What is the public's probable reaction to reporting this story? Should your newspaper take any precautions to prevent public panic? If so, what should they be?
3. How risky is the water compared to risks we take for granted, such as traveling by car? Can you think of a relevant comparison for your article comparing the relative risk of the water to a well-known risk?
4. Is it the media's role to speak for a society that is averse to many risks? How might the media accomplish this function?

CASE 7-C

Painful Images of War: Too Painful for Whom? When?

BEVERLY HORVIT
Texas Christian University

On March 23, 2003, in the first few days of the second Gulf War in Iraq, U.S. troops traveling in a six-vehicle convoy made a wrong turn and were ambushed by Iraqi forces. Six of the U.S. troops were captured, and nine were killed. That news was confirmed when the Qatar-based satellite network Al Jazeera rebroadcast Iraqi television footage of five captured soldiers—four men and one woman—as well as images of slain soldiers. Pfc. Jessica Lynch was among those captured but was not interviewed by Iraqi state television.

The bodies of four of the dead soldiers were filmed as they lay on the floor of a makeshift morgue. Two of the dead soldiers appeared to have been shot in the head. A fifth body was shown lying on the road behind an ambushed U.S. military truck. The tape also showed five of the captured Americans being interviewed by Iraqi officials, who were off-screen.

U.S. officials, including Defense Secretary Donald Rumsfeld, immediately criticized the Iraqi government for allowing those interviews to be recorded and broadcast. By doing so, Rumsfeld argued, the Iraqis had violated the 1949 Geneva Conventions, which mandate how prisoners of war are to be treated. Article 13 states, in part, that "prisoners of war must at all times be humanely treated" and "must at times be protected, particularly against acts of violence or intimidation and against insults and public curiosity."

The International Committee of the Red Cross concurred.

The Geneva Conventions mandates that prisoners only be asked their name, rank and serial number and that they not be subjected to "degrading and humiliating treatment." The Al Jazeera footage shows the U.S. soldiers—some visibly nervous—being asked additional questions about their hometowns and their reasons for coming to Iraq.

Immediately after Al Jazeera began broadcasting the footage, Rumsfeld told reporters, "Needless to say, television networks that carry such pictures are, I would say, doing something that's unfortunate" (Reid and Doran 2003). Lt. Gen. John Abizaid of the U.S. Central Command went further: "We will hold those [in charge] accountable for their actions" (Reid and Doran 2003).

After the Pentagon said the interview footage violated the Geneva Conventions, Al Jazeera pulled the interviews but temporarily continued to broadcast images of slain soldiers (Hamilton 2003). Similarly, although CBS News briefly showed a clip of the Al Jazeera tape, it stopped after the Pentagon complained and e-mailed U.S. news organizations asking them not to use the tape.

The late Peter Jennings, then the anchor of ABC's nightly news show, told viewers that pictures of the captured soldiers and probably slain soldiers "have been seen widely throughout the world, including in Iraq. The Bush administration has said very forcefully this violates the Geneva Conventions governing the treatment for prisoners of war, and the president of ABC News has decided not to broadcast the pictures at this time."

US MILITARY
IRAQ WAR POW

Edgar Hernandez

**Army Spc.
Joseph Hudson**

**Army Spc.
Shoshawna Johnson**

Pfc. Patrick Miller

AP Photo/Iraqi TV via APTN.

Sgt. James Riley

In a "Nightline" edition the next night, Dave Marash of ABC News said "one simple rule" at ABC and other networks is not to use such pictures "until we know that families have been informed that their soldier has been captured." And, even when ABC knew the families had been notified, Marash noted there were other limitations on what ABC would show: "Pictures of dead soldiers, in which their wounds are grotesquely obvious, and their faces, perhaps, identifiable. And the real-time depiction of clearly frightened soldiers being asked questions that go well beyond the name, rank and serial number approved by the Geneva Conventions rulebook."

Newspaper editors around the United States also had to grapple with deciding which images, if any, to publish. Some U.S. newspapers chose to publish neither still photographs from the footage nor the soldiers' names. Others opted to run mug shots of the soldiers that had been cropped from the video footage but not still photographs of the slain soldiers. In many cases, the newspapers felt compelled to explain their rationale to their readers.

The *Orlando Sentinel, Atlanta Journal-Constitution,* Portland *Oregonian* and *Nashville Tennessean* are examples of papers whose editors decided not to use any of the still photographs from the Al Jazeera tapes on the first day. Dan Hortsch, public editor of the *Oregonian,* which published mug shots after the soldiers' names were released, told readers that although the Geneva Conventions applied to governments and not the news media, "the media must consider whether their actions further the intent of the captors" (Hortsch 2003).

In its story for March 24, the *Washington Post* told readers it was "not publishing the names of some of the soldiers because they had not been officially released by the Pentagon." The *Post* and *USA Today* did, however, use the name of Army Spc. Joseph Hudson, 23. Hudson was the second soldier to be questioned. When asked why he was in Iraq, Hudson replied: "I follow orders." Similarly, the *Orlando Sentinel* and *Constitution-Journal* ran a mug shot of Hudson.

Other newspapers, including the *Fort Worth Star-Telegram, Hartford Courant, Salt Lake Tribune* and *Sacramento Bee,* ran photos of the five captured soldiers cropped to mug shots. The *Star-Telegram* and *Sacramento Bee* published the mug shots on their front pages. In a Page 1 note to readers, *Star-Telegram* editors said, "We believe it is important for our readers to know their condition after capture, so we have chosen to run photos of their faces." Their actions and explanation did not impress some readers, many of whom sent angry letters to the editor.

A *Star-Telegram* (2003) editorial argued that publishing the photos would hold the Iraqis accountable for the POWs' well-being:

> The photographs . . . make it impossible for Iraqi officials to deny that they have these brave Americans in custody or to explain away possible injuries after their conditions have been documented. . . . Should the unthinkable happen—that they die after appearing in the news—then it will be clear that the soldiers were mistreated as prisoners. . . . Many families of prisoners held during the Vietnam War said that the media reports at least let them know their husbands, fathers, sons and brothers were still alive.

By the time the Pentagon had notified Spc. Shoshana Johnson's family of her capture, her parents already knew: they "had stumbled across it on their own—on a

Spanish-language television station they had tuned in so that their granddaughter could watch cartoons" (Kenworthy, Willing and Cauchon 2003).

Complaints of media coverage of POWs cut both ways. One Al Jazeera employee told the *Los Angeles Times,* "Everyone showed footage of Iraqi prisoners of war just a day ago, and no one said a thing about that" (Pasternak 2003). Likewise, a Red Cross spokesman said, "Images being shown of POWs on both sides are a cause for concern" (Neuffer 2003).

Gina Lubrano, readers' representative for the *San Diego Union-Tribune,* said readers complained when the newspaper published a photograph of a dead Iraqi soldier, a photograph similar to one that appeared on the front page of the *New York Times.* She told readers (Lubrano 2003):

> The reason photographs of prisoners are permissible in the *Union-Tribune* and other newspapers and suspect when supplied by the Iraqis has to do with who is behind the camera and the intent behind the photo. Government-run Iraqi television represents the government holding the prisoners. Photographing them being questioned can be interpreted by some as an attempt by the Iraqi government to ridicule them and hold them up to public curiosity. . . . The photos of the Iraqi prisoners and the dead published in the *Union-Tribune* and other newspapers have been taken by independent photojournalists, not the government, and are an attempt to show the events of war, not *to ridicule them.*

Micro Issues

1. Critique the *Star-Telegram*'s argument that publishing the photos would make the Iraqis more accountable for the welfare of the soldiers.
2. How should American media respond to the threat by the U.S. Central Command officer to hold those in charge "accountable for their actions"?

Midrange Issues

1. Lubrano makes a distinction between the independent U.S. press and the state-owned Iraqi press in justifying her paper's action while condemning a similar action by Al Jazeera. Is the distinction valid? Justify your answer.
2. Is there a difference between film and still photography of the dead soldiers, and does that difference, if any, justify handling the images differently?

Macro Issues

1. Should the press acquiesce to the government's request to not show photos of the war based on:
   a. notification of families?
   b. taste?
   c. the Geneva Conventions?
   d. national security?
   Justify your answers.

CASE 7-D

For God and Country: The Media and National Security

JEREMY LITTAU
University of Missouri

MARK SLAGLE
University of North Carolina–Chapel Hill

The ethical issues involving the intersection of the media and national security typically revolve around the question of duties and loyalties. Those questions, as the following three-part case demonstrates, are long standing. They also allow journalists to evaluate the consistency of their reasoning over time—something good ethical thinking is supposed to promote. How journalists respond to these cases also may depend on the differing philosophies individual journalists and their news organizations adhere to.

With this introduction, decide each of the following three cases, all of which have an important role in the history of journalism ethics. As you resolve the various issues in each case, ask yourself whether you have been consistent in your decision making and what philosophical approach or approaches best supports your thinking.

Case Study 1: The Bay of Pigs

In 1961, an anti-communist paramilitary force trained and supplied by the CIA, was preparing to invade Cuba and topple Fidel Castro. Although the desire of the American government to overthrow Castro was no secret, the specifics of the invasion plan were not known to the public. On April 6, a *New York Times* reporter filed a story with his editors that declared the invasion was "imminent." The paper prepared to run the story with a page-one, four-column slot using the word "imminent" in the text and the headline.

After much discussion, *Times* managing editor Turner Catledge and publisher Orvil Dryfoos decided to remove the word "imminent" from the story and shrink the headline to a single column. These changes were made, in part, in response to a phone call from President John F. Kennedy, asking the paper to kill the story. On April 17, the anti-Castro forces landed at Cuba's Bay of Pigs, where all group members were either taken prisoner or killed. The botched invasion was a major embarrassment for Kennedy, who later told Catledge that if the *Times* had run the story as planned it might have prevented the disastrous invasion (Hickey 2001).

Micro Issues

1. Did the *Times* act ethically in downsizing and downplaying the story?

Midrange Issue

1. Are there certain categories of information, for example troop movements or the development of new weapons, which journalists as a matter of policy should either downplay or not publish as all?

Macro Issue

1. How should journalists respond if government officials request that specific "facts" (which are not true) be printed as part of a disinformation campaign to confuse our enemies?

Case Study 2: Osama Bin Laden

Since the attacks of Sept. 11, 2001, Osama bin Laden and his deputies have released a series of video and audio tapes containing speeches about their ongoing operations. Many of them have first aired on Al Jazeera, the Arab-language news channel that broadcasts in the Middle East but also can be received in many American and European markets. The U.S. government, specifically President George W. Bush, urged the U.S. media not to rebroadcast these tapes, arguing that they might contain coded messages to al-Quaeda "sleeper cells" and could result in more attacks. Most broadcast networks acquiesced to the request, although it was never made clear whether any of the tapes, in fact, contained such messages (Spencer 2001).

Micro Issue

1. How is this request like and unlike President Kennedy's request to the *New York Times?*

Midrange Issues

1. Does the fact that other news agencies in other countries broadcast the tapes have any bearing on what U.S. broadcasters should do?
2. Should U.S. broadcasters have agreed to this request in October of 2001? Should they agree to the request today? Why or why not?

Macro Issue

1. How would you respond to a viewer who says that broadcasting the tapes is unpatriotic and puts American lives at risk?

Case Study 3: Make News, Not War?

In 1991 CNN correspondent Christiane Amanpour arrived in the Balkans to cover the breakaway of Slovenia and Croatia from Yugoslavia. After witnessing several brutal battles, including the siege of Dubrovnik, she moved on to Bosnia to cover the hostilities there for almost two years. Troubled by the lack of coverage the war was receiving, Amanpour encouraged her editors to devote more time to the issue. In 1994, Amanpour appeared via satellite on a live television broadcast with President Bill Clinton. She asked the president if "the constant flip-flops of your administration on the issue of Bosnia set a very dangerous precedent." Amanpour's pointed questions embarrassed the administration and generated more coverage of the war and of American foreign policy. Amanpour later admitted she wanted to draw more attention to the plight of the Bosnian Muslims (Halberstam 2001).

Micro Issues

1. Should Amanpour consciously have tried to influence U.S. foreign policy in this way?
2. If she had not tried to influence U.S. policy, would she have been complicit in the genocide that followed?

Midrange Issues

1. Are some issues, such as genocide, so ethically reprehensible that journalists should speak out as citizens in addition to fulfilling their professional responsibilities?
2. Is it appropriate for journalists to testify at war crimes trials when they have witnessed and reported on atrocities?

Macro Issues

1. Is it naive for journalists to continue to say that "we just let readers make up their minds" on these issues? If you answer yes, what does that say about the ethical dilemmas that come with the power we have as journalists?

CASE 7-E

Not in Our Name

KARON REINBOTH SPECKMAN
University of Missouri

Whether Great Britain should join the United States in war against Iraq was a hot topic among British citizens in the beginning months of 2003.

America's President George Bush was pushing for war, and Great Britain's Prime Minister Tony Blair was advocating joining the United States. The Blair-Bush partnership was strengthened after the 9/11 attack on the World Trade Center Towers in 2001. Now, Blair was trying to persuade British citizens and his government to join the United States regardless of the outcome of a second United Nations resolution sanctioning the war.

However, many British citizens and even Blair's own Labour Party did not want to join the United States unless the United Nations supported the action. An Independent Television (ITV) poll of Sept. 25, 2002, had showed that 70 percent of the respondents were against Great Britain going to war alongside the United States without a UN mandate. By Jan. 13, another ITV poll showed that 53 percent would have approved taking part in a U.S.-led war on Iraq as long as such action was approved by a fresh UN Security Council motion. The UN Security Council motion wasn't getting support from other Council members, in spite of intense pressure from both countries' leaders. Yet Blair pressed on with his arguments to join the United States, arguing that Iraq posed a threat to world safety. He addressed the House of Commons and also took his case to the British public on television. Blair also spent an hour Feb. 6 defending his reasons in front of a hostile panel of citizens on BBC's "Newsnight" with Jeremy Paxman.

London's 10 daily national newspapers were vocal about their stance on the war, although the message usually focused on the need for another UN resolution. Six papers were for the war, and three were against the war—the *Guardian,* the *Independent,* and the *Daily Mirror.* The London papers are not owned by particular parties. However, excluding the *Independent,* the papers are considered highly partisan. The *Daily Mirror* took partisanship to a new level with an orchestrated effort against the war that involved reader petitions, slanted coverage with inflammatory photo illustrations and involvement in an antiwar rally.

Because British newspapers are quite different than American dailies, it is helpful to look at some of those differences to understand the *Mirror*'s campaign. London's dailies are considered national because the papers have a national reputation, extensively cover national issues and are published in the nation's capital. The dailies are divided in two ways: by size (broadsheet or "quality" and tabloid) and also by audience or socioeconomic market (elite, mid-market, and popular). With a circulation of 2,100,000 of mostly unskilled working class and underclass readers, the Labour-leaning *Daily Mirror* is one of three tabloids at the "bottom" of the socioeconomic categories.

Although London's popular tabloids often are dismissed as "trashy," one of the most famous—the *Sun*—has a readership of more than 3.5 million. In fact, most citizens get their news from tabloids that package rehashed news with a heavy focus on entertainment and celebrities. The broadsheets—the *Times, Financial Times,* the *Guardian* and the *Independent*—usually restrict blatant partisanship to editorial pages. Not so the tabloids. They are very willing to mix comment with news in headlines, stories and photo illustrations. Also, competition for readers is keen among all newspapers but especially the tabloids. The *Daily Mirror* was losing readers at this time to the *Sun* and the *Daily Star* and needed to boost its circulation figures.

So with stiff paper competition and a prospective controversial war, the *Daily Mirror* started a petition drive on Jan. 21, 2003, dubbed "Not in Our Name." Its entire front page had a background picture of a soldier and these words:

> Sign this page and send it back to us. You are NOT powerless.
> You DO have a voice. NO WAR.
> Mr. Blair, I hereby register my opposition to any war with Iraq not justified by unequivocal UN evidence.
> Name
> Address

Thus started a campaign to get reader messages—and e-mail responses—to Blair. The next day's edition also devoted the entire front page to the campaign with the headline "The War is Wrong" and a picture of a Falklands War hero Simon Weston, who was against the Iraqi War. Antiwar coverage consumed six inside pages with several pages of pictures of entertainment celebrities signing the petition.

On Thursday, Jan. 23, the tally of petitions began. The front-page headline read: 15,000 BY FIRST POST, Are you listening NOW Mr. Blair? By Friday, the count was 70,000, and that issue included a giant NO WAR poster. The Friday front page was split into halves—one half devoted to a TV star in a skimpy outfit and the other half devoted to the antiwar campaign.

The number of petitioners continued the second week with 164,500 petitions. The Wednesday Jan. 20 front page had a photo illustration of Blair with bloody hands and the headline: BLOOD ON HIS HANDS. Examples of other front pages that blasted Blair were one with a PRIME MONSTER headline over a picture of Blair, one with a big red VETO stamped on Blair's face and one with Blair kissing Bush that said Make Love Not War. Inside content matched the subjective tone, much of it in first-person editorials mixed with news coverage so that readers would have difficulty separating opinion from fact.

However, the *Mirror*'s involvement did not stop with the petitions and sensationalized content. The largest antiwar rally in Britain's history was Feb. 15 with estimates varying from 1 to 2 million marchers in London. The *Mirror* staff gave out 30,000 placards to marchers—the original NO WAR poster from the first front page of the campaign. In addition, a giant *Mirror* banner with Not in Our Name was a backdrop at the rally in Hyde Park where speakers addressed the marchers. A similar large banner was unfurled in Bush and Blair's flight patterns near Lajes air base in the Azores— where Bush and Blair held a last-ditch summit over the weekend of March 15–16. Newspaper petitions are not new to London papers. The *Sun* started a petition drive earlier in January 2003. But its cause was against what it called "asylum madness." Fear of terrorist acts in London sparked much of the fervor over asylum seekers as well as a killing of an unarmed policeman by an asylum seeker. More than 500,000 people responded to the popular and often xenophobic *Sun* petition drive. Other newspaper-led petitions included a 1990 campaign by the *Daily Mail* and the *Daily Star* against the murder charges of a paratrooper for the death of a Belfast teenager.

Newspaper editors often feel the campaigns are successful; however, critics say that unless focus groups also raise the issues, government will not pay attention. A final problem for those who led antiwar campaigns: What happens when the government goes to war? Britain did join the United States on March 18. By then, almost 225,000 readers had signed the petition. Then the *Mirror* had the challenge of convincing readers that although the paper was against the war, it supported the troops.

Thus, the March 18 front page said:

UNlawful UNethical UNstoppable
Why we blame Blair but back our forces.

By April 2003, the *Mirror*'s circulation had fallen below 2 million. Editor Piers Morgan said in a *Guardian* article that perhaps the antiwar stance could be blamed for the loss in circulation.

Micro Issues

1. Should newspapers or broadcast media openly support or oppose a war or any other cause with petition drives? If yes, who should decide which causes to openly support?
2. How should a media outlet separate or distinguish its "opinion" or analysis from straight news so readers and viewers know the difference?
3. Do photo illustrations have a place in news?

Midrange Issues

1. Is the "objectivity" or fairness standard of American journalism outdated for modern times and in an era of multiple delivery systems for news?
2. What are the dangers of a similar push by an American media company in a time when so many papers are owned by conglomerates?
3. Is partisanship of a media outlet a problem if people know the media outlet's political leanings?
4. What happens when media outlets find themselves on the unpopular side of a cause? Should the financial implications of such a stance be a factor in whether the unpopular leaning should be revealed.

Macro Issues

1. What is the difference between "reflecting" the view of readers and "setting the agenda"?
2. Are editors abusing or misusing political power with petitions or are they giving voice to the voiceless?

CASE 7-F

Mayor Jim West's Computer

GINNY WHITEHOUSE
Whitworth College

The quiet, conservative city of Spokane, Wash., woke up to a surprise on Thursday, May 5, 2005, as residents opened their newspapers. They discovered that Mayor Jim West had used his city computer to solicit young men in gay chat rooms and that two men claimed West had sexually molested them as children.

In the months prior, West had been e-chatting on *Gay.com* with someone he believed to be an 18-year-old recent high school graduate, and offered him a city hall internship, sports memorabilia, help getting into college and excursions around the country. In reality, he had been corresponding with a forensic computer expert hired by the *Spokesman-Review*.

Reporter Bill Morlin had spent two years along with Reporter Karen Dorn Steele tracking down allegations from the 1970s that West had sexually molested boys while he was a county sheriff's deputy and a Boy Scout leader. West had been close friends with fellow deputy David Hahn and fellow Scout leader George Robey, who both committed suicide after sexual abuse allegations were brought against them in the early 1980s.

In 2002, the reporters discovered links to West while investigating abuse by local Catholic priests. West was at that time Republican majority leader in the Washington state senate and was considering running for what he called his "dream job"—being mayor of his hometown, Spokane. During the campaign, the reporters did not believe they had enough information to confirm any allegations. Eventually, they received tips from both anonymous sources and sources who would later go on the record and swear in depositions that West had abused them. One man, Robert Galliher, said West molested him at least four times as a child and that he was assaulted repeatedly by Hahn. Galliher, who says he has struggled with drug addiction as a result of the molestations, said he was in prison in 2003 when West visited him and sent him a message to keep his mouth shut. In addition, other young men reported that they had had sex with West after meeting him on gay chat lines and had been offered favors and rewards.

Spokesman-Review Editor Steven Smith and his staff spent days agonizing over creating a fictional character to go online at *Gay.com* and consulted with ethics experts at the Poynter Institute and elsewhere as they considered options. Smith told Spokane readers that the newspaper would not ordinarily go to such lengths or use deception, "But the seriousness of the allegations and the need for specific computer forensic skills overrode our general reluctance." Most important, Smith said the *Spokesman-Review*'s decisions were based on concerns about abuse of power and pedophilia, and not whether the mayor was homosexual.

The forensic expert, who previously worked for the U.S. Customs' Office, followed strict guidelines. The expert posed online as a 17-year-old Spokane high school student and waited for West to approach him. The expert did not initiate conversation about sex, sexuality or the mayor's office. In the months that followed, the high school student supposedly had an 18th birthday. West then requested meetings with the fictional young man and arrived in a new Lexus at an agreed-upon spot—a golf course. His picture was taken secretly and the forensic expert broke off contact.

West was told about the forensic investigator in an interview with *Spokesman-Review* staff the day before the story broke. He admitted to the offers made within the chat room but denied abusing or having sex with anyone under age 18. When asked about the abuse allegations from the two men, West told the *Spokesman-Review* editors and reporters, "I didn't abuse them. I don't know these people. I didn't abuse anybody, and I didn't have sex with anybody under 18—ever—woman or man."

West insisted that he had not abused his office and that he was not gay. After the story broke, local gay rights advocate Ryan Oelrich, a former member of the city's Human Rights Commission, told the newspaper that he had resigned after coming to the conclusion West appointed him in an effort to pursue a sexual relationship. Oelrich said West offered him at one point $300 to swim naked with him in his swimming pool. Oelrich declined.

A conservative Republican, West blocked antidiscrimination provisions in housing for homosexuals, and voted against health benefits for gay couples while he served in the Washington state legislature and as mayor. He supported legislation barring homosexuals from working in schools or day care centers and called for bans on gay marriage. He told "The Today Show" that he was merely representing his constituents' views.

West asserted a message that he would repeat eventually on CNN, MSNBC and in a host of other national broadcasts: "There is a strong wall between my public and my private life."

Many political scientists disagreed with West's interpretation. Washington State University Political Science Professor Lance LeLoup said using an elected position for personal benefit is both unethical and "a misuse of power." Gonzaga University Political Science Professor Blaine Garvin told the *Spokesman-Review,* "I think it's a pretty bright line that you don't use your command over public resources to earn personal favors. That's not what those resources are for."

At the same time, some media critics criticized the newspaper's choice to use deception. The public cannot be expected to believe journalists and the veracity of their stories if lies are told to get at information, said Jane Kirtley, director of the Silha Center for Media Ethics and Law at the University of Minnesota. Speaking at a Washington News Council Forum on the *Spokesman-Review*'s coverage, Kirtley asserted that police officers can practice deception as part of their jobs, but journalists should not.

"It's one thing for the police or the FBI to pose as a 17-year-old boy," William Babcock, journalism department chair at California State University–Long Beach, told the *Seattle Post-Intelligencer*. "It's another for a journalist to take on the role of junior G-man and do something that essentially is considered police work." Babcock insists that the *Spokesman-Review* should have gotten the information through traditional reporting methods, but he agreed that no one, particularly a city mayor, should expect privacy in an online chat room.

Poytner Ethicist Kelly McBride, who previously was a reporter at the *Spokesman-Review,* said deception should not be normal practice but that the newspaper considered key ethical obligations: that the issue is grave and in the public interest, alternatives are explored, the decision and practice are openly shared with readers and the mayor is given the opportunity to share his story.

Jeffrey Weiss, a religion reporter for the *Dallas Morning News,* said he rarely believes the ends should justify the means, "but some do."

The FBI investigated West on federal corruption charges but did not find his actions warranted prosecution. Special Counsel Mark Barlett said in a media conference, "Our investigation did not address whether Jim West's activities were ethical, moral, or appropriate. . . . We did not attempt to determine whether Jim West should be the mayor of Spokane."

In December 2005, Spokane voters ousted the mayor in a special recall election. West later said the newspaper had created a "mob mentality" and that considering the accusations, even he would have voted against himself. On July 22, 2006, West died following surgery for colon cancer, a disease he had been fighting for three years. He was 55.

Micro Issues

1. Do you agree that police officers are ethically permitted to use deception but journalists are not?
2. Was the *Spokesman-Review* justified in using deception? Under other what extreme circumstances do you believe deception might be justified?

Midrange Issues

1. Some critics claimed that West's story only would come out in a provincial, conservative community, and that his story would not have been news had he been the mayor of Chicago or Miami. Do you agree?
2. Sissela Bok says deception might be permitted if the act passes the test of publicity. Does the *Spokesman-Review* meet that standard?
3. Should the use of a forensic computer expert in this case be characterized as the ends justifying the means? Why or why not?

Macro Issues

1. Should there be a wall between the public and private lives of public officials? At what point do public officials' private lives become public concern? Is public officials' sexuality always part of their private lives?
2. The *Spokesman-Review* is locally owned by the Cowles Publishing Company. The family business includes a downtown mall with a parking garage, which was developed in financial partnership with the city of Spokane. The garage has been subject to repeated lawsuits and controversy. Some critics believed that the *Spokesman-Review*'s delay in reporting about the mayor was due to a conflict of interest. Editor Steve Smith insists that the story was reported as the facts became evident. How do locally owned media companies manage covering their own communities without incurring conflicts of interest?

8

Media Economics: The Deadline Meets the Bottom Line

By the end of this chapter you should be familiar with:

- how the "blockbuster" model influences media content.
- how advertisers gain influence in the media economic equation and the ramifications of that additional influence.
- the economic realities of the social responsibility theory of the press.
- the economic and legislative initiatives that have combined to place control of information in the hands of fewer and larger corporations.
- the "stakeholder" theory of economic success.

INTRODUCTION

In the movie "Absence of Malice," Paul Newman is asked if he has taken his complaint concerning an inaccurate article about him to the newspaper. He replies, "Have you ever tried to talk to a newspaper?" For most Americans, the point is well taken. A faceless, nameless, non–locally owned media is becoming a reality in all but a few communities. Today the media are predominantly corporate owned and publicly traded, with media conglomerates among the largest of the world's corporations. The corporate owners of the average news operation are more insulated from contact with news consumers than virtually any other business owner in America. And, there are fewer of them. At the time this book went to press, most media outlets in the world were owned by six multinational corporations. Those corporations, in most cases, controlled not just the outlet but the content as well, including entertainment programming.

The case of CBS is illustrative. In 2000, the FCC gave its approval to the $46 billion merger between Viacom and CBS. Viacom's assets include MTV, VH1,

Nickelodeon, Paramount, Blockbuster, Simon and Schuster publishers and Spelling Entertainment, producers of television programming. At the time of the acquisition of CBS, Viacom also increased its holdings by acquiring television stations, syndicators KingWorld and Eyemark, a radio and outdoor advertising empire and several cable networks. And even though the merger put Viacom in control of two networks—CBS and UPN—the FCC granted an exception to its rule prohibiting one corporation from owning two television networks. The twin goals of this rush to consolidation were vertically integrated companies with diverse sources of income. Eventually, however, the synergies were so small and the problems so great that in 2006, CBS split the company once again along two lines—CBS and Viacom.

The NBC/Universal conglomerate provides another illustration of this trend. By acquiring the production facilities of Universal, NBC now stands a better chance of owning the shows it puts on its broadcast network. And by acquiring the cable USA network, NBC obtained another outlet for its shows to go into the lucrative phases of syndication—a textbook model of vertical integration of product from beginning to end. Taking advantage of legislation that ended the FCC's old "fin-syn" rule, NBC can now own a show from the filming of the pilot episode to the last airing of the syndicated show sometime in the middle of this century, depending on popularity, and the payoffs for this large "gift" from the FCC are just now being seen.

But well before a show goes into the "aftermarket" of boxed sets at the retail store and unlimited airings on cable, there are now multiple opportunities to access the shows in first run. Are you intrigued with the new show "Heroes" but unable to catch it on Monday night? Don't worry. You can catch that same week's show on the SciFi Channel or on USA network without benefit of any more technology than your television set and a cable box or satellite hook up. Of course, for the more technologically savvy, downloads of popular shows are now available for free from the NBC Web site for those who don't mind watching a few embedded commercials and are available for a small fee commercial-free to such devices as cell phones. In short, by the middle of the first decade of the 21st century, the original airtime of a network television program was becoming increasingly irrelevant, and the media conglomerates had finally found a way to compete with such technologies as TiVo by offering alternative ways to access programming.

Media consolidation allows for a diversification of income. In the case of NBC/Universal, revenues went from 90 percent advertising-based to 50 percent, with the remainder coming from subscriptions, admissions, licensing and other ancillary income. With their dependence on advertising, media companies historically have been subject to the vagaries of recessions, particularly in the United States. Conglomeration added more revenue streams and made things more predictable for stockholders as parent corporations became less subject to localized economic influences.

In June 2003, the Federal Communications Commission, obeying a court order to review all ownership regulations every two years, proposed changes that either eliminated antiquated ownership caps or paved the way to the end of democracy, depending on one's political leanings. The rhetoric was heated in the months leading up to the ruling, with more than 520,000 comments pouring into the commission. The vote for the relaxation of ownership limits was divided 3–2 along party lines, with the Republican majority on the panel casting the deciding votes. Key provisions of the law included:

- Allowing a single company to own multiple television stations in a market.
- Expanding the number of radio stations a company could own in a market.
- Expanding the potential allowable reach of television chains to 45 percent (up from 35 percent) of the total population in the United States.
- Leaving intact a ban on any of the four largest television networks—ABC, NBC, CBS or Fox—from merging their operations.
- Overturning a decades-old rule that prevented newspapers in a monopoly market from owning broadcast properties in the same community.

Groups as diverse as the National Organization for Women and the National Rifle Association criticized the changes. FCC Commissioner Michael Copps, in a minority dissent, called the changes another step in the "Clear Channelization" of American media, a reference to Clear Channel, a media company that had benefited from earlier relaxation of ownership limits in radio, only to become a lightning rod for consumer complaints about nonlocal ownership of radio stations.

Soon after the new ownership rules were announced, they were challenged in court and in Congress. In a historic response, consumers—organized on the Internet—objected so vigorously that Congress ultimately rejected the changes. In their campaign, critics of the ultimately rejected ownership changes claimed that when the local newspaper is allowed to own two or more television stations and up to eight radio stations in the nation's largest markets, competition in news would no longer exist and the public would lose important viewpoints.

Columbia Journalism Review Editor at Large Neil Hickey (2003) summed up the fears of many when he concluded,

> What we risk over the long haul is ownership creep that may eventually see the end of the few remaining rules, and with them, the public's right to the widest possible array of news and opinion—at which point, robust, independent, antagonistic, many-voiced journalism may be only a memory.

How the public interest can best be served through ownership rules will likely be a debate for years to come. The inherent tension created in trying to satisfy competing interests creates many of the ethical problems discussed in this chapter.

ECONOMICS AND ENTERTAINMENT: THE "BLOCKBUSTER" MODEL RULES

While digital technology sent shock waves throughout all media industries, the strongest tremors were felt in the entertainment business. There, digital technology arrived at the same time five global companies—Universal Music Group (owned by Vivendi), Warner Music (a division of AOL Time Warner), Sony Music Entertainment, the German firm Bertelsmann Music Group (BMG) and the EMI Group—took control of about 85 percent of the record industry.

The rationale for the conglomeration in the music industry (labeled "dyssynergy" by *New Yorker* writer John Seabrook) was that profits from established labels and artists would be used to promote new talent. However, the corporate approach meant that managers now focused on quarterly profits and selling records rather than making music and promoting art.

Corporations wanted blockbuster hits. They were difficult and expensive to make and promote, and impossible to predict. Wal-Mart, the largest retailer of music in America, wanted to make their profits from the industry while carrying only about 2 percent of all releases available in a single year (Anderson 2006).

Chris Blackwell, who began a small record label in the 1970s and sold it to Poly-Gram in 1989, said, "I don't think the music business lends itself very well to being a Wall Street business. You're always working with individuals, with creative people, and the people you are trying to reach, by and large, don't view music as a commodity but as a relationship with a band. It takes time to expand that relationship but most people who work for the corporations have three-year contracts, some five, and most of them are expected to produce. What an artist really needs is a champion, not a numbers guy who in another year is going to leave" (Seabrook 2003, 46).

Other industries were affected by the new economic realities as well. In the summer of 2002, one major studio announced that it would no longer make medium-budget films—from $40 million to $80 million. Instead, the corporation announced to its shareholders that it would focus instead on occasional "niche" films for $10 million or less and "blockbuster" films with budgets of $100 million or more. According to executives quoted, films in the middle are now considered too risky to make.

With the average price tag for major films soaring, studios ran for cover. Sequels provided one short-term approach. Some were sequels of classics while others were sequels of movies panned the first time out. Advertising budgets for these sequels were huge, creating large opening weekends that were typically followed by dropoffs in attendance of up to 70 percent as the word of mouth got out that some films were not that good.

The effect of this trend was that midpriced, independent films, with fewer explosions and with no-name actors, have less chance of being made than ever before. True, there was the occasional medium budget breakout such as "Little Miss Sunshine," and Al Gore's Academy winning film suggested that documentaries could be profitable. But the entertainment industry, focused as it was on the "hit" business model, continued to play it safe. It was an instance where the exceptions demonstrated the larger rule.

The new economics of film did open one door, however. Film festivals and movie distributors were looking for the next low-budget breakout film—a trend that started with the "Blair Witch Project" in the 1990s and continues today with new films being discovered at festivals such as Cannes (France) and Sundance (U.S.).

Meanwhile, the music industry was changing. While corporations were merging, CD technology—made possible by the digital revolution—took over what historians now call the "record" market. By 1986, CD sales had climbed to 100 million copies worldwide. In 1999 CD sales eclipsed those of vinyl records. And, then, the bottom fell out due to an unanticipated consequence of the CD (digital) format: CDs made piracy possible. Digital music, uploaded onto the Internet through MP3 files, made enormous inroads with younger listeners and viewers—the generation most comfortable with the computer and its capabilities. In 2002 the industry shipped 33.5 million copies of the year's 10 best-selling CDs, barely half the number it had shipped two years before.

Most industry experts agreed that the MP3 format was a permanent addition to the ways audiences could access music, television and film. The flexibility and specificity of file-sharing programs—and business models such as iTunes and Amazon that take advantage of them—meant that many more people were accessing media content digitally—some of it legally and some of it not. Sir Howard Stringer, the chairman of the Sony Corporation of America, called downloaders "thieves" and compared them to those who shoplift from stores. (For a case study about Napster, the first file-sharing software, go to the Web site for this book.) The recording industry initially filed suit against some select downloaders. But a pricing structure that made downloading inexpensive, and converging media that used devices such as cell phones to access everything from entertainment programming to traditional news, seemed a more effective—and more profitable—remedy.

Some have suggested that the heavy-handed tactics initially employed to discourage illegal file sharing meant the industry regarded its fan base with suspicion and disapproval. However, some artists were not so quick to condemn, noting that music file sharing/piracy could be considered payback for the way giant corporations had exploited artists. Joni Mitchell, songwriter and artist, called the record industry a "corrupt cesspool." Others have said that if the downloading trend continues unchecked, the recording industry as the world currently knows it will die.

The ethical implications of these two now-entwined trends are obvious. As you read this section, ask yourself when was the last time you bought a music CD as opposed to burning one? Do you agree that person-to-person music sharing constitutes theft? Is Joni Mitchell right, and is file sharing a good way to register such a protest? Is Sir Howard Stringer right that it is equivalent to shoplifting? Would you feel the same way if someone shared *your* works? On an industrywide level, how will new artists, especially those who don't fit the corporate view, emerge and prosper? Can music or film fans worldwide "afford" to relinquish an art form that for many sustains an emotional connection to some of the most formative times of their lives? Will creative people, who find their energies unusable in the music industry, turn to other mediums? As is often the case in the mass media, the development and adoption of a new medium or delivery technology often has unanticipated consequences on many mediums and formats as well as on content.

THE PENNY PRESS REVOLUTION

Financing the American media through advertising is so deeply ingrained in the system that it is hard to imagine any other way. Yet newspapers supported solely by their readers thrived in America for more than a century. As recently as 1920, then-Secretary of Commerce Herbert Hoover argued in vain for a commercial-free broadcast industry to be funded by the sellers of the receivers. While the airways eventually became filled with commercials, Hoover and the Federal Radio Commission (now the Federal Communications Commission or FCC) won one important battle: the public is the owner of the airwaves and the station is merely the "trustee" of that commodity.

Today each medium has found its own formula to economic security—from "free" network television on one end of the continuum to books, movies and a handful of magazines such as *Ms.* and *Consumer Reports* on the other—that pass on virtually all of the production costs to the consumer. Most media organizations lie somewhere in between.

That formula for contemporary economic security began more than 170 years ago when Benjamin Day, publisher of the *New York Sun,* started a revolution by lowering the price of his newspaper to a penny at a time when his competition was selling newspapers for a nickel. He gambled that he could overcome the printing losses with additional advertising revenue—if circulation increased. When his gamble paid off, virtually every publisher in town followed his lead. Soon after, Frank Munsey lowered the cost of *Munsey's Magazine* from a quarter to a dime and watched as his circulation increased eightfold in two years to a half million readers.

What Day and Munsey did was farsighted. By pricing their products at or below the cost of printing, they cast their economic future with their advertisers. What was not foreseen, however, was the diminished role the consumer would play in the process.

Under the old pricing structure, subscribers were an end in themselves. Each represented a percentage of the profit, no matter how minuscule. Under this system, readers purchased news, entertainment and opinion content. Under the new system, advertisers purchased readers. The individual subscriber became a means to an end. Content is now relegated to the status of "bait" to catch readers and viewers to be sold to advertisers, as Bill Moyers points out in an interview for PBS's "The Promise of Television":

> Every manager or owner I know in commercial television now simply accepts television as a by-product of the merchandising process. That changes how you regard the people for whom you are producing or creating television. They are there to be seduced, to be sold something that somebody wants to sell. You are simply a transmission belt between someone trying to sell a product and the person who has the money to buy it, and it changes altogether your sense of your mission, your purpose, or your obligations to that viewer.

CASUALTIES FROM THE REVOLUTION

Two problems emerged from the penny press revolution that shifted the profit center from consumers to advertisers. First, in an attempt to attract the largest audience possible, media outlets "homogenized" their content, dealing in topics guaranteed to offend few individuals while hoping to garner large audiences. The result is journalism that takes no risks unless research shows that the audience will follow. In fact, Gannett's *USA Today* was developed from a marketing plan, not as a news concept.

Network news presidents "know," for instance, that the public has an interest in only one foreign story at a time. So while the "pack" went first to the Persian Gulf and then Somalia in the early 1990s, the continuing horrors of Bosnia and the killing fields of El Salvador went unreported or at best underreported. During the buildup and execution of the 2003 war to remove Saddam Hussein, stories of the continuing turmoil in Darfur were virtually nonexistent as were the nuclear buildup of countries such as Iran and North Korea.

Similarly, events are reported more than processes. Stories written for the masses focus on quick-onset disasters such as Hurricane Katrina but not on the slow-onset disaster of global warming that may be spawning ever larger hurricanes. Every summer, stories of forest fires with their made-for-television visuals are played out with only passing reference to the underlying causes of a drought that may be reaching half a century in length now.

Second, the penny press revolution made it more difficult for diverse voices to find a mainstream forum. The late Randy Shilts of the *San Francisco Chronicle,* the first reporter in the United States assigned to the AIDS beat, claimed that AIDS coverage was stymied in its early stages as it was perceived to be a "gay plague" of interest only to the homosexual community (Shilts 1987). Only when celebrities such as Rock Hudson and "innocents" such as Ryan White contracted the disease did it get widespread mainstream media coverage (Rogers and Chang 1991).

The pursuit of financial interests by publicly traded "Big Media" conglomerates has limited the access to mainstream media for anyone whose work (or thought) lies outside the mainstream or goes against the will of advertisers. Scholars (Kessler 1989; Miller 1992) have found a relationship between advertising dollars and editorial content, particularly in the controversial area of tobacco and health. Magazines receiving a great deal of revenue from the tobacco industry were significantly less likely to print articles about the health impact of tobacco. Kessler credits the indirect influence of the tobacco industry on these publications as a factor in the rise of tobacco-related cancers in women during the latter half of the 20th century.

Just what role profit ought to play in the media depends in part on the view you take of the media's role in society. In the next section, we will examine two important descriptive theories of the press that have dominated American thought and look at the role profit and economics play in each.

LIBERTARIAN AND SOCIAL RESPONSIBILITY THEORIES REVISITED

Mass communication research has several descriptive theories. An underlying assumption of these theories is that any media system "takes on the form and coloration of the social and political structures within which it operates" (Siebert, Peterson, and Schramm 1956, 3). Eventually, theorists predict, a media system will reflect the political and social structure of a society. Two of the best known descriptive theories of the press are the libertarian and social responsibility theories. Together they describe more than 200 years of thinking on the role of information in a society and how it should be delivered.

The *libertarian theory* of the press grew out of the changes that swept Europe from the Reformation to the Renaissance. In keeping with the basic tenets of the Enlightenment, libertarian theory assumes that people are rational and that truth is discoverable in a secular, empirical way. According to libertarian theory, political authority rests with the individual. Government's role is to ensure the domestic and foreign peace, but the individual is supreme in politics—a belief spelled out in the

Preamble to the U.S. Constitution. Because the individual is rational, government should do the individual's bidding. People are viewed as having both the time and the inclination to become literate and involved in public affairs.

With these assumptions, the libertarian theory of the press reflects Milton's concept of the "marketplace of ideas." Anyone could operate a printing press, particularly anyone aligned with a political group. Those who ran the presses of the day, because they were partisan, would provide partisan versions of reality. The rational citizen would select the truth from among the partisan versions available.

Within this theory, the press's most potent antagonist would be government, which libertarians viewed as locked in a perpetual power struggle for political supremacy with the individual. The duty of the press was to support the individual in that fight. The result was a media system that supported a well-informed individual in a quest for well-being and happiness.

The ensuing 500 years have done much to change our view of humanity and of society. Three intellectual changes were instrumental in this shift. First, Freud and modern psychology changed our view of rational humanity. We now believe that people are often illogical, sometimes irrational and motivated by a variety of needs and drives. People are not uniformly energetic or educated. For this reason, they will not always seek out and sometimes will not understand information to which they have access.

Second, knowledge, indeed reality itself, has been transformed. Societies have begun to realize that what we think of as a "fact" is subject to both perception and change, a philosophical view known as pragmatism. The "fact" that matter cannot become energy was successfully challenged by Einstein. Truth has become ephemeral.

Third, society has become more cosmopolitan. As people moved to cities and as waves of immigrants reached American shores, people discovered they were as different from one another in culture and language as they were alike in their quest for a better life. What was truth for one group was not truth for another. Literacy, at least literacy in English, was a cherished ideal, not a reality. Mass markets of many sorts emerged.

These shifts transformed the press of the 1800s into the mass media of this century. Life today in the United States often seems to comprise a series of self-interested subgroups. A new media system was required. Today, the mass media are no longer the written word but also television, public relations, advertising, entertainment and every conceivable hybrid, including the Internet. Few people, even in the age of the personal computer, can own a media outlet. Existing outlets are largely corporate owned and eschew partisanship in favor of objectivity. The marketplace of ideas became a monopoly supermarket, and the goods it carried were uniformly "vanilla."

With these changes came a new descriptive theory of the press called the *social responsibility theory*. The theory was developed in the 1940s by a panel of scholars, the Hutchins Commission, with funding from Henry Luce, the conservative founder of *Time* magazine. No journalist sat on the commission. Despite this, the social responsibility theory continues to fascinate both academics and practitioners because it attempts to return to a day when an active recipient of news and information was satisfied by a socially responsible press not bound by financial constraints.

But social responsibility theory even in the 1940s was realistic about the limitations of the press. First, the number of media outlets is limited, and, second, people are often self-interested and sometimes lazy. According to the Hutchins Commission, the media have the following five functions in society:

1. To provide a truthful, comprehensive and intelligent account of the day's events in a context that gives them meaning.
2. To serve as a forum for exchange of comment and criticism.
3. To provide a representative picture of constituent groups in society.
4. To present and clarify the goals and values of society.
5. To provide citizens with full access to the day's intelligence.

The goals of social responsibility theory are troubling to journalists. While the theory acknowledges that the world is intellectually and socially a different place from that of the libertarian view, it provides no clear guidelines for journalistic behavior in this new era.

Indeed, some of the guidelines the theory does provide are ambiguous. How should the forums operate? Whose values should be presented and clarified? Others appear to be mutually exclusive. For example, the media's role as mirror and critic may conflict with some interpretations of media objectivity. Other guidelines might simply be impossible to achieve for example, providing intelligent discourse about the day's events in a nightly newscast of less than 23 minutes.

An even more fundamental problem hobbles social responsibility theory: it gives little attention to modern media economics. This omission occurred in part because multinational corporations and chain ownership were still on the horizon when the Hutchins Commission codified the theory. Because the theory was developed early in the McCarthy period, there also was an unwillingness to link economic and political power for fear of being labeled Marxist. This central omission means that *the social responsibility theory, like libertarianism, does not deal with the realities of concentrated economic power,* particularly in an era when information has become an increasingly valuable commodity. Today some of the most troubling problems in media ethics stem from journalism's dual responsibilities to citizens and to stockholders, and the social responsibility and libertarian views of the press provide little guidance on these issues.

STAKEHOLDER THEORY VERSUS STOCKHOLDER THEORY

The philosophical rationale for the current state of media financial affairs can be readily summarized as an emphasis on corporate fiduciary responsibility to the stockholders of publicly traded corporations—including the six media behemoths. Most succinctly summarized by Nobel-prize winning economist Milton Friedman, stockholder theory says that corporations—and the CEOs and board members who oversee them—have a single, overriding and legally blinding promise to those who purchase stock in the corporations: increase the share price.

Friedman has gone so far as to suggest that increasing the share price is *the* promise that managers make. Provided they stay within the law, a manager's only obligation is to increase share value. Whatever is legally done to promote that end is ethically right.

This standard view of corporate management's responsibility can be illustrated as follows. If you are a member of the Wal-Mart board of directors, you put the corporation—Wal-Mart—in the center of a stakeholder map, and around that center you ring the following "stakeholders": corporate executives, employees, customers, shareholders (some of whom also are customers), the cities in which Wal-Mart operates its stores and suppliers and franchisees. In this way of visualizing corporate responsibility, what's good for Wal-Mart the corporation is assumed to be beneficial for the various stakeholders. Further, by putting the corporation at the center of the map, whether we like to admit it or not, Wal-Mart, Inc. becomes a first of not-quite equals.

We think that the Wal-Mart image is a good parallel for what's going on in the business of the media. In every key media format—radio, television, newspapers, magazines, cable television and motion pictures—more than half of the gross revenues are concentrated in the hands of fewer than six corporations—what media economics researcher Ben Bagdikian (1990, 5) has called "a de facto ministry of information within a democracy." If decisions are made to release only CDs that have a chance to go platinum, the will of one stakeholder—new or emerging artists—bends to the will of the corporation that can scarcely afford to foster unknown talent on the shareholder's dollar. The same can be said of new filmmakers, authors or any other would-be artist wanting to use the engines of the huge corporation to reach mass audiences.

Business ethicist Patricia H. Werhane (2006), has a different vision of the traditional stakeholder map. She says that some sorts of businesses—such as health care—should have a public responsibility that extends beyond individual stockholders. These companies, she says, should operate from an "enriched stakeholder" model as opposed to a "profit-driven stockholder" model. The enriched stakeholder model needs to put something other than the corporation at the center of the "stakeholder" map (she suggests the patient) and ring that central stakeholder with government, investors, the court system, medical professionals, those who pay for medical care, managed care plans and others. By changing the stakeholder map, Werhane suggests that other "promises" surface and that other measures of success beyond a steadily and steeply share price emerge.

Werhane says that this way of thinking—one that relies on a morally informed imagination—can result in some extraordinary things, among them, the Grameen Bank model for the elimination of poverty in Bangladesh. Grameen Bank pioneered the concept of "micro loans"—or the notion of lending very small amounts of money to individuals with good ideas as a way to leverage the "borrowers" (more than 90 percent of them women) and their families out of poverty. The micro-loan concept and its inventor, Muhummad Yunnus, were awarded the Nobel Peace Prize in 2006. And, the bank itself remains both solvent and profitable with a loan repayment rate of more than 98 percent.

We would like to suggest that the stakeholder—as opposed to the stockholder—model of media economics has much to recommend it in this century. We would place two entwined stakeholders at the center of our map: citizen and community, a concept as old as the Greek city-states. Around them, we would ring audiences, creative artists, corporate stockholders, governments, nongovernmental organizations, professional journalists, strategic communication professionals, corporate managers and employees. By asking what benefits citizens living in communities the most, we believe that media corporate managers would begin to use a different gauge of success: one that did not place profits first in every situation. Media corporations would no longer search for a one-time "hit" that can be packaged, imitated (think reality television) and mass reproduced (think movie sequels). Instead, they would make smaller investments in a variety of experiments, allowing creativity and connection to community to help determine what works—in both a stakeholder and stockholder sense—and what does not.

Some great media companies have already learned the lesson. McKinsey and Company made "excellence" a buzzword in business circles with studies that formed the basis of *In Search of Excellence,* the best-selling business book of the 1980s. In 1985, the firm was hired by the National Association of Broadcasters to study 11 of the nation's great radio stations, such as WGN in Chicago, and report to the group's annual convention about what made an excellent radio station. Their findings were:

1. the great radio stations were audience oriented in their programming, often breaking down the traditional walls that defined formats, and
2. the great radio stations were community-oriented in their promotions, becoming synonymous in their communities with charitable events and community festivities.

The attitude is summed up by WMMS (Cleveland) General Manager Bill Smith (National Association of Broadcasters 1985):

> If you want a car to last forever, you've got to throw some money back into that car and make sure that it's serviced properly on a continual basis. Otherwise, it's going to break down and fall apart. We know that we're constantly rebuilding the station one way or another. We throw the profit to the listening audience . . . to charities, to several nonprofit organizations, to free concerts or anything to affect the listeners of Cleveland as a whole. If we can donate the money to light up Terminal Tower, if that's what it's going to take and nobody else is going to do it, we'll do it . . . and we get and hold our listeners, year-in and year-out, because they identify us as being community-minded.

Journalist Reuben Stern has taken the concept of stakeholder theory and applied it to develop a code of ethics for publishers, (Stern, in press). In this view, media corporations are less like Wal-Mart and more like public utilities or health care corporations. Like these organizations that provide a public service—keeping the power on or keeping people as healthy as possible—media corporations with the monopolies they often enjoy would be measured by the informed citizenry or the sense of community that they can foster.

But change will be slow. The current era of cutbacks and consolidations has been noted by media researcher Robert McChesney (1997), who makes this analogy:

> Imagine if the federal government demanded that newspaper and broadcast journalism staffs be cut in half, that foreign bureaus be closed, and that news be tailored to suit the government's self-interest. There would be an outcry that would make the Alien and Sedition Acts, the Red Scares and Watergate seem like child's play. Yet when corporate America aggressively pursues the exact same policies, scarcely a murmur of dissent can be detected in the political culture.

THE MORAL MANDATE OF POWER

As the mass media have themselves become enormous, economically powerful institutions, they have joined what political scientist C. Wright Mills (1956) nearly half a century ago called the "power elite," a ruling class within a democratic society. Time has proved Mills right. Power is found not only in the halls of government but also on Wall Street. And power is found not only in money or armies, it is also found in information. Media organizations, precisely because they have become multinational corporations engaged in the information business, are deeply involved in this power shift.

This emergence of media as economic and political power brokers leads us to question how a powerful institution such as the mass media, which traditionally has had the political role of checking other powerful institutions, can be checked. Can the watchdog be trusted when it is inexorably entwined with the institutions it is watching? For instance, what media can be trusted to take a critical look at the FCC's consideration of loosening the ownership rules when the media stands to profit from the changes? As media corporations expand exponentially in the pursuit of profit, who will watch the watchdog?

Some researchers (see for instance, *What Liberal Media?* by Eric Alterman) have come to the conclusion that the myth of liberal media bias is wrong. While individual journalists still tilt toward the liberal end of the political spectrum, the powerful corporations they work for are often "tamed" by the stockholding public's demand for profits, sometimes following the temptation to self-censor possible offending content for the sake of ratings. The holders of this view got powerful anecdotal evidence when, during the November "sweeps" period of 2003, CBS pulled the plug on a controversial movie, "The Reagans," which purportedly showed the ex-president and First Lady in a negative light. Threatened by protests and threats of advertiser boycotts, CBS pulled the show less than two weeks from its air date and pushed the movie over to its sister property, the premium Showtime channel.

In speaking for those who protested the moving of the program, *USA Today* commentator Robert Bianco (2003) said:

> If nothing else, this act of creative sabotage should put to rest the idea that the media are liberal. The networks aren't driven by ideology. They're driven by the fear of any controversy that would scare off advertisers—which means they bow to the whims of impassioned people on either end of the spectrum.

Government is probably the only institution capable of providing a counter to the massive economic power of the media. Yet government provides a variety of subsidies to the industry. In addition, government functions as a regulator of the broadcast and advertising industries, ensuring profits to both these groups by limiting access to the airwaves and legislating fair play in advertising.

SOCIAL RESPONSIBILITY IN THE NEW MILLENNIUM

Good journalism is often expensive, and in an era of static subscriptions and sometimes unreliable ad revenues, few newsrooms enjoy budgets as large as in past years. The television networks have closed entire bureaus, and many newspapers have pulled back on overseas correspondents, leaving coverage of foreign news to the wires and CNN.

The effect of these cutbacks is lost news for the consumer. One photojournalist, Brad Clift, told the authors that he went to Somalia months before U.S. troops were dispatched, using his own money because he felt the starvation there was an underreported story. Only an occasional network crew and a handful of newspapers pursued the Somalia story until former President Bush committed U.S. troops to the region in December 1992. Most news organizations, like this photojournalist's employer, declined to cover the emerging story, pleading that they had depleted their international budgets by covering Operation Desert Storm. In reading the code of ethics of the Society of Professional Journalists, two of the "guiding principles" of journalism speak directly to the ethics of media economics: (1) seek truth and report it as fully as possible and (2) act independently. Seeking the truth can be personally and financially expensive.

But uplifting examples of corporate enterprise are far too rare in an industry that demands more than 20 percent pretax profit from its holdings. This demand for profits generates subsidiary problems as well. Entry-level salaries for journalists in both print and broadcast are among the lowest starting salaries of any jobs requiring a college degree—under $26,000 at the turn of the century.

When the social responsibility theory was framed in the 1940s, the primary informational concern was scarcity: people might not get the information they needed for citizenship. Today, however, the primary informational concern is an overabundance of raw data: people might not filter out what they need through all the clutter. Media and their distribution systems changed, but the theory remained silent, especially about the role of profit in the development of systems for gathering and disseminating information. This meant that, until recently, government agencies such as the FCC were still basing policy decisions on the scarcity argument when any consumer with cable or a satellite dish knew otherwise.

The Newspaper Preservation Act of the 1970s, the AT&T antitrust suits of the 1980s, the Telecommunications Act of the 1990s, and other battles finally focused the U.S. government's attention on the fact that delivery of entertainment and information is indeed big business and is currently in the hands of a very few—something the libertarian framers of the Constitution sought to avoid.

The clash of large, well-financed institutions for control of information is a modern phenomenon. Classical ethical theory, which speaks to individual acts, is of little help in sorting out the duties and responsibilities of corporations larger than most nations that control the currency of the day: information. Political theory, particularly Marxist theory, is of some help in identifying the problem, but communism has been rejected as a potential solution throughout most of the world.

Americans are equally unwilling to accept government as the solution to counter the concentrated economic power of the media, and government has been loathe to break up the large media conglomerates. During your lifetime, the power and role of "big media," such as AT&T and Time Warner, should emerge as *the* most important issue in media ethics. Can an institution that began as a lone printer with a press "flourish" without a change in vision as a multinational corporation with billions in assets?

History says "no." Adaptability is the key to institutional survival. The Roman Catholic Church lost much of its intellectual and political hold on western Europe when devotion to dogma overruled commitment to parishioners. The Reformation resulted. Likewise, the Mandarin class lost political control in ancient China because it could not change with a country that was moving into the 20th century. Social and political history has not been kind to big entities. Media conglomerates will thrive only to the extent that they can adapt both to serve the diverse communities into which their far-flung empires take them and to react quickly when they fail. The ones that do it well will survive.

Suggested Readings

AULETTA, KEN. 1991. *Three blind mice: How the TV networks lost their way.* New York: Random House.

BAGDIKIAN, BEN H. 2000. *The media monopoly.* 6th ed. Boston: Beacon Press.

GILBERT CRANBERG, RANDALL BEZANSON, and JOHN SOLOSKI. 2001. *Taking stock.* Ames, IA: Iowa State University Press.

MILLS, C. WRIGHT. 1956. *The power elite.* New York: Oxford University Press.

ROBERT W. MCCHESNEY. 1991. *Rich media: Poor democracy: Communication politics in dubious times.* Urbana: University of Illinois Press.

Cases on the Web

"Union activism and the broadcast personality" by Stanley Cunningham

"A salesperson's dilemma: Whose interests come first?" by Charles H. Warner

"Turning on the *Light:* The San Antonio newspaper war" by Fred Blevins

"Calvin Klein's kiddie porn ads prick our tolerances" by Valerie Lilley

"*Ms.* Magazine—No more ads!" by Philip Patterson

CHAPTER 8 CASES

CASE 8-A

Crossing the Line? The *L.A. Times* and the Staples Affair

MEREDITH BRADFORD AND PHILIP PATTERSON
Oklahoma Christian University

The Los Angeles *Times*, in a "special report" on December 20, 1999, called attention to an event its editors perceived as a breach of journalism ethics. The multi-story report was entitled "Crossing the Line." What made this report extraordinary is that it was the *Times* itself that had crossed the line that triggered this journalistic exposé.

A few weeks earlier, the Staples Center, a $400 million sports and entertainment arena in downtown Los Angeles, had opened to great fanfare. Most observers shared the hope that the facility, which would house two basketball franchises and one hockey team, would spark a revitalization of downtown. Staples Inc. had won the naming rights to the arena by paying $116 million.

Tim Lieweke, president of the Staples Center, left with $284 million more to raise, had initiated talks with McDonald's, Anheuser-Busch, United Airlines, Bank of America and others to become "founding partners." He was eager to have the *Los Angeles Times* as a founding partner because of previous joint successes and because he thought the paper could contribute value beyond cash.

The Staples arena already had a promotional arrangement with the *Los Angeles Times* in exchange for cash payments from the *Times* and free advertising in the paper. "The arrangement is similar to that many big-city papers have with their local professional sports teams," said David Shaw, the *L.A. Times* Pulitzer Prize–winning media critic, in an investigative piece on the controversy (Shaw 1999). "But for the Staples Center, Lieweke wanted more. He wanted the *Times* as a founding partner."

Since the Staples Center could be a major contributor to the revitalization of downtown Los Angeles, *Times* executives were "eager to participate," Shaw said. The price for founding partners ranged from $2 million to $3 million per year for five years. Jeffrey S. Klein, then senior vice president of the *Times,* who supervised early negotiations on the Staples deal, "didn't think it was worth what they were asking." Negotiations stalled for several months in 1998 until a "Founding Partner Agreement" was accepted on December 17, 1998, between the L.A. Arena Company and the *Los Angeles Times*. Part of the language in the agreement stated the two companies "agree to cooperate in the development and implementation of joint revenue opportunities."

"Although all of the principals in the negotiations say that the precise terms of the Staples deal are confidential," Shaw reported, "information from a variety of sources shows that in effect the *Times* agreed to pay Staples Center about $1.6 million a year for five years—$800,000 of that in cash, $500,000 in profits and an estimated $300,000 in profits from what Lieweke had called 'ideas that would generate revenue for us.'"

This latter part of the deal was clarified in a clause of the final contract that said, in part, that the *Times* and the L.A. Arena Company would agree to cooperate in the development and implementation of joint revenue opportunities such as a special section in the *Los Angeles Times* in connection with the opening of the arena, or a jointly published commemorative yearbook, Shaw said.

These "joint opportunities" were to create $300,000 of net revenue for each party annually. According to the contract, these opportunities would be subject to the mutual agreement of both parties.

On Oct. 10, 1999, the *Times* published a special 168-page issue of its Sunday magazine dedicated to the new Staples Center sports and entertainment arena.

Only after the section was published did most of the paper's journalists learn that the *Times* had split the advertising profits from the magazine with the Staples Center. Feeling that the arrangement constituted a conflict of interest and a violation of the journalistic principle of editorial independence, more than 300 *Times* reporters and editors signed a petition demanding that publisher Kathryn Downing apologize and undertake a thorough review of all other financial relationships that may compromise the *Times'* editorial heritage.

The petition, in part, stated "As journalists at the *L.A. Times,* we are appalled by the paper entering into hidden financial partnerships with the subjects we are writing about. The editorial credibility of the *Times* has been fundamentally undermined."

Less than two years before the episode, Downing had been named publisher by Mark Willes, the new chief executive of Times Mirror Corporation, parent company of the *Los Angeles Times,* despite having no newsroom background. Her previous experience had been as a legal publicist. Willes had moved from General Mills to Times Mirror in 1995. Willes had made no secret of his desire to "blow up the wall' between business and editorial" (Rieder 1999). He was also on record as telling *American Journalism Review* in 1997 that "[the] notion that you have to be in journalism 30 years to understand what's important, I find rather quaint" (Rieder 1999).

Downing did apologize, calling it a "major, major mistake." After taking questions at a two-hour staff meeting on October 28, she admitted that she and her staff "failed to understand the ethics involved" (Booth 1999). Downing meanwhile canceled all future revenue-sharing deals with Staples, promised to review all contracts with advertisers and ordered up awareness training for the ad side.

For his part, Willes seemed to reverse his earlier stance when he said, "This is exactly the consequence of having people in the publisher's job who don't have experience in newspapers" (Rieder 1999).

On the business side of the paper the arrangement was widely known and discussed openly for most of 1999. Downing says she deliberately withheld the information from Michael Parks, the paper's editor, but did not direct her subordinates on the business side not to talk about it to him or to anyone else in editorial, according to several reports.

Shaw reports that Willes argued that the absence of such discussion only shows the need for "more communications, not less. . . . The profit-sharing deal happened not because The Wall came down," Willes says, "but because people didn't talk to one another when they should have."

In an interesting argument, Downing claimed if the editorial side of the paper did not know about the profit-sharing deal with the Staples Center before printing, then the Sunday magazine devoted to the Staples Center would be unbiased. The uninformed editorial staff would have no reason to be biased.

Many critics from inside and outside the newspaper agree with Shaw that "readers have no reason to trust anything the *Times* wrote about Staples Center, or any of its tenants or attractions, anywhere in the paper, now or in the future, if the *Times* and Staples Center were business partners." He adds that readers will wonder whether other improper arrangements, formal or informal, might also exist or be created in the future with other entities, agencies and individuals covered by the *Times*.

Whether connected to the Staples affair or not, massive changes were in store for Willes, Downing, Parks and the *Times*. The newspaper was bought by the Tribune Company, publisher of the *Chicago Tribune,* in March 2000. All three employees were gone within a year.

Micro Issues

1. Critique Willes' early and late statements about journalistic experience in newspaper management positions.
2. Is the actual loss of credibility as disastrous as the reporters felt, or does the public really have the same sensibilities as those in the profession?
3. How does entering into the contract with the Staples Center differ from the sports department accepting press passes for the events held in the arena?

Midrange Issues

1. If one acknowledges that "the wall" is good and necessary, how does that affect media engaged in advocacy journalism?
2. Shaw entitled his article "Journalism Is a Very Different Business." In what ways do you think journalism differs from other businesses?

Macro Issues

1. In the new information age, where so many competing views can be found on most issues, is "the wall" still relevant?
2. When a newspaper is a publicly traded company, do the loyalties of the paper shift from the public to the shareholders? If not, how can you justify a move that might be counterproductive to profits?
3. After you read the next case, determine if the episode above is a factor in the recent decline in circulation of the *Los Angeles Times*.

CASE 8-B

Profit Versus News: The Case of the *L.A. Times* and the Tribune Company

LEE WILKINS
University of Missouri

Editor's note: *In April of 2007, the entire Tribune Company was sold to entre-preneur Sam Zell for a reported $8.2 billion. He reported he will break up the media conglomerate, including selling off the Chicago Cubs to help pay for the acquisition. The case below is still an excellent example of what publicly-owned newspapers across America face in an era of rising costs and declining revenue sources.*

In October 2006, management of the Chicago-based Tribune Company, the relatively new owners of the *Los Angeles Times,* fired Jeff Johnson, publisher of the newspaper. The reason: Johnson had objected publicly to newsroom staff cuts ordered by the parent corporation.

"Jeff and I agreed that this change is best at this time because *Tribune* and *Times* executives need to be aligned on how to shape our futures," said Scott Smith, president of Tribune Publishing, a subsidiary of the Tribune Company. (Seelye 2006). A memo to the staff distributed at the paper added: "Sorry to tell you that we are told that Jeff Johnson is out as publisher of the *Los Angeles Times.*"

Johnson had not gone quietly. Faced with corporate instructions to boost earnings by 7 percent, which was to be accomplished in part by cutting newsroom staff as well as utilizing increased technological efficiency, Johnson went to the community for support and got it. Twenty Los Angeles civic leaders, among them former U.S. Secretary of State Warren Christopher, the Los Angeles County Federation of Labor chief Maria Elena Durazo, L.A. Police Commission Chairman John Mack and Geoffrey Cowan, dean of the University of Southern California's Annenberg School of Communication, protested, noting, "All newspapers serve an important civic role, but as a community voice in the metropolitan region, the *Los Angeles Times* is irreplaceable" (Rainey 2006).

Instead, they urged the parent corporation to put more money into the paper, not less. In the six years of *Tribune* ownership, the paper had lost more than 200 journalists, moving from a staff of about 1,200 to about 940.

At issue was one central question with a multitude of implications: was the *Los Angeles Times* contributing enough to the bottom line of its parent corporation—a contribution that was reflected in the price of *Tribune* stock. In the 21st century, with chains and conglomerates, media finances are complicated, and those affecting newspapers are no exception.

The Tribune Corporation purchased the paper and its other substantial holdings from the Chandler family in 1999, an indirect result of the turmoil at the paper that erupted after the Staples Center problems (detailed in the previous case). The

Tribune owned additional newspapers, 26 television stations (including Los Angeles' KTLA) and the Chicago Cubs baseball team. Despite this diversity of holdings, the stock price of the Tribune Company had remained relatively stagnant. In the same month as the firing, the Tribune Company announced that its third quarter operating revenues for the entire conglomerate were down 2 percent from the previous year, but publishing profits were off 17 percent. This was attributed to declines of both advertising (down 2 percent from 2005) and circulation (down 8 percent in a year).

In order to boost the price, the corporation had engineered a $2 billion buyback of company stock. The *Tribune* also set a target of $200 million in companywide cost cutting over a two-year period. The company was also selling some of its media holdings but had no plans to sell the baseball team because it would have adversely affected the corporation's synergistic media strategy in its hometown, Chicago.

However, Tribune Corporation stockholders, including the Chandler family—with multiple seats on the Tribune Board of Directors—remained unsettled about their investment. This was despite the fact that the *Times* continued to make a substantial profit. Its operating profit margins were at about 20 percent—ahead of most big metropolitan newspapers. However, its cash flow had declined, according to sources inside the paper (Rainey 2006).

During the same time period, the *Times'* photo department staff had decreased by about a third and the graphics and design department had lost about 40 percent of its staff. Large daily operations in Ventura County and the San Fernando Valley, which had been scaled back previously, had shrunk again to just a handful of reporters. The paper had won 13 Pulitzer Prizes in the previous five years but had lost former editor John S. Carroll, who resigned about a year before Johnson was fired. The pressure to slash newsroom staff had played a role in his decision to leave (Rainey, Sept. 14, 2006).

"This newspaper does so many things well," Dean Baquet, the news editor said. "It is one of only three or four papers in the country with really robust foreign bureaus and that cover the war in Iraq in depth. . . . We have a D.C. bureau that competes on every big story. We cover the most complicated urban and suburban region in America. We do a lot of other things. You can't continue to do that if [staff reductions] keep up" (Rainey 2006).

In response to the newsroom turmoil, Smith affirmed the national stature of the paper but added, "There is a misperception that counting numbers of people is the right way to measure the quality of a great newspaper. You are mixing quality and quantity." (Rainey 2006)

Micro Issues

1. What should individual reporters and editors at the paper do? Should they cooperate with the new editor? Strike?
2. Assuming some cuts will have to be made, which of the activities outlined in Banquet's quote—or others you might think of—do you think the editors should relinquish?

Midrange Issues

1. Was it appropriate that this dispute go public? Who should cover the news of large media organizations?
2. Is the *Los Angeles Times* a national media resource? Should that make any difference— to the staff, to the corporate owners?
3. How might someone like John Stuart Mill, in light of his essay "On Liberty," evaluate this situation?

Macro Issues

1. Several Los Angeles billionaires, including David Geffen, expressed an interest in buying the *Times*. What might local ownership mean to the paper? Are there down sides to local ownership?
2. Would an owner like Geffen, with deep financial and creative ties in the entertainment industry, present important conflicts of interest for any staff? If so, how might they be handled?
3. What is the impact of a "synergistic media strategy" on the way a local newspaper covers its community?
4. Ask you parents about their retirement accounts. Would they be willing to take a lower return on investment in a situation like this to ensure a robust local newspaper? If you have a retirement account, would you?

CASE 8-C

"Bonding" Announcements in the News

JOANN BYRD
Seattle Post-Intelligencer

The "Wedding Book" in the Sunday "Northwest Life" section of the *Herald* in Everett, Washington, includes weddings, engagements and 25th and 50th wedding anniversaries. Each event submitted is reported with a one-column picture and about 2 inches of copy. People who want a more detailed announcement or their own language can buy a reduced-rate display ad, for which they write the copy.

In the fall of 1990, a lesbian couple filled out the form used to collect information and submitted it for the "Wedding Book" page. The women wanted to announce they had made a lifetime commitment to each other in a bonding ceremony attended by family and friends in a local park.

The *Herald* serves an area combining the suburbs of Seattle and surrounding rural communities. Many in the core communities had made it clear over the years that they expected the paper to reflect and reinforce conservative family values. The county had grown 36 percent in the previous decade and showed an increasing diversity of races, cultures and lifestyles. Other institutions, including the state's biggest bank, had adopted policies recognizing unmarried relationships, and the city of Seattle had recently been involved in a visible campaign to have domestic partners of city employees declared eligible for medical insurance.

The decision to accept the announcement was made almost instantly. Simultaneously, Stan Strick, the paper's then-managing editor, suggested expanding the page to include, as the in-paper announcement put it, "significant personal milestones in people's lives, everything from adoptions to retirements."

Readers were notified of the change Sunday morning, Nov. 25, 1990, in a story alongside the jumps of section-front pieces about gay couples who had exchanged vows and ministers discussing church positions on gay commitment ceremonies. The paper, with its page renamed "Celebrations," would be "one of the first in the nation to accept bonding ceremonies other than weddings," said the announcement.

The decision was condemned from pulpits in the county that morning, and people in the community began to protest. The women's announcement ran on the revamped page December 2, under a standing head, "Bondings," that matched the labels for "Weddings," "Engagements," "Anniversaries" and "Birthdays."

The community reaction became intense. Hundreds of angry subscribers canceled their subscriptions (as did some people who didn't have subscriptions). Letters and phone calls flooded the newsroom; a local businessman organized a protest group and visited the *Herald* advertisers, urging, although unsuccessfully, a boycott of the paper. Delegations from the conservative Christian community came to the paper to demand that the policy be rescinded. Seattle television covered the debate, and national media interviewed Strick. The storm continued for months. Letters to the editor and organized letter-writing and telephoning campaigns followed national news stories. As other newspapers across the country were approached to publish gay bonding ceremonies, editors phoned for details of the *Herald*'s experience.

Most of the complaints centered on Biblical interpretations condemning homosexuality. Those callers and letter writers felt the *Herald* was endorsing sin, and giving to homosexual relationships the sanction that should be reserved for heterosexual marriages, engagements and wedding anniversaries.

The *Herald*'s position was that sexual orientation was not a morally relevant basis for refusing to accept the announcements, that a page of reader-generated "significant personal milestones" simply had to give people equal access.

The policy has not been changed, but no other gay couple in the county submitted an announcement in the years following. One advertiser quit advertising for several weeks. Many of those who canceled subscriptions have not returned.

Micro Issues

1. Should the paper have accepted the announcement?
2. What options could you imagine? (Should the paper, for instance, have treated it as a news story rather than institutionalizing gay commitments on its announcement page?)
3. Some critics thought the *Herald* was bragging about being "one of the first" to accept gay bonding announcements. Would it have been better to skip the advance notice and simply publish the bonding ceremony and the new publication procedures for the page?
4. Some defenders likened the paper's decision to publishing mixed-race marriages before such notions were thought "socially acceptable." Is that a legitimate parallel? Are there others?

Midrange Issues

1. Gay commitments are not recognized by most state laws. Should the paper publish any arrangements that do not have legal status?
2. This case arose on a page where "news" is defined by people who want to make the announcements, not by reporters working a beat. Does that raise different ethical questions in the newsroom?
3. How far should the newspaper go in giving people equal access to its pages? Is anything anybody wants to announce okay?

Macro Issues

1. Offending people and their most deeply held beliefs is not morally justified unless there is an overriding moral obligation. How much should the paper weigh the probability of offending a large portion of its audience by doing what it considers morally correct in this case?
2. Chances are that there would have been less dispute if the change had occurred at a paper in a big city. Are the values at stake here different from community to community, and should all newspapers' decisions recognize that?
3. How much should a secular entity like a newspaper reflect religious beliefs?
4. The women involved in this case were harassed by conservative groups for months afterward. Does a newspaper have an obligation to censor news that may harm those submitting it? If so, what are the criteria?

CASE 8-D

Punishing the Messenger: The Tobacco Industry and the Press

STEVE WEINBERG, Former Associate Editor, *Columbia Journalism Review*
University of Missouri–Columbia

When ABC News, under the cloud of a $10 billion libel suit, apologized to Philip Morris in August 1995 for an award-winning investigation entitled "Smoke Screen," most journalists were stunned. The network's action damaged the credibility of a top-notch news organization, perhaps undermined investigative reporting as a journalistic genre, and encouraged lingering questions about the impact of the bottom line on corporate decision making regarding news stories.

The two-part investigative piece reported by Pulitzer Prize winner Walt Bogdanich stated that tobacco companies, including Philip Morris and others, added nicotine to cigarette tobacco with the purpose of keeping smokers hooked on the drug. The story itself had been exhaustively researched for more than a year, and all of the sources but one—"Deep Cough"—had agreed to go on the record with their comments. In the process of researching the story, Bogdanich learned that during the manufacturing process, nicotine is actually removed from tobacco at one point only to be added back into the tobacco later.

Less than a week before the show aired on the news magazine "Day One," the U.S. Food and Drug Administration (FDA) issued a letter stating that it believed there was mounting evidence that nicotine is "a powerfully addictive agent" and that "cigarette vendors control the levels of nicotine that satisfy this addiction" (Weinberg 1995, 27).

Spokespersons for the tobacco industry were quoted in the segments, and Philip Morris, just days before the show was to air, sent ABC News a two-paragraph statement that said, in part, "Nothing done in the processing of tobacco or manufacture of cigarettes by Philip Morris increases the nicotine in the tobacco blend above what is naturally found in the tobacco." The investigative report never made the allegation that nicotine levels were increased beyond those that occur naturally; rather it suggested the tobacco companies had the ability to remove some of the drug from cigarettes and had chosen not to do so.

Controversy erupted after the first part of the story aired on Feb. 28, 1994. A second segment, which aired one week later, focused on the list the tobacco companies had supplied to the federal government of 700 cigarette ingredients. Thirteen of those ingredients are banned in food. Philip Morris was not mentioned at all in the second segment.

Journalists applauded the work. The coverage won a George Polk award and a DuPont/Columbia University award. Congressional hearings into the tobacco industry were called as a result of the story. One day before those hearings were to begin, Philip Morris sued for libel, asking for $5 billion in compensatory damages and $5 billion in punitive damages, despite the fact that Virginia law capped punitive damage awards at $350,000. The story about the libel suit ran nationally, often without the notation about the award restriction. In addition, the tobacco giant gave every indication that it would pursue the suit vigorously, spending more than $1 million per month for more than a year on the litigation.

At ABC, newspeople saw what they perceived as an immediate chilling effect. The day Philip Morris filed the lawsuit, two independent producers were notified by a producer at ABC's program "Turning Point" that their documentary on the tobacco industry's advertising tactics and production transfers to overseas sites was being shelved, despite the outlay of about $500,000.

Legally, the going was equally difficult. Although the network gave every indication that it intended to fight and win the libel suit, discovery tactics by Philip Morris bedeviled the process. Documents that normally would have been public were marked as trade secrets, thus sealing them and making them impossible to report on. Worse yet, from the journalists' point of view, Philip Morris attempted to unearth Deep Cough's identity by subpoenaing records of reporters' phone bills, credit card purchases and travel in an attempt to retrace the journalist's footsteps to Deep Cough's door. A judge initially approved of the subpoenas in the discovery process but later reversed himself after the network contested the decision.

As in many expensive lawsuits, talk about a settlement surfaced from time to time, starting in the summer of 1994, just three months into pretrial discovery—and just as rumors began that Disney might make ABC part of its entertainment empire. Insiders weren't surprised. But it wasn't until almost a year later, on June 30, 1995, that *The Wall Street Journal* reported that settlement talks had begun anew. By that time, and despite assurances from ABC's trial lawyers, other lawyers and some ABC managers had decided that portions of the investigative report would not withstand trial scrutiny.

It turned out that the trial lawyers had been kept away from the settlement negotiations. In-house lawyers, who were joined in the final days by renowned First Amendment lawyer Floyd Abrams, worked with Philip Morris's litigators on the language of an apology to the two tobacco companies. (Abrams had been involved in the case briefly, before the settlement talks began.) The network's statement ultimately ran in more than 700 publications under the headline "Apology Accepted." Philip Morris dropped the suit.

The apology was clearly a victory for Philip Morris, but was it a sellout for ABC? If "Smoke Screen" contained one or more factual errors, it might be possible to consider the extremely limited language of the apology and the absence of any monetary awards (ABC did agree to pay the other side's legal fees, at least $15 million), a victory of sorts for the network. ABC's assertion in the apology letter that it stands behind the show's intended principal focus and the signing of the reporter and producer to new long-term contracts with substantial raises—even though both refused to sign the settlement agreement—are a vindication of sorts for the show.

ABC was purchased by Disney after the suit was settled.

Micro Issues

1. Should Deep Cough have been allowed to remain off the record?
2. What standards of evidence should journalists doing investigative work demand from their sources and documents?
3. How should other news organizations that covered the libel suit have reported it?

Midrange Issues

1. Should journalists work out agreements about legal liability with their editors in advance of broadcast or publication?
2. Should the journalists have been willing to wait on the story and work with government regulators on the issue?
3. What professional values are served by stories such as "Smoke Screen?"
4. Does reporting on undesirable products or issues—toxic waste or tobacco, for example—demand a different professional standard than reporting on city government?

Macro Issues

1. What is the responsibility of "corporate ownership" to encourage and protect investigative reporting?
2. Do journalists, who increasingly work for large corporations, have a responsibility to the public to find mechanisms to counter the demands of the bottom line?
3. Do journalists have a watchdog role when it comes to covering corporations and economically powerful interests?
4. Compare "Smoke Screen" to Upton Sinclair's classic *The Jungle*. Would such a treatment of the tobacco industry be possible today?

CASE 8-E

Digital Manipulation as Deceit? A Case Study of a *Redbook* Magazine Cover

ELIZABETH HENDRICKSON
University of Missouri–Columbia

The June 2003 issue of *Redbook* magazine looked at first glance like many other popular magazines on the newsstand: It featured a cover photo of a popular actress surrounded by multiple cover lines. This particular cover starred actress Jennifer Aniston, wearing a red tee shirt and blue jeans, with hands on hips. The accompanying cover line touted:

> Jennifer's Secret Passion:
> She opens up about making babies, Brad's beard,
> and the tough time that tested—and strengthened—their love
> Plus: The key to her relaxed American Style.

A look inside the magazine credits the Aniston photograph to Barbara Green, for Image Direct/Getty Images, which indicates the cover image was not from a studio photo shoot, but rather, the photo was purchased from a stock photo agency.

While it is not uncommon for a popular magazine to utilize celebrity stock photos within its pages, it is somewhat unusual for a mainstream women's magazine to feature a stock photo of an A-list celebrity on its cover. However, what truly sets this cover apart from other competing women's titles was the public dispute between Aniston's publicist and magazine representatives that followed in the cover's newsstand wake.

According to Aniston's publicist, Stephen Huvane, the cover was procured without his consent, a tacit misstep when booking celebrities for magazine covers. But perhaps more significantly, Huvane claimed the cover photo was not one image but three different photos pieced together to make a composite photo. "The pants and her left hand with the wedding band are from one picture, her right arm, which is thicker and discolored is another, her head is from a paparazzi shot, her shirt is painted on, they changed her hair," said Huvane (Rush and Molloy, 2003).

Additionally, Huvane complained that the inside photo credit gave a makeup credit, "as if she posed for a photo shoot."

A *Redbook* spokeswoman defended the cover, saying, "The only things that were altered in the cover photo were the color of her shirt and the length of her hair, very slightly, in order to reflect her current length." Moreover, *Redbook*'s then Editor-in-Chief Ellen Kunes, responded, "It's 100% her" (Rush and Molloy, 2003).

While Huvane reportedly considered legal action against *Redbook* for "blatant manipulation of her [Aniston's] image," none was ultimately pursued. However, Huvane issued a statement perhaps even more damning to the magazine: that Aniston would never pose for *Redbook*. In 2003, the magazine industry considered Jennifer Aniston newsstand gold, with covers featuring the actress often being a title's top-selling newsstand issue for the year. The publicist's declaration was particularly salient given *Redbook*'s somewhat dire newsstand situation at that time. From 2002–2003, *Redbook*'s single copy sales had dropped 15.2 percent to an average of

471,930 copies sold per month. It may thus seem logical to assume that the magazine was hoping to boost single copy sales with an Aniston cover.

So why did *Redbook* editors seemingly feel compelled to bypass Huvane's approval in lieu of stock photos of the star? It was likely a matter of access. Aniston's publicist manages her image, so in an effort to restrain access to his client and control exclusivity, Huvane was approving very few publicity requests in 2003. The only June 2003 magazine cover Aniston posed for was *Harper's Bazaar.*

While the case of Aniston verses *Redbook* is a recent and palpable example of digital manipulation, the matter has been lurking within the publishing industry for nearly 25 years. The February 1982 cover of *National Geographic* was perhaps the first and most infamous example, done in a pre-PhotoShop age. In order to make a photograph of the Egyptian pyramids fit onto a vertical layout, editors digitally manipulated one of the pyramids closer to another without revealing the manipulation to their readers. Another notorious instance was a 1989 cover of *TV Guide,* featuring Oprah Winfrey. In the image, Winfrey's body was superimposed onto the body of actress Ann-Margret (Kim and Paddon, 1999). The reason given was that no photos were available of the newly-slim Oprah for the *TV Guide* cover, so they manufactured one.

Such cases raise ethical issues within the industry as to what can and should be done with the newly evolving technology. When the tools exist to create an image that appears more attractive, more flawless and possibly, more sellable, are there ethical constraints on publishing a relatively harmless but digitally created image?

Photographic manipulation is commonly considered to be altering or tampering with a photograph, thus shifting it from its truthful, natural state. But there is no general consensus on how much manipulation is allowable before the "truth" of the photo is compromised. For instance, while certain magazine editors do not feel it is wrong to digitally take out wrinkles, undereye bags or stray hairs from a photo image, others feel it is unethical to remove background images from a photo image.

According to sources within the magazine industry, Kunes' decision was not one existing in the industry mainstream, but rather one found on the professional fringes. However, the criticism centered more on professional need for continued access to celebrities, and less on truth or on duty to the reader. As one magazine art director (Hemmel 2006) said:

> It's a perception thing, if you do that you'll never get another cover. Certain people will talk to you but you can't get a shoot with them. It's considered within the industry that if you don't shoot them they shouldn't be on your cover. A lot of times they put them on their cover because they sell. But it's just looked down upon.

Micro Issues

1. Did *Redbook* cross an ethical line when they chose to put Aniston on the cover using a stock photo?
2. If they did, indeed, piece together a photograph from more than one source as Huvane claims, did *Redbook* cross an ethical line?
3. Since an increasing number of readers know how to manipulate digital photos and likely do so on their home computers, is it still deception to manipulate photos in this more media-savvy time?

Midrange Issues

1. Are the ethical standards of photography for *Redbook* different from a news magazine such as *Time* or *Newsweek*? If so, in what way?
2. Does *Redbook* have a duty to not alter photos that occur in a news story within the magazine on a topic such as women's health? Do the rules differ for news stories and features within the same magazine or newspaper?

Macro Issues

1. Who owns the image of Jennifer Aniston? Her? Her publicist contracted to manage her image? A photographer who has a signed contract with her? A medium who buys an authorized photo of her? All of the above?
2. Write a policy that addresses photo manipulation for a magazine such as *Redbook*.

9

Picture This:
The Ethics of Photo
and Video Journalism

By the end of this chapter, you should be familiar with:

- the legal and ethical issues involved in photojournalism in the area of privacy.
- the technology available for altering photos and the ethical and epistemological issues those possibilities raise.
- the legal and ethical problems of file footage and "eyewash."
- the conundrum of open source journalism.

INTRODUCTION

Decades of technological developments have dramatically shortened the time between the occurrence of a news event and the dissemination of photos or video of it to the public. Digital photos can be posted to the Web almost instantaneously. Video is routinely beamed live into television homes across America. Once, the most instantaneous of ethical decisions in the mass media was the one made by the photographer at the scene of a news story: "Shoot or don't shoot?" Today the question has added layers that must be answered: "Post or don't post?" Or: "Go live or not?" Or do we accept this amateur video and post or air it?

Decisions that once could be made in the relative calm of the newsroom after a dramatic tragedy now must be made in the field or at the computer screen immediately in an increasingly competitive media environment. And making the right decision can be the difference in being applauded for beating the competition and bringing a compelling visual to readers or being criticized by thousands of readers or viewers for lack of taste or sensitivity.

How a photographer or editor prepares for such moments, and what decisions he or she makes when a questionable situation arises, is sometimes thought to be the only issue in photo and video ethics. However, a number of ethical issues surround the visual part of the business, many of them evolving rapidly with new technology. In this chapter we will discuss the following:

1. Balancing the right to privacy and newsworthiness.
2. Staging video and news photographs.
3. Changing images electronically.
4. Selective editing to support a point of view.
5. Using unrelated "eyewash," and its first-cousin file footage, in news.
6. Evaluating the visual contributions of citizen journalists.

What do these issues have in common? Perhaps it is that they all seem to center on the twin themes of fairness and accuracy. However, once the problems are identified, the answers are not that simple. What is fair? What is accurate?

While each photographer and photo editor will have to answer these questions individually, perhaps some minimum standard can be established: no image used in the news, whether video or still photograph, is ethical unless it treats the subjects or topics fairly and attempts to present an accurate and unambiguous picture of reality.

We will examine the inherent problems of visual communication, then look at specific ethical issues.

PROBLEMS IN THE PROCESS

Age-old axioms assure us that "The camera never lies" and that "Seeing is believing." Yet no photograph or videotape can be completely accurate, since the mechanics of photography demand that the lens and film make choices the eye is not required to make. These differences between the eye and the camera influence perception, as Arthur Berger (1989) points out in *Seeing Is Believing.* Because of the many variables in photography—camera angles, use of light, texture and focus—Berger says a picture is always an *interpretation* of reality, not reality itself. He adds that a dozen photographers taking pictures of the same scene would produce different views of the reality of it.

For instance, one photographer, Nat Fein, won the Pulitzer Prize for photography while taking a picture of an event dozens of photographers were shooting—the retirement of Babe Ruth. By moving to the rear of his subject, Fein captured a different angle and told a different and more dramatic story with his photo. Not only does the camera differ from the eye in its ability to manipulate angle, light and focus, but cameras also capture an isolated reality by presenting us with a slice of life, free from context. In *About Looking,* John Berger (1980, 14) says:

> What the camera does, and what the eye can never do, is to fix the appearance of that event. The camera saves a set of appearances from the otherwise inevitable supersession of further appearances. It holds them unchanging. And before the invention of the camera nothing could do this, except in the mind's eye, the faculty of memory.

Although the camera and the eye are vastly different in their functions and their abilities, most media consumers believe the photographs they see because most people assume their eyes don't deceive them. In this unguarded assumption lies the possibility for manipulation and deception. Compounding the reality problem is the importance of visuals to the electronic, print and online media. No major story is complete without visuals. In this rush to shoot compelling imagery to accompany a story, photojournalists must juggle deadline and competitive pressures with other, less tangible qualities, such as privacy.

TO SHOOT OR NOT TO SHOOT?

Each day, before photos or video are chosen by the appropriate editor, another important decision is made in the field by photographers. Arriving on the scene of newsworthy events, she must make several decisions. The most basic of these is whether or not to shoot the photo of a subject who is in no position to deny the photographer access to the event. Often these vulnerable subjects are wounded, in shock, in grief. In that newsworthy moment, the subject of the photograph loses a measure of control over his or her circles of intimacy. That control passes to the photographer, who must make a decision.

Goffman (1959) claims people possess several "territories" they have a right to control. Included in Goffman's list are two territories that are problematic to the visual journalist: the right to a personal space free from intrusion (i.e., by a camera lens) and the right to preserve one's "information," such as a state of joy, or grief, from public view.

By its very nature, photojournalism is an intrusive and a revealing process—two violations of Goffman's sense of self. In many cases, it appears that someone else's misfortune is good fortune for the photojournalist. One study (Junas 1980) found that more than half of the winning images in top photography contests were pictures of violence and tragedy. This tendency for professionals also appears to hold true for citizen journalists—most of the amateur images that "make" the news are of violence and tragedy. YouTube content provides a great illustration: in addition to the often zany, campy contributions are videos shot by soldiers serving in Iraq. They are viewed by millions and sometimes make the more traditional news, either in the form of tips or as actual stories.

Inevitably, every photojournalist happens on an assignment that will intrude on a subject's privacy. Garry Bryant (1987), a staff photographer with the *Deseret News* of Salt Lake City, offers this checklist he goes through "in hundredths of a second" when he reaches the scene of events such as the ones just described:

1. Should this moment be made public?
2. Will being photographed send the subjects into further trauma?
3. Am I at the least obtrusive distance possible?
4. Am I acting with compassion and sensitivity?

To this list, however, Bryant adds the following disclaimer (1987, 34): "What society needs to understand is that photographers act and shoot instinctively. We are not journalists gathering facts. We are merely photographers snapping pictures. A general rule for most photojournalists is 'Shoot. You can always edit later.'"

While application of this test might help the photographer make some decisions, the choices will always be tough. They are just as tough for online editors, often dealing with unsolicited but superficially compelling images provided by citizens they don't know. The line between newsworthiness and intrusiveness, between good pictures and bad taste, is often blurry. Donald Gormley, the general manager of the *Spokane Spokesman-Review,* offers some insight into the difference between photos that are universally offensive and photos that are simply tough to view:

> Compassion is not the same as good taste. If a reader knows the person pictured in a very dramatic photograph, he may find it offensive. That's a sin against compassion. If he is offended whether he knows the person or not, the sin is probably one against good taste. (1984, 58)

Editors argue that decisions cannot be made concerning photos that do not exist. Not every picture of grief needs to be ruled out just because the subject is vulnerable. For instance, newspaper readers and television viewers need to know that drinking and driving can kill and leave behind grieving parents and friends. Where to draw the line is a decision best made in the newsroom rather than at the scene. The photographer who attempts to perform a type of ethical triage at the scene of a tragedy might find his career in jeopardy if the assignment fails to capture the pathos of the event when all other photographers succeeded. In addition, the photographer who fails to capture some of the event, for whatever reason, fails to capture some of the truth for the audience.

However, the window of time for deciding later is closing. Today's satellite technology means that television can be "Live at Five" on the scene of a tragedy, broadcasting footage even before the immediate family is alerted. Scenes that might once have been edited as the story was compiled now go straight on the air. An important stage in the ethical decision-making process is bypassed when such stories are aired live. And with the advent of camera phones, even more events are being captured and offered to the media to illustrate stories.

How can the victims of tragedy come to life as vulnerable humans with feelings to a professional who sees the world most of the time through a lens? That question was asked at a conference held on the campus of Texas Christian University entitled "Crime Victims and the News Media." The conference brought together victims of violent crime and the journalists who covered their stories. One participant, Jeff Greenfield, who was ABC's media critic at the time, noted, "Once a journalist hears their simple, eloquent stories of what happened to them, he will never approach the story of a human tragedy in quite the same way."

Essentially, the photographer who is deciding whether and how to photograph a tragedy is wrestling with the dilemma of treating every subject as an end and not merely a means to an end. We can agree that powerful images of accident victims may cause some drivers to proceed more safely, but if that message often comes at the expense of an accident victim's privacy, is it a message that needs to be told? Bovée (1991), in an essay entitled "The Ends Can Justify the Means—But Rarely," offers this set of questions to help the photographer find the answer.

1. Are the means truly morally evil or merely distasteful, unpopular, etc?
2. Is the end a *real* good or something that merely *appears* to be good?

3. Is it probable that the means will achieve the end?
4. Is the same good possible using other means? Is the bad means being used as a shortcut to a good end when other methods would do?
5. Is the good end clearly greater than any evil means used to attain it?
6. Will the means used to achieve the end withstand the test of publicity?

TO ACCEPT OR NOT ACCEPT

It goes by a number of names—open source journalism and citizen journalism being among the most popular. But regardless of the label, the process is essentially the same: citizens, acting as amateur journalists without pay, submit both words and images to various Web sites. Some, such as YouTube, were established by entrepreneurs. But others are established and managed by news organizations. And, even if your local television station or newspaper doesn't have an open source site, increasingly citizens are trying to contribute their efforts to professional news organizations.

Some of those contributions have changed history. For example, amateur video aired first on local and then on national television news of African-American Rodney King being beaten by a uniformed, Caucasian police officer is credited with both riots and racial tensions in Los Angeles. Amateur video first uploaded to the Internet and then later picked up by traditional news organizations, of Republican Senator George Allen of Virginia uttering an apparently racist remark is one of the elements credited with his electoral defeat in 2006. And then, there's the recurrent video of Midwestern tornados—taken at great personal risk by amateurs who aren't paid for their efforts and accepted by media outlets well aware that the weather garners the highest ratings during the traditional local television news show.

Before the Internet opened the possibility of "open source journalism" to thousands of bloggers and videographers, the government could and did exercise control over the media by denying access to information or battlefields or by selectively granting access or leaks to those in favor with the administration. But the Web changed all that, as *Newsweek*'s David Ansen writes in his review of the 2006 film about World War II propaganda, "Flags of our Fathers" (Ansen 2006, 71):

> What the Pentagon didn't foresee, and couldn't control was the rise of new media—the unfiltered images popping up on the Web, the mini-TV cams put in the hands of soldiers that emerge in the recent documentary, "The War Tapes." We don't see much of the real war on network TV, but the unauthorized documentaries—"The Ground Truth," "Gunner Palace" and many more—come pouring out. Just as many people think they get a straighter story from Jon Stewart's mock news reports than from traditional outlets, it's been the "unofficial media" that have sabotaged the PR wizards in the Pentagon. The sophistication of the spinners has been matched by the sophistication of a media-savvy public.

Governments also use the images of amateurs when they help. The men charged with the 2005 subway bombings in London were identified in part through the use of images passengers on the city's underground captured with their cell phones. Those images, together with sophisticated face recognition technology, became a tool of law enforcement.

The emerging ethic of open source journalism has forced some interesting compromises with the emerging ethic of the blogosphere. (For a more detailed discussion, see Chapter 10). But, open source journalism—particularly if it is managed by a more traditional news organization—faces the same ethical tests as more traditional photography. The premiums are accuracy, fairness and originality. Editors at open source cites realize that they must subject amateur content to the same journalistic standards—although not necessarily the same creative and aesthetic standards—as work by professionals. For instance, contributed video cannot be staged or re-enacted and then presented as news. Editors must be able to verify the accuracy, and sometimes the context, of citizen contributions.

STAGING PHOTOGRAPHS

Every photographer has had this feeling: you are about to capture that perfect moment on film, except ———. You can fill in the blank with any number of problems. For the photographer at a birthday party, the issue is inconsequential. You simply remove the offending child, relight the candles or arrange the scene and try again. To the photojournalist attempting to convey the truth of a story, however, the issue is much more complex: to tamper with the subject is to rearrange reality.

The issue is not a new one. As early as 1876, an enterprising photographer staged a picture of his own death allegedly to dodge his creditors (Lester 1992). More than 100 years later, the ethics of the issue of staging remain unresolved, even in major news organizations.

For instance, during the 1992 November sweeps period, NBC's magazine show "Dateline" aired an 18-minute segment on a faulty design of General Motors pickup trucks that concluded with video of a truck exploding into flames immediately after a side-impact collision. More than 300 people had died in such collisions since GM had introduced the trucks. The story included gripping still photographs of charred bodies pulled from accident scenes, court documents from the many suits filed against GM over the truck's design and videotaped testimony from independent auto safety experts and a former GM engineer, all saying that the corporation had known about the design flaw yet had chosen to do nothing.

However, NBC did not inform viewers that, in order to ensure fire in the closing video, "sparking devices" had been mounted on the test cars by the independent testing agency the network had hired as part of its investigation. Even with the addition of the sparking devices, only one of two test vehicles had exploded on cue and the fire had gone out almost immediately. About two months after the story aired, a jury returned a $105 million damage judgment against the automaker in a wrongful death suit that centered on the truck's design flaws. The NBC story had not been introduced in the court case. A week after the jury returned the verdict, General Motors filed a libel suit against the network, charging—among other things—that the network had staged the concluding video. In an unprecedented move, anchors Jane Pauley and Stone Phillips read a 3-minute retraction of the original "Dateline" story, admitting that the network had aired the concluding video even though it was staged. The NBC–General Motors confrontation proved

Calvin and Hobbes

by Bill Watterson

to be the end for network news president Michael Gartner. He resigned less than a month later.

The NBC incident raises several questions. Is there a place for reenactment in the news? If so, when? How should such photos and video be labeled? The issues are not trivial, nor are they resolved. In a poll conducted by the National Press Photographers Association, the number one ethical problem reported by photojournalists was setup shots.

"Your work sounds interesting." Francesca said. She felt a need to keep neutral conversation going.

"It is. I like it a lot. I like the road, and I like making pictures."

She noticed he'd said "making" pictures. "You make pictures, not take them?"

"Yes. At least that's how I think of it. That's the difference between Sunday snapshooters and someone who does it for a living. When I'm finished with that bridge we saw today, it won't look quite like you expect. I'll have made it into something of my own, by lens choice, or camera angle, or general composition or all of those.

"I don't just take things as given; I try to make them into something that reflects my personal consciousness, my spirit. I try to find the poetry in the image."

The Bridges of Madison County
Robert James Waller

The questions surrounding fakery and staging speak to the purpose of news photography. Two possible purposes exist: the "mirror" and the "window" photograph (Szarkowski 1978). The mirror photograph attempts to subjectively re-create the world in whatever image suits the photographer. Anything can be manipulated: light, proportion, setting, even subject. On the other hand, window photographs should be as objective a picture of reality as the medium will allow, untouched by the bias of the lens or the photographer.

Each type of photography has a function. A large percentage of the government-commissioned Dust Bowl–era photographs that have seared our memories of the Depression would fit into the mirror category. Photographers searched for settings, posed people and shifted props to achieve the maximum effect.

On the other hand, the photos that show us the horrors of war and famine, and arouse public opinion, are windows, where the photographer captures the moment with no attempts to alter it. *The problem comes in the substitution of one for the other.* When a photograph mirrors a photographer's bias, yet is passed off as a window on reality, the viewer has been deceived.

ELECTRONIC MANIPULATION

Those who get their news from the Internet could hardly have missed it. The day after the 2005 Madrid train bombings the same photograph appeared on the front pages of a number of European newspapers—sort of. One front page displayed a photograph of the bombing with a bloody, detached limb in the foreground. Another paper displayed the same photograph, but the limb wasn't in it. Other papers cropped the photo so that only a part of the limb could be seen. Still others printed the photo in color, and some of those intensified the color of the blood on the limb, technically called color saturation. It was the same photograph, but the electronic alternations were too obvious to ignore.

The history of photo manipulation is long. It has included such crude drawing-board techniques as cropping with scissors and paste, darkroom techniques such as "burning" and "dodging," and, more recently, airbrushing. Today, technology allows increasingly sophisticated changes to be made to an image after it has been captured.

Any person familiar with InDesign or any of many other software packages is keenly aware of how photos can be manipulated.

Technology has, in fact, made the word "photography"—literally "light writing"—obsolete, as a lighted reality no longer must exist in order for a "photograph" to be created. Photos and video are now what Reaves (1987) calls a "controlled liquid," capable of being manipulated into a seamless, yet totally unrealistic image. What this technology will ultimately lead to, Reaves claims, is an epistemological shift away from photography as irrefutable evidence of a story to photography as changeable story illustration. Eventually, she argues, as the public realizes that photographs can be—and frequently are—electronically altered, photos could lose their "moral authority." Tomlinson (1987) adds that technology could render photos nonadmissible as legal evidence once they lose the assumption of validity.

With an overwhelming amount of technology available for enhancing photos, editors must consider the ethical ramifications of their use. Once expensive technologies such as "morphing" one image into another, creating images directly from pixels with no real image required or the digital insertion of existing images into new contexts are now common software applications on home computers. As a more sophisticated audience approaches the video or photography in the media, viewers will bring with them a skepticism not present in previous generations of consumers.

Most editors and photographers agree that manipulation or staging of news photos is generally more culpable than manipulation or staging of feature photos. During the 2003 war in Iraq, a photojournalist for the *Los Angeles Times* was fired for combining two similar photographs into one more aesthetically pleasing one (see case 9-C). While the resulting photo was so similar to the "real" ones that the difference escaped the eye of the photo editor, a line had been crossed, and the photographer was dismissed. The reasoning for this differing standard for news as opposed to feature photography or advertising photography is a presupposition that *while art may be manipulated, information may not* (Martin 1991). Such a flexible standard would be allowed under a categorical imperative as a permissible act, provided that:

- the photographer's intent is to merely make the photo more aesthetically pleasing and not to deceive; *and*
- the intended audience recognizes the difference; or
- the difference does not make audience members think or act in a manner in which they might not otherwise have thought or acted.

The problem for audiences is compounded by the fact that both advertising and entertainment and even non-news sections of the newspaper make frequent use of these techniques. Confusion over what is appropriate in one context and not another is bound to occur, but we suggest that the same issue of visual truth telling can and should be applied to advertising as well.

SELECTIVE EDITING

Another ethical question centers on the video editing process: whether editing itself renders a story untrue or unfair. While this complaint is not new to television, the charges leveled against video editing are more vociferous, since editing for time considerations is a much more noticeable constraint than editing for space. Scenes aired out of sequence, answers dubbed behind questions that were not originally asked, and a preponderance of one view dominating the final cut at the expense of another view are some of the most frequently cited instances of "selective editing."

Actually, the term "selective editing" is redundant. *All* editing is selective. The issue is who does the selecting, and what predispositions they bring to the process. Some observers have noted that a dual standard has emerged between words and photos. A strange ethical dichotomy has long existed in the business of creating and processing print news and the photos that accompany it. The writer is allowed to reorder facts and rearrange details into an inverted-pyramid story on the rationale that the reader wants the most important facts taken out of sequence, and even out of context, and placed first in the story for more efficient reading. The result is praised as good writing and is taught in every journalism program.

However, should a photographer attempt to do the same thing with a camera— rearrange reality to make a more interesting photo or videotape—the result is called "staged." Our unwillingness to allow visual journalists the same conventions as print journalists says something fundamental about the role of visuals in the news. Media tradition says that while the truth in a print story about an explosion can contain only the highlights, the truth of a photo about the same explosion should be kept in context.

Such an analogy to print is important. When a writer edits, it makes for a more readable story, and the act is applauded. When a photographer or video editor does the same thing, he or she is open to accusations of distortion. That is because we evaluate news photos according to print standards: linear and logical. Yet video and photographs are neither. They have a quality Marshall McLuhan called "allatonceness" that we are not quite comfortable with as a technology. Just what the photographer can do with the visual truth the camera uncovers is still a topic of debate.

Some photographers argue that to take away the possibilities that computer technology allows is to put them at a disadvantage in trying to tell a story visually. Should a photographer attempt to rearrange reality to make a more interesting photo or piece of film, the photograph is denigrated as "staged." And if a computer is used to correct focus or remove distractions, the photograph is derided as being " manip- ulated." In either case, the photographer could face sanctions.

However, as long as readers hold the view that "Seeing is believing," that view—whether based in reality or not—becomes a promise between the media and their audience that photographers and videographers should be hesitant to break. While many photojournalists argue that "Seeing is believing" should have never been a cultural truism (see Lester 1992), others argue that we must work within our readers' or viewers' predispositions about the truth of what they see. Steve Larson, (quoted in Reaves 1991, 181) director of photography for *U.S. News & World Report,* summarized this viewer-based rationale:

> The photo is a record of a moment in time. We're on shaky ground when we start changing that. We must maintain this pact. Catching a moment in time has history. When you look at a Matthew Brady photo there is that sense "this really happened." I believe strongly that's where photography draws its power.

EYEWASH

Another ethical issue in photojournalism is the controversial use of stock photos or file footage to illustrate news stories. Such "eyewash" is used regardless of the context of the original photograph and sometimes without the consent of the subject (Tomlinson 1987).

For instance, an article on compulsive gamblers might show a woman enjoying herself on a sunny afternoon at the races. While her action is taking place in public view, she might or might not be a victim of the syndrome addressed in the article, although the casual reader might infer that she is, indeed, a compulsive gambler. In this context, the photo is serving the purpose of eyewash, decoration for a story that bears no genuine relationship to it.

Eyewash has had a brief history in the courts. A Washington, D.C., television station used a tight shot on a pedestrian facing the camera, chosen at random, to illustrate the "twenty million Americans who have herpes." The court ruled that the combination of the film and the commentary was sufficient to support an inference that the plaintiff was a victim of herpes, which she contended was not true.

However, not all plaintiffs are successful. One young couple photographed in a public embrace in the Los Angeles Farmer's Market later saw their private moment published in *Harper's* illustrating an article entitled "Love Makes the World Go 'Round." The California Supreme Court noted that the couple had "waived their right of privacy" by their voluntary actions and said that publication of the photograph merely extended and increased the public who could view the plaintiffs in their romantic pose.

While the courts' rulings have been ambiguous on the matter of eyewash, the media have created divergent policies to cover the issue. Some newspapers and television stations, for instance, will use no picture not directly related to the story. Others limit the use of file or stock footage to that which is clearly labeled. Others limit the shooting of eyewash only by insisting that it occur in public view.

The issue is exacerbated by the voracious appetite that both television and the print media have for visuals. Virtually all surveys have shown that the presence of a photo adds to the number of readers for a newspaper story, while television news consultants insist that viewers will watch "talking heads" for only a few seconds before diverting their attention elsewhere. The answer to the question "Have you got art?" often means the difference in running or killing a story. At other times, good visuals can get a story in the coveted first slot on the nightly news or the front page of the newspaper.

Given the importance of visuals to a story, it is not surprising that ethical lines blur. Coleman (1987) tells the story of his young son's falling off a horse and breaking his arm. A photographer friend took a picture of the boy "dirty, tear-stained, in great pain, slumped in a wheelchair with his arm in a makeshift sling" on his way to the operating room. About a year later, a textbook publisher ran across the photo and wanted it as an illustration for a book on child abuse. Coleman denied the request but added that the photo could have run with little or no repercussion if he had not been easily available for the publisher to ask. Had that happened, the public would have been deceived by a photograph of a boy who had been a victim of nothing more than a childhood accident.

CONCLUSION

Visual ethics is emotionally charged and constantly changing with new technology. *What this means is that the consumer of news photography is being presented with a product that is sometimes too raw to be palatable and sometimes too polished to be believable.*

The problem lies in the nature of the photojournalist's job. On a day-to-day basis, photography can be a mundane and poor-paying job. When an opportunity for a gripping photo does arise, like word that police are searching for a drowning victim, the desire to break out of the daily grind can lead to one of the two extremes stated above: a photo too raw or a photo too polished.

Photojournalists should operate under this version of Kant's categorical imperative: *Don't deceive an audience that expects your pictures to be an accurate representation of a particular quality of reality.* Fortunately, only a small percentage of photos offend, and only a small percentage of photos are staged or electronically manipulated. However, photographers are dealing with a trust that readers and viewers have placed in them. If that trust is betrayed, it will be slow to return.

Suggested Readings

BERGER, ARTHUR ASA. 1989. *Seeing is believing.* Mountain View, CA: Mayfield Publishing Co.
BERGER, JOHN. 1980. *About looking.* New York: Pantheon Books.
Journal of Mass Media Ethics. 1987, Spring–Summer. Special issue on photojournalism.
LESTER, PAUL. 1991. *Photojournalism: An ethical approach.* Hillsdale, NJ: Lawrence Erlbaum Associates.
———. 2003. *Images that injure.* 2nd edition. Westport, CT: Greenwoood Press.
Newton, Julianne. 2000. *The burden of visual truth: The role of photojournalism in mediating reality.* Hillsdale, NJ: Lawrence Erlbaum Associates.

Cases on the Web

"Film at 10: Handling graphic video in the news" by Sonya Forte Duhé
"Looking at race and sex: When do photographs go too far?" by Beverly Horvitt
"Faking Photos: Is it ever justified?" by James Van Meter

CHAPTER 9 CASES

Case 9-A

Daniel Pearl and the *Boston Phoenix:* Too Much of a Bad Thing?

TIMOTHY RAGONES
WMTV—Grand Rapids-Kalamazoo, Michigan

On January 23, 2002, *Wall Street Journal* reporter Daniel Pearl was on his way to interview an Islamic fundamentalist leader in Pakistan when he was abducted. A month later, on February 21, FBI officials received a video entitled "The Slaughter of the Spy Journalist, the Jew Daniel Pearl" confirming that Pearl's abductors had killed him. The 3-minute video included footage of Pearl confessing his Jewish roots and reading a statement denouncing U.S. foreign policy in the Middle East and Afghanistan. Pearl is then decapitated. Later, an unidentified man holds Pearl's head aloft. That image remained on screen as the National Movement for the Restoration of Pakistan Sovereignty listed demands, among them return of Pakistani prisoners to Pakistan, the delivery of U.S.-made F-16s that Pakistan paid for but which were never shipped, and an immediate end to U.S. presence in Pakistan.

U.S. news media had access to the video in the weeks after it surfaced. On Tuesday, May 14, an edited portion of the tape appeared on the "CBS Evening News." The 4.5-minute story, which was about use of the Internet to spread propaganda, showed about 30 seconds of the Pearl tape, not including the decapitation. In prefacing the story, anchor Dan Rather said, "We're about to show you edited portions of it so that you can see and judge for yourself the kind of propaganda terrorists are using in their war against the United States." Executive producer Jim Murphy noted, "[Dan and I] very, very carefully crafted this story to report what people have to know. We used very little of the video at all."

The network aired the story despite fielding calls from Secretary of State Colin Powell's office, the Justice Department, *The Wall Street Journal* and several members of Pearl's family. After the broadcast, Pearl's family accused the network of playing into the hands of terrorists by airing material that was bound to become propaganda and that spread a message of hate. Barbara Comstock, Justice Department spokeswoman, said the network had opened the door for others to use even more graphic parts of the tape.

Her fears came true on May 31, when the *Boston Phoenix,* an alternative paper that had garnered a Pulitzer Prize for criticism in 1994, posted a link to the unedited tape on its Web site. The paper had a circulation of 118,000 in the Boston area. When the link appeared, traffic on the Web site jumped to 40,000 hits. In an online note below the link, *Phoenix* publisher Stephen Mindich wrote:

> This is the single most gruesome, horrible despicable and horrifying thing I've ever seen. If there is anything that should galvanize every non-Jew hater in the world—of whatever faith, or of no faith—against the perpetrators and supporters of those who committed this unspeakable murder, it should be viewing this video.

The *Phoenix* link connected to **Prohosters.com,** a Virginia-based Web-hosting company. Mindich said he decided to publish the link after learning that the FBI had pressured Prohosters to remove the video from one of its client sites. Prohosters said the FBI had threatened the client with legal action and objected to the government pressure on First Amendment grounds.

The *Phoenix* took another step into the controversy one week later when it published still photographs of Pearl talking to the camera and Pearl's decapitated head in the hard copy version of the paper. Warnings about the nature of the photographs, which had been available on the Web, were not included in the newsprint paper. An editorial defending the decision to run the photos noted, "The silence on this issue— the U.S. government's attempt to censor politically sensitive, yet legal content from our leading pundits and opinion makers has been deafening." The editorial compared footage of Pearl's murder to widely disseminated images of the Nazi concentration camps, the 1986 Challenger space shuttle explosion, and the 9/11 World Trade Center footage.

"Beyond its repugnance, though, it has value in reminding us, as did the September 11 footage, what anti-American terrorists are capable of. It's hard to find language strong enough to decry the impulse to keep this information from the public."

Micro Issues

1. Should CBS have aired even a portion of the tape? Justify your answer.
2. What portion of the tape, if any, should the *Phoenix* have placed on its Web site? Justify your answer.
3. Is there a morally relevant distinction between the tape of Pearl and the 9/11 World Trade Center footage?
4. In considering all the stakeholders in the decision to print the photos, how can the *Phoenix* justify its decision to the wife of Daniel Pearl? Should she be considered in the equation when making the choice whether to run the photos, or does that send the process towards "quandary ethics"?

Midrange Issues

1. Was publication of the video and the stills necessary for the *Phoenix* to accomplish one of its stated goals: educating the American public about terrorism?
2. Is posting on the Web somehow ethically distinct from publication in a tangible newspaper?
3. Does the alternative press, papers like the *Phoenix* and New York's *Village Voice,* play a professionally distinctive role in the American media mix? Do they operate under any different ethical mandates than the mainstream press? Justify your answer.
4. In the 1980s, a Pennsylvania elected official, moments from surrendering to authorities to begin a prison sentence, called a news conference where he was expected to resign his post. Instead, he surprised everyone in the room when he pulled out a gun, put it in his mouth and pulled the trigger. Video and still images were available of the suicide, and some media outlets chose to run them. In what way, if any, does that suicide differ from the Pearl case?

Macro Issues

1. Could words have adequately described what happened to Daniel Pearl? What does your answer say about the role of images in your definition of truth? Of privacy?
2. Is it ever appropriate for the government to pressure news media not to publish? Under what circumstances?
3. What is the relationship between news and propaganda? Is it appropriate for journalists to be concerned about the use others will make of their stories, particularly when that story focuses on hate?
4. How is the government's attempt to censor the tape relevant in the decision to post the tape on the Web or publish the stills?

CASE 9-B

Problem Photos and Public Outcry

JON ROOSENRAAD
University of Florida

Campus police at the University of Florida were called on a Saturday to a dorm to investigate "a large amount of blood on the floor of a women's bathroom," according to police reports. They determined that the blood "appeared to have been from a pregnancy miscarriage" and began searching the dorm area. Some time later a police investigator searching through a trash dumpster behind the dorm found bloody towels, plastic gloves, and a large plastic bag containing more towels and the body of a 6- to 7-pound female infant.

Police discovered no pulse. Rigor mortis had set in. After removing the body from the bag, the police briefly placed the body on a towel on the ground next to the dumpster. The photographer for the student paper, the *Independent Florida Alligator,* arrived at this time and photographed the body and dumpster.

Later on Saturday, the 18-year-old mother was found in her dorm bed and taken to the university's hospital. The hospital exam revealed "placenta parts and the

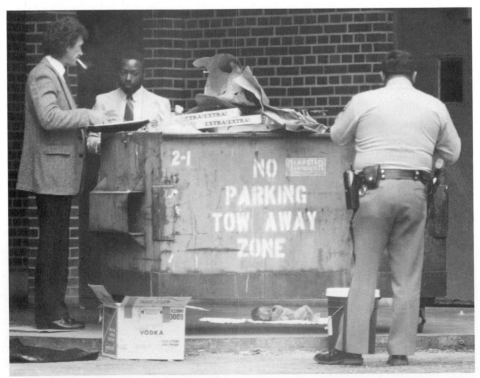

Photo courtesy of the Independent Florida Alligator. *Used with permission.*

umbilical cord in her" and she was released later in good health. A local obstetrician contacted about the case said that judging by the size of the infant, it was likely a miscarriage and not an abortion. The infant was determined to be about seven months developed.

The story began on the front page of the Monday issue, across the bottom of the page, under the headline "UF police investigate baby's death at dorm." It jumped inside to page 3 and was accompanied by the photo.

It was a dramatic photo, contrasting two well-dressed detectives and one uniformed policeman with the naked body and contrasting the fragile human form with the harsh metal dumpster filled with pizza and liquor boxes. The photo was played 7 by 5 inches.

The story was well written and the photo dramatic but likely offensive to many—potentially so offensive that the newspaper's staff debated most of Sunday about how to use it. The editor decided to run it, but in an unusual move she wrote an editor's column explaining why that appeared on the opinion page of the same issue. It showed a scene one might visualize in a ghetto but not on a college campus. It showed that supposedly sexually educated and sophisticated college students still need help. The editor wrote:

> Even with these legitimate reasons we did not run the picture on the front page. This is partially in response to our concern that we do not appear to be exploiting this picture to attract readers. . . . We also examined the photographer's negatives to see if there were any less graphic prints. . . . Is the message perceived by the reader worth the shock he or she experiences? After pondering what we feel is a very profound photo, we decided there is. This was a desperate act in an area of society where it is not expected. The picture shows it.

The local daily covered the story Monday in a police brief. No photo ran. It was determined that the body was from a miscarriage. The woman involved left school. The campus paper got several letters critiquing its coverage of the story. Many chose to criticize the editors for running the photo, while some praised the staff for pointing out the problem and for listing places on campus where sex and pregnancy counseling was available. Some letters did both.

An example of some of the outrage over the running of the photo by the *Alligator* came from a female student who called the coverage "the most unnecessary, tactless piece of journalism I've ever encountered." Another letter from a male student called the photo "in poor taste and extremely insensitive." The writer added, "There are times when good, sound judgment must override 'hot' copy."

Perhaps the most pointed comment came from a female writer who added 24 other names to her letter. The letter stated:

> The incident *could* have been used to remind people that they need to take responsibility for their own sexuality. The story *could* have been used as a painful reminder that there are many un-educated, naïve people out there who need help. But, unfortunately, the *Alligator* chose to sensationalize the story with a picture, completely nullifying any lesson whatsoever that might have been learned.

Micro Issues

1. Should the photographer have taken the picture? Justify your answer.
2. Is this a legitimate story, and if so, does it belong on page 1?
3. If this was the only photo available, did the paper then have to run it?
4. Various letters to the editor called the photo "unnecessary," "tactless," and "insensitive." What would you say to those charges if you were on the staff?

Midrange Issues

1. Does running the photo inside lessen any criticism of poor taste? Did its placement mitigate any ethical criticism?
2. If the staff was so unsure, was the editor correct in writing a same-day rationale for its publication?
3. Critique the reasoning stated by the editor in running the photo. What moral philosophy, if any, would lead one to agree with the action?

Macro Issues

1. Should a paper play a story and photo like this to crusade about a problem?
2. Is the perceived social value of such a picture worth more than the shock and criticism?
3. Was the writer correct in her assessment that the shock of the photo negated any good that might have been done by the story?
4. Should a campus newspaper have a different standard—of taste, play, news value—than a "regular" daily?

CASE 9-C

Manipulating Photos: Is It Ever Justified?

LEE WILKINS
University of Missouri

Author's Note: *By the decision of the* Los Angeles Times, *the photos in question in this case are not available. However, various Web sites have covered this controversy and some include the photos.*

The visual images of the 2003 war in Iraq were extraordinarily controversial. Photo editors, particularly at large media outlets, had to make decisions about hundreds of photographs every day. Sunday, March 30, was no exception. That night, *Los Angeles Times* director of photography Colin Crawford had edited about 500 photos of the war when he saw a picture from staff photographer Brian Walski. The photo depicts a group of Iraqi citizens sitting on the ground as an American soldier, armed with a rifle, stands in the foreground.

The *Times* ran the photo on Page 1, and so did sister publications the *Hartford Courant* and the *Chicago Tribune.* Thom McGuire, the *Courant*'s assistant managing editor of photography and graphics, said, "It was a great image."

But a *Courant* employee, who was looking through the images for a friend, thought he noticed a problem—what appeared to be a duplication of the Iraqi citizens in the background of the picture. He brought the problem to the attention of a copyeditor, who alerted McGuire. "After about a 600 percent magnification in Photoshop, I called Colin to ask for an investigation," McGuire said.

In Los Angeles, Crawford was disbelieving. He thought the apparent duplication of the background crowd was probably due to some sort of technical, satellite-related glitch. "He sent us 13 very good images Sunday," Crawford recalled. "We had to get information and give him the benefit of the doubt."

As it turned out, Walski had used his computer to combine elements of two photographs, taken moments apart, in order to improve the composition. Once that admission was made, Crawford fired him. All the publications that ran the composite photo ran corrections.

In his apology, Walski told other *Times* employees, "I deeply regret that I have tarnished the reputation of the *Los Angeles Times,* a newspaper with the highest standards of journalism . . . and especially the very talented and extremely dedicated photographers and picture editors and friends. . . . I have always maintained the highest ethical standards through my career and cannot truly explain my complete breakdown in judgment at this time."

Another *Times* staff photographer, Don Barletti, told the Poynter Institute's online discussion group that he recalled seeing Walski after he returned. Walski told him, "Now no one will touch me. I went from the front line of the greatest newspaper in the world, and now I have nothing. No cameras, no car, nothing."

Barletti also said he understood how the alteration might have happened. Walski had been in the desert for days under harsh conditions with little sleep and food and under enormous pressure. "He got into a zone," Barletti said. "He was on a head roll, making fantastic images, and it got out of hand. He told me that he did not plan to send the image and was just messing around. He sent it anyway . . . didn't know what he was doing, but he did it. With all that he was facing, how did he have the presence of mind? It just got out of hand."

When asked about the issue, *New York Times* photographer Vincent LaForet agreed that the breach was serious. "There is not ever a good time for such manipulation, but this is the worst time. What really differentiates us from other photographers and media is our credibility. We have a history of getting it right, accurately. . . . Our credibility is all that we have."

Micro Issues

1. How should the newspapers that ran the original photo have corrected the error?
2. Should Walski have been fired? Why?
3. Many journalists who examined the photo did not notice the problem until it was pointed out to them. Is the minor nature of the alteration relevant in the ethical discussion? Why or why not?

Midrange Issues

1. Suzanne Lainson, also commenting on the issue on the Poynter Web site, said, "Why is the culture of the photojournalist supposed to be different than that for the print, audio or video editor . . . rather than condone editing photos, perhaps we should not condone editing print, audio and video data." Evaluate this comment.
2. What should be the role of editors—in an ethical sense—in the newsroom?
3. Should employees blow the whistle on colleagues when they think there has been an ethical breach? If not, why not? If so, how should they do it?
4. How does the electronic manipulation of the persons in the background differ from the photographer simply asking the people to move to a certain location before the photo is taken? Are they equally culpable from an ethical sense?

Macro Issues

1. "People do not expect 'truth' or 'reality' from their media—today's media audience is much more aware of the doctored nature of everything they read, see and hear than we like to think. I'm sure this *LA Times* story did not come as a surprise to most people," wrote Mark Deuze. Analyze this statement. How might media organizations assure viewers and readers of the veracity of the information they publish?
2. Eric Meyer, who commented about the issue on the Poynter Web site said, "A photo is like a direct quote. You chose what to quote or what to photograph. But, when you run a direct quote or a photograph, you don't alter it to 'make it better.' " Evaluate this statement.

CASE 9-D

"Above the Fold": Balancing Newsworthy Photos with Community Standards

JIM GODBOLD, MANAGING EDITOR
JANELLE HARTMAN, REPORTER
Eugene Register-Guard, *Eugene, Oregon*

Author's Note: *On November 10, 1993, a nightmare unfolded in Springfield, Oregon, a quiet town adjoining the university community of Eugene, as Alan McGuire held his 2-year-old daughter, Shelby, hostage in their house. By the end of the standoff both were dead and the media had captured some horrific photos.*

Seven children had died as a result of child abuse in Lane County, Oregon, in the 20 months prior to that day, and the media had just witnessed the eighth. Jim Godbold was the assistant managing editor of the Eugene Register-Guard *at the time. The remarks below are from an interview with him months after the event.*

Godbold: The call came over the police scanner shortly after noon. We responded to a hostage situation, a man holding someone at knife point in a Springfield neighborhood. We knew it was probably 20 minutes from the *Register-Guard* in the best of possible circumstances so we really scrambled. Photographer Andy Nelson and police reporter Janelle Hartman went as fast as they could to the area.

We got there when the police were trying to set up a perimeter to get people away from the area. It was real pandemonium right when Andy arrived. The situation didn't unfold for more than a few minutes before there was a burst of flame inside the house that caught the attention of the police officers, and they immediately made the decision that they were going to have to go inside.

A group of officers ran at the door, and then all of a sudden Alan McGuire, the man who was in the house, came hurtling through the front window on fire. I am not even sure if police officers knew how many people were in the house at the time. His wife had escaped from the home. She had been held at knifepoint and bound, and she had somehow gotten out and she let police know that their two-year-old daughter, Shelby McGuire, was in the house.

Shelby was a hostage and being held at knifepoint. Police saw her and tried to set up a telephone line so they could negotiate with McGuire, but the events unfolded rapidly, and after Alan McGuire jumped through the front window, police broke down the door. Two officers hauled McGuire's flaming body to the ground and tried to douse the flames with a garden hose. Inside the house one of the officers saw Shelby McGuire sitting upright on the couch. She had a plastic grocery produce bag over her head, and it apparently had been duct-taped in some fashion, maybe around the neck.

They immediately tore the bag away. A detective picked Shelby up and sprinted out of the house with her. It was at that moment that Andy Nelson snapped his picture of one of the officers with Shelby's body in his arms, running out, two other officers standing on the side of the doorstep, another officer with a hose near Alan McGuire, and Alan lying on the ground. The flame's now out, but the charred and still smoking body was present in the viewfinder as Andy snapped the picture.

Photo courtesy of the Eugene Register-Guard. *Used by permission.*

At that moment the officer with Shelby McGuire, the 2-year-old, began mouth-to-mouth resuscitation on the front lawn. Andy subsequently took a photograph of that. Then they rushed both Alan and Shelby McGuire to the hospital. We did not know Shelby's condition. The police didn't respond about whether she was able to be resuscitated.

We have a standing policy at the newspaper that as a general rule we don't run photographs of dead bodies of children. That immediately triggered the kind of review that we would go through to determine where this particular incident was going to stand up on our policy, whether or not anyone was going to argue for publication or against publication.

We began to talk about the policy and the potential community reaction that we might face. The discussion was pretty brief. The photo was so compelling and the situation that it sprang from so horrifying that we began looking at the photograph and saying,

"Well, I don't know, but look at what the photo has captured."

"People are going to be upset."

"This is potentially a photograph of a dead 2-year-old child."

"Look at the concern and the expression on the police officers' faces. This is an example of what they deal with day in and day out. They are up against this kind of domestic violence hostage situation and people don't realize that."

So, the debate was intense, and yet pretty short. We prepared a selection of pictures, and we brought those to the then-managing editor Patrick Yak and made the case that this is going to be a tough photograph for us to run. This is going to be one that we are going to have to be prepared to defend. But we believe it's that kind of exception to the rule that we look for.

The public response to the publication of the Shelby McGuire photograph was unprecedented in my 22 years in journalism and unprecedented at this newspaper. I have not come across a case, having been shown a number of them subsequently, that is of the magnitude per capita of reader response to a single photographic image. We received on the order of 450 telephone calls that began the moment people got the newspaper, which started at 6:00 a.m. First they came into our circulation department. The circulation department switchboard became overloaded and gave them the main newsroom switchboard, which didn't open until 7:30. At 7:30 when they threw the switch, all 20 of our incoming phone lines lit up, and the calls began to roll over into a holding pattern that had never been utilized by our switchboard before.

I was called at home by Al Gimmell, the corporate controller, who said, "We are inundated with telephone calls. We need some help." So I immediately came in to try to handle telephone calls, and I tried to find the time in between phone calls to call other editors in, but the calls were coming so rapidly that every time I hung up it rang again. When I picked up my voice mail messages, I had 31 unanswered messages, and that was probably 7:45 in the morning.

Photo courtesy of the Eugene Register-Guard. *Used by permission.*

The range of responses weren't monolithic, except in their anger. But the anger came from different places. For some people the anger came from a belief that we had simply stooped to a tremendously sensational graphic crime picture trying to sell newspapers. For others the anger came from the terrible sense of violation that the surviving mother and brother of Shelby McGuire would have to wake up to the morning after their ordeal and see this on the front page of the hometown newspaper.

Another component argued that this was wholly inappropriate for the kind of newspaper the *Register-Guard* has been and continues to be. That 5-year-olds and 6-year-olds were sharing the newspaper at the breakfast table, and parents were finding themselves in a position of having to explain this horrifying incident and having the question "How is the little girl?" asked again. And there was also a range of response from people who were themselves victims of domestic violence or spouses of victims or had family members who were involved in it. For them it was a combination of anger and pain.

I spoke with literally dozens of people through tears. It was an emotional response that was overwhelming and people were extremely upset by the picture. Most asked the question "Why? I need to understand why the newspaper published this picture."

We were really, I think, at a loss initially to respond to that question. I think a lot of that had to do with being in a very real sense out of touch with a substantial number of readers. The kind of reaction that we had was not anticipated by anyone in the news department.

If we were presented with a similar situation and a similar photograph today, we would absolutely not do it the way that we did it in the Shelby McGuire case. Thousands of our readers have defined for us a boundary in this community and for this newspaper that I don't think until we began to see it materialize we had any sense of exactly where it was.

Micro Issues

1. Look at the photos that accompany this text. The photo of the officer carrying out Shelby McGuire ran in full color above the fold, two-thirds of the page wide and 6 inches tall. Does a photo of that size oversensationalize the story?
2. The photo of Sergeant Swenson's attempts to resuscitate Shelby ran below the fold in a small two-column photo. Why do you think the decision was made to run this photo smaller and lower?

Midrange Issues

1. Does the fact that Shelby died influence your decision on whether to run the photos? If so, in what way?
2. Does the fact that at least one television station and the local Springfield newspaper were there with photographers influence your decision to run the photos? If so, in what way?
3. Does the fact that seven other children had died in Lane County in less than 2 years affect your decision to run the photos? If so, in what way?
4. The biweekly *Springfield News* chose to run a front-page photo of Alan McGuire falling out of the front window of his home, his badly burned flesh still in flames. However, they

covered the front page with a wrapper that read "Caution to Readers" and explained the content of the stories and photos underneath the wrapper. Critique that approach to handling the story.

5. A local television station showed a few seconds of the scene described above after warning viewers of the violent nature of the video that followed. The station got fewer than 20 complaints. How do you explain the vast difference in the reaction to the broadcast and print photos?

Macro Issues

1. What are the privacy rights of:
   a. Shelby McGuire?
   b. Shelby McGuire's mother and 4-year-old brother?
   c. Sergeant Swenson?
2. Critique the argument that these photos should be shown because they illustrate the type of tragedy that law enforcement officers are often called upon to handle.
3. Critique the argument that these photos should be shown because they illustrate the horror of domestic violence.
4. Critique the statement that "If we were presented with a similar situation and a similar photograph today, we would absolutely not do it the way that we did it in the Shelby McGuire case." In your opinion is that based on sensitivity to reader concern or caving in to reader pressure?

CASE 9-E

Horror in Soweto

SUE O'BRIEN, FORMER EDITORIAL PAGE EDITOR
The Denver Post

On September 15, 1990, freelance photographer Gregory Marinovich documented
the killing, by a mob of African National Congress supporters, of a man they believed
to be a Zulu spy.

Marinovich and Associated Press reporter Tom Cohen spotted the man being led
from a Soweto, South Africa, train-station platform by a group armed with machetes
and crude spears. Marinovich and Cohen continued to witness and report as the man
was stoned, bludgeoned, stabbed, doused with gasoline and set afire.

It was one of 800 deaths in two months of factional fighting among blacks as
rival organizations vied for influence in the declining days of apartheid.

The graphic photos stirred intense debate among editors. In one, the victim, con-
scious but stoic, lies on his back as a grinning attacker poises to plunge a knife into
his forehead. In the final photo of the series, the victim crouches, engulfed in fire.

As the series was transmitted, several member editors called up to question what
the photographer was doing at the scene—could he in any way have stopped the
attack? In response, an advisory went out on the photo wire, saying Marinovich had

AP/WIDE WORLD PHOTOS. Used with permission.

tried to intervene and then, when told to stop taking pictures, had told mob leaders he would stop shooting only when they "stopped hurting that man."

Decisions on what to do with the photos varied across the country, according to a survey. If any pattern emerged, it was that newspapers in competitive markets such as Denver, Minneapolis–St. Paul and New York were more likely to go with the harsh graphics.

The burning photo was the most widely used, the stabbing the least. Several editors said they specifically rejected the stabbing as too extreme. "It showed violence and animalistic hatred," said Roman Lyskowski, graphics editor for the *Miami Herald.* Another editor, who agreed that the stabbing was much more disturbing than the burning, said he recalled immolation pictures from the Vietnam era. "That's not as unusual an image as that knife sticking right out of the skull."

When the Soweto series cleared at the *Miami Herald,* the burning photo was sent to Executive Editor Janet Chusmir's home for her approval. At her direction, the immolation picture ran on the front page, but below the fold and in black and white. The detail revealed in color reproduction, Chusmir and her editors agreed, was too graphic.

At the *Los Angeles Times* and *Dallas Morning News,* however, the burning photo ran above the front-page fold—and in color.

The *St. Paul Pioneer Press* chose the stabbing for front-page color. "I look at the moment that the photo freezes on film," said News Editor Joe Sevick. "Rarely do you see a photo where a knife is about to go into somebody." The photo ran in color on the *Pioneer Press* front page, accompanied by the story Cohen had written on the attack and a longer story on the South African government's attempt, announced that day, to crack down on black-on-black violence.

In Denver, at the *Rocky Mountain News,* Managing Editor Mike Madigan wanted to run a comprehensive package on the Soweto story. The tabloid's only open page was deep in the paper, but a page 3 box referred readers to the story with a warning the photos were "horrific and disturbing." Inside, stories on the attack and government crackdown and an editor's note on Marinovich's intervention accompanied three photos: the victim being led away from the train station, the stabbing and the burning.

Most papers that ran the more challenging photos involved top management in the decision. Frequently, top editors were contacted by telephone, or came in from home, to give the photos a final go-ahead.

In most newsrooms, the burning or stabbing photos made it to the news desk for approval or rejection. But there, they sometimes were killed abruptly. "The editors at that point said no," one picture editor reported. "They would not take the heat."

Several editors deferred to the so-called breakfast test. "The question is 'Which of those photos would help tell the story without ruining everyone's breakfast?'" asked Rod Deckert, managing editor of the *Albuquerque Journal.* One editor said his paper is especially likely to de-emphasize disturbing material in the Sunday paper, which children often read with their parents. But many editors who rejected the more brutal pictures said the "breakfast test" is irrelevant. "If you're putting out a paper in New York and don't have something that's going to cause some discomfort over breakfast, then you're probably not putting out the full paper you should," said Jeff Jarvis, Sunday editor at the *New York Daily News*. "I don't think the break-fast test works for [today]."

Others cited distance tests. Some newspapers, in deference to victims' families, are less likely to use death photos from within their own circulation areas. Another editor, however, said his paper is *less* likely to run violent photos unless they are local and have a "more immediate impact on our readership."

Newspapers also differed widely on how they packaged the Soweto story. Some accompanied a photo series with the Cohen and crackdown stories, and a note on Marinovich's intervention. Some ran a single photo, often the burning, with only a cutline and a brief reference to the train-station incident in the "crackdown" story. Two respected big-city dailies, which omitted any reference to the Soweto attack in their accompanying stories, ran cursory cutlines such as "Violence continues: A boy runs away as an ANC supporter clubs a Zulu foe who was beaten, stabbed and set ablaze."

Although 41 papers used at least one of the Marinovich photos, only four—the *Charlotte Observer, Akron Beacon-Journal, Rocky Mountain News* (Denver) and *USA Today*—told the story of Marinovich's attempt to halt the attack.

Among collateral considerations at many news desks was the coverage of South African troubles that had gone before. At least one editor said the Soweto photos, which followed several other beating and killing photographs from South Africa that had been used earlier in the week, were "just too, too much."

AP/WIDE WORLD PHOTOS. Used with permission.

With only three exceptions, editors said race did not figure in their considerations. One white editor said the fact that both attackers and victim were black deprived the series of clarity: "You don't have a sense of one side against another. You don't have a sense of right or wrong." Two editors who identified themselves as African-American, however, argued for aggressive use of the photos. Both work in communities with significant black populations. "I think black readers should be more informed about this," one said. "Across the board, black Americans don't realize what's going on with the black-on-black violence."

Front-page placement and the use of color frequently triggered reader objections, but the adequacy of cutline information and accompanying copy also appear significant. The *Albany Times Union* was flooded by phone protests and subscription cancellations. Two other papers perceiving significant reader unrest—the *Dallas Morning News* and *Los Angeles Times*—ran the burning photo in color on their front pages. But each of the three papers also ran the front-page photos with only cutline accompaniment, referring readers inside to the stories that placed the images in context.

In retrospect, *Rocky Mountain News'* Madigan said he was very pleased with the final Soweto package and readers' reaction to it.

> It wasn't so much the idea that, "Yeah, we ran these really horrific pictures and, boy, it knocked people's socks off." I don't think that was the point. I think it was more the way we handled it. Just one word or the other can make a terrific difference in whether the public starts screaming "sensationalize, sensationalize," or takes it as a thoughtful, important piece of work, which is what we were after.

Micro Issues

1. In all but the most important stories, would you support a ban on dead-body photos in your newspaper or newscast?
2. Some editors believe it is their ethical duty to avoid violating readers' sense of taste or compassion. Others argue that it is their duty to force society to face unpleasant truths, even if it means risking reader anger and rejection. Whose side would you support?
3. Many readers suspect that sensational photos are chosen to sell newspapers or capture rating points by appealing to morbid tastes. Do you believe they're right?

Midrange Issues

1. Editors sometimes justify running graphic photos by saying they can provide a "warning bell," alerting people to preventable dangers in society. What values might the Soweto photographs offer readers?
2. Is the desire to avoid offending readers an ethical consideration or a marketing consideration?
3. Is it appropriate to base editorial decisions on what readers are likely to be doing at home: to edit newspapers differently, for instance, if they are likely to be read at the breakfast table, or present newscasts differently if they are to air during the dinner hour rather than later in the evening?

4. As an editor, would you be more likely to run a photograph of someone being murdered if the event happened in your own community, or if it happened thousands of miles away and none of your readers would be likely to know the victim or his family?
5. Do you see any distinction in:
   a. whether a violent photo is run in color or black and white, or
   b. whether it is run on the front page or on an inside page?

Macro Issues

1. Is aesthetic, dramatic or photographic value ever reason enough to run a picture, regardless of how intrusive it may be or how it may violate readers' sensitivities?
2. Is it your responsibility as an editor to find out if a photographer could have saved a life by intervening in a situation rather than taking pictures of it? Is that information you need to share with your readers?
3. Is it your responsibility as an editor to find out if the presence of the camera at the scene in any way helped incite or distort an event? Is that information you need to share with your readers?
4. When dramatic photographs are printed, how important is it for readers or viewers to be told all the background of the story or situation?

CASE 9-F

Death in Print: Publication of Hurricane Katrina Photographs

ABIGAIL M. PHEIFFER
University of Missouri-Columbia

"Do we publish this photograph of a dead body?" This is one of the most difficult questions newspaper editors can face. Editors at newspapers across the nation faced this question repeatedly as they reviewed wire photographs from the coverage of hurricane Katrina destruction in Louisiana and Mississippi. This case examines the Sept. 2nd photographic coverage of this event in three newspapers—the *Los Angeles Times, Chicago Tribune,* and *St. Louis Post-Dispatch.* Specifically, the study examines whether or not they published James Nielsen's photograph provided by Getty Images. The image depicts a woman standing on a bridge, feeding her dog as a corpse floats in the water underneath her. Sept. 2nd was the fifth day of the Katrina disaster.

All of the newspapers employ a similar process for choosing wire photographs on the day prior to publication of each issue. The first step is for a few wire editors to review the entire collection of photographs provided to them by Getty Images, the Associated Press and other wire services. These editors view hundreds of photographs and narrow the options down to those that they believe have the strongest visual impact.

The second step is to have a morning or early afternoon review of this initial edit. This takes place in the form of a formal meeting of all photo editors, an informal discussion of the photos among the photo editors or a full newsroom staff meeting. At this time the photo editors consider the merits of each photograph and learn the subject matter of the stories for which they must choose photographs. Based on this analysis the initial wire photo edit is narrowed to a smaller group of photos. One editor, often the director of photography or an assistant managing editor, reviews this narrowed edit and decides which photographs he or she believes should be on the front page, also known as A1. This editor then attends an afternoon A1 meeting and makes a pitch to the top editors, usually the executive and managing editors. This pitch includes the photo representative's opinions on where a photo should run in the newspaper and why it should run there. Detailed discussions of each possible A1 photo occur and final decisions are made regarding where photos will run.

St. Louis Post-Dispatch

The *St. Louis Post-Dispatch,* a newspaper that ranks 21st nationally in circulation among American newspapers with 271,386 daily circulation and 428,601 circulation on Sunday, published six Katrina photographs. The Nielsen photograph was published on page A10 and was stripped across the top of the page at roughly 4 inches tall and $11\frac{1}{2}$ inches wide. The photograph was cropped from the top and bottom, cutting out some of the water, bridge and what appears to be the base of a light post. This puts greater visual emphasis on the corpse, woman and the bag of trash in the water. The front-page photograph for Sept. 2nd by Dave Martin of the Associated Press showed thousands of people boarding buses in Metairie, La., a suburb of New Orleans.

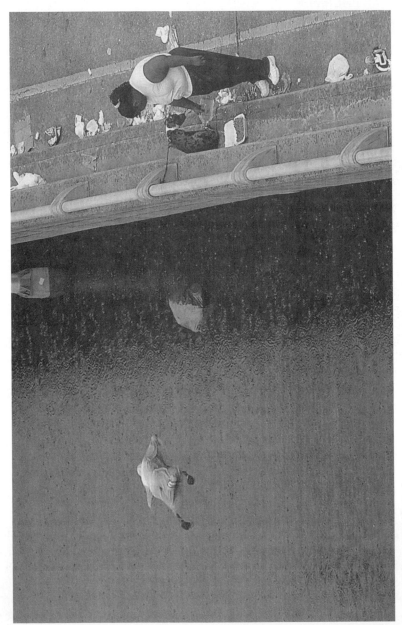

James Nielsen/AFP/Getty Images.

Larry Coyne, Director of Photography for the *St. Louis Post-Dispatch,* presents the photographic options for each day's edition in the A1 meeting. Coyne argued for the Nielsen photo to run on A1 but was in the minority. According to Coyne, the newspaper received many wire photographs that included dead bodies, but the publication was taking a cautious approach to running one, waiting for a photograph that was worthy of such a strong subject matter. Coyne advocated that this photograph run on the front page because it showed not only the tragedy of Katrina, but also how people were attempting to continue with their everyday lives. For him the juxtaposition of these two visual statements summarized the event and the destructive results of Katrina's power. "To get a full understanding you have to see it," Coyne said. "Until you see it, it is a figment of your imagination."

Coyne noted that there was a lively conversation in the A1 meeting regarding the Nielsen photograph, including a focus on whether or not the photograph trivialized the events of Katrina. There was concern that the photograph could offend readers because it included a corpse, but in the end the majority supported running the bus photo as the lead image because they felt it was more relevant to the stories planned for the Sept. 2nd edition.

Los Angeles Times

The *Los Angeles Times,* a newspaper that ranks 4th nationally with 843,432 daily circulation and 1,247,569 circulation on Sundays, published 15 Katrina photographs. The Nielsen photograph was published on the middle of the front page, just below the lead photo. The Nielsen photograph ran at approximately $3\frac{1}{4}$ inches tall and $5\frac{1}{2}$ inches wide. The lead photograph, shot by Michael Ainsworth of the *Dallas Morning News,* showed a mob of evacuees arguing outside of the Superdome as they were boarding buses. The photo editors do work with a page designer early in the photo selection process, before a final decision is made, to determine where each photo will run. Although deference is given to the photo editor, the page designer's opinion is considered regarding where and how large the photographs will run in the publication.

Steve Stroud, the Deputy Director of Photography, represents the national, foreign and often the metro photo desks in the A1 meeting and makes the pitch for the A1 photos. Stroud states that the photo editors did consider not running the Nielsen photograph because of its graphic nature. However, the driving factor in the decision to run the image on the front page was that at the time the staff knew that at least several hundred people had died in New Orleans and there were predictions that the final body count could be in the thousands. Nielsen's work accurately represented one of the major stories that was coming out of the event on that day.

As Stroud stated, "Our role is to inform people and remind people in a way that is appropriate to the event." The Ainsworth photo was selected as the lead image because it is more active, better represents chaos and affects more people.

Chicago Tribune

The *Chicago Tribune,* a newspaper that ranks 6th nationally with 586,122 daily circulation and 950,582 circulation on Sunday, ran 17 Katrina photographs in the Sept. 2nd issue. The Nielsen photograph did not run on Sept. 2nd, but did run in a special section entitled "Special Report: Hurricane Katrina" on Sept. 4th. The image appeared on the bottom of page seven of the special section at roughly $4\frac{1}{2}$ inches tall and $8\frac{1}{2}$ inches wide. The image was cropped slightly from the top. The lead photograph on Sept. 2nd was a Getty Image photo by Mark Wilson that depicted crying women trying to help a relative who appeared to be fighting death outside of the New Orleans Convention Center.

Rob Kozloff, the Metro Picture Editor, was the substitute A section photo editor the week the Sept. 2nd edition was published. Kozloff believed that the Nielsen photograph was probably considered for publication in the Sept. 2nd edition, but was not one of the 15 photos that received serious consideration for A1. He stated that there were many photographs that dramatically depicted the emotion of the day. Some of these images were a better fit than the Nielsen photograph to the storylines planned for the Sept. 2nd edition. However, Kozloff felt that the image provided an accurate perspective once it was placed among many other photographs in the special section. When these images were viewed as a group they accurately represented the entirety of the Katrina disaster. According to Kozloff, Nielsen's work was intriguing because it is not clear to the viewer if the woman is aware of the body.

In all three cases these newspapers made it clear that an extensive discussion involving multiple management members is expected when an image is controversial. Each of the following questions was raised by one or more of the newspapers when deciding whether or not a photo will run and where it will run. Even though none of the newspapers had specific policies that covered the tragedy of Katrina, collectively, these questions form a set of criteria.

1. Is the image relevant to the stories that will run in the issue?
2. Is the photograph in good taste or is it too graphic?
3. Is there a compelling reason for challenging the reader with a controversial image?
4. Is the content of the image newsworthy? Does it educate the reader?
5. Does the image revictimize or embarrass the photo subjects or family members of the subjects?
6. What is the most important news story of that day?
7. Can readers tolerate the image when eating their cereal in the morning?
8. What is the tolerance level of our specific readership?
9. How technically strong is the image?
10. Is it likely that there will be a stronger image for the same topic in the future?
11. Is the image properly stating the case or is it overstating it? Is the image emblematic or gratuitous?
12. Does the event warrant use of a graphic photograph?

None of these editors mentioned selling newspapers as a criterion for deciding which image to use. The editors do consider not running controversial images or placing them inside the newspaper at a smaller size where they are not as startling to a reader.

When discussing controversial images the editors said the discussion often includes weighing the "good" of educating the public versus the "bad" of violating the privacy of the subjects in the photograph. Most of the editors indicated that they felt it was necessary to use a picture that forced the reader to confront death in order to understand the gravity of the situation in New Orleans.

The bottom line is best stated by Greg Peters of the *Kansas City Star,* when he said: "As a picture editor you learn every day and try to get smarter every day. We try to get better every day."

Micro Issues

1. Is the Nielsen photo a page 1 photo on the fifth day of the tragedy? Why or why not?
2. What story does the Nielsen photo tell?

Midrange Issues

1. Does moving a controversial photo to the inside pages of a newspaper allow the editors more latitude in what they show? Why or why not?
2. Does a warning before graphic video is shown on a local newscast give the station more latitude in what they show? Why or why not?
3. If the body had been recognizable, would that change your opinion of running the photo? If the body had been unrecognizable but naked, would that change your opinion?

Macro Issues

1. Is it important that photos pass the "breakfast test" of acceptability before being run in the paper?
2. In weighing the "good" of educating the public to the horrors of the Katrina tragedy versus the "bad" of shocking the readership, where do you stand on running this photo? When the "bad" is the invasion of privacy of the dead individuals, where do you stand on running this photo?

CASE 9-G

Picturing our Fallen Heroes

KATE WEST
University of Texas

On April 7, 2004, Tami Silicio was doing what she had done so many times before: overseeing the loading of coffins onto cargo planes at the Kuwait International Airport bound for Dover Air Force Base in Delaware. On this particular day, 22 of America's fallen heroes from the wars in Iraq and Afghanistan were being shipped back home to their final resting place. As Silicio watched the soldiers carefully secure each casket, she picked up her digital camera and shot one picture.

"When you look at the photo, you will fill with compassion. You can feel grief. That's how I was feeling in my heart when I took the picture. I was thinking about the overwhelming sadness of those irreplaceable lives lost, and the grieving of the families. I was looking at the dignity, respect and care that they are given going home. They were being treated like they were sleeping and the guys strapping them were being very careful as not to wake them," Silicio (2004) told this author.

That night she sat down at her computer and wrote a letter to a friend who lived back in the states and attached the picture. She wrote, "Last night at work we sent home 22." When the friend opened the e-mail she felt the photo should be shared with others. That prompted her to call the *Seattle Times* (Silicio 2004).

The *Times* had received hundreds of calls over the years from readers saying they have a picture that must be published. Barry Fitzsimmons, a veteran photo-journalist, has handled many of these calls but knew that only one in a thousand is a gem. Fitzsimmons said when the picture arrived, he knew it was something the media didn't have access to and it was undeniably newsworthy. Mike Fancher (2004), the *Times* Executive Editor said in an interview for this case study: "We hadn't run a picture like that since the days of the Vietnam War, and I'm not sure what we did back then. Pictures like this one hadn't been available from Iraq."

However, in order to run the photograph the paper needed to get permission from Silicio and to talk with her about the possible consequences. "We felt it as important to not just rush it into the paper because we had the photo. Those conversations took place over a week and helped give the story more context," said Hal Bernton (2004, April 22), the reporter at the *Seattle Times* assigned to cover the story. But he was concerned: Silicio might lose her job if the story was published because the government had banned these types of photographs from being taken.

That ban dates back to President George H.W. Bush, father of President George W. Bush, whose Department of Defense was now enforcing the current ban covering the loading or unloading of flag-draped coffins returning from Iraq or Kuwait. After the invasion of Panama, the elder Bush had complained about an incident in which three television networks broadcast split-screen images of him speaking while at another location coffins were arriving in Dover. Not knowing about the timing or about the video juxtaposition on the nation's screens, the president's remarks during the coffins' arrival had been jocular (CBS/AP 2004) and the result was a presidential ban on any future shots of coffins being unloaded at Dover Air Force Base.

273

WELCOME MAT
OUT FOR RENTERS
HOME / REAL ESTATE, J 1

HOW TO SHACK UP
THE SMART WAY
NORTHWEST LIFE, N 1

MOYER, MARINERS
SHUT DOWN RANGERS
SPORTS, C 1

The Seattle Times

Sunday

Seattle Post-Intelligencer

TODAY'S WEATHER
Partly cloudy, then chance of showers.
High 54; low 42. | B 6

© 2004 • The Seattle Times Company

APRIL 18, 2004

$1.50

The somber task of honoring the fallen

'Everyone salutes with such emotion and intensity and respect ...
So far this month, almost every night we send them home'

Flag-draped coffins *are secured inside a cargo plane on April 7 at Kuwait International Airport. Military and civilian crews take great care with the remains of U.S. military personnel killed in Iraq. Soldiers form an honor guard and say a prayer as, almost nightly, coffins are loaded for the trip home.*

TAMI SILICIO

Military, civilians join in heartfelt rituals

BY HAL BERNTON / Seattle Times staff reporter

The aluminum boxes, in ordered rows, are bound by clean white straps on freshly scrubbed pallets. American flags are draped evenly over the boxes. Uniformed honor guards form on either side of the pallets as they move from the tarmac to the entryways of the cargo planes. There are prayers, salutes and hands on hearts. Then the caskets are carefully placed in cargo holds for a flight to Germany.

In recent weeks, military and civilian contract crews have loaded scores of these caskets onto planes departing the U.S. military area of Kuwait International Airport, south of Kuwait City. And the rituals are repeated over and over again.

"The way everyone salutes with such emotion and intensity and respect. The families would be proud to see their sons and daughters saluted like that," says Tami Silicio, a contract employee from the Seattle area who works the night shift at the cargo terminal.

For U.S. troops, April has been the worst month of this war, with at least 94 service members killed by hostile fire.

"So far this month, almost every night we send them home," Silicio said. " . . . It's tough. Very tough."

The remains arrive at the Kuwait airport ac-

PLEASE SEE **Fallen** *ON A 21*

Despite continued violence, *many Iraqis are enjoying economic recovery: They're shopping. A 22*

5 Marines killed in fierce fighting near Syrian border

SEATTLE TIMES NEWS SERVICES

BAGHDAD, Iraq — Five Marines were killed and scores of insurgents slain in a fierce 14-hour battle yesterday between Marines and mujahedeen fighters who slipped into Husaylah, a town 180 miles northeast of Baghdad near the Syrian border, a St. Louis Post-Dispatch reporter embedded with the Marines reported.

According to Marines, an estimated 300 Iraqis believed to have come west from the Fallujah and Ramadi area launched an assault against the Americans around 8 a.m. local time,

PLEASE SEE **Iraq** *ON A 20*

Gregoire's staff shaped 'independent' investigation of her office

Records reveal bulk of blame in bungled case was shifted

Copyright 2004, The Seattle Times Company

BY RALPH THOMAS AND MIKE CARTER
Seattle Times staff reporters

A review billed as an independent investigation of Attorney General Christine Gregoire's office in 2000 was rewritten to downplay broad management problems at the urging of Gregoire's top deputies.

Internal documents show the investigation — begun after Gregoire's staff missed a deadline to appeal a record $17.8 million verdict against the state — was redirected to focus more blame on one attorney who later was forced to resign.

E-mails, a legal invoice and notes from phone conversations show Gregoire's aides were in almost daily contact with investigator Susan Barnes, a private attorney who had earlier worked as a federal prosecutor. The aides, reviewing Barnes' drafts, suggested making her recommendations "more positive" and asked with respect to one criticism: "Can you give us any leeway here?"

Documents also reveal how concerned Gregoire's senior aides were about media coverage and political fallout. "Insane to write something before the election," say notes from a conversation in September 2000, when Barnes was helping craft a follow-up report for the state. That report, indeed, was not published until January 2001.

Other notes indicate that Gregoire's deputies and Barnes discussed "disposing of our drafts."

Gregoire on Friday denied her office interfered with the investigation or destroyed records. "I find these allegations ridiculous," she said.

Christine Gregoire

A recap *of the case and key players, A 12*

PLEASE SEE **Gregoire** *ON A 12*

Israeli airstrike kills newest Hamas leader

Strike followed Palestinian bombing

BY LAURA KING
AND FAYED ABU SHAMMALEH
Los Angeles Times

GAZA CITY, Gaza Strip — Israeli helicopter gunships incinerated a car carrying Hamas leader Abdel Aziz Rantisi yesterday, killing the firebrand militant and two bodyguards less than a month after his predecessor, Sheik Ahmed Yassin, met the same fate.

The Israeli airstrike came four hours after a Palestinian suicide bombing killed an Israeli border policeman at the main crossing between the Gaza Strip and Israel. It was three days after Prime Minister Ariel Sharon's triumphal visit to Washington, during which President Bush endorsed the Israeli leader's plan to withdraw troops and Jewish settlers from

Abdel Aziz Rantisi

PLEASE SEE **Hamas** *ON A 25*

Practical geniuses
of technology

In a field full of brain power, some individuals stand out because of their unique ability, insight or approach. Working mostly out of the spotlight, these six people have used their brilliance to unravel mysteries, solve problems and improve the way we live.

The quiet prodigy: Alan Lippman

BY MONICA SOTO OUCHI
Seattle Times technology reporter

If Alan Lippman felt uncomfortable at first, no one could blame him.

There he was, this wide-eyed, brown-haired kid taking his first university course, an astronomy class that met at night.

"I remember just feeling very young and out of place for this dark campus," Lippman recalls of his first days at the University of Washington.

He was 11 at the time.

Lippman, now 36, is profoundly gifted by any measure: He graduated

from Garfield High School at 11, earned a college degree three years later, and finished his Ph.D. in applied mathematics by the time he was old enough to vote.

His most well-known contribution, though, is helping transform the Internet into a three-dimensional medium — one that included sound.

Lippman, the first chief engineer of RealNetworks, is among the beautiful minds of technology, the men and women who generate the ideas

PLEASE SEE **Geniuses** *ON A 17*

Alan Lippman *went to college at age 11. In the 1990s at RealNetworks, he helped do the math behind Internet sound and video.*

JOHN LOK / THE SEATTLE TIMES

Since the end of the Vietnam War, presidents have worried that their military actions would lose support once the public glimpsed the remains of U.S. soldier's homecomings on all military bases. But they have continued to allow cameras on the military bases at politically strategic times.

For instance, in 1996, Dover made an exception to allow filming of President Bill Clinton's visit to welcome the 33 caskets with remains from Commerce Secretary Ronald H. Brown's plane crash. In 1998, Clinton went to Andrews Air Force Base to see the coffins of Americans killed in the terrorist bombing in Nairobi. Dover also allowed public distribution of photos of the homecoming of caskets after the terrorist attack on the USS Cole in 2000. And the administration of George W. Bush had allowed photos of coffins returning from Ramstein and other bases during his first two years in office. Then, on the eve of the Iraq invasion, the Pentagon said that other bases were to adopt Dover's policy of making the arrival ceremonies off limits (Milbank 2003).

The editors at the *Seattle Times* were aware of this ban and made sure to tell Silicio about it. "We feared that she might lose her job. She made a tough decision to allow us to publish the photo, and at a crucial time in the war when the government was trying to manage the images coming out of the war zone," said Bernton (2004, April 22). So on Sunday April 18, 2004, the *Seattle Times* published on the front page above the fold in full color the picture of 22 flag-draped coffins leaving Kuwait International Airport for Dover Air Force Base. The headline: "The Somber Task of Honoring the Fallen" (Bernton 2004, April 18).

"Once we determined to run the photo, there was no question in our minds that it belonged at the top of the front page," said Fancher (2004). Other papers and media outlets around the world quickly picked up the photograph. Suddenly the paper and Tami Silicio were in the spotlight. Although some readers called Fancher names, he reports that "the local reader response was very supportive." The photos led to a new debate about the government's ban on photographs of flag-draped coffins arriving from military bases but no change in the administration's policy.

The controversy took another turn when Maytag Aircraft, her employer, reprimanded Silicio the next day. Two days later she was fired (Bernton 2004, April 22). Silicio wrote on her Web site that "word came down from the Pentagon to fire me. I worked very hard 10-hour shifts. I felt I did a great job for the company. I loved my position" (Silicio 2004). Maytag Aircraft said the decision to terminate Silicio was made by the company and not the Pentagon.

In an interview for this case study, Silicio claimed that "my motherly instincts overpowered what was politically correct. My heart took over my brain. I just decided to show how the process of getting home was so respected."

Silicio moved back stateside to the Seattle area where she was from. But life is much different. "Can't make ends meet, losing my home, trying to work," Silicio said, "Spiritually I am staying positive that I am alright. I have even grown more in spirit."

The *Seattle Times* stands by its decision. "If there was an important photo like that, and we had permission to run the photo, I would hope we would run it again," Bernton told this author. "We would run it again even if the majority of readers had objected."

Micro Issues

1. Should Silicio have taken the photo knowing the government ban on such activity? Should she have shared it?
2. Should the friend have forwarded the photo to the *Times?* Is your answer based on whether she has the permission of Silicio?
3. Should the *Times* have run the photo? Justify your decision.

Midrange Issues

1. If the *Times* editors were pretty certain that the fallout from the photo would cost Silicio her job, does this fact outweigh the fact that she was consulted and gave her permission?
2. Is the government ban a morally relevant factor in this case? Why or why not?
3. Are the wishes of the majority of families in this case—whichever way those wishes go—a morally relevant factor in this case?
4. Critique Bernton's last statement. Would you run a photograph (or a video clip) even if you knew most of the readers/viewers would object? In such instances, where does the loyalty of the media outlet lie?

Macro Issues

1. Is this a First Amendment issue? Does the public have a "right to know" in this debate?
2. The Department of Defense claims that it is the wishes of the families of the fallen that the caskets not be shown. However, some families have been vocal in their disagreement of the policy and the war. Similarly, some readers want to see photos like this one and others do not. Whose interests outweigh the others in this debate?

10

New Media:
Continuing Questions
and New Roles

By the end of this chapter, you should be able to:

- **spot "old" ethical issues in their Internet incarnations.**
- **understand the role of copyright law in ethical decision making about Internet content.**
- **develop professional strategies for using the Internet as a reporting and advertising tool.**
- **delineate important policy issues the Internet raises for journalists and citizens.**

The original journalists in America were citizens first and foremost who stepped into the role of pamphleteers or publishers based on a desire to shape an emerging nation through their publications. Most of them, like Benjamin Franklin or Thomas Paine, had sources of income outside of their role as citizen journalists, and indeed many lost money in their publishing pursuits. During the next 100 years, the role of professional journalist emerged in the new democracy and for the next century, the delivery of information was primarily considered the role of the full-time professional.

However, no formal education or license is required to be a journalist. Toward the end of the 20th century—propelled by the emergence of the Internet—it became increasingly evident that the role of "journalist" no longer belonged exclusively to the trained journalist working in a recognizable media outlet.

Today, institutionally employed journalists often step out of their institutional roles through their blogs. Citizen journalists who have never been in a newsroom now create Web sites and write blogs whose readers not only rival in numbers the readers of the mainstream press but whose stories often break important national news. Videos on YouTube often receive a number of "hits" that would rank them among the top rated television programs if they had been measured by the Nielsen ratings. While the delivery methods are new, the concept is old: citizen journalists are a major source of information for the public.

NEW DELIVERY SYSTEMS, CONTINUING ISSUES

Internet-based technologies have allowed those who create information to bypass industry delivery systems and deliver their products directly to the consumer (Halbert 1999). Popular author Stephen King in 1999 bypassed his own publisher and agreed to market a new novel on the Web, providing those who accessed the book chapters would directly pay King $1 for every chapter they downloaded. King curtailed his experiment after about 6 months, but not before he had sent a message to the publishing world that the Internet—at least for popular and well-known artists—could replace some of the marketing support the publishing industry normally provides. King's book, however, remains incomplete.

Today, the King "one-buck-a-chapter" model is emulated by iTunes, Rhapsody and many other online music services that offer consumers just the songs they want for about a dollar a download. And for the not-yet-established artists, often the download is free. While these services slowed the tide of illegal downloads, they did begin the demise of the traditional CD. Since the income from downloads has not yet matched the previous income from CDs, one of the unintended consequences of the new system is that musicians now must depend on live concerts and merchandising at these events for more of their income.

In his book "The Long Tail: How the Future of Business is Selling Less of More," author Chris Anderson (2006) claims that online retailers such as Amazon in books and Rhapsody in music have made entire genres of books and music financially viable by getting around the shelf space and financial overhead constraints of the traditional bookstore or music stores. The upshot is a democratization of a process that, until recently had been controlled by a very few retailers. He writes (2006, p. 5):

> The great thing about broadcast is that it can bring one show to millions of people with unmatched efficiency. But it can't do the opposite—bring a million shows to one person each. The economics of the broadcast era required hit shows—big buckets—to catch huge audiences. The economics of the broadband era are reversed. . . . There's still a demand for big cultural buckets, but they're no longer the only market. The hits now compete with an infinite number of niche markets of any size.

An example of the old economy of music is Wal-Mart, America's largest music retailer, which stocks only 4,500 unique titles in its selection. This means that more than 99 percent of all music albums and CDs on the market today are not in the nation's largest music seller. Similarly, Blockbuster carries only 3,000 of the 200,000 commercially available videos and DVDs today. Even the largest chain bookstores have only about 100,000 titles in stock out of the estimated five million English titles available. This inability to service anything other than a popular "hit" led to what Anderson (2006) calls "the long tail" of online distributors such as iTunes (music), Netflix (video) and Amazon (books). And within a few years, even these new media icons will have to adapt or be replaced by more efficient delivery systems.

But what the new delivery systems also do is place a great deal of responsibility in the hands and minds of the audience. That may work well if you are asked to choose between genres of music. But this portal approach is also being applied to news. One implication is that the traditional gatekeeping function once performed by professionals is now performed "mechanically" by algorithms or by individual audience members. The autonomous journalist has been replaced by autonomous readers or equations. Such a system may promote commerce, but there is less certainty about its impact on democratic functioning.

COOKIES . . . AND THE RIGHT TO READ UNMOLESTED

Academic philosophers sometimes debate whether any really new ethical issues emerge over time, or whether old issues merely resurface. Students of applied ethics (and by reading this book you are one) have a tentative answer to that question. The core ethical issue may remain the same, but its real-world manifestation, and the morally relevant facts, often call for original thinking.

Take cookies, that electronic "marker" particular Web sites attach to your computer when you access them. Those advertising on the Web want to know who is looking at their site and whether they will purchase the advertised product. In rough parallel, cookies might be thought of as a sophisticated version of eye tracking—a research technique used by marketers literally to trace how the human eye moves across the page. The results of eye-tracking studies, for example, have taught us that the upper right hand corner of the newspaper page is where the human eye most often focuses and that a single dominant picture can encourage the eye to move around the page in the way the designer intended. Advertisers also use eye-tracking research to determine what part of a particular design catches and holds consumer attention. Media researchers have used eye tracking for decades, and no one has claimed that it presented an ethical problem. Cookies, the electronic equivalent, should be treated the same way, right?

Not exactly.

Because the cookie is a marker that's attached to your computer hard drive (and in the earliest days of "cookies" you did not know when you had received one), it's capable of providing its originator with a great deal of information about you. What kind of computer do you own? What sorts of Web sites do you visit? For how long? What do you purchase? Did you use a credit card? The cookie gives marketers this kind of information without asking your permission and sometimes, for the Web neophyte, without your knowledge.

In short, a cookie on your computer hard drive can mean that you lose control of a great deal of information about you. Furthermore, the marketers can use the information they gain about you to find better, more effective, ways to sell you things. Law enforcement, or even the spouse you are divorcing, can subpoena such information. Marketers can, and do, sell the same information to other marketers. And, the United States, unlike the European Union, does not make such action illegal.

If phrases in the preceding paragraph sound familiar, they should. Recall that part of the definition of privacy (see Chapter 6) is the ability to control information about you and how that information is interpreted and used. What seemed like a great idea to marketers—to track consumer Web use through the novel approach of a cookie—raises important privacy questions. Those questions seem more urgent because of the nature and amount of information one can collect and connect by accessing the multiple consumer databases of which we are all a part.

The privacy issue raised by cookies, in fact, is so significant that some suggest consumers should have a legal right to access the World Wide Web without fear of their every movement being tracked, analyzed and potentially resold. You have the right to read anonymously (Cohen 2000); information about you is your private property. Your computer constitutes your private space in much the same way your home does. Those who enter your home must do so, except in very rare circumstances, only with your permission.

It is our contention that the Internet, using cookies as a good example, doesn't raise unique ethical questions so much as it asks us to rethink our standard answers to similar questions. The impact of speed—and the trade-off between speed and accuracy in what used to be referred to as the drive for the "scoop"—is another question that the Internet has brought to the foreground. And, because the Internet is a system, it also asks us to broadly consider the systemwide implications of ethically informed choices. Speed, accuracy and privacy are not new ethical issues to journalism and mass communication; the Internet simply asks that we examine them in light of new facts, some of which may be morally relevant.

OWNERSHIP OF INFORMATION: LEGAL HINTS BUT NOT HELP

In October 1995, the *New York Times* found itself under siege from a distinguished group of authors, all of whom contributed occasionally to the paper. More than 300 writers and scholars—among them Norman Mailer, Alice Walker, Garry Trudeau, Kurt Vonnegut, Barbara Raskin, Roger Rosenblatt, Ben Bagdikian and Carolyn Bird—signed a petition protesting the *Times'* newly implemented policy requiring writers to surrender syndication, electronic and other secondary rights to their work after articles were published in hard copy in the *Times.*

In an internal memorandum, the *Times* had announced it would require its freelancers to sign "work-made-for-hire" contracts. It read: "The position on this is unambiguous: if someone does not sign an agreement, he or she will no longer be published in the newspaper." The writers responded that the memorandum was a historic break with publishing tradition where freelancers had been allowed to retain copyright to their own work.

What was really at issue, of course, was money. The freelancers wanted to be paid for the original publication of their efforts and for all subsequent publication of their work—regardless of medium. The *Times,* which was struggling to develop an Internet presence and to make money from that effort, was attempting to cut both costs and subsequent legal problems by demanding copyright ownership of its organizational contribution to the Information Superhighway. Since the *Times,* like all other news organizations, had been unable to turn the Internet into a profit center, it sought to reduce some expenses by curtailing its payments to freelancers. The writers, in turn, wanted the Internet to be governed by the same professional norms that had governed the print media—in other words, the writer retains the copyright and each user must pay for the privilege of reproduction.

Ultimately the protest turned into legal action, and the courts ruled in favor of the writers. But the suit itself still raised a fundamental issue: in an Internet world, who owns—and who can profit from—a work product, be it words, a design, a photograph, a melody or a film?

While the recording industry, and to a lesser extent other media outlets, regard piracy as theft, consumers and some journalists are not so sure. United States copyright law, as it has evolved over the past 200 years, can be boiled down to two succinct concepts. The first is that the courts have repeatedly ruled "You can't copyright an idea." As Justice Louis Brandeis observed in *International News Service v. Associated Press*, "The general rule of law is that the noblest of human productions—knowledge, truths ascertained, conceptions and ideas—become voluntary communication to others, free as the air to common use."

What can be copyrighted, however, is the particular execution of an idea. Mozart could not copyright the order of the keys on the harpsichord, but he could copyright the particular order of notes played on that instrument—the execution of an idea—in "The Magic Flute."

The second basic concept of copyright law is that an idea that is sufficiently novel and concrete enough does warrant protection. This "novel and concrete" approach to ideas is rooted in the 17- and 18-century notion that ideas are like private property and, like private property, are worthy of protection. An entire line of cases involving television and radio formats has developed essentially through regarding particular formats and plot lines as concrete expressions of ideas that can be copyrighted. One legal scholar has noted that the essential feature of this branch of copyright law is "the right to determine what shall be done with an idea."

The courts currently protect ideas that are bound through contracts—what is called "expressed contract theory." This means that copyright is related not so much to ownership as to sales. In fact, some scholars assert that copyright doesn't protect ownership so much as it protects the right to copy (Halbert 1999). A contract may be expressed through money changing hands or a promise to disclose the idea to a third party (for instance, a publisher's promise to publish a novel). Even if an idea is obtained fraudulently, the courts have been willing to protect its originator. The courts also protect ideas under what is called "implied contracts." A freelancer submitting an article to a magazine in the hopes that it will be published is functioning under an implied contract that the publisher will consider the article but not steal it.

Finally, the courts have developed a doctrine designed to impede unjust enrichment. Under this view, ideas should be protected because, failing to do so would allow one person or organization to enrich themselves while failing to compensate the original developer of the idea.

THE LAW LAGS BEHIND

Legal theories and case rulings have not kept pace with the technology. The courts would normally consider a photograph a concrete expression of an idea. But what

Copyright © Ed Stein. Reprinted with permission of Rocky Mountain News.

happens when the photograph has been cut into pixels, the individual pixels' colors changed, the shape of the pixels reorganized—say, from a camel to an elephant—and then the resulting image, which now looks a great deal like an elephant and lacks a negative to indicate that it was once a camel, is downloaded onto a Web site that belongs to your news organization? Is linking to another site some form of copyright infringement? Is it like using "freelance" work in a publication? Could links constitute unjust enrichment? Or are they more like the harpsichord keys—a good idea that cannot be copyrighted although it can be used in many different ways?

Is the execution of the idea that the photograph represents the property of the photographer who shot the original image, the property of the multimedia author who took the photograph of the camel and changed it to an elephant, or the property of the news organization that ultimately distributed it in the form of electrons on a Web site? How about the designer or the content creator of the page you are linking to? Is there an express or implied contract in any of these actions? Does the creator of the elephant image owe royalties or acknowledgement to the creator of the camel?

Adding to the complexity is another question: do these issues persist after death? For example, who gets paid for, and who holds the copyright to, an image of television star Lucille Ball who, years after her death, is electronically reproduced and inserted into a 1996 television ad for Service Merchandise? Furthermore, what if the creator of the ad could prove that the image of Ms. Ball was created out of a group of uncopyrighted pixels? Who then would own the Ball image?

Right now, it is unclear how the use and development of the Internet will influence these trends. Common ownership muddies the professional waters even further. Thinking about copyright has always included an element of "this came first," but that issue was defined in terms of weeks or years rather than nanoseconds.

Historically, when one medium—for example, radio—has surpassed another—say, newspapers—in an important dimension such as timeliness, both mediums have evolved to take advantage of their unique strengths. Thus, as broadcasting developed, that medium tended to emphasize immediacy while print emphasized depth. With the emergence of broadcasting as a dominant medium, journalists began to rethink the ethics of "the scoop" and to insist that accurate news reporting was more important in both a professional and ethical sense than mere speed. This same debate—the balance between accuracy and speed—is now taking place among news organizations with a substantial Internet presence.

This Internet-focused debate has also added renewed energy to questions regarding corrections of inaccurate, but speedy, reports. For instance, a few years ago, John Sigenthaler, former editor of the *Nashville Tennessean,* brought national attention to the way the open-source online encyclopedia Wikipedia works when he called press attention to a posting in his online Wikipedia biography that anonymously and incorrectly claimed he played a role in the assassination of former U.S. President John F. Kennedy. And while Sigenthaler had the stature to get media attention called to the error about him, untold numbers of factual errors race across the Internet each day where few, if any, gatekeepers exist to vouch for the accuracy of the content.

Corrections of news stories, in either the traditional print or broadcast media, have some permanence. On the Internet, it is possible to simply blow away the page—or even the site—that contains an error, leaving no permanent record of either the mistake or attempts to rectify it. But with so many pages out there, and so many links, errors may persist in ways that were unimaginable 20 years ago. Journalists working in many venues, as well as media ethicists, have long agreed that errors merit permanent correction. Should the same professional standard be applied to Internet coverage? If it should, how then might it be achieved so that readers who access the page months, or even years, later know that an error was made and have access to the correct information?

The ability to digitize information also challenges our intuitive assumptions about a variety of things—everything from the "reality" that a picture represents to the external symbol systems that words and images together create. Digitization enables media designers to confound the external referent as never before. Students at the turn of the century will recognize that Audrey Hepburn's image has been digitized and electronically inserted into a Gap ad. But students in 2050 may not recognize the original Audrey Hepburn, may not know that she was a film star and may not be aware that she has been dead for over more than half a century at that point. They will have lost the external referent to the image. One consequence of that loss is that the Gap commercial may not be as meaningful, or seem as clever. There are more sinister possibilities, such as the twisting and destruction of meaning that Orwell raised in "1984."

In addition to what may be copyrighted, the Internet emphasizes questions of when. We now work in a 24-hour news cycle. Stories must be updated almost constantly. The 1990s phrase "All news all the time" has been narrowed in focus to "All terrorism all the time," "All stock market all the time" or "All presidential scandal all the time" by cable and the Internet. Many professionals insist that the 24-hour news cycle has resulted in the trivialization of news and a sensationalistic approach to news. Rumor can pass for information on the Web, further confounding traditional efforts at fact checking and decreasing the time for thoughtful decision making.

Some have suggested that the Web can make news journalists lazy; finding information on the Web in many news organizations has nudged out interviewing as the primary method of information collection. This means journalists have to learn to discriminate between "quality" Web sites and those that, while creative, do not adhere to the facts. The ethical issue—a professional drive for accuracy and, when possible, truth—remains the same. But the Internet requires that journalists not only be able to discern when a source is "lying" (what some professionals refer to as the "sniff" test) but also need to recognize when a Web site is inaccurate, perhaps deliberately so.

Ethical thinking combined with sound professional practice can provide some paths out of this virtual swamp. The first, and probably the most basic, maxim arises from the habits of sound professional performance. Cite the source of your information—or your electronic bytes. After all, journalists are required to note the originators of their information when reporting on documents or interviews. Multimedia designers should be subject to the same standard, just as music arrangers (as opposed to composers) or screenwriters currently are. Just as important, that source needs to be credible—even accurate. Newspapers and broadcast outlets eschew publishing rumors. Internet news—if it is to succeed as a genuine information medium—needs to consider the same standard. Just as in the days of the film "The Front Page," scoops for the sake of scoops are ethically suspect.

If noting the originators of your information creates problems, as it did for the *New York Times,* then be willing to accept those problems as the price of using the information. Many publications require that journalists avoid sourcing their stories exclusively from the Internet; some demand confirmation of an Internet source with additional verification from nonvirtual documents and in-person interviews. In an ethical sense, such professional standards allow news organizations and those who work for them to achieve two results. In the Judeo-Christian tradition, you have avoided information theft, an ethically culpable act, and fulfilled the ethical duty of beneficence, sharing credit with the originator of your information, whether that is a particular author or the source of a quote in a feature story.

In addition, you've also done your best to uphold the professional standards of accuracy and truth. In this world of bits and bytes, application of a maxim of "Cite the source of your bytes" will prejudice you to the development of original and creative work, including multiple sources. And, using your own stuff, and not someone else's, improves performance.

The second maxim that emerges from a discussion of deception is this: information that has the capacity to deceive the rational audience member as to its origin, original referent or source must be regarded as suspect. While journalistic discussion of deception has generally focused on practices used to obtain stories, we believe the concept also applies to the relationship between the journalist and his audience. The issue is whether using digitized information is intended to mislead the audience. Thus, an October 1996 cover of *Life* magazine that combined more than 400 previous covers into an image of Marilyn Monroe does not intend to deceive the audience because the editors clearly explained what they did. But lifting an image from one Web site, downloading sentences from another, and combining them for your own news story without citing your original sources is an attempt to deceive both your editors and your audience.

While both plagiarism and forgery are clearly deceptive practices (Bok 1983, 218), the Web, with its nearly infinite possibilities as a source of information, has highlighted the need for journalists to take care. Even in a new era of pixels and bytes, journalists must maintain old-fashioned credibility with our audiences about the sources of our information and the means and methods of gathering that information.

SOURCES: NEW TECHNOLOGY BUT CONTINUING ISSUES

New technology often raises old ethical issues with additional permutations, and the subtleties of sourcing on the Internet don't all focus on accuracy and speed. Journalists accept that readers and viewers may better understand and evaluate news if those stories identify information sources. Identification often goes beyond a mere name and address: journalists may provide background information so audience members understand why a person or document is cited. The professional standard is that sources should be named and that journalists must have compelling reasons for withholding a source's identity. Implicit in this standard is that sources are aware that they are talking to a journalist, or that a specific document has been requested for a journalistic purpose. The Internet can confound these implicit assumptions.

First, granting anonymity requires a mutual agreement between reporter and source, not a unilateral understanding imposed on one party by the other. Anonymous sources are expected to be the exception rather than the journalistic rule. Professional mores dictate that, should a reporter decide to grant anonymity, she does not have to divulge the source's identity to editors, other supervisors or, in rare instances, the courts.

Even the traditional practice of interviewing, now considered commonplace, was controversial at its inception. The critics claimed that interviewing would destroy reporting. Critics argued that if journalists adapted this reporting technique, they would slip into a moral morass, fall prey to aggressive exploitation and manipulation and would no longer serve the public. Reporters' power grew with the use of the interview because they could select which persons to question and determine which comments to include. As the journalistic practice of the interview developed concurrently with the rise of the professional ideal of objectivity, identifying news sources became accepted professional practice (Schudson 1995, 1978).

The role sourcing plays with readers and viewers has also been questioned in mass communication research. One of the most widely accepted findings in the field is that audience members tend to disassociate the source from the message, what is known as the "sleeper" effect (Lowery and DeFleur 1988). Studies confirm that most people tend to retain the fact of what is said while forgetting the context in which they heard it. Practitioners, from Nazi master propagandist Joseph Goebbels through contemporary political consultants, have intuitively understood this human tendency to disassociate the source from the message. But readers and viewers are morally autonomous actors. Identifying news sources allows audiences to evaluate reports in terms of both content and a source's motives for divulging information.

The motives for providing and withholding information are sometimes central to political coverage, and political reporters have added an element of elasticity to the practice of anonymous sourcing. The phrase "not for attribution" means journalists may quote what is said but agree to veil the source. Thus, the attribution "a high-level White House source" may mean anyone from the president himself to cabinet officers to other, well-connected administrative appointees. The phrase "on background" means journalists should consider the information given as an aid in placing facts in context. Background information also may be used as part of a sourcing trail: journalists in possession of background information may use their knowledge to try to get other sources to provide them with the same information on the record.

Journalists continue to debate allowing sources to go "off the record" or "on deep background." A strict interpretation of these synonymous phrases means that the journalist who accepts such information may not quote the specific source and, in addition, may not use his knowledge to pry the same information from other sources. This stringent interpretation has meant that editors have instructed reporters literally to leave the room when a source asks for such anonymity. Journalists have spent time in jail rather than reveal a source's identity. Less stringent interpretations suggest that journalists who accept information off the record may not name or in any way reveal the identity of the source but may use the information itself to leverage similar or related information from other sources.

Until quite recently such agreements were arrived at through face-to-face conversation and negotiation. However, the advent of the Internet and the ability of journalists to lurk at many places on the Web have changed these dynamics. Journalists surfing for story sources or leads must be careful to identify themselves professionally on the Internet when they begin "conversing" with another Internet user. Concepts such as citizen journalism have also changed the journalist-source relationship. Citizen journalists essentially function as reporters who are most often edited by professionals. But most citizen journalism projects do not attempt to either confirm or police how citizen journalists acquire their information. In some cases, citizen journalists appear to be subject to a different set of rules than are the professionals.

Some publications, for example *The Wall Street Journal,* maintain an informal policy that requires reporters to identify themselves as reporters when they begin their Internet conversations. The reasoning behind such requirements is that people, in this instance people who are "telepresent," need to know that they are dealing with a journalist working in a professional capacity. Since journalists are well aware of the pitfalls of being deceived by a source, "wired" reporters should be more than sensitive to these problems when they become the party to the conversation with the power to deceive. Such professional identification—the Internet version of identifying yourself at the beginning of a telephone conversation—also raises additional professional issues. For example, it is possible for competitors, who also may be surfing the Net, to learn about the direction of a story or even of its specific content during the reporting process. This increases the chance that other news organizations will learn about stories or angles they have missed sometime before actual publication. While this sort of competitive consideration has always influenced journalism, the Internet makes it easier and faster to learn what other news organizations are doing.

Whether in person or through fiber optics, journalists who cover police, the courts and other areas of public life often develop informal agreements with frequent sources about when and how information may be attributed. Such relationships are necessary but risky. Many journalists have had to decide whether they will "burn a source," that is, to reveal the identity of a source who has been allowed to remain veiled in earlier stories for a particularly important story. Burning a source means terminating a relationship that worked well for both parties. It is considered a form of promise breaking. Historically, such promise keeping has been more of a one-way street. However, the capacity of sources to manipulate journalists—and hence news coverage—particularly on issues such as national security, raises important ethical questions, ones we ask you to consider in several cases in this book.

Keeping the trust between reporter and source intact is one reason that larger news organizations will often send an investigative reporter to cover a particularly sensitive story that arises on another reporter's beat. Sending an investigative reporter allows the beat reporter's sourcing agreements to remain undisturbed, ensuring a continuing flow of routine information while the investigation continues. There are significant ethical justifications for using anonymous sources. They are:

- Preventing either physical or emotional harm to a source.
- Protecting the privacy of a source, particularly children and crime victims.
- Encouraging coverage of institutions, such as the U.S. Supreme Court or the military, which might otherwise remain closed to journalistic and hence public scrutiny.

It is this final justification that is used most frequently by journalists. Reporters maintain that only when sources are allowed to remain anonymous will they provide newsworthy information that would otherwise place their careers or their physical safety at risk. While using the Internet as a reporting tool does not alter these justifications, it emphasizes the need for disclosure when working with sources in ways that nonvirtual journalists seldom encounter. The thinking may be the same, but the situation that prompts such reflection may look very different at first glance.

POLICY OPTIONS: THE ROLE OF THE PROFESSION

Unlike some media technologies such as the printing press, the Information Superhighway was initially developed by the government for political reasons. The original Internet was a computer network designed first to support the military and then, in the 1960s, reorganized to allow scientists working primarily at universities and government laboratories worldwide to communicate quickly and easily among each other. This system remained confined to the intellectual and military elite until the early 1980s, when the Internet, as we now know it, began to take shape.

This unusual history—a mass medium that was "invented" to support government policy—has made the Internet a difficult fit for both academic study and journalistic necessity. Unlike the printing press, which began as a private invention and remained private property, the Internet has historically owed a great deal to the government in both conceptual and financial terms. Because journalists never were part of the early history of Internet development, the notion of using the Internet as a profit-oriented mass medium is a very recent invention. Grafting a concept of mass communication onto a system designed for government-supported communication is fraught with the potential to raise some difficult questions.

The contemporary conceptualization of the Internet has government supporting a system that will wire and link all schools, libraries and hospitals. This proposal, which has been partially funded but will cost billions, is rooted in both practical politics and ethical theory.

The political aspects are fairly straightforward: by linking schools, hospitals and libraries, the government is supporting an infrastructure that will promote education and learning and thus strengthen the economy by providing a better-educated workforce. A better-educated workforce is also generally considered a more efficient one, thus making U.S. workers more competitive worldwide as well as driving down production costs domestically. A better-educated populace, of course, also has military implications: it enables the military to draw from a more qualified pool of recruits who are being asked to operate increasingly more complicated weapons. Thus, the reasoning goes, the federal government fulfills its constitutional responsibility to protect Americans from international as well as domestic threats by supporting a system that will promote the country's growth and development in many obvious and subtle ways.

Linking hospitals, of course, is also viewed as one way to simultaneously improve the quality of health care for many Americans while holding down medical costs. Again, the reasoning is that private, for-profit medicine would not be as likely to connect all hospitals; through government support the projected benefit can be distributed throughout American society.

This conceptualization of the Internet is also founded in ethical theory. As you may remember from the discussion of utilitarianism in Chapter 1, the notion of the greatest good for the greatest number has profound democratic implications. Wiring schools and libraries should, in theory, provide access to the Internet for every American. Indeed, some libraries in California have experimented with "Internet addresses" for the homeless. Universal access to the Internet through education also would follow Rawls's theory—it would allow the maximization of freedom (access) while protecting weaker parties (people of color, the poor) who might not have access to many other goods in U.S. society but can use the Internet as a way to better their individual and potentially collective lots in life.

Of course, journalists and journalism have not been included in this conceptualization. Yet many journalists have argued that access is only part of the picture— it does people little good to access information if they can't make sense of it. Some scholars have suggested that, as the Internet develops, journalism itself will change from a profession that primarily gathers facts—something anyone can now do on the Internet—to a profession that places those facts within a context and makes them meaningful. If the development of the Internet does indeed encourage professional development along these lines, then ethical thinking would demand that access to news coverage be distributed as widely as possible among the population and that it remain economically affordable.

That stance, of course, puts journalists at odds with all those segments of U.S. society that view the Internet as another potential profit center, including the multinational corporations for which increasing numbers of journalists now work. Insisting that affordable news become part of the policymaking that is currently swirling around the Information Superhighway would challenge the long-standing U.S. tradition of regarding journalism and government as irreconcilable adversaries. Yet ethical (and in some ways political) thinking would seem to suggest that making news coverage accessible to every American via the Internet has significant potential benefits for the individual and society at large. It also would make journalists and the government partners—a true philosophical shift in the conceptualization of a "free" press.

Finally, such a partnership would demand that journalists themselves take an active part in developing and implementing legislation that will affect their working lives. Such a change in attitude also would require a philosophical shift, one that places journalistic responsibility to political society on an even plane with worker responsibility to profitable media industries.

THE FRAGMENTATION OF POLITICAL CULTURE

In the 1980s, Nicholas Negroponte, the head of MIT's Media Lab and an Internet guru of some note, created a unique publication he called the *Daily Me*. Negroponte programmed his MIT computer to develop a daily newspaper based on his information needs and desires as well as past information preferences. The *Daily Me*, for example, carried a great deal of news about computers and universities and relatively less news about sports, U.S. politics and the environment. Negroponte, acknowledging that he had a good chance of missing stories that he either should know about or would be interested in that would fall outside his desired categories, programmed his computer to select 10 percent of the *Daily Me*'s content literally at random.

Today, all of us now have the capacity to develop a *Daily Me* from the vast collection of information now on the World Wide Web. Of course, reader and viewer selectivity is nothing new. How many people do you know who always read the sports page and never anything else? If most contemporary newspaper readership surveys are correct, about 35 percent of regular newspaper readers fit this profile. Or take the reverse problem. What if something new—say the emergence of a potentially deadly virus—is noted by doctors but given little media attention? How will you know to tell your *Daily Me* that, instead of looking at the *New York Times*, the better sources are the alternative press in the gay community in San Francisco and New York? This was exactly the case from 1981 through 1986, when many major publications, including the *New York Times,* refused to carry front-page stories about the AIDS virus at the same time the gay press was covering the epidemic.

If every member of a society has access to personalized news, the implications for democracy are enormous, as Cass Sunstein (2001) points out in **Republic.com.** He writes that democracy demands two imperatives. First, people must be exposed to materials that they would not have chosen in advance and come across views that they would not have previously selected or even agree with. Second, many, or at least most, citizens should have a range of common experiences. In the absence of shared experiences, society will have a much harder time addressing social problems, Sunstein contends.

Philosopher Jürgen Habermas is another advocate of this approach, arguing that one of the preconditions of a deliberative democracy is a large number of public forums where people meet by chance and begin a dialogue—none of which is possible in a society where everyone subscribes only to the *Daily Me.* Sunstein concludes that "The imagined world of the 'Daily Me' is the farthest thing from a utopian dream, and it would create serious problems from a democratic point of view."

Suggested Readings

ANDERSON, CHRIS. 2006. *The long tail: How the future of business is selling less of more.* New York: Hyperion.

GODWIN, MIKE. 1998. *Defending free speech in the digital age.* New York: Times Books.

HALBERT, DEBORA J. 1999. *Intellectual property in the information age.* Westport, CT: Quorum Books.

NEGROPONTE, NICHOLAS. 1995. *Being digital.* New York: Alfred A. Knopf.

Cases on the Web

"The witch and the woods mystery: Fact or fiction?" by Karon Reinboth Speckman

"The Napster debate: When does sharing become thievery?" by Laura Riethmiller

"Digital sound sampling: Sampling the options" by Don Tomlinson

"Cry Wolf: *Time* magazine and the cyberporn story" by Karon Reinboth Speckman

"Filmmaking: Looking through the lens for truth" by Kathy Brittain McKee

"The Madonna and the Web site: Good taste in newspaper online forums" by Philip Patterson

"The Case of Banjo Jones and his blog" by Chris Heisel

CASE 10 ESSAY

To Post or Not to Post: The Question for Writers in the Digital Age

MICHAEL BUGEJA
Iowa State University of Science and Technology

Increasingly with the advent of interactive, wireless and portable technologies, a reporter or freelance writer, especially, must guard against reacting to comments about his or her work or worse, *person,* in the "add a comment" sections of blogs, listservs or Web sites. This is an ethical issue because it touches on such matters as credibility, conflict of interest, fairness and discretion.

I am a freelance writer contributing regularly to such publications as *Editor & Publisher, The Quill, Inside Higher Ed,* and *The Chronicle of Higher Education.* Typically I report on the impact of technology on ethical standards, not only in journalism, but also in academe.

After an article titled "Facing the Facebook," which questioned the effectiveness of wireless technology in the classroom, ran in *The Chronicle* (see *http://chronicle .com/jobs/2006/01/2006012301c.htm*), making the point that multitasking students were not always doing what they pretended to be doing in college settings an ethical issue associated with deception, not multitasking, by the way—a flurry of criticism was hurled my way in the blogosphere. For example, one post called the article an "anti-technology screed" which blamed "everything bad happening on campus" on Facebook. My arguments were called ridiculous and invalid.

I ignored these posts and other examples critical of my Facebook observations which, in the end, opened debate nationwide on some of the less desirable aspects of social networks, from privacy invasion to sexual predation. As a former wire service reporter, I wanted to give online readers and bloggers the last word, even when they seemed to misinterpret the intent of an article or a fact or two in it. Frankly put, their First Amendment rights supersede my egotistical ones.

Increasingly this is difficult for reporters to do when their e-mail addresses are appended to articles or when they read comments that may misconstrue their work. But the temptation of instant access affects journalists, too, and they may exercise poor judgment in responding to posts appended to their work whereas in the days before Internet they would have to clear any such responses through an editor. (The likelihood of that would be slim unless the reporter was correcting a mistake.) But because the only gatekeeper in the Internet age is your conscience, many reporters have been tempted to respond to readers' comments, which only makes those journalists seem defensive.

To guard against the temptation to reply, you have to ascertain the consequences, just as in any ethics issue. For instance, if I responded to the student blog above, I would have made myself part of the story because most probably he would have replied to me, kicking off a digital chain reaction, not only between us, but among those reading his blog. What appears on one blog soon appears on others because of RSS feeds, a format for syndicating content, and through additional posts. In sum, sooner or later my comments would have gotten back to my editor at *The Chronicle*. Most editors want journalists to stand by their words rather than stand up to readers who question them because the latter can end up maligning the audience.

Journalists need to foresee the consequences of responding to posts and suppressing those urges. But they also need to identify times and occasions when they may want to post comments for the archival record. Admittedly, those times are rare, but they do happen, and when they do, you ought to have conceived guidelines. I decided to do so on blogs of professors or journalists whom I might know or have contact with eventually at a convention or professional forum. My standard was to engage them as a scholar or practitioner seeking to raise the level of dialogue rather than succumb to the lowest digital denominator.

Recently I decided to respond to one professor's blog about my Facebook piece. The opening sentence called my work "Bugeja's rant against technologies newer than the library." He called such thinking *"technostalgia"* (see *http://ghostinthewire .org/archives/01/technostalgia.php*).

I could have responded to the use of my last name without my first and to the word "rant," possibly sparking a personally heated exchange. But in truth, the author's opening sentence does not do justice to the critical thinking in his Jan. 24, 2006 post, where you will also find an expanded dialogue between us.

Here is my initial response:

> Thank you for your well-thought essay on the term technostalgia. There have been a lot of assumptions in "Ghost in the Wire" about me and my research. I am responding now only because of the scholarship in the above piece, "Technostalgia."
>
> Let me give you a bit of background on my concerns about technology as being practiced at universities, especially journalism schools, which have invested heavily in convergence. My concerns about technology are not Luddite-based; they are there because of my work experience, which mandated intimate knowledge of technology, from those 25-pound "Gemini" portable computers in the 1970s to my feather-weight Apple laptop. I have dealt with technology budgets and vendors in one way or another for almost 30 years.
>
> A bit of background might help you understand that my intent is to safeguard the investment in technology rather than use it unthinkingly through the frame of mega-conglomerates rather than pedagogy. We need to be concerned. Never before in our history has technology been as powerful, global and mobile. Never before has our economy rested substantially on commercialization of technology. These devices represent a power that students have not earned, particularly in journalism schools, where we have spent too much time focusing on presentation and too little on fact-gathering. The blogoshpere has always assumed that there would be a record of fact (or the absence thereof) by which to hold media accountable. When media fail to provide fact, opinion prevails, and it is cheaper in corporate journalism to disseminate opinion rather than gather fact. Moreover, a news company can earn more revenue by targeting opinion to clusters of audience. As such, people hear only what they want to hear; they are affirmed rather than challenged or informed. Your essay above does both. I respect it; but I do not entirely agree with it. That is why it has sparked a research-based dialogue.
>
> My own research is based on three types of experience: my career as a journalist for United Press International, my work in the President's Office at Ohio University, and my Ph.D. in English.

Without justifying my work, which is fact-based (even if those facts get trimmed unmercifully in print media so that copy can fit in space), let me briefly state that I saw a major wire service die because of investment in technology at the expense of reporters. Now we have AP and no competition (perhaps a bit from Reuters and Bloomberg). Now corporate journalism is investing in technology at the expense of reporters, just as UPI did. And now higher education is doing the same thing at the expense of teachers. The point is, my calling attention to this is not technostalgia; it is a wake-up call that revenue drives corporate America, especially with respect to technology. I would prefer that we use technology wisely, and that is the thrust of my work. Otherwise we are apt to see standards drop, politicized though they be, and legislators hold educators accountable, even as they cut budgets and even as fewer teachers work not only in physical space but in cyberspace at all hours from myriad locations.

This trend has been long in coming. I worked at Ohio University during the administration of Robert Glidden, one of the first university presidents to install computers in residence halls in the 1990s. We knew that those computers would result in more gaming and other uses apart from research. So we instituted a series of workshops and ethics presentations to help students balance their time in real and virtual habitats. That was a good approach. But education budgets were healthier in the 1990s. Now we simply install technology and hope for the best. That is in part why I am taking a risk in voicing my concerns in the popular print press.

Speaking of print, I have a Ph.D. in English. My major was associated with writing, but my literature specialties were in medieval through Restoration drama. The Enlightenment is responsible for this very blog because print allowed professors like Martin Luther to assert that truth is greater than authority 218 years before we came to that conclusion in Colonial America in the John Peter Zenger case. In sum, my English doctorate taught me the value of the printing press in ensuring the scientific method, especially with respect to footnotes. My research partners and I are working overtime to stabilize the Internet so that digital citations do not lapse. We have submitted National Science Foundation grant applications and have published in a variety of peer-reviewed journals. That is my biggest concern about Internet, a dynamic but unstable medium. Unfortunately, our research methods assume stability. It is a crime, literally, to manipulate books and journals in a library—to cut, mark up and paste. This is what the computer does best. Unless we stabilize the Internet, it cannot reach its full research and educational potential.

Finally, I'll end with an anecdote associated with "technostalgia." It was cut from my recent piece during editing at the *Chronicle*. One of my journalism sources used the word "nostalgia" in a review session for an exam. Immediately his teaching assistant received e-mails asking what the term meant. "Students didn't even think to look it up," he said. "I was tempted to reply, 'Nostalgia' is yearning for a time when students at a major university would not have to ask that question."

The health of the blogosphere may or may not be in your hands. But you can help ensure more respect with the kind of writing and analysis that I see in your post on "technostalgia."

His reply was generous and civil, and we shared a philosophical discussion where both viewpoints could be explored substantively rather than personally. His reply began in the typical way that you would hope would set standards between two communicators who might meet at an academic convention or professional forum: "Michael, thank you for your comment, one both generous and interesting. I would be very interested in reading some of your stabilization pieces, and if you would be so kind as to e-mail either cites or articles to me, I would be in your debt. Indeed, I'd love to even have some of them online for the purposes of discussion, if you're interested or could point me in the right direction."

As our exchange indicates, the Internet can better fulfill its promise of being a medium of information rather than of distraction when basic ethics are followed. In a word, media practitioners, in particular, must foresee the possible consequences of an online response defending their word by:

- *Determining whether your post will undermine your credibility.* It is better to stand by your facts and let them speak for you because they will do a better job.
- *Present a conflict of interest (especially with your editor).* It is better to let the audience have the last word rather than your editor on future assignments.
- *Lapse into unfairness through personal rather than professional rejoinders.* It is better to maintain your cool and credibility rather than lose them online.

Conversely, determine beforehand what your standards are when posting a response. When should you do so, why should you correct the record, to whom should you respond, and how might you elevate discussion? Contemplating these guidelines, you may invite an enlightened online exchange that triggers critical rather than lazy thinking, setting standards in cyberspace.

Editors Note: Michael Bugeja is the author of *Interpersonal Divide: The Search for Community in a Technological Age* (Oxford University Press).

CHAPTER 10 CASES

CASES 10-A

Ethics on the Internet: Abiding by the Rules of the Road on the Information Superhighway

BRUCE LEWENSTEIN
Cornell University

ComNet is a commercial online service with a wide range of options available to its subscribers. These include databases, e-mail capabilities and forums for discussion of many topics. Some of these forums are available to all subscribers, while others require a separate sign-up system and are available only to registered users. In the case of JourForum, a discussion group for journalists, only working journalists may post or read messages to the group. Working journalists are defined as those employed by newspapers, magazines or other legitimate publications; those whose names appear on the masthead of a regularly published magazine; those who belong to one of several professional organizations (such as the Society of Professional Journalists [SPJ] or the American Society of Newspaper Editors); or those who prove their legitimacy by presenting clips of their published work. ComNet is available both through direct modem connection and through the World Wide Web.

Subscribers to ComNet agree to abide by the service's "Rules of Behavior," which include prohibitions against objectionable or lewd language, illegal activity and "abuse of the service." Journalists signing up for JourForum are reminded of these rules and are requested to use only their true names and to limit their discussion to issues directly related to journalism. No specific statements are made about whether JourForum (or other parts of ComNet) are on or off the record. Mark Morceau is the "moderator" of JourForum—as well as its creator—and, through contractual arrangements with ComNet, the person responsible for ensuring that uses of JourForum abide by ComNet's rules.

In a new message to the JourForum, Miriam Zablonsky identifies herself as the editor of a newsletter about "alternative" (nontraditional) medical treatments. She presents many details about a new drug treatment for AIDS, including information about the research leading to the treatment. She wonders why the media has failed to cover the story, she says.

In a response, Harry Lee, a reporter for an online magazine about medicine, suggests that the media usually cover medical stories only after they appear in medical publications such as *The New England Journal of Medicine.*

Zablonsky goes ballistic. In a long, biting, bitter message, she complains about a major medical journal that, she says, refuses to publish information about the new treatment. She calls the editor of the journal, Katherine Kelly, "a fat, sexist, lying slob." Kelly is a well-known commentator on the excesses of tabloid journalism (especially its coverage of medical topics); her columns are often accompanied by her photo, showing a slim, stylish, beautiful woman of 42.

A flood of messages appears, condemning Zablonsky's comments. To each one, Zablonsky responds with long, rambling diatribes about conspiracies of "them" (unspecified) to control the world, about the deep distrust that a journalist should have toward all major institutions, and about her own unwillingness to change or even compromise her positions, no matter what information is presented to her.

At this point (less than a day after the original message from Zablonsky), Mark Morceau posts a message reminding Zablonsky of ComNet and JourForum's rules about objectionable language and abuse of the service (including posting long messages on topics that aren't germane to journalism). In addition, he asks her to apologize to Kelly and to avoid libelous statements in the future.

Zablonsky refuses, citing (among other arguments in another long, rambling message) her rights to free speech and freedom of the press.

Morceau tells Zablonsky that JourForum is not a publication, so it is not subject to rules of free press. It is, he says, more akin to a private club, which can enforce rules on its members. He points to the requirement that contributors belong to professional journalism organizations as one of the ways that JourForum maintains its limited membership. (Zablonsky once worked for a daily paper, and she maintains her membership in SPJ.)

If JourForum is a private club, responds Zablonsky, what she said isn't libelous, because the club isn't a public place or publication. (All of these messages, as with all JourForum messages, are publicly posted so any subscriber to JourForum can view them.)

The next day, Katherine Kelly joins the online discussion. She threatens to sue Zablonsky, claiming that she has been libeled in a public forum. The international community of journalists with access to JourForum is so large that it cannot be considered a "private" club, she argues. Any one of those subscribers can read this forum, she reminds Zablonsky, making it equivalent to a trade paper or magazine. It is as public as any traditional publication, Kelly argues. Moreover, she says, in a landmark decision in June 1996, a federal appeals court described online forums as one of the most important contributions to free exchange of ideas since the development of the printing press. Clearly, Kelly says, the canons of a free press—including the responsibility of avoiding libel—apply to online forums.

Cynthia Smith has been following the online discussion. She finds the issues of potential censorship, free press and free speech fascinating. She writes an article about the fracas for her own newspaper's weekly "News from Cyberspace" page. That page appears on Thursdays in the business section of the paper; it is also available in the newspaper's online edition. In her story, Smith includes quotes from Morceau, Zablonsky, Kelly and other members of the forum; the quotes are taken not from interviews but from the messages those people had posted online.

When Smith's story appears, she is accused (in another round of postings in JourForum) of violating the expectation many journalists had that their words in the online forum were "off the record" and would not be quoted.

Micro Issues

1. Can Zablonsky be sued for libel? Should she be sued for libel?
2. Should Smith have asked for permission to quote?
3. Does Morceau have the right to control what material appears in JourForum?

Midrange Issues

1. Does it matter if Smith's article appeared only in the traditional paper format, only in an online supplement to the newspaper, or in a separate online magazine that does not have ties to a traditional-format publication?
2. Is there a moral difference between Zablonsky's potentially libelous statements and Smith's potential violation of the standards of on- and off-the-record?

Macro Issues

1. Is JourForum a public or private place? What difference would it make if any ComNet subscriber could read messages in JourForum, though only registered members could post messages there? (Compare JourForum to the floor of a convention, where members of the press are often identified with badges so that speakers know they are talking to a reporter.)
2. Under what circumstances does a reporter need to identify himself or herself? At what point do "private" conversations become open to reporting by others?
3. Are online publications subject to different rules than are traditional publications? If so, how do you distinguish between the rules that apply to publications that appear only online and those that appear in both online and offline versions? Does it matter if the online and offline versions are different or edited differently?

CASE 10-B

What Were You Linking?

PAUL VOAKES
University of Colorado

One of the oldest controversies in southern politics helped to create one of the newest controversies in media ethics.

In May 2000, the South Carolina legislature voted to remove the Confederate flag from the Capitol dome in Columbia and to have it placed behind the nearby Confederate Soldiers Monument, but the issue had far broader appeal than just to South Carolinians. Activists on both sides in Alabama, Arkansas, Florida, Georgia and Mississippi were carefully monitoring the debate, expecting it would influence debates in their states over various displays of Confederate symbols. The National Association for the Advancement of Colored People (NAACP) was organizing a national boycott of South Carolina even after the compromise that put the "Rebel" flag behind the monument. The NAACP action included boycotting the products of several manufacturers that had recently built facilities in South Carolina. The national media were paying close attention to the story.

A few months earlier, the Associated Press had begun routinely adding URLs (Uniform Resource Locators, or Internet addresses) to its stories, which would link readers to related sources of information on the World Wide Web. This practice had by now become fairly common on the Web sites of many national news organizations, but the AP's handling of its links on this particular story illustrated the ethical pitfalls that can await online journalists.

For several weeks, at the bottom of every story involving the Confederate flag controversy in South Carolina, the AP listed the Web addresses of three prominent stakeholders in the story: the NAACP, the South Carolina Heritage Coalition, and the Sons of Confederate Veterans. Surfers to the Heritage Coalition's site found the group's position on the flag issue and more: calls for "the confederate curriculum to be taught in all South Carolina public schools," for "recognition of South Carolinians as Confederate/Southern Americans for National Origin status" on government forms, for state holidays commemorating the birthdays of Confederate leaders Robert E. Lee and Jefferson Davis, and for "civil rights protection for Confederate/Southern Americans in the workplace." By providing the link to this organization, the AP had given it unprecedented access to the U.S. public.

When a news organization offers a hypertext link to another site, is it responsible in any way for the content of that site?

This wasn't the first time the question had surfaced. In 1997 the *New York Times* published a story about efforts to establish the innocence of convicted killer Charles Manson, complete with links to "Access Manson" and other sites that suggest Manson's innocence.

In the early days of online journalism—way back in the mid-1990s—few editors thought to provide links to external Web sites as part of a news or feature story. Once editors became more enchanted by the ways in which a Web site "added value" to the printed version, links became frequently embedded in stories. By the end of the decade, however, a modest backlash had occurred as editors realized that (1) readers using the links were leaving the news site and quite often not returning and (2) readers may be associating the tone and views of the linked site with the provider of the original site.

In many cases, the linked Web sites simply add more detailed information or opinions to what was presented in the original story. This is often "unmediated" material that can pass directly from a source or advocate to the reader, without passing through the filters of journalists. Many Web observers and editors celebrate this capability, especially when the link goes to a site produced by a widely known, reliable organization. "I don't see that as a danger to democracy or the public interest," Jonathan Wolman of the Associated Press told the *American Journalism Review.*

But what if the journalist links readers to sites that publish more propaganda than fact or that advocate racism, violence or pornography?

News organizations have taken different approaches to the "linking" debate. Some don't link at all, except to other pages within the same site. **CNN.com** tries to make sure its external links are balanced to represent the major positions of a controversy. The *New York Times* says it will link to no sites that "celebrate violence," present sexual content or advocate bigotry or racism.

Other online newspapers, such as the *Chicago Tribune,* warn readers generally that by clicking on the hypertext, readers will be leaving the *Tribune's* site. Other sites warn readers that not only are they leaving the site but external sites "are not endorsed" by the original site. Other sites warn readers that the information in external sites has not been checked for accuracy by the staff of the original site. Still others offer more specific warnings, such as the *Los Angeles Times'* warning to readers that if they linked to the site of the rock band Rage Against the Machine, they would encounter "adult language."

The AP has instructed its editors to use their "best news judgment" to determine which external sites to include.

As with most ethical controversies raised by fast-changing online technologies, there is no consensus at this time. Most online news providers do agree, however, on this much: linked sites do reflect, at least to some extent, on the journalistic decisions being made by the link provider.

Micro Issues

1. Does each reporter have a responsibility at least to "check out" every Web site his or her story links to, if only to make sure the linked site still exists?
2. Should each reporter be able to vouch for the accuracy and reliability of each linked site?
3. A significant percentage of readers who follow a link will not make it back to the newspaper's site. Is this reality a relevant factor in deciding how often to link or to whom you should link?

Midrange Issues

1. Should news organizations provide any disclaimers about links before taking readers to the linked sites? If yes, what should those disclaimers say?

2. Should mainstream news organizations link only to Web sites of established, "respectable" organizations, in order not to be associated with fringe or extremist positions? Does linking imply endorsement?
3. Who makes the call on what is respectable? Is this decision-making process a form of censorship or is it gatekeeping, or something else entirely?
4. In what way, if any, does checking the accuracy of a cited Web resource differ from checking out the veracity of an individual quoted in the story. Should the same rules apply?

Macro Issues

1. What is the media's responsibility to society in terms of expanding the "marketplace of ideas" via the Web?
2. Will the free exchange of ideas and democratic debate be enhanced, or is widespread, unchecked linking more likely to distort and discourage honest debate?

CASE 10-C

ELLEgirlBuddy: Girl Meets Bot

MARIA CARTER
KCUR Public Radio, Kansas City, Missouri

Author's Note: *The magazine,* ELLEgirl, *is now available only online. The management felt their young female readers could better be reached there. The move also worked synergistically with the very active message board culture that had grown up around the site, so the following case still works well today.*

At the beginning of 2002, teen fashion magazine *ELLEgirl* was looking for a way to increase its readership. The magazine is targeted at teenage girls interested in fashion and beauty. Seeking to establish a larger readership and differentiate itself from other teen magazines, *ELLEgirl* decided to use instant messaging, one of the most popular methods of communication among teenagers, to interest girls in subscribing. *ELLEgirl* teamed up with software developer ActiveBuddy to create an instant message bot to chat with potential *ELLEgirl* readers. The ELLEgirlBuddy chat bot is a software program that works with AOL Instant Messenger and Microsoft Messenger to provide information from *ELLEgirl* magazine while realistically chatting like a teen.

To engage potential subscribers, ELLEgirlBuddy not only uses teenage lingo and chat acronyms but also is given a history and personality. According to an article in the *Los Angeles Times* (Frey 2000), ELLEgirlBuddy represents herself as not just a bot but an actual person. She describes herself as a 16-year-old girl, who is 5'6" tall with straight red hair, green eyes and freckles. She lives in San Francisco with her parents and older brother. Her interests include listening to music, chatting online with friends and polishing her nails. Her favorite band is No Doubt. Her favorite book is *Catcher in the Rye,* and her favorite television show is "Buffy the Vampire Slayer." When she grows up, she would like to own a bookstore café, design handbags or work as a foreign correspondent. These and many other details give ELLEgirlBuddy a personality that appeals to teenage girls.

One month after the launch of ELLEgirlBuddy, traffic at **ELLEgirl.com** increased 83 percent, and *ELLEgirl* magazine subscriptions rose 50 percent. One in 10 people who saw an advertisement on ELLEgirlBuddy visited the advertiser's Web site (ActiveBuddy 2002).

While subscription rates and Web site usage certainly indicate the effectiveness of ELLEgirlBuddy as an advertising tool, the bot does seem to be connecting to its target audience on a personal level. In an e-mail to ActiveBuddy (2002), one ELLEgirlBuddy wrote about the company's various bots: "My favorite so far is ELLEgirlBuddy she is so cool and gives really great tips and quizzes about fashion." Another user wrote, "ELLEgirlBuddy is awesome as well! I love her beauty and fashion tips!"

Anecdotal evidence also suggests that some people use ELLEgirlBuddy and other bots as confidants. They provide the bots with information about their feelings and events in their lives, and in some instances they develop feelings toward the bot. SmarterChild, ActiveBuddy's prototype bot, readily acknowledged that it was not human, although it was also programmed to respond "I love you too!"

ELLEgirlBuddy also collects information provided by the user for future use. For example, if the user says she is looking forward to seeing the next Harry Potter movie, the bot may begin its next conversation with the user by referring her to an article about the film in *ELLEgirl.*

Micro Issues

1. Does creating bots constitute some form of deception?
2. While most teens "catch on" to the fact that the bot is a computer program, should the bots' creators consider the fact that more naive users may not be as quick to catch on?
3. Does the fact that ELLEgirlBuddy was created as an entertaining and informative advertisement pass the TARES test outlined in the advertising chapter?
4. Does collecting information from users raise some privacy questions?

Midrange Issues

1. Anecdotal evidence suggests that users tell ELLEgirlBuddy about breakups with boyfriends, family problems and the rigors of school. Since ELLEgirlBuddy can't gossip and is programmed not to be judgmental, might this be a positive use of the Internet?
2. Would if be appropriate to have ELLEgirlBuddy make its advertising function more prominent? How might that be accomplished?
3. How might the creators of ELLEgirlBuddy respond to questions of authenticity that are raised in discussions of persuasion ethics?

Macro Issues

1. In the late 1930s after the "War of the Worlds" radio program resulted in a national furor, the Federal Communications commission required that broadcast stations regularly identify themselves so audiences would have external cues to help them distinguish entertainment from news. Would it be appropriate for the Federal Trade Commission to adopt a similar policy regarding bots? In what ways are the two different, if at all?
2. At what point should those who provide media content, regardless of the form of transmission, have to consider the impact of that content on naive or psychologically at-risk users as opposed to the much larger, general audience? Are these standards the same for information and entertainment?

CASE 10-D

The Information Sleazeway: Robust Comment Meets the Data Robots

FRED VULTEE
Wayne State University

In detailing the *Washington Post*'s reporting of a congressional lobbying scandal that exploded at the outset of 2006, the paper's ombudsman, Deborah Howell, accidentally touched off a cyber-firestorm. Writing in her weekly column on Jan. 15, Howell noted that Republicans contended that "the *Post* purposely hasn't nailed any Democrats." On the contrary, she wrote, several stories "have mentioned that a number of Democrats . . . have gotten Abramoff campaign money." The *Post* hadn't found any Democrats in the "first tier of people being investigated," she added. "But stay tuned. This story is nowhere near over."

Her assertion was wrong. No Democrats had gotten campaign money from Jack Abramoff, the lobbyist at the center of the scandal, though he had told some of his clients to aim contributions to Democrats as well as Republicans. It was not until a week after her original column that Howell acknowledged her error and stated that the Abramoff matter, far from being bipartisan, was "a Republican scandal."

Having taken a number of bold steps into the information age, the *Washington Post* was caught flat-footed by a barrage of postings, charitably described as obscene, that overwhelmed one of the Web logs it had set up to foster public comment. In navigating the familiar journalistic terrain of correcting an error, the *Post* found itself in a new situation in which any move it made threatened the interests of its own staff, those involved in the issue it was trying to cover or those readers actually trying to get a relevant word in edgewise amid the torrent of personal attacks on the journalist who made the error.

As critics on public discussion boards at **washingtonpost.com** took Howell to task for the error, she wrote a comment for the Web site that satisfied few and angered many with its wording: "I've heard from lots of angry readers about the remark . . . that lobbyist Jack Abramoff gave money to both parties. A better way to have said it would be that Abramoff 'directed' contributions to both parties."

Those who thought the matter was worth a more forthright admission of error were not satisfied. A torrent of comments poured in—enough of them obscenely and viciously personal that the *Post* closed that site to public comment on Thursday of that week. When it reopened, with a much larger investment of staff time, public comments were much more carefully monitored.

The economic and social pressures on the *Post* are hardly unique. Like most metropolitan newspapers, it is losing circulation—down 2.9 percent against the previous year for the six-month period ending Sept. 30, 2004, or more than three times the industry average for that period (Smolkin 2005). Younger readers know its reputation but are intimidated by its bulk and are already quite at ease with finding information they want and need elsewhere.

Like many other papers, the *Post* is aggressively exploring ways to put its journalistic expertise—whether in sports, business, government or international coverage—into play in interactive ways. According to the paper's online editor, that effort includes several dozen staff-run Web logs and 80 to 90 hours of live online discussion a week, almost half involving *Post* staffers.

Mass complaints about media decisions are nothing new, but the e-mail age has given such campaigns a new level of impact. The ethical issue for the *Post,* then, is complicated. Part of a newspaper's job is fostering public debate. Knowing that the practice of journalism is shielded by legal decisions that support the importance of uninhibited debate, how does it act as a forum for debate without exposing its own to scurrilous attacks? What are the standards for debate in an online forum?

The print and online functions are formally separate at the *Post,* but as the executive editor has said, "If it's not something we'd tolerate in the newspaper, it's not something we'll tolerate on the Web site." How does any paper provide a functioning forum for any level of debate when cyber-brownshirts are ready to storm in at any meeting and kick over the tables?

The *Post*'s answer to the dilemma angered a number of vocal critics. It is impossible to know, of course, how many silently approved of the action, but the *Post*'s online editor, Jim Brady, summed up the critical response in a Feb. 12 article: "My career as a nitwitted, emasculated fascist began the afternoon of Jan. 19 when, as executive editor of the *Post*'s Web site, **washingtonpost.com,** I closed down the comments area of one of our many blogs" (Brady, 2006). After Howell's first column, editors had removed about a hundred postings that violated the ban on profanity and personal attacks. Howell's midweek clarification only triggered a larger torrent, leading to Brady's decision to close the blog to comments—and to yet another flood of comments, this time directed at Brady.

Howell told a *Post* reporter that she had not asked for the site to be closed to commenting saying, "I'm a First Amendment freak" (Farhi 2006). And Brady pointed to some irony in the conflict: "It was largely the reporting of the *Washington Post* that brought the Abramoff scandal to light in the first place—an inconvenient fact if one is attempting to assert that the *Post* takes its orders from the Republican White House."

Still, the string of comments on Howell's columns was closed. When comments on Post.blog resumed in February, it was with "minimal but firm rules." These rules included no personal attacks, no profanity and no posing as another writer. A profanity filter was installed, and staffers were assigned to read incoming messages, with the idea that "offensive or inappropriate" ones would be removed at once (Chandrasekaran 2006).

Micro Issues

1. Did the *Post* err in allowing readers to post uncensored messages prior to this problem?
2. Did the *Post* err in instituting profanity filters and staffers to read incoming messages after the problem?
3. How would you have handled the *Post*'s problem?

Midrange Issues

1. Should the original story of the ombudsman have been fact-checked to prevent the mistaken wording or is the copy of an ombudsman "out of bounds" for editorial control?
2. After the error was discovered and the deluge of messages began, was this a news story the *Post* should have covered?

Macro Issues

1. Is the Web site of a newspaper a forum that should be open to everyone without fear of censorship?
2. In the "marketplace of ideas" that is the modern Web log, do the normal rules of libel apply? Is a newspaper more culpable or less culpable for the content of its Web log if it fails to censor the posts?

CASE 10-E

Death Underneath the Media Radar:
The Anuak Genocide in Ethiopia

DOUG MCGILL, EDITOR
The McGill Report

I first learned about the Anuak people while working as a volunteer teacher of English as a Second Language at a school in Rochester, Minn. I had a half dozen Sudanese immigrants in my ESL class, all of them refugees of the Sudan civil war and several of them "lost boys," young men separated from their families who had made their way to safe havens in the Midwest.

One of my students, a man in his late 20s named Obang Cham, was originally identified to me by the ESL school as a Sudanese refugee. But when Obang's English began to improve, and we chatted over coffee, he told me a different story. He was a member of a small tribe called the Anuak who lived primarily in remote western Ethiopia. He said that more than 1,000 Anuak lived in Minnesota, and when I asked him why they had moved here, he gave me an answer I spent another nine months working to verify before committing it to print: "The Ethiopian government is trying to kill my people."

The first thing that I discovered was the Anuak were an invisible people not only in Minnesota but in the world. Although Anuak had been immigrating to Minnesota from the early 1990s, not a single major metropolitan or local paper in the United States had written anything about them. Was it possible that not a single reporter had ever met and chatted with an Anuak before? And if they had done so, and learned the story—of an unreported African genocide no less—why had they not published anything?

According to Obang, he had fled his Ethiopian village of Dimma on foot in 1992 after Ethiopian soldiers surrounded the village and began shooting Anuak. Two dozen died in that attack, he said. Many similar attacks during the early and middle 1990s are why so many Anuak now live in Minnesota. Yet the state had absorbed the cream of the crop of the young, strong male leadership of an entire Ethiopian tribe, and their wives, without notice or knowing. The Anuak were invisible in Minnesota and the world.

On December 13, 2003, my telephone started ringing in the afternoon. One after another, Anuak men whom I'd met in the previous months told me a chilling story—that one of the periodic massacres of Anuak men, women and children was underway at that very moment.

They were having cellular telephone conversations with friends and family in their home villages and were hearing, through their cell phone connections, the sounds of the massacre—shouting and screaming, gunshots, soldiers yelling and people sobbing and crying. Some of my sources described hearing soldiers bashing down doors, yelling "Put down that phone!" followed by gunshots and then silence. I spent hours on the phone that day, gathering every detail I could. Through the cell phone connections, dozens of Anuak had heard essentially the same story over and over—that two troop trucks containing uniformed Ethiopian soldiers had arrived in town and disgorged soldiers who went from hut to hut and home to home in the village, calling out the Anuak men and boys and shooting them dead in the street. Occasionally, the soldiers were joined by non-Anuak citizens, or lighter-skinned Ethiopian "highlanders," who shouted "Today is the day of killing Anuak!" and killed their victims usually with long spears, knives or machetes.

That evening and for several days following, I checked the wire services and the Web sites of the major daily newspapers in the United States, Europe and Africa. Not a word on the alleged massacre was published. On the Web sites of the Ethiopian embassy, the major Ethiopian newspapers and the U.S. Embassy in Addis Ababa: nothing. Finally, around Dec. 17, a small press release from the Ethiopian government came out reporting that "tribal violence" in western Ethiopia had caused up to a dozen deaths. This was nowhere near what the Anuak in Minnesota were claiming based on their knowledge from hundreds of eyewitness accounts, and the Ethiopian government was placing blame in its press releases not on the Ethiopian Army but on tribes fighting each other. I placed a call to the press spokesman at the Ethiopian embassy in Washington, Mesfin Andreas. "The deaths occurred as troops tried to stop people from killing each other," Andreas said.

On the weekend after the first phone calls came in, Anuak refugees from all over the Midwest gathered at a church in St. Paul, Minn. to discuss the crisis. I attended the meeting where I met several hundred Anuak, and interviewed maybe three dozen, only talking to people who said they had spoken directly to people on cell phones who were eyewitnesses as the massacre was happening. The stories that I heard that day were identical to the ones that I'd gotten over the telephone a week earlier. Uniformed Ethiopian soldiers had done the killing with automatic rifles, targeting Anuak men and boys for killing and Anuak women for raping, and they'd gone house to house, sometimes with a list of names in their hands, calling out specific Anuak men by name. Not dozens but hundreds had died.

Back at home, I called an Anuak survivor in Ethiopia on the telephone. He lived in Gambella, the town where the massacre occurred. He told of seeing uniformed Ethiopian soldiers killing Anuak men on the street from the window of his home. He'd hidden under his bed as soldiers marched by his home. His own son had died in the attack. While speaking to me, he said he could still see some bodies in the streets of Gambella, and that at a mass grave on one side of the town, several hundred corpses were strewn in piles. He and other Anuak survivors had counted the corpses and noted how they had died, he said. The total was some 425 killed either by gunshots to the head or back, or by spear thrusts and machete blows.

As a former reporter for the *New York Times* for a decade, I knew I would probably have been unable to publish the story in the *Times* even with all the material I'd gathered. The main problem was, I had not actually been in Ethiopia, nor talked face-to-face with any actual eyewitnesses to the killing. Instead, my sources were a strange new breed of witness—"earwitnesses" to the sounds of a massacre and to direct eyewitness accounts of the massacre, listened to over cell phones. I was not then aware, nor am I aware today, of any report of a massacre or other crime in the media based on witness accounts of this nature. They are the creation of our present strange new world of hypercommunication.

In the end, my decision finally to publish what I'd heard, pointing a finger directly at the Ethiopian army, boiled down to my gut feelings as a journalist and my conscience as a citizen. After a week of solid reporting, interviewing dozens of Anuak in Minnesota, as well as one eyewitness in Ethiopia and the Ethiopian embassy spokesman, I felt that I knew something close enough to the truth to publish. And my conscience told me it was my duty to publish, because even up to Dec. 22, the day I finally did publish an account of the massacre, not a single news publication had done so—anywhere in the world. If I didn't publish, who would?

Within days of my story appearing on the Internet, the leaders of Genocide Watch, a nongovernmental watchdog who investigate new cases of genocide wherever they happen in the world had made enough phone calls to justify hiring an investigator and sending him to Ethiopia to check out the claims made in my article. On Feb. 25, 2004, Genocide Watch published the investigator's report, "Today is the Day of Killing Anuak," based on interviews with dozens of eyewitnesses to the massacre in Gambella (Genocide Watch 2004). The report verified all of the key claims of *The McGill Report* article, including the number of Anuak killed and the fact that uniformed Ethiopian soldiers had carried out most of the killings.

Micro Issues

1. Using a search engine, how much can you find about the genocide of the Anuak that has appeared since McGill's Web site first published the story?
2. Is it fair to say that the international attention being given to the genocide in Darfur distracted the media and the relief organizations from the situation in Ethiopia?

Midrange Issues

1. Following a trip to Ethiopia, McGill still had problems getting the mainstream media to accept the story. What does that say about how mainstream news organizations operate?
2. Is acceptance of this story by a mainstream media outlet such as the Associated Press needed to somehow "validate" the reporting done by McGill?
3. McGill has had a long career in journalism including the *New York Times* and *Bloomberg News,* however, many "bloggers" have not had any journalism experience or training at all. Are traditional media rightfully skeptical about stories that originate in blogs? Should citizens be skeptical?

Macro Issues

1. What does this case tell you about who is a journalist in the Internet era?
2. Why do you think that a massacre of 425 people in Ethiopia wasn't reported in the mainstream media for several months after it happened? Why was it a blogger in southern Minnesota who broke the story?
3. Members of the dispersed tribal communities of Anuak e-mailed the story by McGill all over the world within days of its publication. Is the Internet a more efficient outlet for international stories such as this one?

11

The Ethical Dimensions of Art and Entertainment

By the end of this chapter you should be able to:

- **understand the link between aesthetics and excellent professional performance.**
- **explain Tolstoy's rationale for art and apply it to issues such as stereotyping.**
- **understand the debate over the role of truth in popular art.**

During the 20th century, the predominant use of the media shifted from the distribution of information to entertainment and the popularization of culture. In this chapter we will examine the ethical issues that arise from the field of aesthetics. We will apply these principles, plus some findings from social science, to the art and entertainment components of media industries, focusing on the responsibilities of the public as well as the creators of mediated messages.

AN ANCIENT MISUNDERSTANDING

Plato did not like poets. The ancient Greek's reasoning was straightforward. Poets, the people who dream, were the potential undoing of the philosopher king. They were rebels of the first order, insurrectionists on the hoof. He banned them from the Republic.

But Plato's skepticism about the role of art is alive in contemporary culture. Few weeks elapse without a news story about an artist or entertainment program that has offended. You are probably familiar with at least some of the following:

- Attempts to ban books such as "Catcher in the Rye" or "Lady Chatterley's Lover" from public and/or school libraries for being too sexually explicit. In 2005, Harry Potter was the most banned book, and the book was the focus of unsuccessful attempts to ban it as well.

- The controversy over government funding of art that some claim is obscene.
- Calls by conservatives and liberals to boycott television networks and their advertisers over allegedly objectionable content.
- The furor over rappers, television producers and filmmakers whose homophobic, misogynistic and sometimes clever content offend many while earning nominations for the industry's top awards.
- The public outcry and political posturing that followed Janet Jackson's breast-baring episode at the Super Bowl in January 2004 and Don Imus' statements about the Rutgers' womens basketball team in 2007.

Such a response to works of art and entertainment, whether it is by public officials or individuals, is essentially Platonic. Like Plato, those who would restrict the arts do so because they mistrust the power of the artist to link emotion and logic in a way that stimulates a new vision of society, culture or individuals.

OF TOLSTOY AND TELEVISION

Tolstoy was the sort of artist Plato would have feared. In his famous essay, "What Is Art?" Tolstoy argued that good art had one dominant characteristic: it communicated the feelings of the artist to the masses in the way in which the artist intended.

> To evoke in oneself a feeling one has once experienced and having evoked it in oneself then by means of movements, lines, colors, sounds or forms expressed in words, so to transmit that feeling that others experience the same feeling— that is the activity of art. . . . Art is a human activity consisting in this, that one may consciously by means of certain external signs, hand on to others feelings he has lived through, and that others are infected by these feelings and also experience them.

Tolstoy's application of his own standard—one that sounds remarkably like artistic social responsibility—was so demanding that he rejected the works of both Shakespeare and Beethoven as being incapable of being understood by the masses. While you may not agree with all of Tolstoy's specific applications, we believe his philosophical rationale has much to recommend it.

Tolstoy's rationale is particularly pertinent to photographers and videographers who, through their visual images, seek to arouse emotion as well as inform. Haunting pictures of starvation from Bosnia and Ethiopia have provided a spur for international concerns. Closer to home, televised images of Katrina's victims spurred some political change—the resignation of some of FEMA's top officials—and much political unrest that worked its way to the polls in the 2006 election. Award-winning dramas such as "Angels in America," the AIDS quilt, movies such as "Philadelphia" in which Tom Hanks won an Academy Award for his portrayal of an AIDS victim and obituaries of famous artists who have succumbed to the disease have all aroused both our intellects and our emotions regarding AIDS. They invite action. Television and film documentaries have made viewers more aware of the plight of the mentally ill and homeless, raised important public policy questions and occasionally made us laugh, through a unity of purpose and craft.

Calvin and Hobbes

by Bill Watterson

CALVIN AND HOBBES copyright © Watterson. Reprinted with permission of Universal Press Syndicate. All rights reserved.

Such work reminds readers and viewers of the moral power of art by putting us in touch with characters and situations more complex than our own lives. By thinking about these fictional characters, we enlarge our moral imaginations. Both artists and journalists can provide such a stimulus, although it will not be reflected in every song, story or film.

Unfortunately, Tolstoy's assertion that great art is defined by how it is understood by an audience also includes a genuine dilemma. There are those who, given even Tolstoy's life experiences, could not articulate the deep truths about human nature Tolstoy wrote about in "War and Peace." Worse yet, we might not be able to sell those insights to a sometimes lukewarm public, or to produce them on demand for an hour a week, 36 weeks a year. The result might be popular art that loses its critical edge and takes shortcuts to commonplace insight. In fact, some mass communication scholars have argued that the unstated goal of popular art is to reinforce the status quo; popular culture, they say, blunts the individual's critical-thinking abilities.

Storytellers have a history as popular artists, and the mass media have become the primary cultural storytellers of the era. In "Propaganda," Jacques Ellul (1965) argues that in a modern society storytelling is an inevitable and even desirable tool to stabilize the culture. To Ellul, this "propaganda of integration" is not the deliberate lie commonly associated with propaganda but the dissemination of widely held mores to the culture at large. This is precisely where the entertainment media get their power—not in the overt programming messages but in the underlying assumptions that (if unchallenged) will become widely held societal values. Many observers complain that the media reinforce the status quo by constantly depicting certain social groups in an unflattering and unrepresentative way, presenting a distorted picture of reality to the reader or viewer. For example, when was the last time you saw a person of Muslim heritage on television as anything other than a terrorist or religious fanatic? Or a beautiful blonde woman who also happened to be an engineer? Depictions and omissions such as the ones above reinforce cultural stereotypes and offend the groups involved. They also leave the media in the position of constantly having to explain why the media world is so different from the real world.

At least some such distortion is the natural outcome of compression. Just as substances such as rubber change form when compressed, so do media messages. Given only 15 seconds to register a message in a commercial, an advertising copywriter will resort to showing us the presumed stereotype of a librarian, a mechanic or a pharmacist. Using stereotypes as a form of mental shorthand is a natural way media work and was noted as early as 1922 by Walter Lippmann in his classic work "Public Opinion." Lippmann said that for economy of time and maintenance of the status quo, we hold to stereotypes by "defining first and seeing second." Soon, we expect reality to imitate art. Mass communicators know the power of stereotypes and deeply held notions and use them. According to advertising guru Tony Schwartz (1973), advertising messages are often constructed backward. The communicator actually starts with what the receiver knows—or believes he knows—and then constructs a message that fits within that reality. Schwartz calls it hitting a "responsive chord." It works the same in entertainment.

If you need a pimp to further the plot and time is tight, dress an African-American male appropriately and let the audience fill in the details. If you need a terrorist, anyone of Mid-Eastern descent will usually do. The audience gets the idea of a pimp or a terrorist, but another idea has been planted as well—the racist notion that most pimps are minorities or that all Arabs are terrorists. While these images suit the artist's purposes, they are problematic.

Some scholars have made a more universal argument. Meyrowitz (1985) argues that television has become a "secret-revelation machine," bringing behaviors once confined to the "backstage" to the screen. The result is a loss of faith in institutions such as government, religion and parenthood, with a resulting loss of stability. This loss of stability, Postman (1986) claims, can happen in one of two ways. In the Orwellian concept (found in "1984"), culture becomes a prison; in the Huxleyan concept (found in "Brave New World"), culture becomes a burlesque. Postman believes we are

What Is Art?

Philosophers, sociologists and artists have debated the meaning of art for the past 150 years. Prior to the Industrial Revolution, art was something only the well educated paid for, produced and understood. Mozart had to capture the ear of the Emperor of Austria to get a subsidy to write opera. Such "high" or "elite art" provided society with a new way to look at itself. Picasso's drawings of people with three eyes or rearranged body parts literally provided Western culture with a new way of seeing. Michelangelo's paintings and sculpture did the same thing in the Renaissance.

But patronage had disadvantages. The patron could restrict both subject matter and form, a reality depicted in the film "Amadeus" where the Emperor informed Mozart that his work, "The Marriage of Figaro" had "too many notes." Gradually artists discovered that if they could find a way to get more than one person to "pay" for the creation of art, artistic control returned to the artist. The concept of "popular art" was born.

Scholars disagree about many of the qualities of elite and popular art; some even assert that popular art cannot truly be considered art. While both kinds of art are difficult to define, the following list outlines the major differences between popular and elite art and culture:

1. Popular art is consciously adjusted to the median taste by the artist; elite art reflects the individual artist's vision.
2. Popular art is neither abstruse, complicated nor profound; elite art has these characteristics.
3. Popular art conforms to majority experience; elite art explores the new.
4. Popular art conforms to less clearly defined standards of excellence, and its standards are linked to commercial success; elite art is much less commercially oriented, and its standards of excellence are consistent and integrated.
5. Popular artists know that the audience expects entertainment and instruction; elite artists seek an aesthetic experience.
6. The popular artist cannot afford to offend a significant part of the public; the elite artist functions as a critic of society, and his or her work challenges and sometimes offends the status quo.
7. Popular art often arises from folk art; elite art more often emerges from a culture's dominant intellectual tradition.

in more danger of the latter. Television is a threat to society precisely because most of its messages are so common yet people take them so seriously. Fore (1987) argues that every culture reveals itself through its underlying assumptions—the decisions it makes about what to value, how to solve problems, who is powerful and what is taboo. In earlier cultures, these values were transmitted around the campfire; in our society, they are transmitted via television to a viewer who is separate from feedback and outside points of reference. These conditions, Fore argues, make the viewer subject to "a tunnel vision that encourages unquestioning acceptance of the world view he or she sees on the screen" (Fore 1987, 4).

The unquestioning acceptance of an unchanging reality is the antithesis of the effect Tolstoy intended art to produce. In Tolstoy's vision, art introduces the reader or viewer to the novel with such power and depth that what is novel can become known and what is known can become understood.

TRUTH IN ART AND ENTERTAINMENT

No question in the field of aesthetics is more thoroughly debated with less resolution than the role of truth in art. Most philosophers seem to agree that artists are not restricted to telling the literal truth. Often artistic vision can reveal a previously hidden or veiled truth, a new way of looking at the world or understanding human nature that rings deeply true.

But just how much truth should the audience expect from entertainment? And how entertaining should the audience expect truth to be? There are several opinions. At one point on the continuum is the argument that there is no truth requirement at all in art. At another point on the continuum is the belief that one person's truth should be established as the accepted truth for all. This imposition of a specific moral, as opposed to ethical, "truth" is common to all cultures and political systems. In *The Republic* Plato had Socrates argue against allowing children to hear "casual tales . . . devised by casual persons." Its result, when applied to the mass media, is usually some form of licensing or censorship. In U.S. society, that battle historically has raged over library books. Classics such as "Huckleberry Finn," "Of Mice and Men," "The Grapes of Wrath" and "The Merchant of Venice" are but some of the long-revered and award-winning works that now face censorship by various school systems. The American Library Association reports that incidents of book banning rise each year and now reach more than 1,000 instances annually, with little or no impedance from the courts.

In 1982, the U.S. Supreme Court allowed a lower court ruling to stand that forced the Island Trees, New York, school district to reexamine a list of books considered objectionable (most of them by minority writers or about minority experiences) and to justify the censor's motives, but since that time the high court has not heard another book-banning case. While books are important because they form the most permanent part of our cultural and intellectual web, television has been the medium that has been the most frequent contemporary target of censorship and protest. The protests began early in the medium's history. The 1951 airing of the show "Amos 'n' Andy" was condemned by the National Association for the Advancement of Colored People for depicting "Negroes in a stereotyped and derogatory manner." In the 1960s the United Church of Christ set a legal precedent when it successfully challenged the license renewal of WLBT in Jackson, Mississippi, on the grounds that the owners had blatantly discriminated against African-Americans.

In the latter half of the 20th century, a variety of special-interest groups used more subtle methods to influence entertainment programming. Some, such as the Hispanic advocacy group Nosotros, worked closely with network bureaucracies, previewing potentially problematic episodes of entertainment programs, often altering program content before it reached the airwaves. Other advocacy groups employed strategic campaigns with advertisers and affiliates to influence the airing of certain episodes of popular shows or to make certain that some characters certain segments of society might find objectionable remained scripted in prime time.

The networks opted for a policy of balance, believing that co-option was superior to confrontation and that muting criticism in advance would have a positive impact on the networks' image and the bottom line. Yet, *New York Times* television critic Jack Gould framed the problem of artistic accountability in the early days of the ascendancy of advocacy groups: Such agreements hold "latent dangers for the well-being of television as a whole. An outside group not professionally engaged in theatre production has succeeded in imposing its will with respect to naming of fictional characters, altering the importance of a leading characterization and in other particulars changing the story line" (Montgomery 1989, 21). For the artist, network attempts to "balance" competing advocacy-group interests had come close to recreating the patronage system, albeit a far more sophisticated one.

The struggle over censorship, which some label as disagreement over taste, becomes even more acute when governmental sponsorship is at stake. Some argue that because tax dollars are extracted from all, the programs they fund should be acceptable to all. Federal support for programs such as the National Endowment for the Arts (NEA) has been repeatedly questioned in Congress. Conservatives objected to funding artists such as photographer Robert Mapplethorpe, whose blend of homoerotic photos and traditional Judeo-Christian symbols offended many. Eventually, the criticism was a factor in the resignation of one of the NEA's directors, John E. Frohnmayer.

The government also censors in other ways. On multiple occasions Infinity Broadcasting was fined several hundred thousand dollars for disc jockey Howard Stern's on-air profanity and offensive racial slurs. Stern protested that the FCC's action amounted to an enforcement of political correctness, and his supporters point to Stern's show being dropped by Clear Channel in the spring of 2004 as proof that he was being censored. But those who supported the FCC's action noted that Stern most often castigated disadvantaged people and groups. By 2006, Stern had left terrestrial radio and its rules for satellite radio where he found freedom but a much smaller audience.

In 2006 with the Broadcast Decency Enforcement Act Congress raised the fine for a single count of indecency from $27,500 to $325,000. Because of the potential liability for crippling fines, producers of live programming such as the Grammy awards and the Oscars were forced to put a delay on the broadcast to bleep out indecent language or nudity.

COP TV: ENTERTAINMENT, INFOTAINMENT OR NEWS?

In his ingenious and award-winning satirical film, "Network," the late writer-director Paddy Chayefsky envisioned a time when the lines would be blurred between entertainment and news, rendering them indistinguishable. By the late 1980s, television was proving him right. However, Chayefsky was wrong in one detail. News did begin to take on the look of entertainment as he predicted it would; however, he did not predict that entertainment would also begin to look increasingly like news.

Consider these television shows: "America's Most Wanted," reenactments of crimes with photos or line drawings of the suspects, in which the audience is encouraged to help by calling in tips for police; "Unsolved Mysteries," with its focus on the criminal and the paranormal; "Inside Edition," a voyeuristic look at stories dubbed "too hot to handle" for traditional network news; and others of the same breed, including "A Current Affair," "Hard Copy," "COPS," "Rescue 911" and any number of other spin-offs.

In what genre do these shows belong? When a show such as "America's Most Wanted" follows a bounty hunter on an illegal trip into Mexico to bring home a nationally known fugitive, as it did in the summer of 2003, is the resulting program news or entertainment? If it turns out that the trip to Mexico was illegal under that country's laws, was the media culpable for the act in any way? Which set of standards of truth should the producer of that show (and others like it) operate under—the artistic license of entertainment or the more rigorous truth standard of news?

Currently, dozens of such pseudo-news shows are in production simultaneously. From arrests to court trials to public confrontations, very little escapes our fascination. Dubbed "infotainment" by critics, these shows are hot with television programming executives and audiences alike. Such programming provides relief from reruns of situation comedies and the sameness of game shows and draws large ratings. When produced by syndicators, the shows are prepackaged with ads embedded in them, making them attractive to station owners.

Much attention was focused on the syndicated talk-show genre in the late 1990s when one guest on the "Jenny Jones Show" later murdered another guest when it was revealed on the air that the victim (a male) had a crush on the perpetrator (also a male). The revelation came as a total surprise to the show guest, who admitted to committing the murder. As a condition of being on the show, he had been told that he would be meeting a secret admirer, and was even told that person could be male or female, but he was unprepared for the embarrassment he allegedly felt when it turned out to be a same-sex crush. The family of the victim sued the show for its part in the murder. After a highly publicized trial, the television show won in court, but public opinion was clearly divided on the show's culpability.

CNN's Nancy Grace faced an avalanche of criticism in September 2006 when a guest on her show, Melinda Duckett, committed suicide the day after an extremely confrontational taped interview. However, CNN management allowed the interview to air anyway, with Grace taking most of the criticism from Duckett's family members as well as many in the viewing audience.

Voyeurism can take many forms. In the early days of the Internet, a teenaged girl became a national celebrity when she put her life on the Web for all to view from a camera mounted on a computer in her bedroom that she called "Jennicam." Soon after, a man in Dallas changed his legal name to "dotcomguy" and let the nation watch as he moved into a vacant house with only a computer and lived an online life for 365 days before emerging. Ironically, in his exit interviews, he refused to reveal his real name, claiming that he wanted to retain his privacy. More recently "lonelygirl15" became a celebrity on YouTube watched by more than 15 million viewers before it was revealed that she was an aspiring actress and all three of the people involved in scripting, filming and acting in the "lonelygirl15" postings were represented by a powerful

Hollywood talent agency, Creative Artists Agency. However, even after the ruse was disclosed by mainstream media such as the *Los Angeles Times* and the *New York Times,* the videos continued to be among the most popular on YouTube.

The blending of facts and entertainment is not restricted to the small screen. Films such as "Ray," "Walk the Line," "The Alamo," "Nixon," "Hoffa" and "Thirteen Days" reflect a particular artistic vision based on fact. "Hoffa" director Danny DeVito sought to make an entertaining film of the major facts of the controversial missing labor leader's life, but took symbolic liberties with many events and people. DeVito told the "Today" show audience in early 1993 that what he sought was entertainment—"not sitting down and reading a book."

Though these films and reality-based television shows differ in format and content, they are alike in invoking the license allowed entertainment programming while retaining the authority of fact—a risky combination. By blending information and entertainment into an internally coherent package, the possibility for abuse of an unsuspecting audience exists. To understand how this can happen, we must look to the mass-communication theory of "uses and gratifications." Phrased simply, the theory says audience members will use the media to gratify certain wants and needs. People bring something to the message, and what they bring affects what they take away.

For example, seeking news and information is a common use of the media, with an expected gratification of getting information necessary for citizenship. Entertainment is another common media use, with its own expected gratification. Infotainment, in keeping the look of news yet airing the content of lowbrow entertainment, may be produced to entertain but often has had the unintended "use" of informing. The problem arises when the information such entertainment programming provides about important institutions in U.S. culture, such as the court system or medical practice, or important political figures such as Malcolm X, is fundamentally flawed.

This confounding of unexpected and unintended uses and gratifications is important. *New York Times* columnist A. M. Rosenthal (1989) compared airing these tabloid television shows to buying news programming "off the shelf." The stations airing these programs should add the disclaimer, "We did not put this stuff in the bottle, whatever it is," Rosenthal added.

With a look of authority (an anchor's desk, a courtroom, a police precinct) and the hype of their importance (e.g., "200 lives saved so far!"), these cop-based reality shows appear to be useful for acquiring information, thus gratifying the human need to know. However, by invoking their license as entertainment, such shows are free to bypass accuracy, fairness, balance and other standards normally associated with news and to focus on more sensational elements to gather larger ratings.

REALITY TELEVISION: OXYMORON, PROFIT CENTER AND USING THE AUDIENCE

They eat cow's lips, let their families pick their mates and routinely lie about their financial and physical assets. It's all part of the reality television craze that made strong inroads into prime-time entertainment programming in the new millennium. Most media critics suggest the craze began with the wildly successful "Survivor" series, which ran first as a summer replacement show and garnered ratings that impressed network executives. Since television entertainment is nothing if not imitative and reactive, "Survivor" quickly spawned other reality shows, among them "Amazing Race," "Danger Island," "Wife Swap," "Road Rules" (which actually preceded "Survivor" on MTV), "The Osbornes," "The Real World," "Fear Factor" and "American Idol," again borrowed from the British "Pop Idol."

Why the rush to reality programming? Ratings and money. For three decades, traditional network television programming lost audience share to cable television and more recently the Internet. At their height, the original three American networks, ABC, CBS and NBC, could count on attracting approximately 90 percent of American homes with televisions on any given evening; the rest tuned in a few fledgling independents playing mostly reruns. Today, the audience for what is now five broadcast networks with affiliate stations has plunged to less than half of all households, with the number slipping every season. Compounding the problem, those who continued to watch the traditional networks were an older demographic not popular with advertisers.

Reality television was the first programming genre to pull viewers away from cable and computers and back to the networks. Not only did reality shows draw viewers, but the audience they drew centered on 18- to 49-year-olds, including young men. The result was a ratings bonanza in the preferred demographic, a very potent inducement to produce more reality programming.

Reality programming was not only popular with viewers, but cheap to produce. There was little need to pay writers, since scripts as such weren't generally part of the shows, and the actors who populated them worked for scale or less. Unlike shows such as "CSI," "ER" and others where the popularity of the show caused cast members' salaries to skyrocket, salaries never became an issue for producers of reality programming. Compared to most entertainment shows, including evening news magazines, reality programming costs less to produce and provided bigger, and more demographically desirable, audiences.

But there was a price to pay. The shortsighted view of using cheaply produced reality programming to garner huge ratings will have consequences for years to come. In the financial world of network television, quality shows such as "ER" and "The West Wing" are quite expensive to produce and often take time to find an audience sufficient to sustain these shows. What the producers hope for is a chance to air enough episodes—typically 60 or more—to make it to the lucrative syndication market, where they live on for years and produce a sizable return on the initial investment.

By eating up entire chunks of the network schedule, reality television pushed many quality shows into an early retirement and kept many more out of production. The result will be fewer quality programs in syndication for years to come and, worse than that, fewer producers of quality shows able to get their product an initial airing in the reality-laden schedules of the major networks. The light-viewing months of the summer were once a time when networks took some chances on genre-defining shows to see if they could find an audience. Now that season is given over to reality television that turns immediate profits with no regard for the future.

But with their great popularity, reality shows have even added to American slang. Getting "voted off the island" became a catch phrase for everyone from politicians to news journalists. "You're fired" entered the American vernacular after the popular show "The Apprentice" starring Donald Trump. However, making money is not considered morally culpable. Neither is popularity. So, if there is an ethical angle to reality shows, what might it be?

History provides a partial answer. The new century version of reality was really a second pass at the genre. The first attempt at reality television took place in the 1950s with quiz shows such as "21" and "The $64,000 Question." These shows were enormously popular and, as it turned out, could be rigged. Popular contestants were given the answers to general-knowledge questions beforehand; what the audience saw was a scripted contest with the winner predetermined. Winners came back from week to week to continue the game, and some gained a national following. Not surprisingly, the predetermined winner was the one the various shows' creators believed would sustain the ratings or increase them. The quiz show scandals, as they are referred to in media history, were followed by congressional hearings and even some legislation (for more information on this phenomenon, see the Web site for this text).

The new reality shows suffered from some of the same problems. When it was discovered that those who advanced on one or more popular reality shows had actually been determined in advance, it became national news. Soon after, audiences learned that participants in the various reality shows were not always novices to the medium but were often recruited from ranks of fledgling actors. Furthermore, the notion of spontaneity, crucial to getting the audience to believe the premise of the reality show, was false. The producers of shows such as "Survivor," "Joe Millionaire" and the like most often shot hundreds of hours of video only to edit it into a few hours, confounding the entire concept of viewers "seeing" events as they occurred.

Some reality shows were based on legally questionable premises, such as the series that proposed to capture men hiring prostitutes—the reality of "johns"—or cop shows that allowed media to capture arrests inside homes only to be successfully sued for invasion of privacy later. Others were based on ethically questionable premises, such as the lies told to the female cast of "Joe Millionaire." In the final installment, the truth was revealed and Joe Millionaire didn't get the girl, a conclusion with multiple interpretations depending on your point of view.

While some shows, such as "America's Most Wanted," claimed a purpose more noble than ratings, others seemed notable for their complete lack of a moral compass. "Temptation Island" put couples and relationships in physical and emotional jeopardy for the entertainment of the audience, who became much more like voyeurs than traditional viewers as they watched to see which relationships would end. But, still, America watched.

Reality television raises an important ethical question: what constitutes reality? As you'll remember from Chapter 1, definitions of truth and the relationship between truth and reality have changed throughout the millennia. Reality television is a lot like the computer-generated matrix in the film "The Matrix." Reality shows used participants for other purposes, and along the way, a lot of people in the matrix world of reality TV were entertained. "The Matrix" illustrates how difficult truth and authenticity are to come by. Reality isn't always what we see, and that insight is important, not only because it has philosophical roots but also because it encourages critical thinking.

The early part of this century has been a scary time, and watching Joe Millionaire bungle his relationships is lot easier than taking the chance of going out on a first date. However, that scary first date has the chance of turning into something wonderful or awful—neither outcome one that Joe Millionaire had to face. Truth in relationships matters because it's how people form connections. Reality television was people, inside a box, having a planned and edited experience. That planning wasn't about truth. It wasn't even particularly personal. Just like in the matrix world, it was a code.

The promise of television is found in the Greek roots of its name—"to see from afar." Falling short of the promise of the medium is an ethical issue, one that surfaces again and again as each entertainment craze hits the small screen.

As the reality television craze gathered momentum, a scripted program, "The West Wing," about a fictional president in a fictional White House, gained critical and popular approval while dealing with political questions closely resembling those of the real world. During this time, "The West Wing" was the only television programming (news included) to raise the issue of what constitutes a "just war" simultaneously with America's war against Iraq. "The West Wing" took on social justice, lying to Congress, racism, professional ethics and the trade-offs and the compromises that real public policy requires. Jon Stewart, in the form of comedy, did much the same. In fact, multiple polls found that young people in the 18 to 30 age bracket said they got much of their "news" content from Stewart on "The Daily Show" or Steven Colbert in "The Colbert Report." The fact that both shows feature interviews with real political figures, include "real" news footage of actual events, and have the license to be satirical rather than fair and balanced was more mind-bending yet.

In the process of entertaining us, "The West Wing," "The Daily Show" and "The Colbert Report" also help us understand ourselves. The shows let us "see from afar" some of the difficulties of governing in a democracy, and in doing so fulfilled the promise of art in general and television as an artistic medium. Philosophers would suggest that reality television at the height of its popularity threatened to drive out the opportunity for such higher quality programming. In fact, the final episode of "Joe Millionaire" trounced "The West Wing" in the ratings, even though the latter show had garnered multiple Emmy awards for its scripts and its cast.

AESTHETICS IS AN ATTITUDE

Artists see the world differently. While most people perceive only what is needful for a particular purpose, the artist works with what some philosophers call an "enriched perceptual experience." This aesthetic attitude is one that values close and complete concentration of all the senses. An aesthetic attitude is a frankly sensual one, and one that summons both emotion and logic to a particular end.

For example, the theatre audience knows that Eugene O'Neill's plays are "merely" drama. But they also provide us with an intense examination of the role of family in human society—an experience that is both real and personal to every audience member. Such intense examination is what gives the plays their power to move.

We believe that the makers of mediated messages, whether they are the executive producers of a television sitcom or the designers of a newspaper page, share this aesthetic impetus. These mass communicators are much like architects. An architect can design a perfectly serviceable building, one that withstands the elements and may be used for particular purposes. But great buildings—St. Paul's Cathedral in London or Jefferson's home at Monticello—do more. They are tributes to the human intellect's capacity to harmoniously harness form and function.

In fact, philosophers have argued that what separates the commonplace from the excellent is the addition of an aesthetic quality to what would otherwise be a routine, serviceable work. These qualities of excellence have been described as:

- An appreciation of the function realized in the product.
- An appreciation of the resulting quality or form.
- An appreciation of the technique or skill in the performance.

These three characteristics of aesthetic excellence characterize excellence in mass communication as well.

Take the newspaper weather page. Before *USA Today* literally recalibrated the standard, weather pages were generally restricted to the upper right hand quadrant of the second page of a newspaper section. They were printed in black and white, in columns of tiny type. Newspaper editors believed that most people weren't interested in the weather—unless it was weird—and designed their pages accordingly. *USA Today* editors, on the other hand, understood that their readers agreed with the observations of the late political columnist Molly Ivans: when people aren't talking about football, they talk about the weather. The editors devoted more space to it and printed it in color. They added more information in a more legible style and form. In short, they gave newspaper weather information an aesthetic quality. While much about *USA Today* has been criticized, its excellent weather page has been copied.

Although mass-communication professionals are infrequently accused of being artists, we believe they intuitively accept an aesthetic standard as a component of professional excellence. As philosopher G. E. Moore (1903, 83) noted in "Principia Ethica":

> Let us imagine one world exceedingly beautiful. Image it as beautiful as you can; put into it whatever on this earth you most admire: mountains, rivers, the sea, suns and sunsets, stars and moon. Imagine these all combined in the most exquisite proportion so that no one thing jars against another, but each contributes to increase the beauty of the whole. And then imagine the ugliest world you can possibly conceive. Imagine it just one heap of filth, containing everything that is most disgusting to you for whatever reason, and the whole, as far as may be, without one redeeming factor. . . . Supposing (all) that quite apart from the contemplation of human beings; still it is irrational to hold that it is better that the ugly world exist than the one which is beautiful.

Substitute film, compact disc, poem, news story, photograph or advertising copy for Moore's word "world" and we believe that you will continue to intuitively agree with the statement. While we may disagree on what specifically constitutes beauty in form and content, the aesthetic standard of excellence still applies.

Philosopher John Dewey noted, "Aesthetic experience is a manifestation, a record and celebration of the life of a civilization, a means of promoting its development, and is also the ultimate judgment upon the quality of a civilization." Perhaps the most important positive effect is the media's ability to pull people away from the routine of everyday life and provide an outlet for escape. In an interview on the PBS series "The Promise of Television," commentator Bill Moyers (1988) said:

> The root word of television is vision from afar, and that's its chief value. It has brought me in my stationary moments visions of ideas and dreams and imaginations and geography that I would never personally experience. So, it has put me in touch with the larger world. Television can be a force for dignifying life, not debasing it.

Though Moyers' comments were made specifically about television, the same argument can be made for a good book, a favorite magazine, music or a film. And whether the media are a force for dignifying humanity or debasing it is largely in the hands of those who own it and work in it.

Suggested Readings

CALVERT, CLAY. 2000. *Voyeur nation: Media, privacy and peering in modern culture.* Boulder, CO: Westview Press.

JENSEN, JOLI. 2002. *Is art good for us? Lanham,* MD.: Rowman & Littlefield, Publishers.

LIBERTY, ROBERT M., JOYCE N. SPARKING, and EMILY S. DAVIDSON. 1982. *The early window: Effects of television on children and youth.* New York: Paragon Press.

MEDVED, MICHAEL. 1992. *Hollywood vs. America.* New York: HarperCollins Publishers.

MONTGOMERY, KATHRYN C. 1989. *Target: Prime time. Advocacy groups and the struggle over entertainment television.* New York: Oxford University Press.

POSTMAN, NEIL. 1986. *Amusing ourselves to death: Public discourse in the age of television.* New York: Penguin Books.

Cases on the Web

"How to remember Malcolm X" by Dennis Lancaster

"Beavis and Butthead: The case for standards in entertainment" by Philip Patterson

"Joe Klein and the authorship of "Primary Colors" by Lee Wilkins

"'Bamboozled:' Truth (or prophesy) in satire" by Lee Wilkins

"Truth in filmmaking: Removing the ugliness from 'A Beautiful Mind'" by Philip Patterson

"Playing hardball: The Pete Rose–Jim Gray controversy" by Ben Scott

"How much coverage is appropriate? The case of the highly paid athlete" by Matt Keeney

CHAPTER 11 CASES

CASE 11-A

Up for Debate: NBC News Logo Decorates "The West Wing"

REUBEN STERN
University of Missouri–Columbia

It's 8:15 p.m. on a Sunday night. In three days votes will be cast for local initiatives in several states. A channel-surfing TV viewer stumbles on a political debate on one of the three major broadcast networks. The debate is moderated by a prominent national news anchor, and is branded in the lower right corner of the screen with the logo of the network's news division and the word "Live" above it. Thinking it is some unscheduled special report, the viewer keeps watching. After 10 minutes of trying to catch up, he finally realizes the debate is not real. Instead, the program in question was a live performance of a mostly scripted episode of the NBC political drama "The West Wing." This lone viewer (real or hypothetical) could hardly have been the only one fooled. According to NBC's own poll, conducted by professional polling firm Zogby International, 26 percent of responding viewers said the debate "seemed realistic."

Lasting seven seasons, "The West Wing" was an hour-long weekly show that chronicled the behind-the-scenes activity within a fictional U.S. presidential administration. Although the show was clearly made up, it prided itself on incorporating current events into the story lines and on presenting a believable yet idealized representation of the character and motives driving the people who run the government of the United States, led by the show's fictional president, Jed Bartlet.

After series creator Aaron Sorkin left the show in 2003, "The West Wing" veered more toward typical formulaic television, and ratings for the show slowly began to slip. In 2005, with many loyal fans having tuned out, the network moved the show from Wednesday to Sunday night, pitting it directly against the wildly popular new program "Desperate Housewives" on ABC. The switch caused ratings for "The West Wing" to drop immediately by about a third, to an average of 8.2 million viewers during the season.

The live debate episode was timed to draw additional viewers during "sweeps" week. The live episode of "The West Wing" fit well with the season's continuing story line, which involved the race for a new president to replace Bartlet, who was nearing the end of his second term. This larger narrative pitted a Democratic candidate played by Jimmy Smits against a Republican candidate played by Alan Alda, both highly recognizable television series veterans.

NBC had heavily promoted the live "West Wing" episode in advance, with news of the broadcast appearing as early as a month beforehand. The publicity included a conference call with journalists the week before the show aired that involved both Smits and Alda, along with executive producer John Wells. Newspapers across the country carried advance stories previewing the debate program a day or two before the show, and the Associated Press also moved several stories over its news wire service.

The debate episode was performed live two times that night to accommodate different time zones. After a brief introduction by comedian Ellen Degeneres, the show began with the usual "West Wing" opening credits, after which it cut to moderator Forrest Sawyer and the debate format. In both showings, an NBC News "bug" remained on the screen for the duration of the show. The insignia that appeared on-screen featured the network's signature rainbow peacock tail and the words "NBC News" and "LIVE." Although it looked almost identical to the real thing, an online message-board posting from one viewer asserted the logo was slightly different from the actual news logo the network uses.

The program was moderated by Forrest Sawyer, a prominent former news anchor who has worked as a journalist in the news divisions of all three major networks, including NBC. Articles in at least three major newspapers about the actual "West Wing" episode incorrectly identified Sawyer as still working at NBC News. Because anchoring at NBC and its sister cable channel MSNBC was Sawyer's most recent network news position (Sawyer had filled in as anchor of the "Nightly News" for a week in August 2005, a little more than two months before the "West Wing" debate), many viewers may have reasonably believed Sawyer was representing the network's news division during the show. A Lexis-Nexis search of the five years before the "debate" failed to turn up a single news article reporting that Sawyer had departed NBC or MSNBC.

According to an AP report, the use of the NBC News logo was requested by the episode's producer and writer, Lawrence O'Donnell, and approved by NBC Universal Television Group president Jeff Zucker. O'Donnell, who at one time worked for the late Democratic Sen. Daniel Patrick Moynihan, also serves as a senior political analyst on MSNBC. His responsibilities included both onscreen appearances in MSNBC's political coverage and the behind-the-scenes work on "The West Wing."

Did the live episode staging accomplish its goals? In terms of attracting additional viewers, the answer is clearly yes. The live episode drew an estimated 9.6 million viewers, a 17 percent increase from the 8.2 million the show had been averaging. However, "The West Wing" still lagged behind other programs that night. First-place network ABC drew more than twice as many viewers (18.4 million) with "Home Edition." CBS' "Cold Case" program drew 16.2 million viewers, and Fox's "The Simpsons" drew 11.6 million viewers.

The reviews were mixed with critics largely unimpressed. A *New York Times* reviewer called the debate "the quintessence of wishful writing," while a *Hartford Courant* writer called the program "every bit as boring" as a real presidential debate. Tom Shales of the *Washington Post* declared the show "a failure, yet not a complete waste of time."

But even critics who panned the show overall noted how well the debate simulated the real thing. As the *Hartford Courant's* reviewer pointed out: "It sure looked real, with flat video stock, plain two-shots of a conventional TV debate, and a fake NBC News logo subbing for the luxurious film gloss, glamorous lighting and arty angles of the weekly series." As noted in the *Los Angeles Daily News,* "the trappings of the debate sure looked real enough: In their dark business suits, both candidates were stationed at lecterns in front of the customary blue background." The reviewer for the *Tampa Tribune* was equally convinced: "NBC's live 'West Wing' debate Sunday was so realistic that five minutes into it I was ready to switch channels."

The larger intent of the show—indeed the entire series—was to give the American public an idealized vision of political behavior, thus enabling voters to more effectively set standards for real politicians while encouraging more widespread participation in the democratic process. Actor Jimmy Smits stated the mission even more directly: "What John (Wells, the executive producer) really wants to do is try to give the audience what a real debate should be. . . . Hopefully, with this, maybe we'll give a little lesson or two to the way the next one should be—the next real one."

According to a reviewer at the *Hollywood Reporter,* the episode "showed what a real debate might be if candidates ever decided to risk being themselves and confronting the issues and each other. Odd as it may seem, it gives viewers a basis for comparing actual presidential debates and what is possible." Another reviewer completed the thought: "By contrast, too many real politicians seem to have been hollowed out and stuffed with straw polls by party taxidermists, the better to mouth platitudes devoid of meaning or passion."

While much of the written coverage of the show highlighted differences between fictional and real political exchanges, the majority of newspaper stories at the same time adopted traditional news reporting formats to focus on the question of who "won" the debate. In this way a large portion of the coverage both before and after the show, including stories moved over the wire by the AP, furthered the goals of "West Wing" producers by lending an air of validity to the evening's event and the fictional political race overall.

This type of coverage was cleverly stirred up by NBC, which hired an independent polling firm, Zobgy International, to gauge and report viewer response. At least two major West Coast newspapers also ran their own online polls asking readers to vote on which fictional candidate "won" the debate. This not only furthered the illusion of a real contest but also mirrored the typical "horse race" coverage of an election that is widely decried by a number of media scholars.

Although the fictional candidates conspicuously steered clear of a few important topics (most notably abortion), the hour-long program was filled with statistics and references related to real-life policies and issues, including taxation, Medicare, Head Start, oil drilling in Alaska, debt relief for African countries, etc. Perhaps the most extreme example involved one candidate's assertion that the government-run Medicare insurance program is about six times more efficient than private health insurance companies.

Micro Issues

1. Does the use of the NBC News logo "cheapen" the NBC news division and its programs? Did the logo enhance the fictional debate on "The West Wing"? Justify your answer.
2. Does the selection of Forrest Sawyer as the moderator cheapen any future journalistic enterprises he might attempt? Justify your answer.
3. Do you think many viewers were like the man in the opening paragraph of this case who admitted on his blog that he was fooled by the presentation?

Midrange Issues

1. If it is true that the logo was slightly changed from the NBC logo, does that make a difference?
2. Does it make a difference if Forrest Sawyer was currently employed by NBC? Why or why not?
3. In what ways does this episode of "The West Wing" differ from the admittedly fake news programming nightly on Comedy Central?

Macro Issues

1. Is it the role of entertainment media to foster political debate in the United States?
2. Some polls showed that a significant number of Americans would have voted for the fictional Jed Bartlet for president. What does this say about the power of the media? What does it say about the U.S. electorate?
3. What do you see as the differences in this program, which is admittedly about fictional characters running for president, and a made-for-television movie about an actual incident like, for instance, the attack on the World Trade Center on 9/11? Are the standards different for fiction based on factual events?

CASE 11-B

Hate Radio: The Outer Limits of Tasteful Broadcasting

BRIAN SIMMONS
Cascade College

Trevor Van Lansing has what some would call the greatest job in the world. He is employed by KRFP-AM, an all-talk-format radio station in a large city in the West. His program airs weekdays from 3:00 p.m. to 7:00 p.m., and he is currently rated number one in his afternoon drive-time slot. Van Lansing is, quite simply, the most popular radio personality in the market. He is also the most controversial.

Each afternoon Van Lansing introduces a general topic for discussion and then fields calls from listeners about the topic. However, Van Lansing's topics (and the calls from his listeners) revolve around a recurring theme: the world as viewed by a Caucasian, Anglo-Saxon Protestant who also happens to be vocal, uncompromising and close-minded.

A sampling of his recent programs typifies his show. On Monday, Van Lansing discusses a woman in a small Indiana town who quits her job in a convenience store to go on welfare because there is more money to be made on the federal dole than in the private sector. Says Van Lansing, "All these irresponsible whores are the same. They get knocked up by some construction worker, then expect the taxpayers to pay for them to sit around the house all day and watch Oprah Winfrey."

Callers flood the airwaves with equally combative remarks in support of and opposition to Van Lansing's comments. On Tuesday, the topic of racial discrimination (always a Van Lansing favorite) comes up. According to Van Lansing, "Those Africans expect us Americans to make up for 200 years of past mistakes. Forget it. It can't be done. If they are so keen on America, let them compete against Caucasians on an equal basis without the 'civil rights crutch.'"

When one African-American caller challenges Van Lansing's thinking, the host responds, "Why don't you tell your buddies to work for what they get like us Caucasians? All you do anyway is steal from the guys you don't like and then take their women."

Wednesday finds Van Lansing lashing out against education: "The problem with today's schools is that our kids are exposed to weird thinking. I mean, we tell our kids that homosexuality is okay, that we evolved from a chimp, and that the Ruskies are our friends. It all started when we elected women to school boards and started letting fags into the classroom. It's disgusting."

Thursday features an exchange between Van Lansing and an abortion-rights activist. At one point they are both shouting at the same time, and the airwaves are peppered with obscenities and personal attacks. By comparison, Friday is calm, as only a few irate Jews, women and Mormons bother to call in.

Critics have called Van Lansing's program offensive, tasteless, rude, racist, obscene and insensitive. Supporters refer to the program as enlightening, refreshing, educational and provocative. The only thing everyone can agree on is that the show is a bona fide moneymaker. Van Lansing's general manager notes that the station's ratings jumped radically when he was hired, and that advertising revenues have tripled.

In fact, Van Lansing's popularity has spawned promotional appearances, T-shirts, bumper stickers and other paraphernalia, all designed to hawk the station. "Sure, Trevor is controversial, but in this business that's good," says KRFP's general manager.

"Van Lansing is so good that he will make more money this year than the president of the United States. Besides, it's just a gimmick."

Does Van Lansing see a problem with the content and style of his program? "Look," he says, "radio is a business. You have to give the audience what they want. All I do is give them what they want. If they wanted a kinder, gentler attitude, I would give it to them." He continues, "Don't get mad at me. Thank God we live in a country where guys like me can express an opinion. The people who listen to me like to hear it straight sometimes, and that's what the First Amendment is about, right?"

Finally, Van Lansing points out that if people are really offended by him, they can always turn the dial. "I don't force these people to listen," he pleads. "If they don't like it, let them go somewhere else."

Others disagree. The National Coalition for the Understanding of Alternative Lifestyles, a gay- and lesbian-rights group, calls Van Lansing's show "reprehensible." "Trevor Van Lansing is hiding behind the First Amendment. What he says on the air isn't speech; it's hate, pure and simple," says the group's director. "His program goes well beyond what our founders intended."

Adds a representative of the National Organization for Women: "Van Lansing is perpetuating several dangerous stereotypes that are destructive, sick and offensive. Entertainment must have some boundaries."

Micro Issues

1. Would you be offended by Van Lansing's program? If so, why?
2. Would Van Lansing's program be less offensive if the station aired another talk show immediately after his that featured a host holding opposite views?
3. How are the lyrics of rapper Eminem like or unlike Van Lansing's rants? Is an artist subject to different restrictions?

Midrange Issues

1. Who should accept responsibility for monitoring this type of program? Van Lansing? The radio station, KRFP? The Federal Communications Commission? The courts? The audience?
2. What, if any, are the differences between Van Lansing's *legal* right to do what he does and the *ethical* implications of what he does?
3. Legal scholar Mari Matsuda (1989) has called for a narrow legal restriction of racist speech. She notes, "The places where the law does not go to redress harm have tended to be the places where women, children, people of color, and poor people live" (Matsuda 1989, 11). She argues that a content-based restriction of racist speech is more protective of civil liberties than other tests that have been traditionally applied. Could such an argument be applied to entertainment programming?
4. In the current American media landscape, talk radio is supposedly the stronghold of the right while the majority of major daily newspapers are supposedly controlled by the left. Does the evidence validate this widely held assumption? Is democracy well-served by this arrangement of entire media systems leaning to one side of the political spectrum?

Macro Issues

1. Are entertainers relieved of ethical responsibilities if they are "just giving the audience what they want"? Do Van Lansing's high ratings validate his behavior, since many people are obviously in agreement with him?
2. How does Van Lansing's narrow view of the world differ from a television situation comedy that stereotypes blondes as dumb, blue-collar workers as bigoted, etc.?
3. Van Lansing says that it's great that a guy like him can have a radio show. Is tolerance one of the measures of a democracy? If so, are there limits to tolerance, and who draws those lines?
4. Supreme Court Justice William O. Douglas has said, "If we are to have freedom of mind in America, we must produce a generation of men and women who will make tolerance for all ideas a symbol of virtue." How should democratic societies cope with unpopular points of view, particularly as expressed through the mass media?
5. Compare and contrast the rantings of Van Lansing to the real-life incident that resulted in shock-jock Don Imus being fired from his radio and television shows following racially insensitive remarks about the Rutgers women's basketball team.

CASE 11-C

"Schindler's List": The Role of Memory

LEE WILKINS
University of Missouri–Columbia

In 1982 director Steven Spielberg purchased the rights to Australian novelist Thomas Keneally's retelling of the story of the "Schindler Jews," a group of about 1,100 Krakow, Poland, residents who survived the Holocaust because Czech businessman Oskar Schindler was willing to cajole, bribe and bully the Nazis for their lives. Today, Schindler, a Roman Catholic by birth, is known in Israel as a "righteous person"; he is the only Nazi buried in Jerusalem's Mount Zion cemetery.

By 1992 when Spielberg began work on the film, both he and the world had changed. Bosnia was in the midst of "ethnic cleansing," as were nations in Africa and in the Far East, such as Nepal. Some polls indicated that more than half of the U.S. teenagers living in that decade had never heard of the Holocaust; about 23 percent of the U.S. public at the time maintained the gassing of 6 million Jews plus 5 million other "undesirables" in Germany and its occupied territories never happened.

"I think the main reason I wanted to make this film was as an act of remembrance," Spielberg told the film editor of the *Atlanta Journal-Constitution.* "An act of remembrance for the public record. Maybe it won't be seen by gallons of people who see my other movies, but it might be the kind of movie shown one day in high schools. I also wanted to leave this story for my children. I wanted to leave them a legacy of their Jewish culture."

What Americans, as well as Spielberg's children, will see is a 3-hour-and-15-minute examination of the conscience of Oskar Schindler, who entered World War II on the side of the Nazis, intending to make a profit. He hires Jews to work in his enamelware factory because they work for less than slave wages. Initially, he befriends the Nazis and the SS to help expedite his purchase and takeover of the plant. Later, after the Nazis have first ghettoized and then attempted to exterminate the Jewish population of Krakow, Schindler uses his personal charm, his connections and most of his war-amassed wealth to have "his" Jewish workers first labeled as essential to the German war machine and later moved from Germany and into Czechoslovakia for safekeeping. None of the bombs manufactured at Schindler's plant ever exploded.

Spielberg shot the film in black and white on location in Poland. Much of the movie has a documentary feel; cinematography is at eye level. It was often Spielberg himself who focused the handheld camera. Hitler appears only once—in a photograph on someone's desk. And, by centering on Schindler, Spielberg captured the conscience of an uneasy hero.

As Keneally's book indicates, Oskar Schindler was a complex man. He managed to maintain outward friendships with many Nazis whom he despised. He was a sensualist who enjoyed good food, expensive possessions and carnal knowledge of women who were not his wife. Spielberg's film, which was rated "R," depicted all of this, including scenes of lovemaking that involved full, frontal nudity and more distant shots of concentration camp existence in which Jewish inmates were required to run naked in front of their guards to determine who remained well enough to work and who was sick enough to be murdered.

Perhaps the most disturbing element of the film was Spielberg's portrait of the violence embedded in Hitler's "final solution" and of the banality of evil (Hannah Arendt's phrase used to describe convicted war criminal Adolph Eichmann) that individual human beings can come to represent. That sundered humanity is symbolized by Amon Goeth (played by Ralph Fiennes), the amoral and, some have suggested, sociopathic commandant of the labor camp from which many of the people who worked for Schindler survived. Whether it is the Nazis hunting the Jews who remain in hiding in the Krakow ghetto or Goeth's randomized murder of the men and women who lived in his camp as before breakfast sport, the violence in the film is devastating not just for its brutality but also for its casualness.

When Spielberg's mother told him making "'Schindler's List' would be good for the Jews," Spielberg responded that "it would be good for all of us."

Critics, who had a difficult time accepting that the same man who directed "Jurassic Park" could also produce "Schindler's List" in the same year, praised the film for its aesthetic qualities and for its retelling of the story of the Holocaust in such a powerful fashion. The film also brought Spielberg multiple Oscars, an award that had eluded him despite his enormous popular success. After the film's release, President Bill Clinton said that every American should see it.

Writing in the *Washington Post,* Rita Kempley saw more than a superficial resemblance between Schindler and Spielberg. "And Schindler, played with élan by [Liam] Neeson, is really a lot like Spielberg himself," she wrote, "a man who manages to use his commercial clout to achieve a moral end."

Micro Issues

1. Should a film like "Schindler's List" receive the same "R" rating as films such as "Road Trip"?
2. What is the appropriate role of a film critic for films such as "Schindler's List?" Should different standards be used to evaluate this film than some other Spielberg successes, such as "E.T." or "Jaws"?
3. Would you allow a child under 17 to see this film?

Midrange Issues

1. Should news accounts focus on events such as the ethnic cleansing in Bosnia with the goal of changing public opinion?
2. Are docudramas that focus on social issues such as spouse abuse or child molestation the appropriate mechanism to engage the public in debate or discussion about such serious questions?
3. Some people have argued that certain historical events, such as the Holocaust or the recent genocide in Rwanda, should never be the subject of entertainment programming because entertainment can never capture the true horror of what has happened. How would you evaluate such an assertion?

Macro Issues

1. Compare the moral development of Oskar Schindler with that of the main characters in a film such as "Gandhi."
2. John Dewey wrote about "funded memory," by which he meant how a culture remembers and reconstructs its own history. What is the role of entertainment programming in funded memory? What should be the role of news programming in such cultural constructions?
3. Tolstoy argues that good art communicates the feelings of the artist to the masses in such a way that others may experience the same feeling as the artist. How does this film accomplish that purpose?

CASE 11-D

Naomi Campbell: Do Celebrities Have Privacy?

LEE WILKINS
University of Missour–Columbia

Supermodel Naomi Campbell is an international celebrity. Campbell was discovered in London's Covent Garden when she was only 15 and soon became one of the best paid and most often photographed supermodels, earning more the $1 million a year. Her worldwide celebrity was helped, in part, because of her physical image; a native of the United Kingdom, Campbell is black. She was often the focus of media coverage in both Britain and the United States and, in the years after her discovery, developed a reputation for being a prima donna—irritable and manipulative. She was dropped by her agency in 1993, although she was later reinstated, and she was once arrested for assaulting her personal assistant. These stories about Campbell were news.

Campbell often sought the media spotlight. And, like many models, among them Britain's Kate Moss, Campbell was rumored to use drugs—specifically cocaine, which depresses the appetite and hence helps with weight control. Campbell publicly denied any drug addiction on multiple occasions, including in 1997 when she had been rushed to a hospital in Gran Canaria following an alleged drug overdose. After that incident, she told Britain's *The Daily Telegraph,* "I didn't take drugs." Then, in February 2001, London's *Daily Mirror,* one of Britain's most widely read tabloids, published a photograph of Campbell leaving a Narcotics Anonymous meeting in King's Road, Chelsea, a wealthy London neighborhood. The article that appeared with the photograph included details of the meeting she attended.

Campbell sued in British courts—not for libel but for invasion of privacy. The suit was the first brought under laws governing the European Union (EU), which includes in its charter protection of individual privacy under the Human Rights Convention. Britain is a member of the EU. Campbell's attorneys reasoned that the EU statutes, which are more specific about privacy than legal precedent in either Britain or the United States, gave them the best chance of winning the suit.

Speaking later, Campbell said the *Mirror* photograph and articles made her feel as if she had been raped. She characterized the article as "very damaging." However, things got more complicated when the case actually went to Britain's High Court. During that proceeding, Campbell maintained that she was not a drug addict and denied that she had been receiving therapy for some years. She did admit that she was "notorious for tantrums."

In its ruling in March 2002, the High Court awarded Campbell 3,500 pounds (about $6,000) in damages and ordered that the newspaper pay additional court costs equal to about $110,000 (70,000 pounds). The judge in the case noted that even celebrities were entitled to some privacy. "Although many aspects of the private lives of celebrities and public figures will inevitably enter the public domain, in my judgment it does not follow that even with self-publicists every aspect and detail of their private lives are legitimate quarry for the journalist." The judge noted that Campbell's attendance at the Narcotics Anonymous meeting and the details of her therapy clearly related to her physical and mental health and therefore met the standard of "sensitive personal data."

However, the judge also noted that the public clearly had an interest in knowing that Campbell had been misleading them by her denials of drug addiction. "Clearly *The Mirror* was fully entitled to put the record straight and publish that her denials of drug addiction were deliberately misleading. She might have been thought of and, indeed, she herself seems to be a self-appointed role model to young black women." The judge also noted, "I am satisfied she lied when making denials about her drug addiction."

News organizations in Britain generally treated the ruling as a victory, noting that the small damage award served as much as a rebuke to Campbell than as a punishment to the often invasive tabloids. Campbell, too, seemed to regret many aspects of the suit. She said the case had left her unable to sleep. "I didn't expect it to be the way it's blown up like this. . . . Recovery is something that takes time. You feel that you're getting better in the right direction. I wasn't hiding. But first of all an addict had to admit to themselves that they have a problem before they can admit it to anybody else. That is the first step."

Piers Morgan, editor of the *Mirror,* characterized the judgment as ". . . derisory. . . . This is a case that should never have been brought. It is quite clear that the judge thought we had every right to say she was a drug addict. We have every right to tell the public that she was having treatment. The only thing we couldn't do—and this was what the whole case came down to—was say she was going to Narcotics Anonymous."

Micro Issues

1. If Campbell had admitted her drug addiction when first asked, would it have been ethical to publish the story?
2. Was it appropriate for other media outlets—the mainstream press in both Britain and the United States—to publish the *Mirror* photo and story details once the *Mirror* had published them?
3. Are the details of Campbell's drug treatment ethically distinct from the fact that she is in treatment? Justify your answers in terms of ethical theory.

Midrange Issues

1. How should Campbell's character influence media coverage of her, particularly her private life?
2. Are celebrities morally distinct from other categories of people when it comes to privacy issues? Would you make the same or a different argument for public officials?
3. Is there something more invasive about a photograph of Campbell leaving the meeting than a story that recounted the event? Was a photograph necessary for a journalistic purpose?
4. Should there be different standards for the tabloid press than for more mainstream media? If there are different standards, how do you account for them?

Macro Issues

1. In a commentary that ran after the court decision was announced, British journalist Kim Fletcher noted: "There is more at stake here than the right to write about what famous people do in their own time. The fear is that lawyers will extend the notion of what can be regarded as confidential—conversations between business colleagues, tax discussions—to prevent newspapers gaining and publishing information that may be of greater significance and more in the public interest than a model's drug addiction." Analyze and evaluate this statement based on ethical theory.

2. How do you believe this case would have been resolved in the United States, had Campbell chosen to sue there? Is your analysis based on legal precedent? On ethical theory? Which is more appropriate in privacy cases?

CASE 11-E

Does Jon Stewart Have a Point?

LEE WILKINS
University of Missouri–Columbia

Jon Stewart, host of Comedy Central's "The Daily Show," has always insisted that, by profession, he is a comedian and that he reports "fake news." Stewart follows a long tradition of news being incorporated into entertainment programming, beginning with Orson Wells' 1939 radio play "War of the Worlds" (which featured news bulletins as a part of the well-orchestrated ruse to make the "Martian invasion" seem more real) and continuing through several generations of "Saturday Night Live" performers.

What makes Stewart's contributions unique is that his "fake news" programs often incorporate actual news video and direct quotes from news makers, most of them political officials. Sometimes, Stewart interviews political officials, and he often features book authors who write about real politics and public policy debates.

Viewers have recognized Stewart's contributions. Not only is the "Daily Show" popular, but also multiple public opinion polls have documented that young people, particularly between the ages of 18 to 30, get "some" or "most" of their public affairs information from Stewart. The critics—many of them somewhat older than the prized 18 to 30 demographic—also have praised Stewart's show. He has won both an Emmy and a Peabody Award, the latter of which is given for programming that raises important public issues.

At the same time, Stewart continues to work as a comedian. At the height of the show's popularity, Stewart also hosted the Academy Awards, arguably the most watched television show on the planet, and one that is designed to entertain rather than inform.

So, when Stewart appeared on "Crossfire" with Tucker Carlson during the 2004 presidential campaign, both hosts and the audience had every reason to believe they were booking a comedian. But on this night, Stewart was far from funny. Instead, Stewart lambasted Carlson, "Crossfire," and the television news media in general, when he accused them of doing bad political theater rather than their jobs. Among his comments (transcript found at: **http://transcripts.cnn.com** accessed on October 27, 2006) were the following:

Stewart: "But the thing is that this—you're doing theater, when you should be doing debate, which would be great."

Carlson: "You had John Kerry on your show and you sniff his throne and you're accusing us of partisan hackery?"

Stewart: "Absolutely. . . . What is wrong with you?"

Stewart: "You know, the interesting thing I have is, you have a responsibility to the public discourse, and you fail miserably."

Carlson: "You need to get a job at a journalism school, I think."

Stewart: "You need to go to one. The thing that I want to say is, when you have people on for just knee-jerk, reactionary talk . . . "

Carlson: "Wait. I thought you were going to be funny. Come on. Be funny."

Stewart: "No. No. I'm not going to be your monkey. . . . I watch your show every
day. And it kills me."

Carlson: "I can tell you love it."

Stewart: "It's so—oh, it's so painful to watch. You know, because we need what you
do. This is such a great opportunity you have here to actually get politicians off
of their marketing and strategy."

Carlson: "Is this really Jon Stewart. What is this, anyway?"

Stewart: "Yes, it's someone who watches your show and cannot take it anymore. I
just can't. And come work for us, because we, as the people . . . "

Carlson: "How do you pay?"

Stewart: "The people—not well. . . . But you can sleep at night."

Micro Issues

1. Are shows such as "Crossfire" and other cable network shows obligated to provide viewers with public affairs programming?
2. What is the role for debate and disagreement in news coverage? What other sorts of issues should news about politics focus on?
3. Does the fact that Stewart is an entertainer who is not obligated to be fair or objective
alter what he is able to accomplish?

Midrange Issues

1. Go to a city council meeting or a zoning meeting. How much of what you see there is theater? How would you report on it?
2. If you consider Stewart a "liberal," do you think his comedy would work as well with a
democrat in the White House?
3. In the exchange between Stewart and Carlson, who, if anyone, is not doing his job? Stewart as a comedian? Carlson as a journalist?
4. If a significant number of young adults report getting their political news from "The Daily
Show," does that change the ethical mandate of the show? If so, how?

Macro Issues

1. Does the recent downsizing of MSNBC and other cable outlets confirm Stewart's analysis?
2. Compare Stewart to other political commentators such as Upton Sinclair and Jonathan
Swift. What role does biting and satirical political commentary play in the public sphere?
3. Is Jon Stewart a journalist? Is Tucker Carlson? Is it Carlson's role to find "truth" or to find
"controversy"? How do the two differ?
4. Can comedy uncover underlying truths about our society that no objective journalist can
mine? Is that the role of comedy?

12

Becoming a Moral Adult

By the end of this chapter you should:

- **know the stages of moral development as described by Piaget and Kohlberg.**
- **understand the ethics of care.**
- **understand the stages of adult moral development.**

INTRODUCTION

Graduation is not the end of the educational process; it is merely a milestone marking the beginning of a new era of learning. If delivered properly, college studies not only equip you for entry into the workforce (or for the adult student, perhaps a promotion in the workplace) but also equip you to be a lifelong learner.

The same is true about moral development. There is no "moral graduation," marking you as an upright person capable of making right choices in all of life's personal and professional dilemmas. It is a lifelong process of steps, some of which you have taken, while others lie ahead. Where you are now is a function of both age and experience, but no matter what your circumstances, the person you are now is not the person you will be 10 years from now. In a decade, you will have added insight. Growth may, and probably will, change your decisions. This process is not only inevitable but also desirable.

This chapter is designed to provide you with an overview of some psychological theories of moral development. It attempts to allow you to plot your own development not only in terms of where you are but also in terms of where you would like to be.

BASIC ASSUMPTIONS ABOUT MORAL DEVELOPMENT: THE RIGHTS-BASED TRADITION

People can learn to develop morality just as they can learn to think critically (Clouse 1985). Scholars base this assertion on the following premises.

First, *moral development occurs within the individual.* Real moral development cannot be produced by outside factors, nor can it be produced merely by engaging in moral acts. People develop morally when they are aware of their reasons for acting a certain way.

Second, *moral development parallels intellectual development.* Although the two may proceed at a slightly different pace, there can be little moral development until a person has attained a certain intellectual capacity. For this reason, we exempt children and people of limited mental ability from some laws and societal expectations. While you can be intelligent without being moral, the converse is not as likely.

Third, *moral development occurs in a series of universal, unvarying and hierarchical stages.* Each level builds on the lower levels, and there is no skipping of intermediate stages. Just as a baby crawls before walking and babbles before speaking, a person must pass through the earlier stages of moral development before advancing to the later stages.

Fourth, *moral development comes through conflict.* As moral development theorist Lawrence Kohlberg notes (1973, 13), "A fundamental reason why an individual moves from one stage to the next is because the latter stages solve problems and

CALVIN AND HOBBES copyright © Watterson. Reprinted with permission of Universal Press Syndicate. All rights reserved.

inconsistencies unsolvable at the present developmental stage." Just as a baby soon learns strategies other than crying to get its needs met, the developing moral being learns more complex behaviors when older, more elementary strategies no longer work.

The two developmental psychologists who are the most cited experts in the field did their work decades and continents apart yet came to remarkably similar conclusions. Jean Piaget conducted his research in Switzerland in the 1930s by watching little boys play marbles, and in the 1960s Lawrence Kohlberg studied Harvard students. Together they have produced many of the most provocative insights in the rights-based tradition. They are often called "stage theorists" for their work in identifying and describing the stages of moral development.

THE WORK OF PIAGET

Swiss psychologist Jean Piaget turned his attention to children's moral development in the 1930s. He watched as boys between the ages of 3 and 12 played marbles, and he later tested his assumptions about their playground behavior in interviews. The box below presents the basics of Piaget's theory.

The children under ages 5 to 7 didn't really play a game of marbles at all. They made up their own rules, varied them by playmate and game and delighted in exploring the marbles as tactile objects. Their view of the game-playing universe was centered exclusively on what each individual child wanted.

Piaget found that younger boys (ages 7 and 8) played marbles as if the rules had been taught to them by their parents or other authority figures and as if violations of those rules would result in punishment. The boys believed the rules were timeless and that "goodness" came from respecting the rules. Boys in this stage of moral development believed "Right is to obey the will of the adult. Wrong is to have a will of one's own" (Piaget 1965, 193).

Children progressed to the next stage of moral development when the boys began to develop notions of autonomy. As they became more autonomous, they began to understand the reasoning behind the rules, and that the reasons (i.e., fair play and reciprocity) were the foundation of the rules themselves. Children in this stage of moral development understood that the rules did not originate from some outside authority figure but rather received their power from the group consensus.

These children had internalized the rules and the reasons behind them. Understanding the rules allowed the boys to rationally justify violating them. For example, children in this stage of moral development allowed much younger children to place their thumbs inside the marble circles, a clear violation of the rules. But the younger boys' hands were smaller and weaker, and by allowing them a positional advantage, the older ones had—in contemporary language—leveled the playing field. They had ensured fairness when following the rules literally would have made it impossible.

Although Piaget worked with children, it is possible to see that adults often demonstrate these stages of moral development.

Piaget's Stages of Moral Development

EARLY DEVELOPMENT (before age 2)

- Interest in marbles is purely motor (e.g., put the marbles in your mouth).

FIRST STAGE—egocentrism (years 3–7)

- Children engage in "parallel play"; there is no coherent set of rules accepted by all.
- The moral reasoning is "I do it because it feels right."

SECOND STAGE—heteronomy (years 7–8)

- Children recognize only individual responsibility; obedience is enforced through punishment.
- Each player tries to win.
- Rules are regarded as inviolate, unbreakable and handed down from outside authority figures, usually older children.
- The children do not understand the reason behind the rules.

THIRD STAGE—autonomy (begins about age 11)

- Children internalize the rules; they understand the reasons behind them.
- They develop an ideal of justice and are able to distinguish between individual and collective responsibility.
- They ensure fair play among children.
- Children can change the rules in responses to a larger set of obligations.
- Authority is internal.
- Children understand universal ethical principles that transcend specific times and situations.

Take the videographer whose primary motivation is to obtain a great shot, regardless of the views of those he works with or his story subjects. This journalist operates within an egocentric moral framework that places the primary emphasis on what "I" think, "my" judgment, and what's good for "me."

Beginning journalists, the ones who find themselves concerned with the literal following of codes of ethics, may often be concerned with the heteronomy stage of development. This journalist knows the rules and follows them. She would never accept a freebie or consider running the name of a rape victim. It's against organizational policy, and heteronomous individuals are motivated largely by outside influences.

Just as the boys at the third stage of moral development were more willing to alter the rules to ensure a fair game for all, journalists at the final stage of moral development are more willing to violate professional norms if it results in better journalism. The journalist at this stage of moral development has so internalized and universalized the rules of ethical professional behavior that he or she can violate some of them for sound ethical reasons.

Proceeding with a story that is unpopular, expensive or out of the norm could be considered an example of journalism at the highest level of Piaget's schema. For instance, the Pulitzer Prize–winning series by the *Des Moines Register* regarding the rape, recovery and trial ordeal of a victim who volunteered to have her story told is an example of journalism that breaks the mold and goes far beyond the norm of stories of its type. Also indicative of this level of journalism is the painstakingly detailed series of articles written by two enterprising *Detroit Free Press* reporters who read volumes of the federal tax code and found it to be loaded with one-of-a-kind tax loopholes for individuals and businesses with political connections.

However, people seldom remain exclusively in a single stage of moral development. New situations often mean that people, including journalists and their sources, regress temporarily to a previous stage of moral development until enough learning can take place so that the new situation is well understood. But, such regression would not include behaviors that would be considered morally culpable under most circumstances, for example, lying or killing, despite the new context.

THE WORK OF KOHLBERG

Harvard psychologist Lawrence Kohlberg mapped six stages of moral development in his college-student subjects. The accompanying box outlines Kohlberg's stages of moral development, divided into three levels.

Kohlberg developed a lengthy set of interview questions to allow him to establish which stage of moral development individual students had achieved. He asserted that only a handful of people—for example, Socrates, Gandhi, Martin Luther King or Mother Teresa—ever achieved the sixth stage of moral development. Most adults, he believed, spend the greater portion of their lives in the two conventional stages. They are motivated by society's expectations.

Doing right, fulfilling one's duties and abiding by the social contract are the pillars upon which the stages of Kohlberg's work rest. Under Kohlberg's arrangement, justice—and therefore morality—is a function of perception; as you develop, more activities fall under the realm of duty than before. For instance, reciprocity is not even a goal for students in the earliest stage, yet it is an essential characteristic of people in upper stages of moral development. Conversely, acting to avoid punishment is laudable for those in the first stages yet might not be as praiseworthy for someone who is operating on universal ethical principles. The further up Kohlberg's stages students progressed, the more they asserted that moral principles are subject to interpretation by individuals and subject to contextual factors.

Kohlberg's stages are descriptive and not predictive. They do not anticipate how any one individual will develop but suggest how most will develop. In addition, there is a difference in moral reasoning and moral behavior. They are correlated but not totally overlapping phenomena. Kohlberg focused not on the goodness of moral decisions but on the adequacy of the cognitive structures underlying them.

Kohlberg's formulation has much to recommend it to journalists, concerned as they are with concepts such as free speech, the professional duty to tell the truth and their obligations to the public and the public trust. However, Kohlberg's work was not without its problems. At least two aspects of his research troubled other moral development theorists.

Many scholars have argued that any generalizable theory of moral development should allow people who are not saints or religious leaders to attain the highest stages of moral development. While it has been argued that only saints can be expected to act in a saintly manner most of the time, history is replete with examples of ordinary people taking extraordinary personal or professional risk for some larger

The Six Moral Stages of Kohlberg

LEVEL 1: PRECONVENTIONAL

Stage 1: Heteronomous morality is the display of simple obedience.

Stage 2: Individualism is the emergence of self-interest. Rules are followed only when they are deemed to be in one's self-interest and others are allowed the same freedom. Reciprocity and fairness begin to emerge, but only in a pragmatic way.

LEVEL 2: CONVENTIONAL

Stage 3: Interpersonal conformity is living up to what others expect, given one's role (e.g., "brother," "daughter," "neighbor," etc.). "Being good" is important and treating others as you would have them treat you becomes the norm.

Stage 4: Social systems is the recognition that one must fulfill the duties to which one has agreed. Doing one's duty, respect for authority, and maintaining the social order are all goals in this level. Laws are to be upheld unilaterally except in extreme cases where they conflict with other fixed social duties.

LEVEL 3: POSTCONVENTIONAL

Stage 5: Social contract and individual rights is becoming aware that one is obligated by whatever laws are agreed to by due process. The social contract demands that we uphold the laws even if they are contrary to our best interests because they exist to provide the greatest good for the greatest number. However, some values such as life and liberty stand above any majority opinion.

Stage 6: Universal ethical principles self-selected by each individual guide this person. These principles are to be followed even if laws violate those principles. The principles that guide this individual include the equality of human rights and respect for the dignity of humans as individual beings regardless of race, age, socioeconomic status or even contribution to society.

ethical principles. Many scholars felt that Kohlberg's conception—unlike Piaget's—was too restrictive.

Still more troubling was how those students who were tested on Kohlberg's scale performed. In study after study, men consistently scored higher than women on stages of moral development. This gender bias in Kohlberg's work—coupled with other findings from developmental psychology—prompted discussion about a different concept of moral development founded on notions of community rather than in the rights-based tradition. It is called the ethics of care.

PARALLEL ASSUMPTIONS ABOUT MORAL DEVELOPMENT: THE ETHICS OF CARE

The psychologists who developed the ethics of care disagree with at least two of the fundamental assumptions underlying Piaget and Kohlberg.

First, while moral development occurs within the individual and parallels intellectual development, moral development does not always occur in a series of universal, unvarying and hierarchical stages. Second, moral growth emerges through understanding the concept of community, not merely through conflict.

The rights-based scholars believe that moral development emerges from a proper understanding of the concept "I." Proponents of the ethics of care say that moral development arises from understanding the concept of "we."

Carol Gilligan's (1982) work provides the clearest explanation of the ethics of care. Gilligan studied women who were deciding whether to have abortions. As she listened to them, she learned that they based their ethical choices on relationships. The first thing these women considered was how to maintain a connection. Gilligan argued that the moral adult is the person who sees a connection between the "I" and the "other." The women spoke in a "different voice" about their ethical decision making.

For example, Gilligan presented the women with Kohlberg's classic ethical dilemma: the case of the desperate man and the greedy pharmacist. In this scenario, a man with a terminally ill spouse doesn't have enough money to purchase an expensive and lifesaving drug. When he explains the situation to the pharmacist, the pharmacist refuses to give him the medication.

Under Kohlberg's system, it would be ethically allowable for a man at the highest stages of moral development to develop a rationale for stealing the drug, an act of civil disobedience for a greater good. However, women made this particular choice less often. Instead, they reasoned that the most ethical thing to do was to build a relationship with the pharmacist, to form a community in which the pharmacist viewed himself or herself as an active part. In that situation, the women reasoned, the pharmacist ultimately would give the man the drug in order to maintain the connection.

Gilligan proposed that the women's rationale was no more or less ethically sophisticated than that expected under Kohlberg's outline. However, it was different, for it weighed different ethical values. Whether those values emerged as the result of how women are socialized in Western culture (an assertion that has often been made about Gilligan's work) or whether they merely reflected a different kind of thinking still remains the focus of heated academic debate. For our purposes, the origin of the distinction—and whether it is truly gender-linked—is not as important as the content of the thought itself.

Gilligan's notion of moral development is not neatly tied into stages and does not borrow as heavily from the tradition of logic and rights-based inquiry. Her closest theoretical counterpart is probably communitarianism with its emphasis on connection to community and its mandate for social justice.

If you were to carve stages from Gilligan's work, they would resemble:

- **First**—an ethic of care where the moral responsibility is for care of others before self.
- **Second**—an acknowledgment of the ethic of rights, including the rights of self to be considered in ethical decision making.
- **Third**—a movement from concerns about goodness (women are taught to believe that care for others is "good" while men are taught that "taking care of oneself" is good) to concerns about truth. It is at this stage of moral development where commitment to a universal ethical principle begins, with truth at the core of that universal principle.

A complete sense of moral development, Gilligan observed, requires the ability "to [use] two different moral languages, the language of rights that protects separations and the language of responsibilities that sustains connection" (Gilligan 1982, 210).

Contemporary journalists have struggled with the issues of connection. Since much of our profession is based on an understanding of rights as outlined in various legal documents, ethical reasoning for journalists almost always assumes a rights-based approach. This historically well-founded bias, however, has led journalists into some of their more systematic and profound errors in decisions about privacy, attitudes of arrogance toward sources and readers and an unwillingness to be genuinely accountable to anyone.

News organizations can work to sustain community. If journalism as a profession is to mature ethically, it must see itself as the vehicle to help people become the citizens they can be and to help reconnect and sustain communities that have become increasingly fragmented, often by the very media that should have brought them together.

In 1992, the streets of Los Angeles erupted into deadly riots when a jury acquitted two L.A. police officers in an assault trial, despite videotape evidence that the officers had beaten the detainee, Rodney King, into submission. In an essay entitled "Whose Values," written in the wake of the Los Angeles riots following the Rodney King verdict, *Newsweek* author Joe Klein wrote:

> Television brought the nation together in the '50s; there were evenings when all of America seemed glued to the same show—Milton Berle, "I Love Lucy" and yes, "Ozzie and Harriet." But cable television has quite the opposite effect, dividing the audience into demographic slivers. . . . Indeed, if you are a member of any identifiable subgroup—black, Korean, fundamentalist, sports fan, political junkie—it's now possible to be massaged by your very own television and radio stations and to read your own magazines without having to venture out into the American mainstream. The choices are exhilarating, but also alienating. The basic principle is centrifugal: market segmentation targets those qualities that distinguish people from each other rather than emphasizing the things we have in common. It is the developed world's equivalent of the retribalization taking place in Eastern Europe, Africa and Asia. (Klein 1992, 21–22)

If there was one common denominator from the vast variety of projects that claimed to fall under the "civic journalism" umbrella in the late 1990s, it was the fact that almost all of them had as a goal to bring people back together and foster a sense of community using the media as a primary tool in the process. To that end, the movement was a laudable one.

DEVELOPING AS AN ETHICAL PROFESSIONAL

Moral development theory helps to explain the decisions of everyday people. However, for the past three decades, scholars have attempted to apply the understandings of moral development to professionals—among them journalists.

James Rest, a psychology professor at the University of Minnesota, took Kohlberg's schema of moral development and used it to create a paper-and-pencil test to measure moral development among various professions. In the ensuing 30 years, the test, called the Defining Issues Test (DIT), has been administered to more than 20,000 professionals, among them doctors, nurses, dentists, accountants, philosophers and theologians, members of the U.S. Coast Guard, surgeons, veterinarians, graduate students, junior high students, prison inmates and others. Those taking the test read four to six scenarios (including the Heinz dilemma used by Kohlberg and described earlier in this chapter). They are then asked to make a decision about what the protagonist should do, and then to rate the factors that influenced that decision. Because the test is based in Kohlberg's understanding of moral development, those who take the test who rely on universal principles and who consider issues of justice score well. In general, most people who take the DIT score in the range of what Kohlberg would have called conventional moral reasoning— stages three and four on the Kohlberg scale.

Recently, scholars (Wilkins and Coleman, 2005) asked journalists to take the DIT and compared journalists' scores to those of other professionals. Perhaps to the surprise of the general public, journalists do well on the DIT, scoring below only three other professions: philosophers/theologians, medical students and practicing physicians. This finding is significant because the single biggest predictor of a good score on the DIT is education, and journalists as a group have less formal education than the three professions with scores "above" those of journalists as well as several professions, for example orthopedic surgeons, that score lower on the test.

In a follow up study (Coleman & Wilkins 2006), public relations professionals also did well on the DIT, suggesting that knowing how to make good ethical decisions may be a component of professionalism in a way that the literature on that question has not yet addressed.

The scenarios on the DIT are not directed at any particular profession but rather try to determine how people think about "average" moral questions. When journalists are presented with scenarios that deal directly with journalism, for example, problems involving the use of hidden cameras or whether to run troubling photographs of children, they score even better. In these tests, journalists often score in the fourth and fifth stage of Kohlberg's moral development schema, indicating not only that professionals are capable of thinking well about these issues but also that when their domain (journalism) is the issue, they are very good ethical thinkers indeed. In studying journalists, scholars have also learned that having a visual image, such as a photograph, of some of the stakeholders in an ethical dilemma elevates ethical reasoning.

Scholars have studied journalists' ethical decision making in other ways. Investigative reporters make moral judgments about the subjects of their stories, even though when they talk about their work they are reluctant to leave the terrain of professional objectivity (Ettema and Glasser, 1998). Journalists who have been sued for invasion of privacy don't often think about the ethical issues their reporting creates, an indirect indication that solid ethical thinking may sometimes keep journalists out of court—an indirect measure of professional performance (Voakes 1998).

Finally, journalists do agree on what constitutes "good work" in their profession— an emphasis on truth telling, taking a role as government watchdog, investigative reporting and treating the subjects of their stories with dignity. However, journalists believe that the single biggest threat to continuing professional excellence is the in-creasing pressure to make a profit that characterizes so many media and corpora-tions. Professionally, journalists are out of joint with a mission that includes both public service and profit making (Gardner et al. 2001). How that tension is resolved will either help to create a professional environment that encourages ethical behav-ior and sparks better performance or help create an environment where money mat-ters more than content.

WHERE DO YOU GO FROM HERE?

Perry (1970) postulates that one of the major accomplishments of college students is to progress from a simple, dualistic (right versus wrong) view of life to a more complex, mature and relativistic view. Perry states that students must not only ac-knowledge that diversity and uncertainty exist in a world of relativism but also make a commitment to their choices (i.e., career, values, beliefs, etc.) out of the multi-plicity of "right" choices available. And ethical choices abound in mass media ca-reers. For instance, even the daily routine of setting the news agenda is an ethical issue, since those decisions are often made by Caucasian males for others who are unlike them in significant ways. Even word choice is an ethical issue. Why do we see stories about "working mothers," yet none about "working fathers"? Why are criminal suspects more often referred to by ethnicity when they are black than when they are white?

Unlike physical development, moral development is not subject to the quirks of heredity. Each individual is free to develop as keen a sense of equity as any other in-dividual, yet few reach their full potential. About your attempts to "grow" ethically, Kohlberg (1973) has offered one observation: we tend to understand messages one stage higher than our own moral judgment stage. Through "aspirational listening"—that is, picking an ethical role model on a higher level and observing that person—you can progress to a higher stage of moral development. This observation is not a new one. In fact, it dates to Aristotle, who suggested that virtues could be learned by observing those who possess them.

This book uses the case study method so that you may see ethical decisions that were made at higher and lower levels of moral reasoning and aspire to the former. Often in case studies, it is the reasoning behind the answer rather than the answer it-self that is the best determiner of moral growth (Clouse 1985). *An important part of moral development is the recognition that motive, not consequence, is the critical factor in deciding whether an act is ethical.*

Elliott (1991) illustrates the difference in the following scenario. Imagine a sit-uation where you are able to interview and choose your next-door neighbor. When you ask Jones how she feels about murder, she replies she doesn't kill because if she got caught she would go to jail. When you interview Smith, he says he doesn't kill people because he believes in the sanctity of life. It takes little reflection to decide which neighbor you would prefer. Elliott concludes: "Ethics involves the judging of actions as right or wrong, but motivations count as well. Some reasons for actions seem better or worse than others" (1991, 19).

Suggested Readings

BELENKY, MARY F., et al. 1988. *Women's ways of knowing: The development of self, voice and mind.* New York: Basic Books.

COLES, ROBERT. 1986. *The moral life of children.* New York: Atlantic Monthly Press.

ETTEMA, JAMES, and THEODORE CLASSER. 1998. *Custodians of conscience: Investigative journalists and public virtue.* New York: Columbia University Press.

GARDNER, H., CSIKSZENTHMIHALYI, MIHALY, and DAMON, WILLIAM. 2001. *Good work: When excellence and ethics meet.* New York: Basic Books.

GILLIGAN, CAROL. 1982. *In a different voice: Psychological theory and women's development.* Cambridge, MA: Harvard University Press.

LEVINSON, DANIEL J. 1978. *Seasons of a man's life.* New York: Alfred A. Knopf, Inc.

WILKINS, LEE, and COLEMAN, RENITA. 2005. *The moral media.* Mahwah, NJ: Lawrence Erlbaum Associates.

Bibliography

ActiveBuddy (2002). Case D Study: ELLEgirlBuddy. Retrieved November 21, 2002. **http://www.activebuddy.com/welcome/**

Agence France Presse (2003, March 26). "The war as seen on US TV: More sand sweat than blood and tears." Accessed on LexisNexis Academic.

Alderman, E. and Kennedy, C. (1995). *The right to privacy.* New York: Alfred A. Knopf, Inc.

Alderman, Eric (2003). *What liberal media? The truth about bias and the news.* New York: Basic Books.

Allossery, P. (2000, January 21). Benetton sparks controversy again: Series of magazine ads attack death penalty. *Financial Post,* p. C3.

Anderson, C. (2006). *The long tail: How the future of business is selling less of more.* New York: Hyperion.

Ansen, D. (2006, Oct. 23). "Inside the hero factory." *Newsweek,* p. 70–71.

Arendt, H. (1970). *The human condition.* Chicago: University of Chicago Press.

Aristotle. *The Nicomachean ethics.* Book II 4–5. (1973). Trans. by H. Rackham. Ed. by H. Jeffrey. Cambridge, MA: Harvard University Press.

Associated Press (2006, Oct. 6). "NBC plans live episode of 'The West Wing' for presidential debate." AP wire story.

Audit Bureau of Circulation. (2006, January). Available from **http://www.accessabc.com;** Internet.

Auletta, K. (1991). *Three blind mice: How the TV networks lost their way.* New York: Random House.

Axelrod, R. (1984). *The evolution of cooperation.* New York: Basic Books.

Bagdikian, B. H. (1990). *The media monopoly.* (3rd ed.). Boston: Beacon Press.

———. (2000). *The media monopoly.* (6th ed.). Boston: Beacon Press.

Baker, S. and Martinson, D. (2001). "The TARES test: Five principles of ethical persuasion." *Journal of Mass Media Ethics, 16,* 2 & 3, pp. 148–175.

Bauder, D. (2005, Nov. 7). "Blurring lines between entertainment and news on 'The West Wing' and 'Sports Center.'" Associated Press News Wire.

Beasley, M. H. and Harlow, R. R. (1988). *The new majority: A look at what the preponderance of women in journalism education means to the schools and to the professions.* Lanham, MD: University Press of America.

Becker, L., et al. (2000). "Undergrad enrollments level off; graduate enrollment declines." *Journalism and Mass Communication Educator, 55:* 3, pp. 68–80.

Belcher, W. (2004, Nov. 8). "Fictional live presidential debate comes up short on excitement." *Tampa Tribune,* Baylife, p. 4.

Belenky, M., et al. (1988). *Women's ways of knowing: The development of self, voice and mind.* New York: Basic Books.

Bennett, L. (1988). *News: The politics of illusion.* Longman: New York.

Benoit, William (1999). *Seeing spots: A functional analysis of Presidential television advertisements.* Westport, CT: Praeger.

Bentley, R. (1986, August 4). "Lessons sought from tragic events." *Bakersfield Californian,* p. 15.

Berger, A. (1989). *Seeing is believing.* Mountain View, CA: Mayfield Publishing Co.

Berger, J. (1980). *About looking.* New York: Pantheon Books.

Bernton, H. (2004, April 18). "The somber task of honoring the fallen." *Seattle Times,* p. A1.

———. (2004, April 22). "Woman loses her job over coffins photo." *Seattle Times,* p. A1.

Bianco, R. (2003, Nov. 5). "Cowardly CBS unfair to viewers, not Reagans." *USA Today,* p. D1.

Black, J., Steele, B. & Barney, R. (1993). *Doing ethics in journalism.* Greencastle, IN: The Sigma Delta Chi Foundation and The Society of Professional Journalists.

Bok, S. (1978). *Lying: Moral choice in public and private life.* New York: Random House.

———. (1983). *Secrets: On the ethics of concealment and revelation.* New York: Vintage.

Boorstin, D. (1962). *The image.* New York: Antheneum.

Booth, C. (1999, November 15). "Worst of times." *Time,* pp. 79–80.

Borden, S. (in press). *Journalism-as-practice: MacIntyre, virtue ethics and the press.* Hampshire, United Kingdom: Ashgate Publishing.

Boulware, J. (2006, Oct. 15). "Everybody's watching." *American Way,* pp. 98–104.

Bovée, W. (1991). "The end can justify the means—but rarely." *Journal of Mass Media Ethics, 6,* pp. 135–145.

Brady, Jim (2006, February 12). "Blog rage." *Washington Post,* p. B1.

Braun, S. (1994, November 2). "Tuning out the hype and gore." *Los Angeles Times,* p. 1.

Brooks, D. E. (1992). "In their own words: Advertisers and the origins of the African-American consumer market." (A paper submitted to the Association for Education in Journalism and Mass Communications), Montreal, Canada, August 5–8.

Bryant, G. (1987, Spring–Summer). "Ten-fifty P.I.: Emotion and the photographer's role." *Journal of Mass Media Ethics,* pp. 32–39.

Buckner, J. (2000, Jan. 30). "Horrific photo forces us to face a painful past." *Charlotte Observer,* p. 3C.

Calvert, C. (2000). *Voyeur nation: Media, privacy and peering in modern culture.* Boulder, CO: Westview Press.

Carey, J. W. (1989, Autumn). "Review of Charles J. Sykes' Profscam." *Journalism Educator,* p. 48.

Cassier, E. (1944). *An essay on man.* New Haven, CT: Yale University Press.

Catlin, R. (2005, Nov. 8). "'West Wing' debate didn't fly." *Hartford Courant,* p. D-2.

CBS/AP (2004, April 23). "Pentagon: Families want photo ban." **www.cbsnews.com.**

Chaffee, P. (2006). "How the *Times* sells genocide." **www.pulitzer.org.**

Chandrasekaran, Rajiv (2006). "Comments resuming in *Post*.blog." *Washington Post* memo retrieved 17 February from **Poynter.org.**

Chow, Sher-Min (March 22, 2005). *Rodeo Houston ropes in records.* Retrieved from **www.khou.com/news/rodeo/stories.**

Christians, C. (1986). "Reporting and the oppressed." In D. Elliott (ed.). *Responsible journalism* (pp. 109–130) Newbury Park, CA: Sage Publications, Inc.

Christians, C. G., Ferré, J. P. & Fackler, M. (1993). *Good news: Social ethics and the press.* New York: Longman.

Christians, C., Rotzoll, K. & Fackler, M. (1987). *Media ethics: Cases and moral reasoning.* (2nd ed.). New York: Longman.

Christians, C., K. Rotzoll, M. Fackler, K. McKee & R. Woods, Jr. (2005). *Media ethics: Cases and moral reasoning.* Boston: Pearson Education, Inc.

Clark, C. (1997, Summer). "In favor of civic journalism." *Harvard International Journal of Press/Politics, 2, 3,* pp. 118–125.

Clegg, A. (2005). "Dove gets real." **www.brandchannel.com.**

Clouse, B. (1985). *Moral development.* Grand Rapids, MI: Baker Book House.

CNN Transcripts (accessed October 27, 2006), **http://transcripts.cnn.com.**

Cohen, A. (2000, Oct. 2). "A crisis of content." *Time,* pp. 68–73.

Coleman, A. D. (1987, Spring/Summer). "Private lives, public places: Street photography ethics." *Journal of Mass Media Ethics,* pp. 60–66.

Coleman, P. A. (2000). "Fighting a fair war or tilting at windmills?" An unpublished master's thesis. University of Missouri. Columbia, Missouri.

Coleman, R. and Wilkins, L. (2006). "The moral development of public relations practitioners." Presented at AEJMC, August, 2006, San Francisco.

Coles, R. (1986). *The moral life of children.* New York: Atlantic Monthly Press.

Commission on Civil Disorders. (1989). "The role of the mass media in reporting of news about minorities." In T. Goldstein (ed.), *Killing the messenger: 100 years of media criticism.* New York: Columbia University.

Committee on the Judiciary—Task Statement. (May 21, 2000). Available: **http://www.house .gov/judiciary/10148.htm.**

Costello, A. (2004). "Chad/Sudan: A question of genocide." From PBS "Frontline." **www.pbs.org.**

Coyne, L. (2005). Interview by case study author.

Cranberg, Gilbert, Randall Bezanson, and John Soloski. 2001. *Taking Stock.* Ames, IA: Iowa State University Press.

Cranberg, G., Bezanson, R. & Soloski, J. (2004). *Taking stock.* Ames, IA: Iowa State University Press.

Crouse, T. (1974). *The boys on the bus: Riding with the campaign press corps.* New York: Ballantine.

Cunningham, B. (2003, July/August). "Re-thinking objectivity." *Columbia Journalism Review,* pp. 24–32.

Cutlip, S. (1994). *The unseen power: Public relations—A history.* Hillsdale, NJ: Lawrence Erlbaum Associates.

D'Agostino, J. (2004, Sept. 20). "Reports debunk documents Rather used to attack Bush." *Human Events, 60,* 32.

Daniel, C. (1989). "National security and the Bay of Pigs invasion." In T. Goldstein (ed.), *Killing the messenger: 100 years of media criticism.* New York: Columbia University.

Daniels, J. (1965). *They will be heard: America's crusading newspaper editors.* New York: McGraw-Hill.

Dates, J. L. (1990). "Advertising." In J. L. Dates and W. Barlow (eds.), *Split image: African Americans in the mass media.* Washington, DC: Howard University Press.

Davies, J. C. (1963). *Human nature in politics.* New York: John Wiley & Sons.

Davis, M. (2005). Interview by case study author.

Day, L. A. (1991). *Ethics in media communications: Cases and controversies.* Belmont, CA: Wadsworth, Inc.

Deaver, F. (1990). "On defining truth." *Journal of Mass Media Ethics, 5* (3), pp. 168–177.

Dionne, E. J. (1991). *Why Americans hate politics.* New York: Simon & Schuster.
———. (1996). *They only look dead.* New York: Simon & Schuster.
Doyle, M. (2003, March 26). "Photos of POWs raise legal questions." *Star Tribune* (Minneapolis), p. 10A.
Dyck, A. (1977). *On human care.* Nashville: Abingdon.
Eisenberg, E. M. (1984, September). "Ambiguity as strategy in organizational communication." *Communication Monographs, 51,* pp. 227–242.
Elliott, D. (1986). "Foundations for news media responsibility." In D. Elliott (ed.), *Responsible journalism* (pp. 32–34). Newbury Park, CA: Sage Publications, Inc.
———. (1991, Autumn). "Moral development and the teaching of ethics." *Journalism Educator,* pp. 19–24.
Ellul, J. (1965). *Propaganda* (Trans. by K. Kellen and J. Lerner). New York: Alfred A. Knopf.
Emery, E. and Emery, M. (1978). *The press and America: An interpretative history of the mass media.* (4th ed.) Englewood Cliffs, NJ: Prentice-Hall.
Encabo, N. (1995). Ethics of journalism and democracy. *European Journal of Communication, 10* (4), pp. 513–526.
Epstein, E. J. (1974). *News from nowhere.* New York: Random House.
Ettema, J. and Glasser, T. (1998). *Custodians of conscience: Investigative journalists and public virtue.* New York: Columbia University Press.
Etzioni, A. (1993). *The spirit of community.* New York: Crown Publishers, Inc.
Fallows, J. (1996). *Breaking the news: How the media undermine American democracy.* New York: Pantheon.
Fancher, M. (2004, April 18). "Powerful photograph offered chance to tell an important story." *Seattle Times,* p. A1.
Farhi, P. (2006, Jan. 28). "Deluge shuts down *Post* blog." *Washington Post,* p. A8
Farhi, P. (2006, June 3). "U.S. media settle with Wen Ho Lee." *Washington Post,* p. A1.
Feldstein, D. (2005a, Feb. 27). "The big business of rodeo." *Houston Chronicle,* p. A1.
Feldstein, D. (2005b, April 10). "Is rodeo's spending justified?" *Houston Chronicle,* p. B1.
Feldstein, D. (Nov. 4, 2005). Personal communication with the author.
Festinger, L. (1957). *A theory of cognitive dissonance.* Stanford, CA: Stanford University Press.
Fischer, C. T. (1980). "Privacy and human development." In W. C. Bier (ed.), *Privacy: A vanishing value?* (pp. 37–46). New York: Fordham University Press.
Fitzgerald, M. (1995. Nov. 11). "Decrying public journalism." *Editor and Publisher,* p. 20.
Fitzpatrick, K. and Bronstein, C. (2006). *Ethics in public relations: Responsible advocacy.* Thousand Oaks, CA: Sage.
Fletcher, G. P. (1993). *Loyalty: An essay on the morality of relationships.* New York: Oxford University Press.
Fore, W. F. (1987). *Television and religion.* New York: Augsburg Publishing House.
Fort Worth Star-Telegram unsigned column. (2003, March 26). "Painful images." *Fort Worth Star-Telegram,* Metro, p. 14.
Frey, C. (2002, July 18). "Web friend or faux." *Los Angeles Times,* p. C-1.
Fuss, P. (1965). *The moral philosophy of Josiah Royce.* Cambridge, MA: Harvard University Press.
Gans, H. (1979). *Deciding what's news: A study of CBS Evening News, NBC Nightly News, Newsweek and Time.* New York: Vintage.
Gardner, H., Csikszenthmihalyi, M. & Damon, W. (2001). *Good work: When excellence and ethics meet.* New York: Basic Books.
Garron, B. (2005, Nov. 8). "The West Wing." **www.hollywoodreporter.com.**
Genocide Watch (2004, Feb. 24). "Today is the day of killing Anuaks." **www.genocidewatch .org.**

Gerbner, G. (1987, Summer–Fall). "Television: Modern mythmaker." *Media and Values,* pp. 8–9.

Gert, B. (1988). *Morality, a new justification of the moral rules.* New York: Oxford University Press.

Gilligan, C. (1977). "In a different voice: Women's conceptions of self and morality." *Harvard Educational Review, 47,* pp. 492–505.

Gilligan, C. (1982). *In a different voice: Psychological theory and women's development.* Cambridge, MA: Harvard University Press.

Godwin, M. (1995). "The shoddy article." *JournoPorn on HotWired* (Online).

Godwin, M. (1998). *Defending free speech in the digital age.* New York: Times Books.

Goffman, E. (1959). *The presentation of self in everyday life.* New York: Anchor.

Gogoi, P. (2005, Aug. 17). "From reality TV to reality ads." **www.businessweek.com.**

Gogoi, P. (2006, Oct. 17). "Wal-Mart vs. the blogosphere." **www.businessweek.com.**

Goldstein, P. (2000, Jan. 1). "The year of unconventional wisdom." *Los Angeles Times,* p. 1F.

Gormley, D. W. (1984). "Compassion is a tough word." *Drawing the Line,* pp. 58–59. Washington, DC: American Society of Newspaper Editors.

Graham, B. and Weisman, J. (2003, March, 24). "Display of 5 POWs draws firm rebuke." *Washington Post,* p. A1.

Grcic, J. M. (1986). "The right to privacy: Behavior as property." *Journal of Values Inquiry, 20,* pp. 137–144.

Gross, L., Katz, J. S. & Ruby, J. (eds.). (1988). *Image ethics: The moral rights of subjects in photographs, film and television.* New York: Oxford University Press.

Grunig, J. E. and Hunt, T. (1984). *Managing public relations.* Fort Worth: Holt, Rinehart and Winston.

Grunig, L., E. Toth, & L. Hon (2000). "Feminist values in public relations," *Journal of Public Relations Research, 12,* 1: 49–68.

Gunther, M. (2006, Oct. 18). "Corporate blogging: Wal-Mart fumbles." Posted on **www .cnnmoney.com.**

Gurevitch, M., Levy, M. & Roeh, I. (1991). "The global newsroom: Convergences and diversities in the globalization of television news." In P. Dalhgren and C. Sparks (eds.), *Communication and citizenship.* London. Routledge.

Hadley, C. (2006) Personal interview with case study author.

Haiman, F. (1958). "Democratic ethics and the hidden persuaders." *Quarterly Journal of Speech, 44,* pp. 385–392.

Halberstam, D. (2001). *War in a time of peace.* New York: Scribner.

Halbert, D. J. (1999). *Intellectual property in the information age.* Westport, CT: Quorum Books.

Hamilton, A. (2003, March 25). "5 GIs held in Iraq, shown on Arab TV." *The Dallas Morning News,* p. 1A.

Hanson, K. (1986). "The demands of loyalty." *Idealistic Studies, 16,* pp. 195–204.

Hart, A. (2003, July/August). "Delusions of accuracy." *Columbia Journalism Review,* p. 20.

Hemmel, P. (2006, June 11). Personal interview with author.

Hess, S. (1981). *The Washington reporters.* Washington, DC: The Brookings Institution.

Hickey, N. (2001, November/December). "The cost of not publishing." *Columbia Journalism Review.*

Hickey, N. (2003, July/August). "FCC: Ready, set, consolidate." *Columbia Journalism Review,* p. 5.

Hixson, R. F. (1987). *Privacy in a public society.* New York: Oxford University Press.

Hobbes, T. (1958). *The Leviathan* (Reprints from 1651). New York: Bobbs-Merrill.

Hodges, L. W. (1983). "The journalist and privacy." *Social Responsibility: Journalism, Law, Medicine, 9,* pp. 5–19.

——. (1986). "Defining press responsibility: A functional approach." In D. Elliott (ed.), *Responsible journalism.* (pp. 13–31). Newbury Park, CA: Sage Publications, Inc.

Horn, B. (2004, January 10). "Any more questions?" *Dallas Morning News,* p. C-2.

Hortsch, D. (2003, March 30). "Photos of dead and POWs raise thorny questions." *The Oregonian,* p. C1.

House, D. (2003, March 30). "Worth a thousand words." *Fort Worth Star-Telegram Weekly Review,* p. 3.

Houston Livestock Show and Rodeo (2005). *Economic impact.* Retrieved from **http://www.hlsr.com.**

Houston Livestock Show and Rodeo (2005). *Frequently asked questions: Houston Livestock Show and Rodeo scholarships.* Retrieved from **http://www.hlsr.com.**

Houston Livestock Show and Rodeo (2005). *HLSR homepage.* Retrieved from **http://www.hlsr.com.**

Houston Livestock Show and Rodeo (2005). *Ticket availability.* Retrieved from **http://www.hlsr.com.**

Howell, Deborah C. (2006, 22 Jan.). "The firestorm over my column." *Washington Post,* p. B6.

Hoyt, M. (1990, March/April). "When the walls come tumbling down." *Columbia Journalism Review,* pp. 35–40.

James, C. (2000, Dec. 3). "In a gay world, without the usual guides." *New York Times,* Section 2, p. 27.

Jamieson, Kathleen Hall (1983). *The interplay of influence: Mass media and their publics in news, advertising, politics.* Belmont, CA: Wadsworth Publishing.

——. (1992). *Dirty politics.* New York: Oxford University Press.

Jamieson, K. H. (2000). *Everything you think you know about politics . . . and why you're wrong.* New York: Basic Books.

Jamieson, K. H. and Campbell, K. K. (1992). *The interplay of influence: News, advertising, politics and the mass media.* (3rd ed.). Belmont, CA: Wadsworth, Inc.

Jensen, J. (2002). *Is art good for us?* Lanham, MD: Rowman & Littlefield, Publishers.

Junas, L. (1980, Feb. 23). "Tragedy and violence photos dominate in news prizes." *Editor and Publisher,* p. 17.

Kaid, L. L. (1992). "Ethical dimensions of political advertising." In R. E. Denton (ed.), *Ethical dimensions of political communication,* (pp. 145–169). New York: Praeger.

Kalson, S. (2005, Nov. 9). "Fictional debate easily trumps the real thing." *Pittsburgh Post-Gazette,* p. A-2.

Kant, I. (1785). *Groundwork on the metaphysics of morals.*

Keleny, G. (2003, March 25). "The Iraq conflict: Prisoners of war, photographs used for propaganda, and the Geneva Convention." *The Independent* (London), p. 9.

Keleny, G. (2003b, March 25). "The MoD wants face of Iraqi POWs to be obscured." *The Independent* (London), p. 9.

Kenworthy, T., Willing, R. & Cauchon, D. (2003, March 28). "TV coverage takes toll on families of POWs." *USA Today,* p. 9A.

Kessler, L. (1989). "Women's magazines' coverage of smoking-related health coverage." *Journalism Quarterly, 66,* pp. 316–322, 445.

Kim, G. and A. Paddon (1999, Sept.). "Digital manipulation as new form of evidence of actual malice in libel and false light cases." *Communications and the Law, 21,* p. 3.

Klein, J. (1992, June 8). "Whose values?" *Newsweek,* pp. 19–22.

Koehn, D. (1998). *Rethinking feminist ethics.* New York: Routledge.

Koff, S. (2003, March 25). "Did the U.S. violate Geneva Convention?" *The Cleveland Plain Dealer,* p. A9.

Kohlberg, L. (1968, September). "The child as a moral philosopher." *Psychology Today,* pp. 25–30.

———. (1973). "The contribution of developmental psychology to education." *Educational Psychologist, 10,* pp. 2–14.

Kozloff, R. (2005). Interview by case study author.

Kristof, N. (2005, Nov. 22). "Sudan's department of gang rape." *New York Times,* p. 23

Kristof, N. (2005, Nov. 27). "What's to be done about Darfur? Plenty." *New York Times,* p. 27.

Kristof, N. (2006, March 7). "Where killers roam, the poison spreads." *New York Times,* p. 19.

Kurtz, H. (2005, Jan. 18). "Administration paid commentator." *Washington Post,* p. A01.

Landsman, S. (1984). *The adversary system: A description and defense.* Washington, DC: American Enterprise Institute.

Lebacqz, K. (1985). *Professional ethics: Power and paradox.* Nashville: Abingdon Press.

Ledford, J. (2005). Interview by case study author.

Leiss, W., Kline, S. & Jhally, S. (1986). *Social communication in advertising: Person, products and images of well being.* New York: Methuen Publications.

Lester, Paul (1991). *Photojournalism: An ethical approach.* Hillsdale, NJ: Lawrence Erlbaum Associates.

Lester, P. M. (1992). *Photojournalism: An ethical approach.* Hillsdale, NJ: Lawrence Erlbaum and Associates.

———. (1996). *Images that injure.* Westport, CT: Greenwood Press.

———. (2003). *Images that injure.* Westport, CT: Greenwood Press.

Liberty, Robert M., Joyce N. Sparking & Emily S. Davidson. (1982). *The early window: Effects of television on children and youth.* New York: Paragon Press.

Linsky, M. (1986). *Impact: How the press affects federal policymaking.* New York: W. W. Norton.

Lippmann, W. (1922). *Public opinion.* New York: Free Press.

———. (1982). *The essential Lippmann.* Cambridge, MA: Harvard University Press.

Lippmann, W. and Merz, C. (1989). "A test of the news." In T. Goldstein (ed.), *Killing the messenger: 100 years of media criticism.* New York: Columbia University.

Littleton, C. (2005, Nov. 8). "'Housewives' hotter than ever.'" **www.hollywoodreporter.com.**

Los Angeles Daily News. (2005, Nov. 8). "If only real debates were this exciting," **www.dailynews.com**

Lowery, S. & DeFleur, M. (1988). *Milestones in mass communication research* (2nd ed.). New York: Longman.

Lubrano, G. (2003, March 31). "Images of POWs—and questions." *San Diego Union-Tribune,* p. B1.

Madison, J., Hamilton, A. & Jay, J. *The Federalist papers.*

Manly, L. (2005, Oct. 3). "U.S. network TV shows turn props into dollars." *International Herald Tribune,* pp. A14, 16.

Mapes, Mary (2005). "*Truth and duty: The press, the president, and the privilege of power.*" NY: St. Martin's Press.

Martin, E. (1991). "On photographic manipulation." *Journal of Mass Media Ethics, 6,* pp. 156–163.

Martinson, D. (1999). "Is it ethical for practitioners to represent 'bad clients'?" *Public Relations Quarterly, 44,* 22–25.

Matsuda, M. (1989). "Public response to racist speech: Considering the victim's story." *Michigan Law Review, 87,* pp. 2321–2381.

Matthews, A. W. and Steinberg, B. (2003, Nov. 19). "FTC examines health claims in KFC's ads." *Wall Street Journal,* p. B1, 2.

May, William F. (2001). *Beleaguered rulers: The public obligation of the professional.* Westminster: John Knox Press.

McChesney, R. (1991). *Rich media, Poor democracy: Communication politics in dubious times.* Champaign-Urbana: University of Illinois Press.

———. (1997). *Corporate media and the threat to democracy.* New York: Seven Stories Press.

Medved, Michael. (1992). *Hollywood vs. America.* New York: HarperCollins Publishers.

Merrill, J. C. (1974). *The imperative of freedom: A philosophy of journalistic autonomy.* New York: Hastings House.

Merritt, Davis. (1995). *Public journalism and public life.* Hillsdale, NJ: Lawrence Erlbaum Associates.

Meyers, C. (2003). "Appreciating W.D. Ross: On duties and consequences." *Journal of Mass Media Ethics, 18*(2), pp. 81–97.

Meyrowitz, J. (1985). *No sense of place: The impact of electronic media on social behavior.* New York: Oxford University Press.

Milbank, D. (2003, Oct. 21). "Curtains ordered for media coverage of returning coffins." **www.washingtonpost.com.**

Mill, J. S. (1859). *On liberty.*

———. (1861). *Utilitarianism.*

Miller, K. (1992, December). "Smoking up a storm: Public relations and advertising in the construction of the cigarette problem, 1953–1954." *Journalism Monographs,* p. 136.

Miller, S. and A. Marks. (2005, March 9). "Dan Rather: A pioneer and a lightning rod." *Christian Science Monitor,* p. A1.

Mills, C. W. (1956). *The power elite.* New York: Oxford University Press.

Mills, K. (1989, Winter). "When women talk to women." *Media and Values,* p. 12.

Molotch, H. and Lester, M. (1974). "News as purposive behavior: On the strategic use of routine events, accidents and scandals." *American Sociological Review, 39,* pp. 101–112.

Montgomery, K. C. (1989). *Target: Prime time. Advocacy groups and the struggle over entertainment television.* New York: Oxford University Press.

Mooney, C. (2000, Nov. 6). "The virtual campaign." *The American Prospect, II* (23), pp. 36–39.

Moore, G. F. (1903). *Principia ethica.*

Morton, J. (2003, June/July). "Less of a loss." *American Journalism Review,* p. 68.

Moyers, B. (1988). Quoted in "The promise of television," episode 10. Produced by PBS.

MSNBC website (2005, Nov. 7). "Viewers give Santos the victory in debate, barely." **www.msnbc.com.**

Murrdow, A. (2000, January). "Ad men walking—Benetton is facing its biggest advertising backlash yet, with a new campaign about Death Row." *The Irish Times,* p. 61.

Nasar, Sylvia (1998). *A Beautiful Mind.* New York: Simon & Schuster.

National Association of Broadcasters. (1985). *Radio: In search of excellence.* Washington, DC: NAB.

Negroponte, Nicholas. (1995). *Being digital.* New York: Alfred A. Knopf.

Nelkin, D. (1987). *Selling science: How the press covers science and technology.* New York: W. H. Freeman.

Neuffer, E. (2003, March 24). "Airing of POW footage blasted." *The Boston Globe,* p. A19.

Neville, R. C. (1980). "Various meanings of privacy: A philosophical analysis." In W. C. Bier (ed.), *Privacy: A vanishing value?* (pp. 26–36). New York: Fordham University Press.

Newsom, D., Turk, J. V. & Kruckeberg, D. (1996). *This is PR: The realities of public relations.* Belmont, CA: Wadsworth.

Newton, Julianne (2000). *The burden of visual truth: The role of photojournalism in mediating reality.* Hillsdale, NJ: Lawrence Erlbaum Associates.

Nimmo, D. and Combs, J. (1985). *Nightly horrors: Crisis coverage in television network news.* Knoxville, TN: University of Tennessee Press.

O'Toole, J. (1985). *The trouble with advertising.* New York: Times Books.

Oldenquist, A. (1982). "Loyalties." *Journal of Philosophy, 79,* pp. 73–93.

Orwell, G. (1949). *1984.* San Diego: Harcourt, Brace, Jovanovich.

Pasternak, J. (2003, March 24). "Treatment of POWs is said to violate treaty." *Los Angeles Times,* p. 4.

Patterson, T. E. (1980). *The mass media election.* New York: Praeger.

Patterson, T. E. and McClure, R. D. (1972). *The unseeing eye.* New York: G. P. Putnam's Sons.

Perry, W. O. (1968). *Intellectual development in the college years: A scheme.* New York: Holt, Rinehart and Winston.

Perry, William (1970). *Forms of ethical and intellectual development in the college years.* New York: Holt, Reinhart & Winston.

Peters, G. (2005). Interview by case study author.

Peters, J. (2000). *Speaking in the air: A history of the idea of communication.* Chicago: University of Chicago Press.

Pfanner, E. (2005, Oct. 3). "Product placements cause a stir in Europe." *International Herald Tribune,* pp. A14–15.

Piaget, J. (1965). *The moral judgment of the child.* Translated by Marjorie Gabain. New York: Free Press.

Pierce, S. (2005, Nov. 4). "Vote Vinick? Or Santos?" *Deseret Morning News,* p. C-1.

Plaisance, Patrick L. (2002). "The journalist as moral witness: Michael Ignatieff's pluralistic philosophy for a global media culture." *Journalism: Theory, Practice & Criticism, 3*(2), pp. 205–222.

Plato. *The republic.*

Pojman, L. (1998). *Ethical theory: Classical and contemporary readings.* Belmont, CA: Wadsworth Publishing Co.

Postman, N. (1986). *Amusing ourselves to death: Public discourse in the age of television.* New York: Penguin Books.

Powell, T. F. (1967). *Josiah Royce.* New York: Washington Square Press, Inc.

Rainey, J. (2006, Sept. 14). "Local leaders urge owner of the *Times* to avoid cuts." **www.latimes.com.**

Rather, D. (1987, March 10). "From Murrow to mediocrity?" *New York Times,* Sec. I, p. 27.

Rawls, J. (1971). *A theory of justice.* Cambridge, MA: Harvard University Press.

Reaves, S. (1987, Spring-Summer). "Digital retouching: Is there a place for it in newspaper photography? *Journal of Mass Media Ethics,* pp. 40–48.

———. (1991). Personal correspondence to the author quoted in digital alteration of photographs in consumer magazines. *Journal of Mass Media Ethics, 6,* pp. 175–181.

Reid, T. and Doran, J. (2003, March 24). "Mistreating prisoners is a war crime, says Bush." *The Times* (London), p. 2.

Rieder, R. (1999, November/December). "A costly rookie mistake." *American Journalism Review,* p. 6.

Ripley, A. (2004, Sept. 27). "How did Dan Rather get in this fix?" *Time,* p. 28–29.

Robertson, N. (1992). *The girls in the balcony.* New York: Random House.

Robinson, M. and Sheehan, G. (1983). *Over the wire and on TV.* New York: Basic Books.

Rogers, E. M. and Chang, S. B. (1991). "Media coverage of technology issues: Ethiopian drought of 1984, AIDS, Challenger and Chernobyl." In L. Wilkins and P. Patterson (eds.), *Risky business: Communicating issues of science, risk and public policy,* pp. 75–96. Westport, CT: Greenwood Press.

Rosen, J. (2000). *The unwanted gaze: The destruction of privacy in America.* New York: Random House.

Rosenthal, A. M. (1989, Oct. 10). "Trash TV's latest news show continues credibility erosion." Syndicated column by *New York Times* News Service.

Ross, W. D. (1930). *The right and the good.* Oxford, England: Clarendon Press.

Ross, W. D. (1988). *The right and the good.* Hackett: Indianapolis, IN.

Royce, J. (1908). *The philosophy of loyalty.* New York: Macmillan.

Rush, G. and J. Molloy (2003, May 16). "Cut and cover." *New York Daily News,* p. D1.

Russell, B. (ed.). (1967). *History of Western philosophy.* New York: Touchstone Books.

Sabato, L. J. (1992). *Feeding frenzy: How attack journalism has transformed American politics.* New York: Free Press.

Safer, M. (1992, Jan. 30). Keynote address at the annual Alfred I. DuPont–Columbia University Awards ceremony.

Salmon, F. (2006, March 27). "Blood money." **www.democracynow.org.**

Sandel, M. J. (1982). *Liberalism and the limits of justice.* Cambridge, MA: Harvard University Press.

Sanders, M. and Rock, M. (1988). *Waiting for prime time: The women of television news.* Champaign-Urbana: University of Illinois Press.

Schaffer, J. and Miller, E. D. (1995). *Civic journalism: Six case studies.* St. Petersburg, FL: The Poynter Institute.

Schoenbrun, D. (1989). *On and off the air: An informal history of CBS news.* New York: E. P. Dutton.

Schoeman, F. D., (ed.). (1984). *Philosophical dimensions of privacy: An anthology.* Cambridge, MA: Harvard University Press.

Schudson, M. (1978). *Discovering the news.* New York: Basic Books.

——. (1984). *Advertising: The uneasy persuasion.* New York: Basic Books.

——. (1995). *The power of news.* Cambridge, MA: Harvard University Press.

Schwartz, T. (1973). *The responsive chord.* Garden City, NY: Anchor Press.

Seabrook, J. (2003, July 7). "The money note." *New Yorker,* p. 46.

Seelye, K. (2006, Oct. 5). "Publisher is fired at *Los Angeles Times.*" **www.nytimes.com.**

Shales, T. (2005, Nov. 7). "A debatable ploy by NBC: Live 'West Wing' earns no points for substance." *Washington Post,* p. C-1.

Shaw, D. (1999, December 20). "Journalism is a very different business—Here's why." *Los Angeles Times,* p. V3.

Shilts, R. (1987). *And the band played on.* New York: St. Martin's Press.

Siebert, F. S., Peterson, T. & Schramm, W. (1956). *Four theories of the press.* Champaign-Urbana: University of Illinois Press.

Silicio, T. (2004) Tami Silicio's official website. **www.tamisilicio.net.**

Silver, R. (1989, Winter). "The many faces of media women." *Media and Values,* pp. 2–5.

Simpson, Christopher (1996). *Science of coercion: Communication research and psychological warfare, 1945-1960.* Oxford: Oxford University Press.

Smith, C. (1992). *Media and apocalypse.* Westport, CT: Greenwood Press.

Smith, R. (2000, Jan. 13). "Critic's notebook: An ugly legacy lives on, its glare unsoftened by age." *New York Times,* p. E1.

Smolkin, Rachel (2005, April/May). "Reversing the slide." *American Journalism Review.*

Snow, Nancy (2002). *Propaganda Inc.: Selling America's culture to the world.* New York: Seven Stories Press.

Spencer, J. (2001, Oct. 1). "Decoding bin Laden." *Newsweek.*

Squires, J. (1997). *Read all about it! The corporate takeover of America's newspapers.* New York: Basic Books.

Stanard, A. (2006, Oct. 12). "Facebook privacy charges raise student ire." **www.detnews.com.**

Stanley, A. (2005, Nov. 8). "Engrossed in a world of political idealism." *New York Times,* p. E–1.

Stein, M. L. (1986, June 21). "Covering a disaster story." *Editor & Publisher,* p. 17.

Stern, Reuben (In press). "Stockholder theory and media management: An ethical framework for news company executives." *Journal of Mass Media Ethics,* anticipated publication 2008.

Sterngold, J. (2006, Nov. 6). *San Francisco Chronicle.*

Stone, I. F. (1988). *The trial of Socrates.* Boston: Little, Brown and Co.

Stroud, S. (2005). Interview by case study author.

Sunstein, C. (2001). *Republic.com.* New Haven: Princeton University Press.

Szarkowski, J. (1978). *Mirrors and windows.* New York: Museum of Modern Art.

Thomas, B. (1990, Jan. 19). "Finding truth in the age of 'infotainment.'" *Editorial Research Reports.* Washington, DC: Congressional Quarterly, Inc.

Tomlinson, D. (1987). "One technological step forward and two legal steps back: Digitalization and television news pictures as evidence in libel." *Loyola Entertainment Law Journal, 9,* pp. 237–257.

Toppo, G. (2005, Jan. 7). "Education Department paid commentator to promote law." *USA Today,* p. 1A.

Toronto Star unsigned column (2003, March 23). "A note to readers about photos." *Toronto Star.* p. A2.

Toulmin, S. (1988). "The recovery of practical philosophy." *The American Scholar,* Summer, p. 338.

Unilever Corporation (2005). **www.campaignforrealbeauty.com.**

Voakes, P. S. (1998). "What were you thinking? A survey of journalists who were sued for invasion of privacy." *Journalism and Mass Communications Quarterly,* 75(2): pp. 378–393.

Vonnegut, K. (1952). *Player piano.* New York: Dell Publishing Co.

Ward, Stephen J. (2004). *The invention of journalism ethics.* Montreal: McGill-Queens University Press.

Watkins, J. J. (1990). *The mass media and the law.* Englewood Cliffs, NJ: Prentice-Hall.

Weaver, D. H. and Wilhoit, G. C. (1986). *The American journalist: A portrait of U.S. newspeople and their work.* Bloomington, IN: University of Indiana Press.

Weaver, David H., Randal A. Beam, Bonnie J. Brown Lee, Paul S. Voakes, G. Cleveland Wilhoit (2007). *The American journalist in the 21st century: U.S. news people at the dawn of a new millenium* (LEA's Communication Series). Mahwah, NJ: Lawrence Erlbaum & Assoc.

Weber, H. (2006, July 23). "Richard Jewell's fortunes changed in a split second." Associated Press article retrieved on **www.news.yahoo.com.**

Weiss, A. (2006). "*New York Times* probed on Sudan ad insert." **www.forward.com.**

Weinberg. S. (1995, Nov/Dec.). "ABC, Philip Morris and the infamous apology." *Columbia Journalism Review,* pp. 29–37.

Werhane, P. (1999). *Moral imagination and management decision-making.* London: Oxford University Press.

Werhane, Patricia (2006). "Stockholder ethics in health care." Presented to the Association of Applied and Professional Ethics, February 2006. San Antonio, Texas.

Werner, M. R. and Starr, J. (1959). *Teapot Dome.* New York: Viking.

Westin, A. F. (1967). *Privacy and freedom.* New York: Atheneum.

Wicker, C. (1990, March 7). "A while back, everyone was doing it—but not anymore." *Dallas Morning News,* pp. 1–2C.

Wilkins, L. (1987). *Shared vulnerability: The mass media and American perception of the Bhopal disaster.* Westport, CT: Greenwood Press.

Wilkins, L. and Christians, C. (2001). "Philosophy meets the social sciences: The nature of humanity in the public arena." *Journal of Mass Media Ethics,* 16 (2,3): pp. 99-120.

Wilkins, L. and Coleman, R. (2005). *The moral media.* Mahwah, NJ: Lawrence Erlbaum and Associates.

Wilkins, L., and Coleman, R. (2006). "The moral development of public relations practitioners: A comparison with other professions." Presented to the Public Relations Division of the Association of Educators in Journalism and Mass Communication for the annual conference, August 2–5, 2006, San Francisco, CA.

Williams, Bruce. In press. "The ethics of political communication." In Lee Wilkins and Clifford G. Christians, eds., *Handbook of Mass Media Ethics.* New York and London: Taylor & Francis.

Williams, B. A. and Carpini, M.X.D. (2002, April 10). "Heeeeeeeeeeere's democracy!" *Chronicle of Higher Education,* p. B14.

Winslow, D. (2004). "Peter Turnley's photo-essays to debut in *Harper's Magazine.*" **www.digitaljournalist.org.**

Woods, G. (1996). *Advertising and marketing to the new majority.* Belmont, CA: Wadsworth.

Woodward, K. (1994, June 13). "What is virtue?" *Newsweek,* p. 38–39.

Index